PAUL THE APOSTLE

Wisdom and Folly of the Cross

A THEOLOGICAL AND EXEGETICAL STUDY

Volume 2

PAUL THE APOSTLE
Wisdom and Folly of the Cross

by

ROMANO PENNA

translated by

THOMAS P. WAHL, O.S.B.

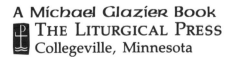

A Michael Glazier Book
THE LITURGICAL PRESS
Collegeville, Minnesota

The Translator:
Thomas P. Wahl, O.S.B., S.T.L., The Catholic University of America, S.S.L., Pontifical Biblical Institute, Ph.D., Union Theological Seminary, New York City. Father Wahl taught Scripture at St. John's University, Collegeville, Minnesota, from 1967 to 1993. He is a member of St. Anselm's Benedictine Priory, Tokyo, Japan, a foundation of St. John's Abbey, Collegeville, Minnesota.

A Michael Glazier Book published by The Liturgical Press.

Cover design by David Manahan, O.S.B. St. Paul; detail of iconostasis beam, St. Catherine's Monastery, Sinai.

Paul the Apostle: Wisdom and Folly of the Cross is the authorized English translation of *L'apostolo Paolo: Studi di esegesi e teologia*, published by Edizioni Paolini, Turin, Italy, in 1991.

Manufactured in the United States of America.

Library of Congress Cataloging-in-Publication Data

Penna, Romano.
    [Apostolo Paolo. English]
    Paul the Apostle : a theological and exegetical study / by Romano
Penna ; translated by Thomas P. Wahl.
       p.   cm.
    "A Michael Glazier book."
    Originally published in Italian in a single vol.
    Includes bibliographical references and index.
    Contents: v. 1. Jew and Greek alike — v. 2. Wisdom and the folly
of the Cross.
    ISBN 0-8146-5912-8
    1. Bible. N.T. Epistles of Paul—Theology. 2. Paul, the
Apostle, Saint. 3. Bible. N.T. Epistles of Paul—Criticism,
interpretation, etc.   I. Title.
BS2651.P37513 1996
225.9'2—dc20   95-37825
                                                                CIP

PETRO ROSSANO

MAGISTRO INCOMPARABILI

in memoriam

Contents

APPENDIX

Preface

There are two ways to present the theology of Saint Paul, or for that matter the thought of any brilliant and prolific writer. One is to offer as complete a picture as possible, inserting each component into a systematic whole. The other does specialized investigations, dwelling on the individual components, digging ever deeper into specific lines of research. The difference is evident. The former achieves a synthesis, which, however, is in danger of being excessively abstract. The latter, preferring analysis, reaches more profoundly into the author's mind, but with the risk of never achieving an overview.

This book chooses the second method, with its attendant danger. This choice can surely claim theoretical justification in the complexity of Paul's thought, which is scarcely amenable to an ironclad Aristotelian logic. For Paul's charism, as has been said, is more one of richness than of clarity. But this observation also accords with the purpose of this book, which is to gather the best things I have written on the Apostle over the past twenty years and present them in an organic structure.

Each chapter represents a different earlier publication of mine, revised here and there in text and notes alike. Most of these were prepared for specialized periodicals or miscellanies, thus meeting the demands of rigorous scientific research. Nevertheless, there are among them some slightly less meticulous articles, and even conferences, that betray their original oral character. I have omitted some less important pieces and also some works on Deutero-Paul, especially the Letter to the Ephesians. At any rate, the variety should make the present work accessible to a varied audience.

One thing is certain: An encounter with Paul, even if relatively superficial, cannot help but stir the waters of one's life of faith and witness. Paul has always found eloquent praise in the Church, from John Chrysostom:

> Can you name me a better possession [than Paul's faithfulness to the Cross]? Or an equal one? How many angels and archangels is he not worth who uttered this word? (*Paneg.* 7:3);

to Martin Luther:

> Nothing has ever entered the world so daring as the preaching of Paul (*Tischreden* 2:277);

and on into our own day:

> One who is an honor to humanity (Daniel Rops, 1951);
> It is he who originated the completely modern sense of the scandal of faith (Mario Luzi, 1991).

Still, let us not be carried away by the rhetoric. The best way to escape this is simply to take his letters in hand and weigh them with one's own study and meditation, in order to recognize that from these letters there always flows clear, cool water, capable of quenching the thirst of even the most parched spirits.

In all simplicity I offer this volume to help with such an approach, with the wish that it may succeed.

ROMANO PENNA

Rome
29 January 1991

Abbreviations

AB	Analecta Biblica
ABR	American Benedictine Review
AJut	Acta Jutlandica
AnglThRev	Anglican Theological Review
ANRW	Aufstieg und Niedergang der Römischen Welt
AThANT	Abhandlungen zur Theologie des Alten und Neuen Testaments
BB	Biblioteca Biblica
BBB	Bonner Biblische Beiträge
BCM	Biblioteca di Cultura Moderna
BCR	Biblioteca di Cultura Religiosa
BET	Beiträge zur biblischen Exegese und Theologie
BETh	Beiträge zur evangelischen Theologie
BEThL	Beiträge Ephemeridum Theologicarum Lovaniensium
BFChrTh	Beiträge zur Förderung Christlicher Theologie
B.G.U.	Aegyptische Urkunden aus den Koeniglichen Museen zu Berlin: Griechische Urkunden
BhTh	Beiträge zur historischen Theologie
Bib	Biblica
BiblArchRev	Biblical Archeology Review
BibKir	Bibel und Kirche
BibOr	Bibbia e Oriente
BibTrans	Bible Translator
BJ	Bible de Jérusalem
BJRL	Bulletin of the John Rylands Library
BOr	Biblica et Orientalia

BSR	Biblioteca di Scienze Religiose
BT	Biblioteca Teologica
BTB	Biblical Theology Bulletin
BThN	Bibliotheca Theologica Norvegica
BU	Biblische Untersuchungen
BUL	Biblioteca Universale Laterza
BZ (NF)	Biblische Zeitschrift (Neue Folge)
BzHTh	Beiträge zur historischen Theologie
BZNW	Beihefte zu der Zeitschrift für die neutestamentliche Wissenschaft
CalvTheolJour	Calvin Theological Journal
CB NTS	Coniectanea Biblica, New Testament Series
CBQ	Catholic Biblical Quarterly
CII	Corpus inscriptionum iudaicarum
CNT	Commentaire du Nouveau Testament
Conc	Concilium
C.R.	Corpus Reformatorum
CTNT	Commentario Teologico del Nuovo Testamento
EB	Etudes bibliques
EKK	Evangelisch-Katholischer Kommentar zum Neuen Testament
EstBibl	Estudios Biblicos
EThL	Ephemerides Theologicae Lovanienses
ETThRel	Etudes Théologiques et Religieuses
EvQ	Evangelical Quarterly
EvTh	Evangelische Theologie
ExpT	The Expository Times
FRLANT	Forschungen zur Religion und Literatur des Alten und Neuen Testaments
FzB	Forschung zur Bibel
GLNT	Grande Lessico del Nuovo Testamento
GNS	Good News Studies
GThA	Göttinger Theologische Arbeiten

HistRel	History of Religions
HNT	Handbuch zum Neuen Testament
HThKNT	Herders Theologischer Kommentar zum Neuen Testament
HThR	Harvard Theological Review
HUCA	Hebrew Union College Annual
HUTh	Hermeneutische Untersuchungen zur Theologie
ICC	The International Critical Commentary
Int	Interpretation
IrThQuart	Irish Theological Quarterly
JAAR	Journal of the American Academy of Religion
JB	Jerusalem Bible
JKZ NF	Internazionale Kirchliche Zeitschrift, Neue Folge
JournBiblLit (JBL)	Journal of Biblical Literature
JournJewStud (JJS)	Journal of Jewish Studies
JournRomStud	Journal of Roman Studies
JournStudJud (JSJ)	Journal for the Study of Judaism
JQR	Jewish Quarterly Review
JSNT	Journal for the Study of the New Testament
JTSt (JThS)	Journal of Theological Studies
LAB	Pseudo-Philo, Liber Antiquitatum Biblicarum
LD	Lectio Divina
LOS	London Oriental Series
MBS	Message of Biblical Spirituality
MRB	Monographische Reihe von Benedictina
MThZ	Münchner Theologische Zeitschrift
NA NF	Neutestamentliche Abhandlungen, Neue Folge
NCBC	New Century Bible Commentary
NEB	New English Bible
NHC	Nag Hammadi Codices
NIGTC	New International Greek Testament Commentary

NKZ	Neue Kirchliche Zeitschrift
NRT	Nouvelle Revue Théologique
NT	Novum Testamentum
NT Suppl.	Novum Testamentum, Supplements
NTD	Neues Testament Deutsch
NTOA	Novum Testamentum et Orbis Antiquus
NTS	New Testament Studies
NTTS	New Testament Tools and Studies
NVB	Nuovissima Versione della Bibbia
OBO	Orbis Biblicus et Orientalis
PG	J. Migne, Patrologia Graeca
PL	J. Migne, Patrologia Latina
PS	Patristica Sorboniensia
QD	Quaestiones Disputatae
RAC	Reallexikon für Antike und Christentum
RB	Revue Biblique
RechScRel	Recherches de Sciences Religieuses
RestorQuart	Restoration Quarterly
RevEtJuives	Revue des Etudes Juives
RGG	Religion in Geschichte und Gegenwart
RHPhR	Revue d'histoire et de philosophie religieuses
RHR	Revue de l'Histoire des Religions
RivArchCrist	Rivista di Archeologia Cristiana
RivBibl	Rivista Biblica
RivStLettRel	Rivista di Storia e Letteratura Religiosa
RNT	Regensburger Neues Testament
RQ	Revue de Qumran
RSB	Ricerche Storico-Bibliche
RSPhTh	Revue de Sciences Philosophiques et Théologiques
RSR	Religious Studies Review
RSV	Revised Standard Version
RTP	Revue de Théologie et de Philosophie
RvSR	Revue de Sciences Religieuses

SB	Studi Biblici
SBEC	Studies in the Bible and Early Christianity
SBL DS	Society for the Biblical Literature, Dissertations Series
SBM	Stuttgarter Biblische Monographien
SBTh SS	Studies in Biblical Theology, Supplementary Series
SC	Sources Chrétiennes
ScottJourTheol	Scottish Journal of Theology
SDB	Supplément au Dictionnaire de la Bible
SIDJC	Service International de Documentation Judéo-Chrétienne
SNT	Studien zum Neuen Testament
SNTS MS	Society for New Testament Studies, Monograph Series
SNTU	Studien zum Neuen Testament und seiner Umwelt
SOC	Scritti delle Origini Cristiane
SPAA	Spicilegium Pontificii Athenaei Antoniani
SPCIC	Studiorum Paulinorum Congressus Internationalis Catholicus
ST	Studia Theologica
StEv	Studia Evangelica
STh (StTh)	Studia Theologica
StiZt	Stimmen der Zeit
StPat	Studia Patavina
Sum.Th.	Summa Theologiae
SUNT	Studien zur Umwelt des Neuen Testaments
SVF	Stoicorum Veterum Fragmenta
TAPA	Transactions of the American Philological Association
TB	Babylonian Talmud
TDNT	Theological Dictionary of the New Testament
TgJo	Targum Pseudo-Jonathan
TgN	Targum Neofiti
ThB	Theologische Beiträge

ThBl	Theologische Blätter
ThEx	Theologische Existenz Heute
ThF	Theologische Forschung
ThGl	Theologie und Glaube
ThHNT	Theologischer Handkommentar zum Neuen Testament
ThJb	Theologische Jahrbücher
ThLZ	Theologische Literatur-Zeitung
ThQ	Theologische Quartalschrift
ThSK	Theologische Studien und Kritiken
ThSt	Theological Studies
ThZ	Theologische Zeitschrift
TrThZ	Trierer Theologische Zeitschrift
TU	Theologische Untersuchungen
TZ	Theologische Zeitschrift
TZTh	Tübinger Zeitschrift für Theologie
USQR	Union Seminary Quarterly Review
VT	Vetus Testamentum
WA	D. Martin Luther's Werke (Weimar Ausgabe)
WBC	World Biblical Commentary
WdF	Wege der Forschung
WMANT	Wissenschaftliche Monographien zum Alten und Neuen Testament
WUNT	Wissenschaftliche Untersuchungen zum Neuen Testament
ZAW	Zeitschrift für die Alttestamentliche Wissenschaft
ZNW	Zeitschrift für die Neutestamentliche Wissenschaft
ZRG	Zeitschrift für Religions- und Geistesgeschichte
ZThK	Zeitschrift für Theologie und Kirche
ZWTh	Zeitschrift für die Wissenschaftliche Theologie

Chapter 17

Preaching as Sacrament of Salvation in Paul and the New Testament

Catholic theological reflection is not much inclined to think of preaching as a "sacrament." Having limited this term, and hence the concept, to the traditional seven cultic actions—baptism to matrimony—we have pretty well lost sight of the *word*, which according to the Bible is by itself able to create (Gen 1:3-4) and to save (James 1:21). It is not difficult, then, to understand the uneasiness of many before the decisive declaration of Paul, "Christ sent me not to baptize but to preach the gospel" (1 Cor 1:17). And yet even here Paul has no intention to set up an opposition between "sacrament" and word, but rather simply a hierarchy of values between two equally sacramental realities, as we shall see. The New Testament text that more than any other shows the sacramental structure of preaching is 1 Thess 2:13: "We give thanks to God without ceasing, for when you received the word of God preached by us, you accepted it not as a human word but as God's word, which it truly is and which has been active in you who believe." We consider here the three classical aspects of the sacrament that we will use in developing our explanation: the *sacramentum tantum, res tantum,* and *res et sacramentum.*[a]

I. "The word preached by us"

The first aspect, which we are all too likely to forget, is basic. As Vatican II expressed it, "The economy of revelation is made up of deeds and words that are closely connected" (*Dei Verbum,* 2). Now, in Scholastic terms, the word functions as *form,* that is, it confers meaning on the deed,

a. Though I make no attempt to translate these technical terms of Scholastic sacramental theology, they are roughly explained in context below.—T.P.W.

1

revealing its true salvific sense. Apart from the proclamation, all the events of what we call "salvation history" would remain neutral, meaningless; we would not even know what meaning to attribute to the cross. But in fact we should note that revelation is completely dependent on the word, and indeed on the human word. Phenomenologically speaking, in preaching all that we see are human persons, all that we hear are words derived completely from the most ordinary human speech. Paul writes: "When I came to you, I came not with lofty words or wisdom, but I appeared in weakness, with great fear and trembling, and my words and preaching were not in persuasive words of wisdom" (1 Cor 2:1, 3-4).

On this extreme, defenseless fragility of the naked human word depends every prophetic intervention from Elijah to Saint Paul. Even Jesus of Nazareth, appearing as a rabbi on the roads of Palestine, entrusts his message to simple speech: "He came into Galilee, *announcing* the gospel of God and *saying* that the time was fulfilled and the reign of God was at hand" (Mark 1:14-15; cf. 2:2). Jesus went like a sower of the word (Mark 4:14), scattering his seed generously, unconcerned whether some of it fell on the path or among thorns (Mark 4:15-19). He speaks with confidence and courage (Mark 8:32), but even so, *this frail word always remains his only weapon* against the Pharisees (Matt 22:46; cf. John 10:19) and the crowds (Matt 26:55; Luke 4:22) alike. He desires that all should hear his voice (John 10:16), even if it may seem harsh (John 6:60); "blessed are the ears that hear" what he says (Matt 13:16). Like John's activity (Mark 1:3), that of Jesus can also be identified as a "voice" that cries, that rejoices (John 3:9), and that becomes familiar, like that of a shepherd to his sheep (John 10:3-4) or of the bridegroom to his friend (John 3:29), until the supreme moment, when on the cross it becomes only an inarticulate cry (Matt 27:50).

And after Easter and Pentecost the early Church in presenting itself to the world knows no other arms with which to protect itself save the word (Acts 4:29-31). It is a public, official "testimony" (Acts 4:33), a "voice" that cannot be stopped, that cannot help but speak of what has been seen and heard (4:20). And for that matter, it was precisely for this that Jesus had chosen the apostles: "He chose twelve to be with him and to be sent out to preach, with power to drive out demons" (Mark 3:14-15). And Paul also found it an inescapable necessity (1 Cor 9:16). Speech, then, remains the only, or at least the primary, means the Christian community has available. Her fragility is comparable to that of "vessels of clay" (2 Cor 4:7). Her humility involves the life and fate of the preacher as well, who is exposed to others with the same simplicity and selflessness (1 Thess 2:1-12), doomed to death, considered a pure spectacle by the world, with no way out (1 Cor 4:9-13).

Even so, Paul recognizes the absolute priority that this task has over every other sacramental action: preaching is equivalent to the task of planting (1 Cor 3:6), of laying a foundation (1 Cor 3:10), without which nothing can grow or be built. This is truly the beginning of everything: "How beautiful are the feet of those who bring the good news!" (Rom 10:15). Just as one cannot celebrate Eucharist without at least a bit of bread and wine, likewise, "How will they believe in him unless they have heard? And how shall they hear if no one preaches?" (Rom 10:14). No wonder we find the urgent exhortation in 2 Tim 4:1-2: "I charge you before God and Jesus Christ . . . preach the word, be insistent in season and out of season."

II. ". . . which has been active in you who believe"

The value of the preached word is not just that of being a mere external sign, a *sacramentum tantum*. Preaching is certainly not merely "sounding brass or a tinkling cymbal" (1 Cor 13:1). It is rather a truly "efficacious sign." It is a question of faith. Even the preacher is called to believe in something extra that characterizes and distinguishes the word that is spoken; this preacher is a vessel of clay, but one that contains a treasure. The New Testament is clear about it: "Meekly accept the word implanted within you that has the power to save your souls" (James 1:21; cf. 1:18).

The proclamation, then, necessarily entails a dynamic aspect that makes it an act unlike any other. All human language has this dimension: the effect of somehow stimulating or provoking the hearer to a reaction. The human word is always an appeal or a challenge that compels the hearer to take a stance in regard to it. But when it comes to the preaching of the gospel, this "is the power of God for the salvation of whoever believes" (Rom 1:16). If it is true that the human being is saved only through faith (Rom 3:28) in God's saving intervention, we must still remember that such faith comes to the individual not from a direct, interior revelation but "from hearing" (Rom 10:17; Gal 3:2, 5). By analogy, compare what Elizabeth says to Mary: "Scarcely had the sound of your greeting reached my ears when the child in my womb leapt for joy" (Luke 1:44). Hence the Pauline saying that provides the title of this second section can also be translated: ". . . which has been active in you, bringing you to believe." "For speech about the cross is folly for those who are perishing, but for those who are being saved, for us, it is the power of God" (1 Cor 1:18).

It appears evident here that preaching always accomplishes a "critical-eschatological" function, i.e., the hearers encounter a distinction, even a separation, between "those who are being lost" and "those who are being saved." Thus, at the moment of the proclamation there takes place an intervention of God that corresponds to the final judgment. When the cross is proclaimed, the hearers find themselves in a situation with es-chatological resonances or consequences (see also John 12:47-49). Thus, the word is "God's power." The expression means not only to empha-size the saving power of the gospel as some sort of static privilege inher-ing in it like a hidden treasure, but even more, to demonstrate the fact that the gospel or kerygma is "power" essentially when it is active and calls forth a response. On the other hand, only if this human response is one of acceptance will the "power" of the kerygma actually have achieved its goal, namely, of being "salvific." In fact, in 1 Cor 1:18 and Rom 1:16 alike the proclamation is identified as salvific only "for those who are being saved" or "for everyone who believes"; about those who do not accept it Romans says nothing, but First Corinthians specifies "it is foolishness for those who are being lost."

And so we understand Saint Paul when he protests, "Christ sent me not to baptize, but to preach the good news" (1 Cor 1:17). Indeed, it all begins here. I would even say that this act of preaching already contains within itself an eschatological completion: salvation, in fact, is not based primarily on the sacrament or on moral works. This is so first of all for Jesus himself, who solemnly declares: "Amen, amen, I say to you, the one who hears my words has eternal life" (John 5:24); "you are already clean because of the word I declared to you" (John 15:3). But it is also true for the post-Easter Church: "All I want to know from you is this: Is it from the works of the Law that you have received the Spirit or from faith in what you heard [lit.: the hearing of faith]?" (Gal 3:2). Now, the person who is confronted with the preached word and actually believes becomes "a child of Abraham" (Gal 3:7), i.e., the former gentile receives the "blessing" given to the first "believer," "so that we receive the prom-ise of the Spirit through faith" (Gal 3:14). It is thus that we are incorpo-rated into the new people of God, which is the body of Christ (Gal 3:25-29). Baptism will be the public and official seal of this new belonging.

It is preaching, therefore, that puts a person into the living fabric of the history of salvation. The preacher's mission, then, is actually not just to explain the content of the Christian mystery but also, and above all, to bring it about. This is actually what is said by a Pauline letter: "The gentiles have become co-heirs, members of the same body, and sharers in the same promise in Christ Jesus through the gospel, of which I have become minister" (Eph 3:6). And so the preaching of the gospel becomes the instrument through which non-believers come to share in the in-heritance of Israel's salvation history and have access to the Father through Christ's mediation in the one Spirit (Eph 2:11-18).

Consequently, the plan of salvation is not just that it be revealed or announced by preaching, but that it actually be *brought about* through the preaching, that through this it reach its proper fulfillment. We could say that preaching is the first effective element in the realization of the history of salvation, for it is thanks to it that the Spirit still intervenes again (Eph 1:13-14) and the long line of believers continues from Abraham all the way to the response in our own days of the most recent person to have heard the good news and come to believe. We realize that the revelation of God's merciful justice came in history precisely with the cross and blood of Jesus on Calvary (Rom 3:25); but it also comes in the preaching of the gospel (Rom 1:17).

So it is fair to say that revelation is always in process, that it is renewed in every act of faith aroused by the proclamation of the gospel. In fact, if by "revelation" we mean a reciprocal gift not just of God to us but also of us to God, this is actually the full salvific event par excellence: it is only here that something really new happens under the sun. And precisely this eschatological newness makes preaching a sacrament.[1]

III. "Not a human word . . . but God's word"

If the preached word has the "power" to bring about the accomplishment of this *res mysterii*, which is the faith and hence the justification of the hearer, this is then clearly not just a "human word." Like the Eucharistic Bread, if it brings about the communion of the Lord with the sisters and brothers (1 Cor 10:16-17), it is obviously not a food like any other but is the "body of Christ" (ibid.) present in the midst of the assembly united in his name. Thus it is with the proclamation of the gospel: this is "God's word." The dimension of "mystery," then, exists not only on the level of the hearer who believes but also on the level of the simple word that is proclaimed *(res et sacramentum)*. Note 1 Pet 1:23-25: "You have been reborn, not from corruptible seed but from incorruptible, through God's living and abiding word. For 'all flesh is grass, and all its glory is like the flowers of the field: the grass withers and the flower falls, but the word of the Lord remains forever.' Now, this is the word of good news brought to you."

The one who preaches, then, presents Christ, and the one who listens encounters him. The phenomenon that takes place in preaching is just this: Christ becomes present in it, and through it is encountered by the

---

1. Compare also the concept of "prophecy" in 1 Cor 14 and what H. Schlier says in *Zeit der Kirche* (Freiburg, 1956) 258–264 (Italian ed. Bologna, 1965, 420–423).

hearers. "In the proclamation of God's word, its 'content' is revealed and becomes present: the Cross rises up before me in the 'word of the Cross,' reconciliation appears in the 'word of reconciliation,' glory radiates in the word of glory, and life and immortality shine forth. . . ."[2] (see also 2 Tim 1:10). There is, then, the presence of Jesus even in the preached word: "Who hears you, hears me" (Luke 10:16). It is a presence of a dynamic order because it is always a question of a living word directed to someone specific; it is the presence of one who extends an invitation, who converses with us, as we said above. In preaching, "the claim made in the word is the very means of his presence" (H. Schlier). But all this depends precisely on the specific "content" of the proclamation being made. Jesus is not present in all the words of our day but only in those of preaching, and precisely because of what this proclaims and communicates.

Then here is the question that the Athenians posed to Paul: "Can we know what is the new doctrine you are speaking? For as you bring strange things to our ears, we want to know what they mean" (Acts 17:19-20). What is the primal message of the Christian proclamation? As a general response, we could say it is the coming of salvation in Jesus Christ (Eph 2:17; Acts 4:12). But the earliest preaching, according to the New Testament, was not content with this level of abstraction. It passed immediately to the concrete: the earliest formulas deal with the death and resurrection of Jesus Christ (1 Cor 15:3-4; Rom 4:24-25; 10:9; Luke 23:34; etc.) in their salvific meaning. This is the kerygma, which announces its fulfillment in these events of the merciful justice of God toward the sinner. In other words, it announces that the "Go in peace, and sin no more" (Luke 7:50 and John 5:14) was pronounced not just verbally by the earthly Jesus but effectively by God himself in the destiny of the death of this same Jesus. This event in its historical individuality ("once for all": Heb 7:27; 9:12, 26, 28; 10:10, 12, 14) indicates and guarantees the enduring availability of the liberating mercy of God to humanity and to the individual human tormented by sin (note Heb 12:24: the blood of Jesus *speaks* better than that of Abel).

Even if Jesus' words had an individual validity limited to the persons whom he actually encountered, still the eschatological occurrence of the paschal events has a universal validity. Henceforth every generation can say, "In him we have redemption through his blood, the remission of offenses . . . since the justice of God is now revealed for all who believe, without distinction" (Eph 1:7 and Rom 3:21-22). This is why this "gospel"

---

2. H. Schlier, *Wort Gottes* (Würzburg, 1958 [Italian, 1963, 58f.]) 40–41. The following quotation from Schlier is from pp. 41–42.

must be proclaimed to every generation, so that everyone may know and be able to say, "He loved me, and gave himself over for me" (Gal 2:20) and then reach complete freedom (Gal 5:1).

But then secondarily the proclamation contains also the invitation to conversion (it is useful, for instance, to study the general structure of the great letter to the Romans or Peter's discourse at Pentecost in Acts 2:14-40 to see the relationship between the two great elements of the Christian proclamation). Moreover, Paul and John trace the message back to the incarnation of Christ, interpreted as pure gift for us (Gal 4:4f.; John 3:16f.). Other themes are those of the creation (Rom 1:20), our election from eternity (Eph 1:4), the whole salvation history of Israel (Rom 9–11), and the new salvific situation that finds its place in the Church (Eph 3:10).

All this is "the word of faith that we preach" (Rom 10:8); "we do not preach ourselves" (2 Cor 4:5) but "the gospel of God" (1 Thess 2:9): "Christ crucified" (2 Cor 1:23) and "risen" (1 Cor 15:11-12) "for us" (Rom 8:32), without whom we would have nothing to say (1 Cor 15:14). Evidently this is all understood on a level of faith; but actually our kerygma can be considered a scandal or a folly by some (1 Cor 1:23). Indeed, "it pleased God to save the believers by means of the folly of the proclamation" (1 Cor 1:21).

A necessary aspect of the preacher's mission is to present the message in all its "scandalousness" (Gal 5:11). The Cross must always stand in the foreground, not so much an unexpected cross imposed by human beings (see Mark 8:34), but rather the very Cross of Christ in its salvific quality (see Rom 3:25; 1 Cor 1:18; Rev 12:11). To water it down with compromise or "anonymity" would be to betray it. But the Lord is near to the preacher, whom he strengthens so that through this servant the message of salvation may come to completion (2 Tim 4:17; cf. Acts 18:9-10; Titus 1:3; Rom 16:25).[3]

IV. Conclusion

What we have said above permits us now to draw some conclusions concerning the relationship between the preacher and the concrete proclamation. Of course, the Church's sacramental theology has never accepted the Donatist doctrine that the minister who does not have God's grace can transmit nothing to others. But if there is any place where the Donatist doctrine is closer to the truth, it is precisely in the question of the sacramentality of preaching. In some cases an anti-Donatism can dan-

---

3. See also M. Chevallier, *Esprit de Dieu, paroles d'hommes* (Neuchâtel, 1966).

gerously divide the person of the minister from the action this person accomplishes, like a bureaucrat dispensing a perfunctory function. But the Christian proclamation must be something quite different: "We cannot help but speak of what we have seen and heard" (Acts 4:20). As with Jeremiah: "I said, 'I shall speak no more in his name.' But in my heart it was like a burning fire. . . . I tried to contain it but could not" (20:9), it is actually the preacher, in all the subjectivity of the person, that becomes the issue, for the "matter" of this sacrament is not something extraneous to the "minister." Nor can the reason be different from what Paul declares, "We, having the same spirit of faith of which it is written, 'I have believed and so I spoke,' we also believe, and therefore we speak" (2 Cor 4:13). While the hearer moves from the word to faith, the Christian preacher moves from faith to the word.

1) Between preacher and word there arises a common destiny. The "folly of the kerygma" (1 Cor 1:21) finally makes the one who proclaims it also to be "foolish" in human eyes but wise in God's eyes (1 Cor 4:10-11). As in the case of Jesus, whose person is not distinguished from the word, "You are trying to put *me* to death because there is not room for *my word* in you" (John 8:37, 40; cf. John 1:1, 14), the principle applies analogously to the preacher. Thus, for the one who follows in the footsteps of Jesus, "to be a minister of Christ among the gentiles" means in the first place "to do the sacred work of preaching God's good news" (Rom 15:16).

2) The preacher should always remember that what is being handled is the property of another. It is "God's" word, not something to manipulate for our own satisfaction. It is not at our disposition; we are at its disposition. It does not serve us, but we serve it. As with John the Baptist, "the word of God came *upon* John, son of Zechariah" (Luke 3:2); like "those who were eyewitnesses from the beginning and have become servants of the word" (Luke 1:2). "We shall continue to be assiduous in prayer and the service of the word" (Acts 6:4): it is precisely this service that is the sign that always distinguishes every prophet and every apostle within God's people (note the important text 2 Cor 2:17).

3) It is not enough, then, to say that we must "respect" God's word; if it is "light for my feet" (Ps 119:105), we must adhere to it and reverence it like Samuel, who "did not let a single word of the Lord fall to the earth" (1 Sam 3:19). Otherwise the word proclaimed can become a cause of condemnation for the very one who proclaims it (cf. John 12:48).

4) Since we are not dealing with what belongs to ourselves, we are only "ambassadors for Christ, so that God is exhorting through us" (2 Cor 5:20). But precisely because of this we can speak with confidence and boldness.

If we were preaching ourselves or our own ideas, we might have reason to fear for our "image"; but "fear not, but speak and do not be silent, for I am with you" (Acts 18:9f.) The concept of *parrhēsía*, "bold speech," so frequent in Acts and in Saint Paul, identifies one of the most indispensable qualities of the apostle (see Acts 4:29, 31; 2 Cor 3:12; Eph 6:20; Phil 1:20).

To conclude, we affirm the primary value of the proclamation of the word in the framework of a sacramental theology. Actually there is no other sacrament about which the New Testament has so much to say as about preaching. Of course, a distinction must be made: "There is a preaching that leads to baptism and a preaching that leads to the eucharist" (von Allmen); but if the latter is not yet included in the former, the former must always remain as a constant in every later phase. And certainly, in the Christian understanding the "word of salvation" (Acts 13:26) can never be neglected; without this the only possible alternative would be religion as magic.

It is, then, fair to say that the first Christian sacrament administered is that of preaching. Such a "primacy" is not just genetically true but axiologically so, i.e., not only in the phase of missionary conquest but also in that of normal Christian life (see, for example, in Matt 28:19f. the relationship between "making disciples" through the word and "baptizing").

Chapter 18

Sin and Redemption: A Synthesis

I have been invited to speak on the basically complementary subjects of sin and redemption. However, I shall not examine the whole Bible but shall limit myself to the New Testament. Nor can I be exhaustive. Very schematically, I divide my talk into the two parts of the title: sin and redemption.

I. Sin

I begin with an observation that seems noteworthy to me. In the New Testament, sin never becomes part of the kerygmatic formulas, of the first confessions of faith, at least not as the subject of the confession. What did the first Christians proclaim? What was it that struck them, that overwhelmed them? It was the fact of Christ, his person, and even more it was what took place in him. They did not proclaim sin; sin is never the subject of proclamation in the New Testament. We see this already in the very first formulas of Christian faith that can be isolated here and there in the New Testament. I mean that sin is at least never a primary subject but an indirect subject, a reflex subject, a subject that may be brought in, of course, but at least never in the foreground.

We must at least quote the First Letter to the Corinthians, where we have this archaic formulation of faith: "Christ died for our sins according to the Scriptures, and was buried, and rose on the third day according to the Scriptures, and appeared to Cephas and then to the Twelve" (1 Cor 15:3). Now, we do have mention of sin here, but in the background, insofar as Christ died because of it. The confession of faith is Christological, and the theme of sin, which is secondary here, is quite absent in the other creedal formulas (see 1 Thess 1:9-10; 1 Cor 8:6; Phil 2:6-11; Rom 1:3b-4a; 10:9; Col 1:15-20; 1 Tim 3:16).

1) *Sin and sins*

This said, let us read a text that we are putting *in capite libri*[a] for our consideration, without doing an exegesis for the time being. We take it from Rom 5:12 and follow the standard Italian translation of the C.E.I.: "Hence, just as because of the sin of one single person sin entered the world, and with sin, death, so too death has reached all because all have sinned." I have said we will not do the exegesis of this passage now, which is in any case very complex and difficult. Rather, we make a basic observation about the terminology regarding sin. At least in Paul—but also in John—we must distinguish clearly between *sin* and *sins;* hence between a singular and a plural.

A statistic or two first. We will briefly consider the Letter to the Romans, considered the high point of the Pauline corpus, and the Gospel of John. We are thus looking at the two preeminent New Testament theologians. Now, in Romans the term "sin" (ἁμαρτία in Greek) occurs forty-seven times, only three of which are plural. The term "sins" is used only three times, and of these three, two are in Old Testament quotations and so are not really Pauline texts. It is evident, then, that Paul normally thinks of the concept of "sin" in the singular. Etymologically the term means "missing, error," that is, "missing a target or goal, missing the right thing." But in the letter there are other related words: the term "fall" (παράπτωμα) nine times, seven of which are in the singular; the term "transgression" (παράβασις) three times in the singular; the term "disobedience" only once, in the singular; and then the term ἁμαρτήματα, that is, "sins, concrete errors," only once. This is the situation. Hence, Paul thinks of sin considered as a reality in itself but prescinding from its multiplication.

The same can be said of John's Gospel. In John, where only the term "sin" occurs, it is found seventeen times, thirteen of which are in the singular. Moreover, in John there are no catalogues of vices such as we encounter in the Synoptics and Paul alike, which give detailed examples of sins (see Mark 7:21-22 and 1 Cor 6:9-10). John, then, like Paul, dwells on this fundamental reality of sin.

What does this mean? Paul and John alike have a basic reality in mind, something antecedent to individual sins. For them sin is a primary datum, a presupposition, something in which human persons find themselves, prescinding from the fact of this reality springing up in specific sinful acts.

---

a. "At the head of the book," Ps 40:8 (7) in the Vulgate. This is Penna's little joke, as he knows perfectly well that his use has nothing to do with the meaning of the phrase in its context.—T.P.W.

It is, I repeat, a reality that stands behind individual sins considered concretely.

What is the cultural background of this conception? Not the Old Testament. The Old Testament speaks of sins (or of a sin in the singular, but this will be a single transgression) precisely as considered fundamentally as rebellion against God, and so as incurring a debt that is owed to God, but always in reference to the behavior of the individual (see Exod 32:20; Deut 24:15; Ps 51:21 [19 "due sacrifices"], etc.). The same is true of rabbinic thought, that is, the religious-cultural environment on which Paul is partially dependent. Let us not forget that Paul was a disciple of one of the major rabbis of the first century, Gamaliel I. However, quite another thing is the thought of Qumran. This is a location on the western bank of the Dead Sea, where a number of manuscripts were found after the Second World War, texts that have modified, or at least in many ways have deepened, our understanding of the New Testament. They demonstrate that certain parts of the New Testament have their roots in a specific preexisting religious-cultural environment.

Now, the Pauline—and also the Johannine—conception of "sin" as an antecedent reality that totally confronts and involves the human person is to be found at Qumran as well. It is rather characteristic of this so-called apocalyptic Judaism, whose thought is tendentially dualistic, comparing if not contrasting the historical human situation, which is specifically immersed in evil, with the eschatological situation of purification, of renewal, of the new creation. But, I repeat, at Qumran the human person is clearly said to be radically a sinner. The writer of the Hymns affirms straightforwardly, "I am a structure of sin" (1QH 1:22), that is, from my roots I am immersed in sin.

And here is the key text of Paul that we have read: "Hence, just as because of the sin of one single person sin entered the world, and with sin, death, so too death has reached all because all have sinned" (Rom 5:12). Let us make some brief considerations of the reality of sin.

2) What is sin

Sin is, to put it in our terms, a situation of alienation from God. In every case—and this is always characteristic of biblical tradition, whether of the Old or the New Testament—the fundamental reference is to God, i.e., sin is the situation of alienation from God—not so much from oneself but primarily from God. The Bible does not have so much to say about the intrahuman issues, but it does always speak of relationship: the human person is always a being in relation, specifically in relation with God. Now sin means reference to God, specifically to God's will, that will that is expressed in Torah, in the Law.

For example, 1 John 3:4: "Whoever commits sin also commits violation of the law, for sin is violation of the law," at least according to the C.E.I., the official Catholic Italian translation. Others would understand the text differently: "violation of the law" can be understood not in the episodic sense of violation of a specific precept but in the sense of a fundamental disorder (the Greek is ἀνομία, "lawlessness"), a fundamental situation that stands behind everything. This is the understanding, for instance, of Ignace de la Potterie, who has done a study of the text.[1]

But the first half of the verse is clear: "Whoever commits sin also violates the law." But the "law" in question is normally understood by New Testament authors not so much as civil law but as the Torah, the body of books (to treat the literary aspect) that embody the will of God as revealed in the Old Testament tradition.

That is why the Lord's Prayer asks, "Pardon our debts," i.e., the debts we owe to you. That is why Jesus in Matt 18:23-35 tells the fundamental parable of the ruthless servant, whose debt is canceled but who then is unable to pardon the debt of his peer. In this parable the primary relationship is with the master, who generously cancels the debt.

And that is why the prodigal son says, "I shall arise and return to my father, and shall say to him, 'Father, I have sinned against heaven and against you' " (Luke 15:21). And when they meet he repeats this clause, "I have sinned against heaven and you" (Luke 15:21). This expresses precisely the situation of personal relation with God. Apart from this idea there is no biblical concept of sin, no concept of sin. Sin could become synonymous with generic infraction, as it basically is in Greek tradition: an infraction, an error, the missing of something, but a reality that essentially confronts me only with myself.

But here I should like to quote a text from Saint Thomas that not only is illuminating but somehow clarifies and integrates this idea of relationship with God. In the *Summa contra Gentiles* he says, "God is offended by us only because we are acting against our own good" (III 122: *Non enim Deus a nobis offenditur, nisi ex eo quod contra nostrum proprium bonum agimus.*) We should try to recover this understanding. In the Bible, it is true, it is not formulated so clearly, not even in the New Testament, but it is always presupposed: sin against God implies a degradation of oneself (see Psalms 32 and 51). In the parable of the prodigal son, in description, narration,

---

1. See I. de la Potterie, "Sin Is Iniquity (1 Jn 3,4)" in I. de la Potterie and S. Lyonnet, *The Christian Lives by the Spirit* (Staten Island, N.Y., 1971) 35-55.

metaphor if you will, Jesus expresses this reality: the sin against the father has brought on the son that social and personal degradation that touches us all.

There is, then, no need to insist so much on sin as offense against God. We must beware of certain anthropomorphisms that seem to have entered our current speech, when God is described as offended, as if God bore a grudge and so we must make reparation or propitiation, must appease God. This is not the meaning. God is offended only insofar as our attitudes and our behavior are contrary to our welfare. Here, if anywhere, is the offense against God's self.

We find in 1 Cor 8:12 an important aspect to recover in this observation on the nature of sin: "When you sin against your brother or sister and injure their weak conscience, you sin against Christ." Here is a typically Christian expression of reality: in this case one sins against Christ as well as one's brother or sister because Christ identifies himself in them. And this transcends a purely Jewish—or, if you will, purely natural—conception of sin in relation to God, and we find something more, a new relationship with Christ. But not as a relationship with him directly; the direct relationship is with the brother or sister, with whom Christ stands shoulder to shoulder.

And here we see the emergence of the new law, which for the Christian no longer consists of the Jewish list of hundreds of precepts but is synthesized in the commandment of love.

3) *The origin of sin*

A word about the origin of sin. We have read in Rom 5:12: "Just as because of the sin of one single person sin entered the world, and with sin, death, so too death has reached all because all have sinned." Paul here refers to a common, universal, primordial origin. Actually, the theme does not receive much emphasis. Jesus says nothing of it. And even Paul does not have much to say about it, though he does in any case state it. But we must be careful in our interpretation of the text. At least we must reject the Vulgate's Latin translation that conditioned the exegesis of the early Church writers, including that of Saint Augustine. They read the last words of the passage as *in quo omnes peccaverunt*, understanding the pronoun as referring to Adam, "in whom all sinned": in Adam all sinned as if in Adam were present all human beings, and hence in a sense all their sins. But this translation does not exactly correspond to the Greek.[2]

2. See S. Lyonnet, "Le péché originel en Rom 5,12. L'exégèse des Pères grecs et les décrits du Concile de Trente," *Biblica* 41 (1960) 325–355.

Modern translations (including the C.E.I.) change the perspective and render it thus: not "in whom" or "in which," all have sinned but "because" all have sinned. Two realities are, then, to be respected. First is the fact of the first sin of Adam, a first man, an individual person—who, however, is not even named here—:[b] through him sin has entered the world. Why has it entered the world? "Because all have sinned." There are, as I said, two realities: the original sin and the fact that this sin has been somehow taken up, repeated, ratified by all human beings, "because all have sinned." Then here at any rate is the affirmation of a personal free will ("because all have sinned"), and this expression refers to the fact that *each one* of the "all" has sinned, without exception.

Paul's declaration is universalizing, and in any case is different, for example, from the idea in a contemporaneous first-century Jewish book, the *Apocalypse of Baruch*, which says that Adam sinned for himself, but that then in turn everyone sinned for his or her own self, i.e., as if there were no connection between Adam and us. In Paul there is a connection: "Because of just one person sin entered the world . . ." And it is precisely this fundamental reality that Paul personifies in this chapter of the Letter to the Romans; that is, *this sin* becomes the subject of various actions; this sin it is that makes slaves, and pays the wages, the wages of death, etc. It is precisely this reality that implicates and encompasses humanity, as a prior and fundamental datum.

And yet, still in line with this personal free will, we must recognize the inward character of sin, as we read for example in Mark 7:18, 23, where Jesus says clearly: "It is not what enters one that renders one unclean, but what comes out. . . . For from the heart come thefts and adulteries and enmities." This is a text that confronts one with one's own responsibility, not with alibis, where sin is really sin and there are no alibis, not even the devil.

---

b. Note, when Penna is attempting to describe the thought of the ancient author, the cultural distance of that author is respected in the description. That Paul in this case ignores Eve may be jarring to us, but so is the fact that he assumes the old story's unitary biological origin of the human race, an understanding that seems quite out of line with findings of archaeological anthropology. Our theological task is not to misrepresent Paul's thought but, having understood it, to seek to understand how it best addresses us in our different cultural world, to determine how to distinguish between the case in which the alien thought is a compelling evangelical challenge to us and the case in which the strangeness must be criticized in the light of valid and even evangelical differences between our culture and that of the ancient thinker.—T.P.W.

4) *The spread of sin*

A final obvious observation concerns the spread of sin; it is universal: "All have sinned." Here is also the place to refer to John 1:29: "Behold the lamb of God, who takes away the *sin* of the world." We must note the singular, despite the variant in the Eucharistic liturgy, which uses the plural in the *Agnus Dei* (but the singular in the *Gloria*). The biblical text is singular, "the *sin* of the world." We could do a lengthy disquisition on this text. At least this must be understood in the context of Johannine theology, both in its understanding of sin and in its concept of the world. "The sin of the world," then, is somehow explained by John himself. Jesus, in the last discourse, says: "When the Spirit comes, he will convince the world of sin, of justice, of judgment. Of sin, because they do not believe in me. . . ." (John 16:8-9). What is sin? In Johannine theology sin is the failure to accept the *Logos*—to use the terms of the prologue—failure to embrace Christ as the one who reveals God, and hence ultimately the failure to restore fundamental relations with God. This is the sin of the world, as it is precisely this that puts the world in a situation of sin. We note that for John the concept of "world" has for the most part a decidedly negative resonance.

In concluding this treatment of sin, I should like to make a final observation: sin is an objective reality. Surprising as this may sound, we must note that the New Testament has a dearth of terminology for "guilt," especially in Paul, the author who has the most ample treatment of sin. The language, and essentially the idea of guilt, is lacking. We find here no Greek vocabulary to express this reality.[3] Only once, in 1 Cor 11:27, do we read "guilty of the blood [of Christ]." According to this text, there is question of guilt for one who does not think and receives unworthily. But in any case, apart from the uniqueness of the allusion, we have something limited to the eucharistic celebration, and moreover in the context of the failure of judgment in the Corinthian Church.

Sin is an objective reality that does not necessarily lead to feelings of anxiety or some such psychological state of mind. It is a reality that is, I say, judged in the light of reason, but especially of faith, in the logic of faith. It is judged to be present where it is observed. Perhaps with bitterness (note Luke 22:62: "Peter went out and wept bitterly"), but without mental anguish. The most appropriate reaction is humility, awareness of one's own limits, yes, one's moral limits before thethrice-holy God (note Peter also in Luke 5:8 and the publican in Luke 18:13).

---

3. See E. P. Sanders, *Paul and Palestinian Judaism: A Comparison of Patterns of Religion* (Philadelphia, 1977) 500–503 (Italian ed. 1986).

II. Redemption

We have come to the second panel of our diptych, the treatment of redemption. As a general statement we can say that in contrast to sin, redemption is the restoration of human dignity insofar as it is a restoration of relations with God, the proper focusing of the relationship to which we are called by our nature, indeed by our character as creatures. But here too we shall do a brief study of the terminology used by the New Testament, much more varied than that of sin and far more important and rich. We note first of all that the vocabulary of redemption comes from various spheres of human experience (and already in choosing this term "redemption" I use only one among many possible terms).[4]

1) *The terminology of "redemption"*

1) First, there is *the sphere of social institutions*, originally of the Greek world, at least in its vocabulary, whether redemption from slavery or payment for merchandise or more generically the liberation of one who is subject to repressive realities or principles. Here we have three verbs and their related nouns. A first verb, "redeem" or "ransom," provides the predominant vocabulary for redemption (ἀπολυτροῦν: redeem from slavery, ransom, buy back). Thus, in Mark's Gospel we find a fundamental text: "The Son of Man came not to be served but to serve, and to give his life as a ransom for many" (Mark 10:45); and Rom 3:24: "[All] are justified free of charge by his grace through the ransom/redemption in Christ Jesus."

A second verb means "to buy in the market" (ἐξαγοράζειν); e.g., 1 Cor 6:20: "You were bought at a price" (the Vulgate, the C.E.I., and the Douai translated "at a great price," but the Greek reads "at a price," that is, "for cash"!). The third verb is "liberate" (ἐλευθεροῦν), related to the noun "liberty/freedom" and the adjective "free." For example, Rom 6:18: "Thus, freed from sin, you have become servants to righteousness." We do not here emphasize the evident paradox, but it is, of course, obvious that the verb "freed" refers to a previous state of slavery, of servitude, that is quite different from what Paul refers to in the new state of service. Likewise Rom 6:22: "But now, freed from sin, and made servants of God. . . ." See also Rom 8:2: "The law of the Spirit of life in Christ Jesus has freed you from the law of sin and death."

---

4. See S. B. Marrow, "Principles for Interpreting the New Testament Soteriological Terms," *NTS* 36 (1990) 268–280.

2) The *second conceptual sphere* from which the language of redemption is derived is that of *common daily or existential experience.* Here we locate two verbs. The first is ῥύομαι, which means "release" or "deliver." From what? From a danger or a calamity. For example, in Matt 6:13 the Lord's prayer ends, "Deliver us from evil." The Latin Vulgate and the Italian translation use the verb "liberate," but the original carries a different nuance, more like "deliver" or "rescue," with the suggestion of the use of force. See also Rom 7:24: "Miserable man that I am, who will deliver me from this body of death?" And in Col 1:13: "He has released us from the power of darkness and transferred us into the kingdom of his beloved Son." Here the idea of a movement, a change of place, is explicit, and hence radical alteration of relations.

The second verb belonging to this semantic group is "save" (σώζειν), which basically means to rescue from death, that is, from extreme danger. One who is saved is one in whom life has triumphed: this is salvation. The word occurs frequently in the Synoptics, precisely in the sense of saving from death, for example with Jesus's miracles: "Save us, we are perishing!" in the straightforward miracle of the calming of the storm (Mark 4:35-41); or else with regard to spiritual reality: "Dead though we were through sins, he has brought us back to life together with Christ; by grace you have been saved. . . . By grace you have been saved, through faith" (Eph 2:5-8). Here the antithetic relationship between salvation and death is obvious.

In Paul, the vocabulary of salvation refers primarily to the eschatological rather than the immediate future. Only then will salvation be complete. See, for example, Rom 5:9: "All the more so, justified by his blood, we shall be saved from the wrath"; and in Pauline language "the wrath" is the eschatological wrath, judgment and condemnation.

3) *A third sphere* from which the imagery of redemption is derived is *religious, and specifically cultic.* The Greek verb is ἰλάσκομαι, which means "expiate" rather than "propitiate." Studies of the use of this verb indicate that in Greek tradition it does mean to propitiate an offended, angry god, whom one must appease, with whom one must ingratiate oneself, changing the god's attitude from rage to cheerfulness (the etymologically related word *hilarotēs*) and benevolence. But in biblical tradition (see Lev 6–7 and 16, *passim*) the verb means not to propitiate the deity but to expiate the sin, precisely as an obstacle, a screen that prevents full communication with God, a God who is well beyond these wretched anthropomorphic categories of rage or good cheer.

We have here the important text of Rom 3:25: "God predestined him [Jesus] as the *means of expiation [ἰλαστήριον]*, by means of faith. . . ." The reference is actually to the cover "expiatory/mercy seat" *(ἱλαστήριον)* of the Ark of the Covenant, which was placed in the Holy of Holies, the last chamber of the Jerusalem Temple (at least until the time of Nebuchad-nezzar, for after the Exile it existed no more, its place being simply com-memorated by a low base stone). Here the high priest entered only once a year, to sprinkle this *ἱλαστήριον* with the blood of a bullock. Thus was accomplished the purification of the people from their sin, their redemp-tion, called *kippur* in Hebrew (cf. Lev 16). This is the great Day of Atone-ment. Now, Jesus on the cross is the instrument of expiation for Christians. He is simultaneously Priest, Victim, and Ark of the Covenant, who re-stores our relationship with God. Similarly we can cite Heb 2:17, with the same kind of cultic language and imagery, and also 1 John 2:2, where the etymologically related *ἱλασμός* reflects the same theme.

4) *A fourth sphere* of origin for salvific terminology is that of *interper-sonal relations*. Here we have the language of reconciliation with the word *ἀποκαταλλάσσειν* ("reconcile"), i.e., to restore friendship between partners, a pure, transparent relationship. We have this in Rom 5:10-11, and 2 Cor 5:18-20 as well: "All this comes from God, who has reconciled us to him-self through Christ, and has confided to us the ministry of reconciliation; indeed God was, in Christ, reconciling the world to himself." Note also the Gospel text "If you are making your offering . . . and remember that your brother has something against you, go first and be reconciled with your brother" (Matt 5:23-24). And again we will find the same terminol-ogy in Col 1:20-21.

5) *A fifth sphere* from which the language of redemption is derived is the *forensic sphere*, that of the court of law and the administration of jus-tice. The language here is typically Pauline: that of justification *(δικαιοσύνη)*. I believe we are all aware of it because it is a classical term in the history of theology, especially since Luther. According to Paul, this justification is altogether different from normal human practice, insofar, as Paul says in Rom 4:5, as "God justifies the impious!" No more remarkable religious message could be proposed or proclaimed. It is the complete overturning of human logic, since the one who is a sinner is declared by God himself to be just, but declared just, not as a sinner but insofar as the person's sin is now eliminated. Here is accomplished precisely the opposite of what takes place in the human court of law, where the guilty is condemned and the innocent is acquitted, i.e., declared just. But God amazingly reverses the terms. There is a text of which everyone is aware, though it may not have penetrated all hearts: "While we were still weak [or sin-ners], Christ died for the impious. Why, one would hardly die for a just

person, though one might actually die for a good person. But God shows his love for us because while we were sinners Christ died for us. All the more so, then, now that we have been justified by his blood will we be saved from the wrath by him" (Rom 5:6).

So this vocabulary does come from a very specific sphere of human experience, but with a stupefying subversion. To perceive the unheard-of dimension of this reality is to perceive the heart of the Christian message. We here encounter something utterly without parallel, with God showing what it means to be God, that is, utterly different from us. To this the only possible reaction is humble and joyful adoration.

Let us listen to another text, Rom 3:28; this is a first principle, of which every Christian ought always to be aware, pondering the words repeatedly in the heart: "We maintain that a person is justified by faith, apart from works of the Law." This is the first principle for Christians—and not just for Luther and Protestants, who have made this their battle cry, only because Catholics have neglected it. It is simply a Pauline text, which in itself can be labeled neither Protestant nor Catholic. Note also the parallel passage of Gal 2:16.

6) *We can note one last expression* in reference to the terminology of redemption: *to have life.* I am not sure what sphere this derives from— perhaps simply from the realm of nature, of simple existence: to have life, to be alive. This expression is especially characteristic of John, who closely links "life" with the adjective "eternal." For John, to believe in Christ is to have eternal life right now, fully anticipated. For example, John 5:24: "Amen, amen, I say to you [the introduction is solemn], the one who hears my words and believes in the One who sent me, *has* eternal life and does not enter into judgment, but has passed from death to life." We might well ask to what extent Christians are aware of this rather than projecting, as is typical, eternal life only into the hereafter.

2) *The foundations of redemption*

From this diverse vocabulary let us identify certain fundamental bases of the speech about redemption.

1) *Modality of the event.* Salvation is an event. Salvation, redemption, liberation, justification—all that is signified by the terminology we have considered has a very precise point of reference or of origin that is an event, a historical event, namely the Cross of Christ. We cannot speak of salvation in the Christian sense unless we start from there, or at least include the Cross of Christ.

The fact stands out overwhelmingly if we compare the Christian language about salvation with the Jewish background of the period, where salvation could be achieved by various means.

a) One of these means consisted of the sacrifices of the Jerusalem Temple, which ceased to exist after the year 70.

b) Another means consisted of the sufferings, the tribulations, of life.

c) Another means was death; death itself, accepted as God's commandment, was considered a source of salvation.

d) Finally, repentance, which also retains a basic salvific reality in Jewish tradition. We need think only of the Old Testament and of Jesus's preaching, but also of rabbinic teaching (see Abot 4:17: "One hour of repentance and good works in this life is worth more than all the life to come"). But here we must make an astounding observation: Paul never speaks of repentance, or at least for him repentance does not have a true soteriological value. Why? Because he stands face to face with the Cross of Christ, and this alone is the origin of salvation. It is not my retreat into myself or my asking pardon of God that has salvific value; rather, I am encountered by an event, namely, the Cross of Christ. There it is that my salvation is decided. Instead of speech about repentance we have speech about faith, i.e., about accepting the Cross and the Blood of Christ insofar as they concern me, since they took place for me. This is the event, and such is the modality of the event; it is a modality that can seem banal, accidental, but that cannot help but be historic, since it expresses something so provocative, goes too much against the current, namely, a salvation embodied in a crucifix, a stumbling-block to Jews and foolishness to gentiles.

2) *This redemption has an agent* that is actually twofold, God in Christ. As it says in Rom 8:32: "He who did not spare his own Son but gave him up for us all, how can he help but give us everything along with him?" No division, then, can be made between God and Christ. The Cross is not just a Jesus fact, something that concerns only Jesus in his human and simply individual reality. In the Cross, God is in action: "He gave him up for us all."

Here we must also be careful not to insist too much on this terminology about a God who hands his own Son over to death, a bloody God who inhumanly sacrifices his own Son. In the background of this usage (which is very rare in any case—we have it here and can also see it in John 3:16: "God so loved the world as to give his own Son") is the biblical text of Gen 22 with its rabbinic re-reading.[5] In Gen 22 we read of Abra-

5. See vol. 1, chap. 9.

ham sacrificing his own son, Isaac. This story is paradigmatic in the history of Israel. And rabbinic literature returns to it, reflects on it, develops it until this offering becomes a sacrifice of expiation, emphasizing the fact that Abraham in offering his own son, and Isaac in accepting his own immolation (even if the sacrifice did not actually take place, but it is as if it were accomplished) have made expiation for all their descendants, with the result that this act becomes a source of merits for Israel, for all generations to come. This conception is known as the '*Aqedah* (an Aramaic word that literally means "binding" and refers to Isaac being "bound" by Abraham and placed on the altar); this is still a key element of Jewish liturgy for the feast of the New Year.

We must always read this story of Gen 22, about the sacrifice of Isaac, against the background of the New Testament language about the Son who is handed over to death. The Christian key to the interpretation of this story in patristic tradition has been to read this as a reference to the one who carries the wood, i.e., the cross, on his back, etc.

3) *What is the essence of this event?* Or better, what is the essence of God's salvific intervention in Christ? The essence is the gift of self, i.e., a supreme act of love—the gift of self rather than an act of raw power, which God could theoretically have performed for the salvation of the world. We might consider the opposite alternative of Jewish conceptions of the triumphant eschatological exploits of the Messiah. No, on the cross there is nothing but the total gift of self. This is where other texts come into play, such as Gal 1:20: "He loved me, and gave himself up for me." Note how personalized the discourse has become. In Rom 8:35, 37, 39 the love of God and the love of Christ are superimposed, identified; the love with which God loves is the very love with which Christ loves.

4) *The essence of redemption on the part of the recipient,* on the part of the human person, the believer, is a communion of love. It is a communion of love which derives from this gift and which in turn impels one to give oneself. Here we really ought to consider everything concerning *agápe,* or the love that is giving, to read 1 Cor 13,[6] and reflect that Paul's speech about Law sums up the whole Law in the law of agape, the law of love; for if God has so loved us, we ought to love one another. In this regard see Eph 4:32, but also chapter 4 of the First Letter of John, where this theme is developed.

5) Simultaneous with this is *the interior dynamism of the Spirit,* which we can see in Rom 8:2: "The law of the Spirit that gives life in Christ Jesus

6. See vol. 1, chap. 12.

has freed you from the law of sin and death.'' It is precisely the Spirit, poured out in our hearts, that formulates for us the invocation ''Abba, Father'' (Gal 4:6). Thus we have the complete restoration of a relationship of the utmost friendship, even the family ties of child and parent. And what is the result? What Paul calls the ''new creation'' (2 Cor 5:17). The believer, the Christian, is for Paul already today a new creation, not according to the apocalyptic Jewish conception, which uses this expression only to refer to the eschaton. But it is not only then that there will be a new creation; it already exists at this moment in the baptized person.

All this is possible *in* Christ, because, we read in Rom 8:1, ''there is now no condemnation for those who are in Christ Jesus.''

Chapter 19

The Blood of Christ in the Pauline Letters

In all the Pauline letters the word "blood" (αἷμα) occurs scarcely a dozen times—not very many if we take into account the considerable bulk of these works within the New Testament. Still, when the word occurs in connection with Christ, we are dealing with passages of powerful theological significance.

Preliminaries

First of all, we briefly note the texts, four in number, where there is no relationship between the blood and Christ.

The first is Rom 3:15: "Their feet are quick to shed blood [ἐκχέαι αἷμα]." Paul is here simply quoting Ps 14:1-3 (LXX), to describe the fact that there is not a single person who is righteous before God. Our verse fits into the general picture sketched by the psalmist, taken up by the Apostle, describing the general, gloomy human situation of all who are far from God and have no fear of the Lord. One element of the picture is just this declaration of v. 15. "To shed blood" is a typical biblical-Semitic expression found again and again in the Old Testament that can stand, as it does here, for "kill," i.e., take the life of a living person, with the implicit idea of sacrilege, since the blood belongs to God (see, for example, Gen 9:6; Lev 17:4, 13; Deut 21:7; 1 Sam 25:31; Prov 1:11; Sir 11:32; Isa 5:7; 59:7; Jer 22:3; Pss 79:3; 106:38; 1 Macc 1:37; etc.); or else it can refer to a ritual gesture in the execution of a bloody sacrifice (see Lev 4:7, 18, 25, 30, 34). The quotation makes it clear that Paul shares a basic component of the biblical anthropology; but the fact that the expression occurs only in a text cited from Scripture and is never taken up elsewhere in Paul's own writing gives us no reason to associate Paul with a semiticizing Greek.[1] In fact, he does not even use the expression ἐκχέειν αἷμα to identify or describe the death of Christ, neither in reference to the Cross nor to the Eucharist, while the three Synoptics all have the participle ἐκχυννόμενον in connection with the Eucharist.[2] Paul's language itself thus represents a tendency to transcend old and traditional patterns of expression.

The expression "flesh and blood" (σάρξ καὶ αἷμα), on the other hand, is better attested. It occurs three times: 1 Cor 15:50; Gal 1:16; Eph 6:12 (in this last text the terms are inverted.) We have here evidently the use of two nouns to describe the principal components of the living animate creature. It can have two meanings: either sacrificial (see below), or simply anthropological to designate "man as a transient being in contrast to God or supernatural powers."[3] It is in this second sense that the expression is used in the three passages noted; as such it is much used by the rabbis,[4] whereas elsewhere in the New Testament it is found only in Matt 16:17 and Heb 2:14. In Paul it is contrasted on the one hand with "the reign of God" and "the revealing of the Son," and on the other "the world rulers of this darkness, the spirits of wickedness in the heavenly places." By contrast, then, "flesh and blood" indicates creaturely human weakness, human nature itself insofar as it is not equal to the task of competing with what is greater than it, which normally belongs to the sphere of the divine. We might note that such terminology is more frequent and more standardized than that of the Eucharist in Paul, who will substitute the expression σῶμα, "body," for σάρξ (unlike John 6:54, 56).

There remain, then, eight texts that provide us with a Christological use of αἷμα, "blood": Rom 3:25; 5:9; 1 Cor 10:16; 11:25, 27; Eph 1:7; 2:13; Col 1:20. This Pauline use represents the most concentrated utilization of the theme by any New Testament writer except the author of Hebrews. Still, we must at once observe that while Hebrews clearly develops the meaning of the theme through an explicit comparison with Jewish sacrificial worship, in Paul this happens only rarely, and without much logical development. Throughout it looks as if it represents an already existing motif, or at least refers to a historical event already known to everyone,

1. Still, even classical Greek provides instances of the expression "shedding blood" for "killing" (see Aeschylus, *Eumenides*, 653: αἷμ' ὅμαιμον ἐκχέας πέδοι, "who has shed kindred blood"; cf. *ibid.*, 259–261); but the expression is infrequent and poetic.

2. The verb "shed" (ἐκχέειν or ἐκχύννειν) recurs with "blood" also in Matt 23:35; Luke 11:50; Acts 22:20; Rev 16:6.

3. J. Jeremias, *The Eucharistic Words of Jesus*, trans. N. Perrin (Philadelphia, 1977) 221.

4. See H. L. Strack, P. Billerbeck, *Kommentar zum Neuen Testament aus Talmud und Midrasch* (Munich, 1922) 1:730-731; also: Mishnah *Nazir*, 9:5 (twice; here the Italian version of V. Castiglioni translates it as "person"); *Sotah*, 8:1.

concerning which there is no need to enter into any particular speculation based only on its bloody character.

I. The kerygma as point of departure

Let us, then, identify just how we will approach the Pauline theme.
We will not come to it by beginning with Old Testament sacrificial texts,
as do, for example, W. D. Davies and Da Cruz Fernandes,[5] who consider
the New Testament theme only in the light of the Jewish conceptual
scheme, as though it were a normal and direct result thereof. While such
a treatment has the value of placing the "blood of Christ" against the background of an undeniable sacrificial influence, it brings the risk of suggesting that the death of Jesus can be understood in Jewish terms, can be
absorbed back into the Jewish cultic system, thus overemphasizing the
element of blood in its physical and material aspect, and thus isolating
it from the larger context of the death on the cross, and its motivation.

But in fact, the Cross of Christ actually represents the rupture of such
themes,[6] and is revealed as something new, irreducible to explanations
of an Old Testament nature. For the early Christian reflection on the death
of Jesus, the Old Testament sacrificial texts are not a point of departure,
in such a way that the blood of Christ could simply be referred to such
categories as if they constituted its one hermeneutical matrix; on the contrary, paradoxically they are rather the point of arrival, or better, a means
for understanding such a datum as the death of the cross, the modalities
of which do not coincide with those of the liturgy, and the proclamation
of which did not emphasize a cultic dimension.

It must be emphasized that if Paul uses the term αἷμα, "blood," eight
times in reference to Christ, he employs the noun "cross" (σταυρός) ten
times (and furthermore, in Eph 2:16 this is in synonymous parallelism with
"blood" in Eph 2:13, while in Col 1:20 it is an eloquent specification of
the "blood") and the verb "crucify" (σταυρόω) at least six times; also the
noun "death" (θάνατος) in a Christological sense is used at least eight times
(once in synonymous parallelism with the blood of Christ, Rom 5:9-10);
moreover, we must consider the verbs "die" (ἀποθνῄσκω—some fifteen

---

5. See W. D. Davies, *Paul and Rabbinic Judaism: Some Rabbinic Elements in Pauline Theology*
(London, 1965); A. J. A. Da Cruz Fernandes, *Sanguis Christi. Ricerca del senso e dell' ambito
sacrificale di questa espressione neotestamentaria alla luce del concetto e dell'uso ebraico del sangue* (Rome,
1971).

6. Whether because it is a question of human rather than animal blood (see Philo of
Alexandria, *De specialibus legibus*, 1:254: τὸν δ'ἱερὸν βωμὸν οὐ θέμις αἵματι ἀνθρωπίνῳ μιαίνεσθαι:
"It is not permitted to stain the sacred altar with human blood"), or because it was not shed
in any ritual context.

times) and "deliver" (παραδίδωμι—six times), which describe the death of Jesus rather in personalistic terms.[7] Now within this rich vocabulary the term "blood" is only one element, which is then part of a much larger linguistic context, from the whole of which it derives its own basic semantic value. But the oldest kerygmatic formulas never mention the blood, but only the death in general, understood globally as redemptive event.[8]

This means the recognition that the point of departure for a proper understanding of the death and the blood of Christ is simply the earliest Christian kerygma,[9] which immediately perceived in that event a special salvific dimension and expressed it in lean but eloquent terms. Actually, from the beginning, what is determinative for the understanding of the death of Christ is the frequent use of the preposition ὑπέρ, "for," found in connection with the verb "die" (e.g., 2 Cor 5:14-15; Rom 5:6-8) or "deliver" or "deliver oneself" (e.g., Gal 2:20; Rom 8:32). The most typical passage, 1 Cor 15:3, must stand for them all: "Christ died for our sins" *(Χριστὸς ἀπέθανεν ὑπὲρ τῶν ἁμαρτιῶν ἡμῶν).*

Whether this formula alludes to the Servant Song in Isa 53 (Cullmann, Lohse, Jeremias, Conzelmann) or not (Barrett, Hahn), it cannot but allude in all its richness to a vicarious and expiatory sacrifice.[10] This is even more apparent elsewhere, where in place of the term for things, "sins," we have the personal pronoun "us" (Rom 5:8) or "all" (2 Cor 5:14-15), or else a substantive referring to persons, "the impious" or "sinners" (Rom 5:6, 8; cf. "brother" in 1 Cor 8:11). The expiatory sacrificial value derives also from the fact that the effects of this death come not to good persons or to positive values being promoted,[11] but to persons to be purified or realities to be destroyed. But as we see, the lack of a specific reference to the bloody nature of this sacrifice is surprising. Only Rom 5:9, δικαιωθέντες νῦν ἐν τῷ αἵματι αὐτοῦ, "justified by his blood," is close to a ὑπέρ-formula

7. We should add the following to these terms: κρεμάννυμι, "hang" (Gal 3:13); ἀποκτείνειν, "kill" (1 Thess 2:15); παθήματα, "suffering" (2 Cor 1:5; Phil 3:10); θλίψις, "tribulation" (Col 1:24); στίγματα, "marks" = "wounds" (Gal 6:17); νέκρωσις, "putting to death" (2 Cor 4:10).

8. See G. Delling, *Der Kreuzestod Jesu in der urchristlichen Verkündigung* (Göttingen, 1972); see also F.-J. Ortkemper, *Das Kreuz in der Verkündigung des Apostels Paulus* (Stuttgart, 1967).

9. Note the good methodological observation of E. Lohse, *Märtyrer und Gottesknecht. Untersuchungen zur urchristlichen Verkündigung vom Sühntod Jesu-Christi* (Göttingen, 1955) 139, n. 1. See also E. F. Siegman, "The Blood of Christ in St. Paul's Soteriology," *Contemporary New Testament Studies* (Collegeville, Minn., 1965) 359–374.

10. In other instances we encounter other prepositions meaning "for": διά (1 Cor 8:11; 2 Cor 8:9; Rom 4:25) and περί (1 Thess 5:10); and related to these, ἀντί (Mark 10:45; Luke 20:28).

11. The formulation "to die for" does also appear in secular Greek, but with reference to a person who is loved or else to noble ideals; likewise, even in Hellenistic Judaism one can die "for the Law of God" (2 Macc 7:9), even with an expiatory *effect* (2 Macc 7:37-38); see M. Hengel, "1. Preliminary Questions," *The Atonement* (Philadelphia, 1981) 1–32 = *The Cross of the Son of God* (London, 1986) 189–220.

of the preceding v. 8 (Christ died for us); but the expression about the blood is here parallel to the reference to the cross in the following v. 10 (We have been reconciled with God *through the death of his Son: διὰ τοῦ θανάτου τοῦ υἱοῦ αὐτοῦ*), not to mention the simple personal pronoun "through him" *(δι᾽ αὐτοῦ)* of v. 9 itself.

We can also affirm that Paul regularly uses the expression αἷμα Χριστοῦ in passages in which he employs traditional expressions.[12] This affirmation, of course, must not be accepted uncritically but should be verified each time (and for more detail we refer to the commentaries). But it is certainly true with regard to the three eucharistic uses (1 Cor 10:16; 11:25, 27). The same can be said essentially of the texts of Col 1:20 and Eph 1:7 found in two hymnic fragments held to be pre-Pauline.[13] As for Rom 3:25, many authors there perceive a borrowing from tradition.[14] There remain Rom 5:9, which can be explained in the light of the preceding 3:25 and the following v. 10, and then Eph 2:13 (but here the whole letter is probably deutero-Pauline.

In any event, we must remain aware that the eight Pauline occurrences appear in only a very few thematic contexts and are certainly of some theological relevance, not to say originality. It is our intention to make a brief exegetical analysis of each one, grouping them according to their theological contexts, of which we identify four: Eucharist (1 Cor 10:16; 11:25, 27); justification (Rom 3:25; 5:9; Eph 1:7); cosmology (Col 1:20); and Church (Eph 2:13). These are also arranged in chronological order.

II. The blood of the eucharistic meal (1 Cor 10:16; 11:25, 27)

In 1 Cor 11:25, 27 we have a double mention of the blood of Christ in a traditional context (on which the understanding of the preceding text 10:16 also depends). The reference to the *paradosis*, "tradition" (11:23), says clearly that Paul is simply transmitting material that already belonged to the earlier Church. Actually, these verses find an eloquent parallel in the threefold Synoptic tradition (Mark 14:22-23; Matt 26:26-27; Luke 22:19-

---

12. See E. Lohse, *Märtyrer*, 139.

13. These fragments show evidence of redactional intervention, to which precisely the mention of the blood probably belongs (at least in Col 1:20); however, even more authors consider these letters deutero-Pauline (see, e.g., G. Barbaglio and R. Fabris, *Le lettere di Paolo*, 3 vols. [Rome, 1980]).

14. In favor of the "traditional" character of this passage and of vv. 25-26a, U. Wilckens, *Der Brief an die Römer*, I (Zurich–Neukirchen Vluyn, 1978) 183, provides these arguments: the "relative-style" of v. 25; the repetition of "to manifest his justice" in vv. 25b-26a; the cumbersome expression "by means of faith" in v. 25; the number of non-Pauline expressions (προτίθεσθαι in the sense of "propose publicly," ἱλαστήριον, πάρεσις, and the very allusion to the "blood" of Christ); for other authors see ibid., nn. 488 and 490.

20), though of these, the Lukan version is the nearer to the Pauline text.[15] But there are obvious signs of redactional work by Paul himself. What strikes us first, to limit ourselves to the saying about the chalice, is the absence of the present participle ἐκχυννόμενον, "poured out," which is present not only in Matthew and Mark but even in Luke. Additionally, we look in vain for the expiatory theme expressed with the preposition "for," ὑπέρ (πολλῶν, "many," in Mark/Matthew; ὑμῶν, "you," in Luke), something all the more surprising in that it is to be found in v. 24 concerning the body/bread. Thus two terms typically associated with sacrificial language are missing.[16]

Furthermore, in Paul (as also in Luke) the "blood" is not the direct predicate as it is in Mark and Matthew ("This is my blood of the covenant"), but rather is in a modifying phrase within the predicate, thus fulfilling a secondary role: "This cup is the new covenant in my blood." The Semitic-sounding preposition "in" (ἐν) makes an instrumental (or causal, according to Jeremias) clause. Apart from any other considerations,[17] it is obvious that this formulation gives priority to the effect or result mediated by the blood rather than the instrument or cause that brought it about, i.e., the "new covenant" rather than the "blood" of Christ, even though the two are linked precisely as cause (or instrument) and effect.

On the whole, we get the impression that the Pauline formula has a more static, "realistic" interest, that is, inclined to consider the actual and personal presence of the Lord during the celebration. The impression is further evidenced by v. 26, which, as if by way of compensation, feels the need to relate the celebration itself with the past "death of the Lord," and by v. 27, which declares the unworthy participant to be "guilty of the body and blood of the Lord."[18] Actually, to drink the cup means to communicate in the "blood of Christ" (10:16), even if this affirmation is polemically conditioned in the context of a warning against "communion with demons" by eating food offered to idols (see 10:20-21).

15. On all the issues, see J. Jeremias, *Eucharistic Words*, chap. 4.
16. See Jeremias, op. cit., 226.
17. The complicated Lukan-Pauline formula had "the intention of warding off the misunderstanding that the Lord's supper was a Thyestian meal where blood was drunk" (J. Jeremias, op. cit., 170).
18. The repeated use of the title κύριος in 11:23, 26, 27 (twice) rather than "Christ" or the like confirms the fact of an actual, "present" encounter with him: see W. Kramer, *Christ, Lord, Son of God* (London, 1966) 181-182. As for the blood of Christ (10:16), in which one shares by drinking, it must be said that it "is not the substance, but the death of Jesus as a saving event," and that this "finally involves the question of faith, [which] alone makes one 'worthy' of the community meal (1 C 11:18ff; R 14:23"—L. Goppelt, "πίνω," TDNT 6:143, n. 70 and n. 72). For a parallel with the cultic "meals" of antiquity, see H. Lietzmann, *An die Korinther I-II*, ed. W. G. Kümmel (Tübingen, 1949⁴) 49-51; see also F. Hauck, "κοινωνός," TDNT 3:805-806, and especially H.-J. Klauck, *Herrenmahl und hellenistischer Kult*, NA 15 (Münster W., 1982).

Thus, in Paul the motif of the blood is subordinated to that of the covenant.[19] This is also emphasized by the fact that the addition of the adjective καινή, "new," to the noun διαθήκη recalls the prophetic text Jer 31:30-31
(31-32) more than the cultic text of Exod 24:8, which is clearly the background of Mark/Matthew. Hence, the "blood" of the Pauline formula
seems to be meant less as the material element of the sacrifice and more
as an effective symbol of the violent death of Christ. As P. Neuenzeit rightly
observes, "to indicate the blood alone, and mean it as sacrificial matter,
would have required further reflection; after all, the death on the cross
was not a particularly bloody execution, and moreover a theological base
would have to be found before applying the reference to the sacrificed
animals to the death on the cross, since human blood was unknown in
Israel as sacrificial matter."[20] These words need not indicate a relativiza-
tion of the blood, which is spoken of in relation to the institution of the
Eucharist.

Precisely because the crucifixion was not particularly bloody (but we
must remember the flagellation, the nails, the lance), and precisely because human blood was not common sacrificial matter, it is surprising that
Jesus still makes reference to his blood. Rather, the Pauline connection,
even if only instrumental, with the New Covenant clearly indicates that
the latter actually came about no more and no less than because of the
blood and therefore the death of Christ. Even the separation of the "blood"
from the "body," by means of a separate formula for each element, may
allude to a sacrificial victim, the two constitutive elements of which are
separated when it is killed; but this remains problematic.[21] Still, at least
the Pauline (and Lukan) redaction of the story means to use the αἷμα,
"blood," as a synecdoche, as representing (surely significantly) the whole
event of the death of Christ.

We must, then, observe that it is only in recounting the institution that
the blood is associated with the covenant in Paul (indeed throughout the

---

19. See M.-L. Gubler, *Die frühesten Deutungen des Todes Jesu* (Freiburg in Schweiz-Göttingen,
1977) 239.

20. P. Neuenzeit, *Das Herrenmahl. Studien zur paulinischen Eucharistieauffassung* (Munich,
1960) 161. Concerning crucifixion and capital punishment in antiquity, see M. Hengel, "3.
Docetism as a Way of Removing the 'Folly' of the Cross," and "4. Crucifixion as a 'Barbaric'
Form of Execution," *Crucifixion*, 15–21, 22–32 = *Cross*, 107–113, 114–124 (on the explicit
connection cross/blood, this author, whose documentation is generally very copious, can cite
only one, Flavius Josephus, *Jewish Antiquities*, 19:94); see also L. Díez Merino, "La crocifis-
sione nella letteratura ebrea antica," in *La sapienza della Croce oggi*, I (Turin, 1976) 61–68.

21. In favor, see J. Jeremias, op. cit., 221–222; concerning the fact that in the Synoptics
and Paul the usual pair "flesh/blood" become "body/blood," see ibid., 199–201. Against this
sacrificial opinion see, for example, H. Schürmann, *Der Einsetzungsbericht, Lk 22,19-20*, II,
(Münster, 1955) 98–110, esp. 109; he interprets the two terms in a purely anthropological sense:
"body" (σῶμα) in place of *baśar* for the bodily totality, and αἷμα as a description of the violent
death of the martyr (thus also E. Lohse, *Märtyrer*, 124–125).

whole New Testament besides); the other allusions to the term διαθήκη, "covenant," in the Pauline corpus (Rom 9:4; 11:27; 2 Cor 3:6, 14; Gal 3:15, 17; 4:24; but note Eph 2:12-13) make no allusion at all either to the Eucharist or even to the death on the cross. This also may be an indication that the appearance of "blood" in this context is a traditional datum that Paul never repeats on his own because it has no role in his personal vision. It is still possible to maintain, along with certain scholars, that it is the eucharistic context that is the original *Sitz im Leben* of the soteriological interpretation of the death of Jesus as an expiatory sacrifice.[22]

III. The blood of justification (Rom 3:25; 5:9; Eph 1:7)

In the two passages from Romans we find the same grammatical construction, an adverbial clause of means or instrument with a marked Semitic flavor, "in his blood," ἐν τῷ αὐτοῦ αἵματι (3:25) and ἐν τῷ αἵματι αὐτοῦ (5:9). The simple transposition of the personal pronoun in the former phrase gives it a special personalistic emphasis. Actually, of the two texts this 3:25 is the richer in meaning, and it is this one that we must treat in greater detail.

In 3:24-25 we read, "Justified gratis by his grace through the redemption in Christ Jesus, whom God displayed (or planned) as a ἱλαστήριον ('expiation'. . .), through faith, in his blood." In this phrase[23] the most difficult issue, and also the most important, is trying to determine the exact meaning of the word ἱλαστήριον. Apart from some less important interpretations,[24] the strongest possibilities are two: either to see it as a neuter adjective used as a substantive, to be translated as "instrument of expiation" (thus the Bible de Jérusalem and the Italian Episcopal Con-

---

22. See M.-L. Gubler, *Die frühesten Deutungen*, 325–327 (with other authors); we must be clear about it: the Eucharist is not divorced from the motif of servanthood, which informed the whole of Jesus' earthly existence. At any rate, this origin of the theme in the Eucharist at least outweighs, if it does not actually contradict, derivations from conceptions of Old Testament sacrifices or of the expiatory death of martyrs (Lohse), or recourse to Isa 53 (Jeremias).

23. Some authors, especially Bultmann and Käsemann, perceive in vv. 24-26 a fragment of pre-Pauline faith; among the most recent commentaries, U. Wilkins is favorable, while Schlier rejects it; see n. 14 above. Also D. Greenwood, "Jesus as Hilasterion in Romans 3:25," BTB 3 (1973) 316–322.

24. E.g., E. Lohse, *Märtyrer*, 152, interprets it as a neuter adjective, which he associates with the noun θῦμα, "offering" (the adjective is found in 4 Macc 17:22, but explicitly modifying the noun θάνατος, "death"); see also L. Morris, "The Meaning of Hilasterion in Romans III, 25," NTS 2 (1956), 33–43; but in Romans the supposition is gratuitous, since 4 Macc does not necessarily imply the idea of offering. Another solution is that of some Vulgate manuscripts (FDKB) and ancient Latin writers (Ambrose, Ambrosiaster, Jerome, Pelagius), who read a masculine adjective "propitiatorem" modifying the preceding relative pronoun ὅν, "whom"; but the reading is late and would actually better correspond to the noun *hilastēs*, which, however, is not the reading of the Greek.

ference) in a general sense, equivalent to a simple "expiation,"[25] or else to discover there a specific allusion to the "propitiatory," *kapporet*, of Exod 25:17; Lev 16:15-16 as cultic location in the (first) Jerusalem Temple. Each of these exegetical choices is favored by excellent authorities[26] and also good arguments, which we have no intention to summarize here. In any case, the first explanation obviously puts less emphasis on the specifically cultic background of the concept. And in fact, as rightly noted by J. Cambier, "the bloody death of Christ, described as *hilastērion*, cannot be simply identified with any sacrifice offered by human beings, and so we must not stress the terms borrowed from ordinary sacrificial usage."[27]

Perhaps the texts that are closest to ours thematically are the passages about the martyrdom of Eleazar and of the seven brothers in 4 Macc 6:29 (καθάρσιον αὐτῶν ποίησον τὸ ἐμὸν αἷμα καὶ ἀντίψυχον αὐτῶν λαβὲ τὴν ἐμὴν ψυχήν: "Make my blood a purification for them, and take my life as their ransom") and 17:21-22 (ἀντίψυχον γεγονότας τῆς τοῦ ἔθνους ἁμαρτίας. καὶ διὰ τοῦ αἵματος τῶν εὐσεβῶν ἐκείνων καὶ τοῦ ἱλαστηρίου τοῦ θανάτου αὐτῶν ἡ θεία πρόνοια τὸν Ἰσραὴλ προκακωθέντα διέσωσεν: "they became a ransom for the sin of the nation. And through the blood of these pious ones and their atoning death, divine providence saved Israel, which had been afflicted").

Hellenistic Judaism, then, knew of the atoning character of the death of martyrs and accepted it, and described it by using terms from sacrificial speech (e.g., substitution, purification, atonement, blood) but in a non-cultic context. This is precisely the case with Jesus, the "faithful and true

25. The sense would be similar to that of ἱλασμός, which in the New Testament is found in 1 John 2:2; 4:10 (see O. Michel, *Der Brief an die Römer* [Göttingen, 1955] ad loc.).

26. For the first, the commentaries of W. Sanday and A. Headlam, M.-J. Lagrange, J. Huby, O. Michel, O. Kuss, C. K. Barrett, E. Käsemann, C. E. B. Cranfield, H. Schlier, and also studies by C. H. Dodd, "Ἱλάσκεσθαι, Its Cognates, Derivatives and Synonyms in the Septuagint," JTS 32 (1931) 352–360; V. Taylor, *The Atonement in New Testament Teaching* (London, 1946); J. Cambier, *L'évangile de Dieu selon l'épître aux Romains*, I (Bruges, 1967) 92–112. Supporting the second, the commentaries of A. Nygren, F. J. Lehnhardt, U. Wilckens; also the studies of F. Büchsel in TDNT 3:318–323; T. W. Manson, "ΙΛΑΣΤΗΡΙΟΝ," JTS 46 (1945) 1–10; W. D. Davies, *Paul and Rabbinic Judaism*, 237–242; S. Lyonnet, *De Peccato et Redemptione* (Rome, 1960) 106–117 (S. Lyonnet-L. Sabourin, *Sin, Redemption, and Sacrifice* [Rome, 1970] 157–166); P. Stuhlmacher, "Zur Neueren Exegese von Röm 3:24-26," in *Festschrift W. G. Kümmel* (Göttingen, 1975) 315–333.

27. J. Cambier, *L'évangile*, 97. The principal arguments against the cultic interpretation are the following: the term would make a better "type" for the cross than for Jesus, for otherwise he is simultaneously antitype of both the *kapporet* and the sacrificial victim, whose blood is sprinkled on this cultic object. Moreover, the context of the term is so lacking in cultic allusions that the readers would really have had to work to discover the hidden meaning—and all the more so if they were of gentile origin. On the other hand, the argument often adduced against the cultic understanding based on the lack of the article that is regularly used by the Septuagint does not hold up, for when ἱλαστήριον is in the predicate position, as it is here, the article can be omitted (as in Philo, *De vita Mosis*, 2:96 and 97). Among the early Church writers, Origen (PG 12:515, 523) understands the term in reference to the *kapporet*, while Chrysostom (PG 60:444) refers it only to a sacrificial animal.

martyr'' (Rev 3:14); but Paul, in a more original and suggestive manner, presents and, as it were, comments on his immolation by means of a discreet emphasis on the love that informed him from within (note the eloquent texts Gal 2:20; Rom 5:8; 8:35, 39; Eph 2:4; 5:2, 25). It is precisely in virtue of this basic disposition that Jesus rises above any cultic context as the consummately personal and free victim. And it is as such that through him (v. 24: "in Christ Jesus") God completes the expiation, that is, the removal of every impurity in human beings, all of whom are "deprived of God's glory" (v. 23), as if to say that it is not the mere material or bloody immolation that brings about justification or the "new creation" (2 Cor 5:17), but the loving and obedient offering of self with full conviction. And therefore it is brought not only to "sins," as objective, neutral cause, but rather to "sinners/the impious/the weak, enemies" (note Rom 5:6-8).

Our text actually reveals a basic preoccupation that becomes apparent through the insistence with which Paul treats the effects of the death of Jesus while quite significantly ignoring how this comes about. Such a contrast of effects and means is revealed specifically by the substantially secondary role of "the blood" compared with the concepts of "faith" and "justification." In the whole letter to the Romans we note that "blood" *(αἷμα)* occurs only in the two passages cited, and in the form of modifiers at that. On the other hand, the verb "believe" *(πιστεύειν)* is present twenty times and the noun "faith" *(πίστις)* thirty-seven times, while the term "righteousness" *(δικαιοσύνη)* is found thirty-three times, the verb "justify" *(δικαιοῦν)* fifteen times, the adjective "righteous" *(δίκαιος)* six times, and another word for "righteousness" *(δικαίωσις)* twice, to all of which should be added the related concepts of "grace," "gift," "life."

But to limit ourselves to our present passage, it is important to note the singular construction of the phrase ἱλαστήριον διὰ πίστεως ἐν τῷ αὐτοῦ αἵματι: "as an expiation, through faith, in his own blood." It is so evident that the modifier "in his own blood" *(ἐν τῷ αὐτοῦ αἵματι)* refers to ἱλαστήριον that according to R. Bultmann and others, the phrase διὰ πίστεως, "through faith," would be a Pauline addition to an earlier confession of faith that is here quoted and retouched. Thus "faith" is as it were wedged in between "expiation" and "in his blood," to show that this is an integrating and essential part of the process of salvation, which results not just from the material sprinkling of blood, much less from a cultic procedure, but depends on a conscious and free appropriation of the meaning inhering in this event.

Thus, the blood of Christ is determinative for justification, but more for what it signifies than for its merely being shed physically, considered

as an isolated fact standing on its own. This is so much the case that in
5:9 the instrumental phrase (Semitic in form) ἐν τῷ αἵματι αὐτοῦ, "by his
blood," is only a synonymous parallel to the corresponding phrase (more
Greek in form) that occurs in the following v. 10: διὰ τοῦ θανάτου τοῦ υἱοῦ
αὐτοῦ, "through the death of his Son," where both formulas pick up and
develop the simple confession of faith of the preceding v. 8, Χριστὸς ὑπὲρ
ἡμῶν ἀπέθανεν, "Christ died for us." So the "blood" becomes almost a
cipher for the "death" of Jesus, of which it is the most vivid, concrete,
and striking exponent, especially because of the violence of the death. It
is just because of humiliation and obedience "unto death, even the death
of the cross," (Phil 2:8) that "the grace of God and the gift in the grace
of the one man Jesus Christ abounded for the many" (Rom 5:15). Precisely in the section Rom 5:15, 21, where Paul sets up an opposition between the sin of Adam and the redemption in Christ, this is traced back
at various points not to the blood but to the "grace" of Christ (v. 15: ἐν
χάριτι τῇ τοῦ ἑνὸς ἀνθρώπου Ἰησοῦ Χριστοῦ, "in the grace of the one man Jesus
Christ," with a modifier similar to that of the "blood" of 3:25; 5:9), simply
to "only Jesus Christ" (v. 17), to the "one person's work of righteousness" (v. 18), to "one person's obedience" (v. 19).

To these passages we can also add Eph 1:6-7: "the grace he lavished
on us in the Beloved, in whom we have redemption through his blood,
the forgiveness of sins." The association of the blood with sins demonstrates the expiatory character, desired and accomplished by God, of whose
"grace" it is both sign and instrument. The context of this mention is traditional in character, since Eph 1:3-14 almost certainly includes a preredac-
tional *berakhah*.[28] Given the presence of the "Beloved," ἠγαπημένῳ, we
should perhaps not exclude from the background of the text at least a tenu-
ous reference to the *'aqēdah*, i.e., the sacrifice of Isaac (according to Gen
22 and the Jewish speculations about it), with a thematic linkage to Rom
8:32.[29] Nevertheless, in the context of the *eulogia*, the mention of the blood
and of the relationship to the forgiveness of sins appears only as an intermediate state in the process of realization (and of proclamation) of "the
mystery of God's will" (v. 9) and the plan to recapitulate all things (or
bring them together) in Christ, whether they be in heaven or on the earth
(v. 10). Actually, this is the high point of a text that is thematically mid-

28. On the isolation of these verses as an independent passage, see the commentaries,
e.g., R. Penna (Bologna, 1988) 109.
29. In the Jewish tradition of the sacrifice of Isaac, mention of the blood is rare (still, note
Pseudo-Philo, LAB 18:5: *et pro sanguine eius elegi istos*, "and because of his blood I chose them");
on the various problems raised by the comparison of this theme with the New Testament,
see M. L. Gubler, *Die frühesten Deutungen*, 336–375, and especially vol. 1, chap. 9, of the
present work.

way between the soteriological passages of Rom 3:25; 5:9 on the one hand, and the cosmological passage of Col 1:20 on the other.

IV. The blood of cosmic reconciliation (Col 1:20)

A highly original treatment of the blood of Christ concerns its connection with the establishment of cosmic peace, on which the hymn of Col 1:15-20 ends: "God was pleased . . . through him to reconcile all things in heaven and on earth to himself, bringing about peace through the blood of his cross."

The precise understanding of this literarily weighty statement depends on what relationship one can establish between it and the whole context of which it is part. Contemporary exegesis unanimously recognizes that Col 1:15-20 is the repetition and to some extent the reworking of a pre-Pauline (if not pre-Christian) hymn.[30] Its general interpretation depends not so much on an undemonstrated pre-Gnostic background,[31] as it does on the use of categories from the Jewish milieu,[32] especially from Wisdom circles.[33] In this sense Christ is sung as center and ruler of the universe, as the one in whom the variety and even the contradictions of the universe are gathered into unity, just as the old Wisdom had been considered such a divine cohesive element of the universe and of human experience (see, above all, Prov 8:22-31; Sir 24:3-12; Wisdom *passim*).

This perspective, however, of Christ as unifying principle of all things under his transcendent lordship comes to be treated according to a substantially cosmological point of view. That is, Christ emerges as Παντόϰρατωρ, both insofar as his divine nature places him above all "things visible and

---

30. See H. J. Gabathuler, *Jesus Christus, Haupt der Kirche—Haupt der Welt. Der Christushymnus Colosser 1:15-20 in der theologischen Forschung der letzten 130 Jahren* (Zurich, 1965); A. Feuillet, *Le Christ, sagesse de Dieu d'après les épîtres pauliniennes* (Paris, 1966) 163–273; R. Deichgräber, *Gotteshymnus und Christushymnus in der frühen Christenheit. Untersuchungen zu Form, Sprache und Stil der frühchristlichen Hymnen* (Göttingen, 1967) 143–155; K. Wengst, *Christologische Formeln und Lieder des Urchristentums* (Gütersloh, 1973²).

31. Against E. Käsemann, "Eine urchristliche Taufliturgie," in *Festschrift R. Bultmann* (Stuttgart, 1949) 133–148.

32. The comment of E. Lohmeyer, *Die Briefe an die Philipper, an die Kolosser und an Philemon* (Göttingen, 1964¹³) 43–47, tries to explain the whole hymn precisely on the basis of v. 20, in which he sees an echo of the great Jewish Day of Atonement *(yom kippûr)*, while S. Lyonnet, "L'hymne christologique de l'Épître aux Colossiens et la fête du Nouvel An," RechScRel 18 (1960) 93–100, here perceives a resonance of the Jewish New Year festival, *ro'š ha-šanah* (basing himself primarily on a text of Philo, *De specialibus legibus*, 2:192).

33. See A. Feuillet, *Le Christ*; F. Montagnini, "Linee di convergenza fra la sapienza veterotestamentaria e l'inno cristologico di *Col* 1," in *Atti della XXIII Settimana Biblica dell'A.B.I.* (Brescia, 1976) 37–56; S. Lyonnet, "Ruolo cosmico di Cristo in *Col* 1,15ss alla luce del ruolo cosmico della Torâ nel giudaismo," ibid., 57–59.

invisible" (in the so-called first strophe of the hymn, vv. 15-18a, where the genitive "of the Church" should probably be considered a redactional addition), and also insofar as his resurrection has conferred on him a primacy over all things (vv. 18b-20a); this second motif will, then, be taken up and developed in the sister letter to the Ephesians (esp. in 1:10, 22), but still in the sense of a summing up of the cosmos in the risen Christ.[34]

But then, the phrase of Col 1:20b turns up a bit unexpectedly, chronologically out of order after what precedes it. In fact, the expression about the "blood of the cross" not only appears out of place after the mention of the resurrection but adds a completely new reason after the two already mentioned: even the death of Jesus has an essential part in the unification and pacification of the universe under the Christological sovereignty. It is as though the author of the letter had, before the end of the hymn, finally found the right place to put a theological insertion that was especially dear to his heart (or which he could not avoid). But then in the cosmological context of the hymn this means that what has been described earlier finally "receive[s] solid historical reference," so that "the right understanding of the cosmological statements of the first part of the hymn is disclosed only by the soteriological statements of the second strophe."[35] I dare say that it is actually this last part that turns the hymn into a specifically Christian text, raising it above the perspective of simply a quasinatural theology that would risk the mortal danger of being detoured into a theology of glory, disincarnated and especially triumphalistic. But the determined return to an inevitable theology of the Cross reminds the Christian that Christ's lordship over the cosmos was not established without a specific historical drama, yes at a high price, most realistically expressed by the "blood."

This suggests to us how we must understand the instrumental modifier "*by means of (διά)* the blood of his cross." In this formula the main accent falls on the "cross"; this is actually a genitive of specification, and is in turn specified by the possessive pronoun "his"; the "blood," then, serves to emphasize all the more the dramatic dimension of the event here recalled. And then v. 22 will speak of "reconciliation . . . in the body of his flesh by means of *(διά)* [his] death," taking up the fact of the supreme sacrifice of Jesus as a whole, considered in its general physical reality apart from specific attention to the blood.

---

34. See R. Penna, *Il "mysterion" paolino: Traiettoria e costituzione* (Brescia, 1978) 58–63.

35. E. Lohse, *Colossians and Philemon*, Hermeneia (Philadelphia, 1971) 43 and 61. The commentary by E. Schweizer, *Der Brief an die Kolosser* (Zurich-Neukirchen Vluyn, 1976 [English edition: *The Letter to the Colossians* (Minneapolis, 1982)]) actually speaks of "competition" between the perspective of resurrection and that of the cross (p. 70).

At this point we may be asking ourselves, In what does this reconciliation of which we speak consist? In answering, we must distinguish between the "reconciliation" found in our v. 20 and that mentioned in v. 22. Actually, vv. 21-22 represent a shifting to an anthropological form of discourse more familiar to Paul (and furthermore without reference to the blood). But in v. 22 the perspective is cosmological, even though anchored in history. The two verbs "reconcile" and "make peace" are synonymous and refer to concepts of unity, friendship, harmony, tranquility, order, and prosperity.

It may well be that in the background is the apocalyptic theme of the "new creation" (see 1 Henoch 72:1; 91:16; Jubilees 1:26-29; Rev 21:1-5; 2 Peter 2:13).[36] But we must recognize that our text refers not to a future reality but to one that is already brought about by the resurrection of Christ (vv. 18b-19), and especially by "the blood of the Cross" (v. 20). That is, the event of the Cross is already considered that which brings about the eschatological hopes concerning harmony between humanity and the cosmos (cf. Isa 11:1-9; 65:17-25), which, at least in the Christian community, should be recognized and experienced as a fact. Philo of Alexandria had written about the Jewish New Year that it is meant to "give thanks to God, the maker and guardian of peace [εἰρηνοποιοῦ . . . εἰρηνοφύλακος], who, after destroying the divisions that threaten the city and the regions of the universe as well, has brought about prosperity, fertility, and the abundance of all good things."[37] Changing the terms, we could say that the Crucified One is the sign for us of an altogether definitive New Year, rich with a peace which is more than promise but which can already be experienced in him, since "whoever belongs to this Lord is free from enslavement to the cosmic powers and from the compelling force of fate"[38] (see Col 2:8-23).

V. The blood of Church unity (Eph 2:13)

The text of Eph 2:13 reveals to us a new dimension of the manifold fruitfulness of the blood of Christ: "But now, in Christ Jesus, you who were far off have come near *in the blood of Christ (ἐν τῷ αἵματι τοῦ Χριστοῦ)."*

This affirmation as a whole refers to a preceding situation of alienation proper to the gentile recipients of the letter ("you"!) over against the

---

36. See A. Succhi, "La riconciliazione universale (*Col* 1:20)," *Atti della XXIII Settimana Biblica dell' A.B.I.*, 221-245, esp. 229-230.

37. *De specialibus legibus*, 2:192; see also *De vita Mosis*, 2:117-133.

38. See E. Lohse, *Colossians . . .*, 60, n. 208. For documentation of the sense of a destruction of the world perceived in Greek tradition, see E. Schweizer, "Versöhnung des Alls. Kol. 1:20," in *Festschrift H. Conzelmann*, ed. G. Strecker (Tübingen, 1975) 487-501.

chosen people (v. 12: "excluded from the commonwealth of Israel, strangers to the covenants of the promise, without hope and without God in this world"). The previous condition, then, is a state of utmost division between the gentiles and Israel, or better, of separation of the former from the latter. The context, in fact, clearly suggests that to become Christian is to be joined to the people of Israel, of which the Church is the most direct heir.[39] The Christian community is, thus, the single result of the joining of the two families, which in salvation history had been enemies; and thus the Letter to the Ephesians is the only New Testament letter that explicitly treats the unity of Jews and gentiles joined in Christ.[40] Now, in 2:13 we read that this is verified "in the blood of Christ." What does this mean?

First there is one interpretation to eliminate,[41] which would see the "blood" of v. 13 as simply one element in the anthropological pair (noted above) that would be completed in v. 14 with a parallel phrase, "in his flesh." For the context gives no support for an allusion to the incarnation; and furthermore, simply the unusual character of the division of the elements of the pair would incline us to reject the explanation, which in fact today finds no followers. The same can be said for an unlikely eucharistic interpretation of the passage, opposed by the repeated aorists in the text if nothing else.[42] What remains is the most obvious probability: to refer the mention of the blood to the saving event of the sacrificial death of Jesus.

Our phrase is, in fact, instrumental[43] and finds its best parallel in the adverbial phrase of means in the following v. 16, διὰ τοῦ σταυροῦ, "through the cross." Our v. 13 has all the appearance of functioning as a title or at least as an introduction to the pericope vv. 14-18. Various contemporary authors believe that they find here a recasting of a pre-redactional hymn,[44] the content of which is certainly Christological, with an ecclesiological function. Actually, in vv. 14-18 it is important to note how the verbs are used: only in the first and last verses, 14a and 18, do we find two present indicatives ("He *is* our peace" and "through him we both *have* access to

39. On this thematic, see R. Penna, *Il "mysterion" paolino*, 68–75.

40. See R. Penna, "La proiezione dell'esperienza communitaria sul piano storico (Ef 2,11-22) e cosmico (Ef 1,20-23)," RivBibl 26 (1978) 163–186.

41. Thus already proposed by Calvin, and more recently by J. A. Robinson, *St. Paul's Epistle to the Ephesians* (London, 1922).

42. Against this position, see M. Barth, *Ephesians*, I-II (Garden City, N.Y., 1974) 1:302-303.

43. See H. Schlier, *Der Brief an die Epheser* (Düsseldorf, 1957) ad loc.; as such, the phrase is different from the similar phrase in the same verse, "in Christ" (ἐν Χριστῷ Ἰησοῦ), which has rather a local or modal character, and describes the present Christian existence "in Christ"; see also H. Merklein, *Christus und die Kirche. Die theologische Grundstruktur des Epheserbriefes nach Eph 2,11-18* (Stuttgart, 1973) 23–26.

44. See K.-M. Fischer, *Tendenz und Absicht des Epheserbriefes* (Göttingen, 1973) 131–137.

the Father in one and the same Spirit"), the latter of which significantly has the ecclesial "we" as subject; but all the other intermediate verbs are in effect aorist and have only the initial αὐτός, "he" (i.e., Jesus Christ) as subject: "he made *(ποιήσας)* of the two one single people," "broke down *(λύσας)* the wall of division," "annulled *(καταργήσας)* . . . the Law," "to create *(κτίσῃ)* one single new man," "to reconcile *(ἀποκαταλλάξῃ)* them both," "destroyed *(ἀποκτείνας)* the enmity," "came to announce *(ἐλθὼν εὐηγγελίσατο)* peace."

We note immediately that the establishment of peace and unity accomplished by Christ is described as a *creation* (v. 15b: ἵνα . . . κτίσῃ . . .). The theme is already present in the Old Testament, referring to Yhwh, who "created" Israel as his people (see Deut 32:6; Isa 43:1, 15; Mal 2:10); but the passage in Eph 2:15b is the only case in the whole New Testament in which a new creation of his own is attributed to Christ in his own person, that is, where he no longer appears simply as mediator of the first cosmic creation (see 1 Cor 8:6; Col 1:16; Heb 1:2; John 1:3), but as agent in himself, bringing into being a new reality of communal and ecumenical character, namely, the Church insofar as it is composed of Jews and gentiles alike, finally made brothers and sisters, cemented together by his "blood."

But here we must add something about the literary-thematic procedure in the passage. If, as we have said, v. 13 amounts to a title or thesis to be demonstrated, vv. 14-18 provide its development or something of a proof. This amounts to a fourfold insistent repetition (vv. 14-15a, 15b, 16-17, 18), through the appearance of three constants that occur each time, namely, the mention of the previous situation of duality or division (v. 14: τὰ ἀμφότερα, "both"; v. 15b: τοὺς δύο, "the two"; v. 16: τοὺς ἀμφοτέρους, "both"; v. 18: οἱ ἀμφότεροι, "both"); emphasis on the unity achieved (v. 14: ἕν, "one"; v. 15b: εἰς ἕνα καινὸν ἄνθρωπον, "into one man"; v. 16: ἐν ἑνὶ σώματι, "in one body"; v. 18: ἐν ἑνὶ πνεύματι, "in one spirit"); and the remembrance of the means whereby this result was brought about (v. 14: ἐν τῇ σαρκὶ αυτοῦ, "in his flesh"; v. 15b: ἐν αὐτῷ, "in him"; v. 16: διὰ τοῦ σταυροῦ, "through the cross"; v. 18: δι᾽ αὐτοῦ, "through him"). This last element, as we see, is Christological in character. And it is precisely to this category that the instrumental phrase of v. 13 belongs by way of anticipation: ἐν τῷ αἵματι τοῦ Χριστοῦ. Now, it is interesting to note that of the various Christological allusions ("his body," the "cross," "him" himself), this is the first to appear; in other words, the author begins by recalling the αἷμα, "blood," of Christ as the factor of mutual communion between Israel and the gentiles. And it is difficult to find a cultic explanation for this fact; perhaps in the background of the expression there is the memory of a covenant sacrifice.

Still, we must remember that the communion and peace to which it refers (v. 15: "He is our peace") does not consist so much in vertical relationships with God, except only secondarily (v. 16: τῷ θεῷ, "to God"; v. 18: πρὸς τὸν πατέρα, "to the Father"), as it does primarily in mutual horizontal relationships between Jewish and gentile Christians. The "wall of division" (v. 14) and the "enmity" (vv. 14-16) in all probability refer not to a rupture of relations with God but to the Mosaic Law, understood as a fence, and hence carrying the motif of mutual incommunicability between human beings.[45] Now, we must recognize that the "blood" is here somewhat lost from view, since the language at once becomes frankly personalistic with the immediately following αὐτός, "he." The passage actually concentrates its attention on the fact of Christ's death in general and what springs from it; in the words of Saint Augustine: "At Christ's death the Church comes into existence" (*Moriente Christo, Ecclesia facta est*).[46] The theology of the Cross and not of the Incarnation explains and requires Church unity (note also by analogy the treatment of a similar theme in 1 Cor 1-4, where, however, there is no mention of the "blood").

VI. Some conclusions

The position of J. Behm on the word αἷμα, "blood," in volume 1 of the *Theological Dictionary of the New Testament* is rather well known. As he expresses it, "The interest in the NT is not in the material blood of Christ, but in his shed blood as the life violently taken from him. Like the cross, the 'blood of Christ' is simply another and even more graphic phrase for the death of Christ in its soteriological significance.[47] This statement concerns the whole New Testament, and its verification on such a broad scale is beyond the limitations of the present contribution. Nevertheless, insofar as it concerns the Pauline letters, I believe I must subscribe to it.[48] However, I propose that for clarity we must make distinctions, with the following thesis: It is the whole event of the death of Jesus that has sacrificial value, and not only the shedding of his blood. Let us examine the two elements of the proposal.

45. See, for example, the *Letter of Aristeas* 139: Moses "has surrounded us with a palisade without a breach and with bastions of iron to prevent any free association with the other peoples"; see R. Penna, *Il "mysterion" paolino*, 72-73. On the social and communitarian significance of peace in the Letter to the Ephesians, see M. Barth, *Ephesians*, 44-45.

46. *Enarrationes in Psalmos*, 127:11.

47. J. Behm, αἷμα, TDNT 1:174; this contention is regularly cited by Pauline commentaries regarding passages on the blood. And Behm, in turn, cited in his bibliography C. A. Anderson Scott, *Christianity According to Saint Paul* (Cambridge, 1927) 85-89. Also see C. Ryder-Smith, *The Bible Doctrine of Salvation* (London, 1941) 211-212.

48. *Pace* W. D. Davies and A. J. C. Da Cruz Fernandes: see the bibliography in note 5.

1) The sacrifice of Christ does not consist only in the shedding of his blood. As we have seen, the allusions to the "blood of Christ" in Paul are rather rare, and almost accidental, in passing. Especially, Paul never builds any particular theological development thereon. This is quite evident in 1 Cor 10:16-17, where in the eucharistic context he sets the reference to the cup before treating the bread, because it is only on the latter that Paul goes right on to elaborate a rich ecclesiological development, playing on a new dimension of the "body of Christ," understood dialectically in both individual and communitarian senses (thus in 10:16b-17 and then in chapter 12).

In none of the letters does Paul develop the theme of the αἷμα Χριστοῦ, and this is especially observable, for instance, in contrast to the role that this motif plays in the Letter to the Hebrews. This alone would suggest that it is misleading to imagine that the Pauline uses of the "blood" are governed by the text of Leviticus that says: "The life of the flesh is in the blood, and I have given it to you [to sprinkle] to make expiation for your lives, for the blood atones insofar as it is life" (Lev 17:11).

It is, of course, difficult if not impossible to deny that the original *Sitz im Leben* of the memory of the blood of Christ was a cultic perspective of Jewish origin; the same is surely the case for the mention of the blood of Jewish martyrs in the apocryphal 4 Macc 17:22 (διὰ τοῦ αἷματος τῶν εὐσεβῶν ἐκείνων, "through the blood of those pious ones"). However, the fact that in our literature the reference to the blood of Christ is mostly found in passages from pre-Pauline tradition (or passages of post-Pauline redaction; see Col 1:20; Eph 2:13) simply indicates that Paul is indebted to an antecedent theological tradition. He makes use of it but does not stress it.

This is confirmed by the silence about the blood in the unquestionably Pauline texts, where mention would have been appropriate and illuminating. For example, in 1 Cor 5:7 (*"Christ, our Passover, has been immolated"*) the passive verb ἐτύθη reflects the ancient expression θύειν τὸ πάσχα, "immolate the Pasch" (Exod 12:21 LXX = MT: šāḥaṭ ha-pesaḥ); but while Exod 12:22 immediately mentions the blood of the lamb to be sprinkled on the lintels and doorposts of the Hebrews' houses to avert the entrance of the Destroyer, Paul completely ignores this apotropaic role of blood and only stresses the paschal component of the unleavened bread (1 Cor 5:6, 8) and its allegorical meaning for Christian life. Such a procedure is in contrast even with the Jewish midrashic treatment of the same passage from Exodus.[49]

---

49. Compare *Exodus Rabbah*, 15:3 (on Exod 12:10) ". . . as a king said to his son, 'You know that I am the one who judges capital crimes and pronounces the sentence; so give me a gift, in order that I may dismiss the accusation against you when you appear before my

Moreover, in 1 Cor 6:20; 7:23 the declaration ἠγοράσθητε γὰρ τιμῆς, "for you have been bought at a price," appears in slightly variant forms. Here we can ask what this τιμή, "price," consists of (a phrase amplified by the Vulgate as "a great price," *pretio magno*), and all the more so since 1 Pet 1:19 specifies "you have been redeemed . . . τιμίῳ αἵματι by the precious *blood* of Christ, as of an innocent lamb without stain." But in the two Pauline texts there is no mention of blood whatsoever, nor is the context sacrificial; "the point is merely that you belong to a new master; beyond this the metaphor should not be pressed.[50]

In all probability Paul thinks of the death of Jesus only in a general sense, as a giving of ransom. This is confirmed by the other Pauline passages using the same verb, redeem *(ἐξαγοράζω)*, namely, Gal 3:13 ("Christ ransomed us from the curse of the Law by becoming a curse for us," alluding to the non-cultic legal text Deut 21:23) and the synonymous but more vague Gal 4:4-5 ("born under the Law to redeem those who were under the Law"). Therefore (like 1 Pet 1:19) the specification of Rev 5:9 should be considered secondary to the motif and so not part of the Pauline conception: ἠγόρασας τῷ θεῷ ἐν τῷ αἵματί σου, "You bought us for God with your blood."

Also, in 2 Cor 5:21 ("God made him to be sin for us"), if we are to follow the New Jerusalem Bible (text and footnote) in recognizing an allusion to "victim for sin" or ḥaṭṭāʾt (Lev 4:1-5, 13), it is surprising that there is no mention of the blood.[51]

As for the vocabulary derived from λυτρ-, we should note that neither the various nouns (ἀπολύτρωσις, λύτρον, λυτρώτης, "redemption, ransom . . .") nor the verb λυτροῦσθαι in biblical Greek ever occurs in a cultic context along with the expression "blood."[52] So in the two Pauline texts where the blood of Christ is associated with the ἀπολύτρωσις, "redemption" (Rom 3:24 and Eph 1:7), we probably need not perceive there an indissoluble link between the two elements, but rather should understand "redemption" in its general sense of liberation associated with the death of Christ and our faith in him (see 1 Cor 1:30; Col 1:14); in fact, even the late 1 Tim 2:6 speaks simply in these terms: "He gave himself as *a ransom for all*, ἀντίλυτρον ὑπὲρ πάντων" (thus also in Titus 2:14), not to mention that in

---

tribunal.' In the same way the God of Israel has said, 'I pronounce the death sentence, but I declare to you that in my mercy I shall spare you *because of the blood of Passover* and of the circumcision, and that I will expiate for you.' "

50. H. Conzelmann, *1 Corinthians* (Philadelphia, 1975) 113.

51. Less likely is an allusion to the rite of the "expiatory goat" of Lev 16, which would, indeed, be unbloody; see S. Lyonnet, *De peccato*, 2:135–138.

52. See S. Lyonnet, op. cit., 2:35–40; the same is true in profane literature (ibid., 30–32).

Rom 8:23; Eph 1:14; 4:30 the noun is used with an eschatological reference, and hence outside our perspective. And finally, this whole lexical family derives from the sphere of social relationships rather than cult.

2) The whole of Christ's death, including his blood, has sacrificial value, even if the allusion specifically to the blood puts more emphasis on this meaning. At this point we should recall all the terms mentioned above (see I), i.e., "cross/death/die/give oneself up," which constitute the more usual Pauline vocabulary to refer to the supreme event of the life of Christ; in this greater linguistic context the blood is just one element, but an especially vivid one (see Behm). In any case, it is precisely the tragic final event of Christ's life that is characterized by the dimension of sacrifice, and not the mere material shedding of blood so much as the incomparable *agape* that informed it from within.[53]

In this sense, the most eloquent text is surely Eph 5:2: "Walk in love, just as Christ *loved us and gave himself up for us (ἠγάπησεν ἡμᾶς καὶ παρέδωκεν ἑαυτὸν ὑπὲρ ἡμῶν)* as an *offering and sacrifice to God, in a sweet smell (προσφορὰν καὶ θυσίαν τῷ θεῷ εἰς ὀσμὴν εὐωδίας).*" Here in the last part of the phrase certain technical terms of sacrificial language are used, with no insistence on the element of blood, though it is certainly presupposed. The two nouns "offering" and "sacrifice" (προσφορά and θυσία, only the latter of which originally had a bloody sense) are apparently a hendiadys.[54]

Actually, I should think that the second term is defined by the first; that is, the death of Christ is "sacrifice" only insofar as it involves a free and loving "offering" of self. This is suggested by the preceding "gave himself up" (see also 5:25), as if to say that only on the basis of a gift of self can one speak of sacrifice; and here the language is certainly Pauline (see Gal 2:20; Rom 4:25; 8:2). Finally, the term "sacrifice" in Paul (except 1 Cor 10:18, where it refers to the sacrificial victim of Jewish worship) always refers to the concrete Christian life (Rom 12:1; Phil 2:17; 4:18); and the same is true of "offering" (Rom 15:16).[55]

As we see, the ground we are treading is personalistic, to which corresponds the Christian's attitude of faith. And when this faith alludes to Christ, it always turns toward him as a person, in his complete stature as Redeemer and Lord (and not toward partial aspects or "things," such as "cross," "death," or "blood").

53. See K. Romaniuk, *L'amour du Père et du Fils dans la sotériologie de Saint Paul* (Rome, 1961).
54. See M. Barth, *Ephesians*, 2:558.
55. The same must be said for other sacrificial terms, which are actually never referred to Christ, such as ἱερουργέω, "doing priestly service" (Rom 15:16), and σπένδομαι, "poured out as a libation" (Phil 2:17; 2 Tim 4:6).

The fact thus remains that in Saint Paul the mention of the "blood of Christ," as we have seen, occurs only in contexts of considerable richness and even originality. The Eucharist (1 Cor 10:16; 11:25, 27), justification, or pardon of sins (Rom 3:25; 5:9; Eph 1:7), cosmic reconciliation (Col 1:20), the ecumenical unity of the Church (Eph 2:13) are, after all, matters of no small moment. The connection of Christ's death with these basic themes that determine the identity and the very existence of the baptized tells by itself how fruitful for life is his death,[56] and how indelible is the love which it reveals, because it is written in blood: a love from which the Christian can never again be separated (cf. Rom 8:35, 38-39).

56. See E. Grandchamp, "La doctrine du sang du Christ dans les épîtres de Saint Paul," RTP 11 (1961) 262-271.

Chapter 20

The Wisdom of the Cross and Its Foolishness
as Foundation of the Church

A clear relationship between the cross of Christ and the Church is affirmed here and there in the New Testament, but it is rare to find a whole passage that deals with the theme at any length. Only in the first chapters of 1 Corinthians is this developed with some breadth, but rather from the viewpoint of the "word of the cross," i.e., the gospel proclamation. But concerning the cross itself, which logically precedes this proclamation, what is said about it is sporadic and undeveloped, but all the more intriguing. Let us begin here.

I. The cross, historical foundation of the Church

The most important text concerning this is doubtless Acts 20:28, where Paul, on his way on his last journey to Jerusalem, finds himself in Ephesus and addresses the presbyters of the Christian community there. In a speech that can properly be called his pastoral testament, he exhorts his hearers thus: "Watch out for yourselves and for the whole flock, in which the Holy Spirit has set you as overseers to shepherd the Church of God, which he acquired for himself with his blood" (after the translation of the C.E.I.) The translation of the final phrase is disputed, and there are those who prefer to translate "which he acquired for himself with the blood of his own Son."[1]

There is also a text-critical question, and the second translation makes the Christological element of the drama of the cross more evident, since

---

1. Thus J. Dupont, *Le discours de Milet. Testament pastoral de Saint Paul (Actes 20,18-36)* (Paris, 1962 [Ital. 1967]) 150ff.; C. M. Martini, *Atti degli Apostoli* (Rome, 1976); R. Fabris, *Atti degli Apostoli* (Rome, 1977); E. Haenchen, *The Acts of the Apostles: A Commentary* (Philadelphia, 1971); G. Schneider, *Die Apostelgeschichte* (Freiburg–Basel–Vienna, 1982).

the blood (unless one will hold to the improbable heresy of Patripassian-ism) is only and wholly that of the Son of God, Jesus of Nazareth. But in either case a tight link, a direct line, is established between the blood of the cross and the reality of the Church. The declaration, rich as it is in content, is developed no deeper. At any rate, the affirmation is there that in the genesis of the Church, "his own blood" (i.e., that of the Son of God) has played a fundamental role, provided a fundamental initiat-ing element, as it were, the purchase price, considering that the verb used here (περιποιήσατω: "acquire, gain for oneself") recalls the words of Isa 43:21 LXX ("I shall make water flow in the wilderness . . . to give drink to . . . the people I have acquired" (λαόν . . . ὃν περιεποιησάμην): as if to say that precisely the blood of Christ generates, brings into being, a people that belongs to him. And it is the same theme that resonates in Titus 2:13-14: "Our great God and Savior, Jesus Christ. . . . gave himself up for our sake, to redeem us from all lawlessness and cleanse himself a people of his possession [λαὸν περιούσιον], zealous for good works." And even though it may be veiled, we definitely find here the linkage between the gift of self (characteristic formula of the Pauline corpus to designate the supreme sacrifice of Christ) and the establishment of a people "of his own" (cf. Isa 19:5; Deut 7:6), where the expression used indicates the threefold con-notation of election, possession, and preferential relationship.

This same conception is taken up again in a passage of the New Testa-ment epistles, where precisely the idea of creation appears. We read in Eph 2:14-16: "He is our peace, having made the two one . . . so as to create of the two one single man in himself . . . and reconcile both to God through the cross." The purpose clause in Greek, (ἵνα κτίσῃ, "so as to create") expresses precisely one of the most singular salvific effects of the crucified Christ: the raising up of the Church from nothing, or better, from its opposite, which is the separation and opposition of Jews and gentiles.[2] Thus, the only time the New Testament attributes a creative activity to Christ himself and to his cross, this work has a twofold significance. On the one hand, it refers to the Church itself, which as Church is totally based on nothing but the blood of Christ, as Saint Augustine well expresses it: "When Christ died, the Church came into being" (*Moriente Christo, Eccle-sia facta est*).[3] On the other hand, this creative work is ecumenically

2. See R. Penna, "La proiezione dell'esperienza communitaria sul piano storico (Eph 2:11-22) e cosmico (Eph 1:20-23)," *RivBibl* 26 (1978) 163–186, esp. 172–174.

3. *Enarrationes in Psalmos*, on Ps 127:11. See R. Schnackenburg, *Ephesians: A Commentary*, trans. H. Heron (Edinburgh, 1991) 117: "The Church is thereby pulled into the immediate vicinity of the Cross, exists in fact in the Crucifixion event. In that Christ dies on the Cross, the Church is born. . . ."

oriented, since it aims to overcome a sad state of division and so to unite two opposite poles, which precisely "through the cross" amazingly come together to form one single new man (see Col 1:21-22). This same letter resumes the theme in 5:25-27: "You husbands, love your wives as Christ loved the Church, and gave himself up for it," and goes on to say that the love of Christ is still present and active to make his Church always beautiful; but everything is based on the past "loved," thus indicating that everything began at the moment of his supreme gift on the cross, when he wholly "gave himself up," thus beginning and also assuring the continuation of an incomparable love story.[4]

The theme returns in Rev 5:9-10: "Worthy are you to receive the book and to open its seals, because you were slain, and have redeemed for God with your blood persons of every tribe and tongue, people, and nation, and made for our God a kingdom of priests." Here also we find an explicit connection between the blood of Christ on the cross, the immolated Lamb, and the establishment of a priestly people, composed of elements of the most varied origin. This very multitude emphasizes the generative power of this blood, and so of the cross.[5] Thus the immolation of Christ has as its direct consequence the formation of a community of universal dimensions. But both realities, i.e., the blood and the immense people that derives from it, are taken up as motives for the praise of Christ as being "worthy to receive the book and open its seals," that is, to be established as God's eschatological plenipotentiary and spokesperson. This means that not only the cross but also the Church is the basis of the glory of Jesus Christ.

From these texts we draw two important conclusions. First of all, they demonstrate clearly that the salvific effects of Christ's cross are not to be sought on the anthropological level. It is true that the aspects most stressed in Paul's letters are the soteriological effects of the cross and the forgiveness of sins (see 1 Cor 15:3: a pre-Pauline formula; also perhaps Rom 3:25), or more exactly of sin (see Rom 5–8), resulting in a "new creation" (Gal

---

4. See C. L. Mitton, *Ephesians*, NCBC (London, 1981 = 1973) 201; M. Barth, *Ephesians*, II, AB 34A (Garden City, N.Y., 1974) 684–687; R. Penna, *Il "mysterion" paolino. Traiettoria e costituzione* (Brescia, 1978) 75–79.

5. Unfortunately the commentaries put very little emphasis on this aspect, even the recent major one of P. Prigent, *L'Apocalypse de Saint Jean* (Lausanne-Paris, 1981). But see Ch. Brütsch, *La clarté de l'Apocalypse* (Geneva, 1966⁵) 113–114: "Here the Cross of Christ is exalted in its true meaning: *Ave crux, spes unica.* Thanks to his sacrifice and to his paschal victory, Jesus Christ has established a new order; from the midst of the tribes, tongues, peoples, and nations he has raised up a new royal and priestly people, called to serve God freely and to reign on earth in his spirit. Having suffered our shame, Christ gives over his glory to us. We who were once abandoned to the depths of hell are now united by him with God and with one another."

6:15; 2 Cor 5:17) that makes each person a true son or daughter of Abraham, justified, reconciled, redeemed, liberated, etc. In this vision of things the negative state from which one is redeemed is essentially described by the concepts of flesh, Law, sin, death; and the result is considered to be primarily on the individual level—at least in the traditional hermeneutic. However, such an understanding of things, which in practice slips into an individualistic conception of salvation, is only partial. For it does not adequately address the ecclesiological results of the cross of Christ. But this dimension is already inherent in Paul's discussion of the redemption of the sinner. So true is this that even the Lutheran camp today is rediscovering the linkage between the event of justification by faith (which has its essential point of reference in the cross of Christ) and the reality of the Church. A doctoral thesis recently defended in the Protestant faculty of theology at the University of Tübingen addresses this specific question.[6] Acknowledging that there is an "ecclesiological deficit" in Paul (pp. 9, 11), in the sense that Paul never expressly treats the Church in speculative terms,[7] the author nevertheless demonstrates that the communal life of Christians is actually a reality that Paul actually does address (p. 58) and that it is especially his treatment of justification that has an ecclesiological dimension: "The existence of the community is a sign of the efficacy of the revelation of God's righteousness. It is when the Creator reveals his faithfulness and reaffirms his justice that there arises a new creation. And since Christ offers himself in love for all, communion in his body increases as a communion of service and mutual self-giving. . . . And this is why the Apostle in his ecclesiological paraenesis can never argue in isolation from the nature of the Church, but precisely in order to define this nature must always keep referring back to the Christ event, and the justifying intervention of God that is revealed in him."[8]

But besides this basic theological observation, we must also note that in the texts briefly analyzed above, a direct relationship is established be-

6. W. Klaiber, *Rechtfertigung und Gemeinde. Eine Untersuchung zum paulinischen Kirchenverständnis*, FRLANT 127 (Tübingen, 1982).

7. The author rejects the Pauline authenticity of the Letter to the Ephesians, correctly I believe. See R. Schnackenburg, *Ephesians*, 24–29 and 33–37.

8. W. Klaiber, *Rechtfertigung und Gemeinde*, 193; on p. 192 he also cites an axiom of K. L. Schmidt from 1927, according to whom "the correct understanding of what the Church is, stands or falls with the correct understanding of what justification is." Moreover, one of the contemporary masters of Lutheran New Testament exegesis writes pertinently and convincingly: "Paul's doctrine of the charismata is to be understood as the projection into ecclesiology of the doctrine of justification by faith, and as such makes it unmistakably clear that a purely individualistic interpretation of justification cannot be legitimately constructed from the Apostle's own teaching" (E. Käsemann, *Essays on New Testament Themes* [London, 1964 = selections from *Exegetische Versuche und Besinnungen*, I (1960)] in "Ministry and Community in the New Testament," 75–76.)

tween the cross of Christ and the Church. Even if none of these goes back to the historical Paul, they nevertheless reveal a Christian understanding that ultimately was affirmed in the New Testament writings, therefore in the primitive Christian literature. These respond quite clearly to the traditional question in the theology of the manuals: When did Jesus found the Church? During his earthly life? Or at the moment of his death on the cross? Or during the period of the paschal Christophany? Or on Pentecost day?

Strictly speaking, we cannot exclude any of these points, since each of them contributed to the final outcome, so that we can maintain that "the origin of the Church is actually a long and continuous path, with various stages and moments, but no one 'zero point' where it all began."[9] However, this judgment is basically valid on the level of a historical but not a theological consideration of the question. It is, of course, true that *in the Gospel accounts* of the passion and death of Jesus, not only is there not the least allusion to a founding of the Church, but we actually do read in Mark 14:50 that even those closest to him, the Twelve, "all abandoned him and fled"! Now, if the Church is a community of believers united with the Savior and one another, in Gethsemane we had quite the opposite! And Mark, who is surely a qualified spokesperson for the Church, or at least for one ecclesial community, notes it bluntly without any false shame, whereas when it comes to the other moments suggested above, at least we have there evidence of aspects that are ecclesiomorphic. During his public life Jesus brought together a group of disciples, from which he chose the Twelve, even though it says nowhere that by doing so he intended to found a Church.[10]

Then, during the apparitions of the Risen One, we see a slow regrouping around him of that union that the tragic events of the Passion had shattered (Matt 28:16: "the eleven disciples"; Luke 24:33: the disciples of Emmaus "found the Eleven gathered together, and the others who were with them"; John 20:19ff. Jesus confers the ministry of forgiving sin on the disciples); yet, neither does this announce the true, actual founding of a Church. Finally, on the day of Pentecost, the community (perhaps consisting no longer only of the Twelve but also of the hundred and twenty persons mentioned in Acts 1:15), through the pouring out of the Holy

9. G. Lohfink, *Die Sammlung Israels. Eine Untersuchung zur lukanische Ekklesiologie* (Munich, 1975).

10. And actually in the Gospels the term ἐκκλησία is found only in Matthew, three times, two of which do not carry the technical meaning (Matt 18:17 [twice]: "tell the ἐκκλησία"; at least on the level of the earthly Jesus the phrase can allude to a Jewish practice, though on the level of the evangelist it may have acquired the sense of "Christians"), and once it occurs specifically with regard to the future (Matt 16:18: "Upon this rock I shall build my Church").

Spirit, acquires a more clear-cut identity that consists essentially in a new missionary consciousness, so that even if there is no mention of a real founding, the books of the Acts of the Apostles is the New Testament writing that most uses the word "Church" (twenty-three times, followed by the twenty-two times in 1 Corinthians), but regularly to indicate specific local Churches (of Jerusalem, Antioch, etc.; note the plural "churches" in 16:5).

And so, in the narrative texts, where such a notice could be made most aptly, there is never any mention of the founding of a Church by Jesus. This is all the more curious in that the persons who wrote these pages were certainly men of the Church, who not only presuppose its existence but play their part in it, their lives defined by its vital needs, so that their writings are composed for Church far more than for outsiders. Specifically, the redaction of the Gospels and the Acts is a great act of ecclesial responsibility (note Luke 1:1-4), meant for the living faith of the baptized, to preserve the historical foundation of their present and enduring identity by recalling the memory of the beginnings. And yet, these writers do not determine the moment of the beginning of their "being Church." In truth, only the text cited at the beginning of this essay mentions anything of the sort: "to shepherd the Church of God, which he acquired for himself with his blood" (Acts 20:28: it is the last occurrence of the word "Church" in the whole book). But the phrase comes here quite unexpectedly because it is pronounced at a time that is at a considerable distance from the event of Calvary, but also because it is *not* mentioned where it would be most appropriate, i.e., in the description of the events themselves. This declaration certainly has its determining value here,[11] but note that it is not written up in a biographical context but rather takes up elements of the kerygma in a paraenetic context.

But it is only in *texts of theological reflection* that the reality of the connection of cross and Church rises to the surface of Christian consciousness. This is the case in Acts 20:28; Titus 2:14; but also in Eph 2:14-16; 5:25; Rev 5:9; other texts to consider would be Heb 2:10; 1 Pet 1:18-19. And it is highly instructive, especially if we consider the paradox between this relationship and the situation described above, in that at the very time of the crucifixion of Christ the Church factor seemed to be most absent, both in deeds and in words. Inevitably the question will arise: How could

11. As G. Lohfink, *Die Sammlung*, 91-92 recognizes: "The blood of Christ was the price that made the very existence of the Church possible. There are events in the life of Jesus— Acts 20:28 mentions the death on the cross as the most important—that are both revelatory and determinative for the Church. Luke is well aware of the fact that there is a profound dimension to the Church, and that if one is to do justice to this inward dimension, one must go beyond the story of its outward growth."

this linkage ever arise? How could the origin of the Church be anchored precisely in the moment of Christ's greatest abandonment, the moment when the least is said concerning Church?[12]

It seems to me that there can be only one response: We are evidently standing before a conclusion of faith, the result of a true and appropriate deepening of the Christian message and experience. It is no accident that the texts cited all belong (Acts, Ephesians, Titus, Hebrews, 1 Peter, Revelation) to Christianity's third generation, with all that this chronological observation means in suggesting a true intensive search by the believing community to determine better what belongs to the mystery, including the origins of the community.[13] And the outcome of this search, the conclusion that was finally drawn, was not so much narrative in character (probably because the narrative had no appropriate material for this issue); rather, the answer was grafted onto that which from the beginning was the characterizing and typical possession of the Christian group, i.e., the content of the kerygma. For it is the cross that was always considered the ultimate reality, the solid, stable foundation, and hence the point of departure for Christian faith, the indispensable element from which it springs.

12. Actually, in the most common interpretation, in John 19:26-27 ("behold your son . . . behold your mother") Mary at the foot of the cross is proposed as an image of the Church, so that by means of the new spiritual motherhood of Mary a link would be forged between Jesus on the cross and the reality of the Church. For such understanding, see A. Feuillet "Les adieux du Christ à sa Mère (Jn 19,25-27) et la maternité spirituelle de Marie," NRT 86 (1964) 469–489; I. de la Potterie, "La maternità spirituale di Maria e la fondazione della Chiesa (Gv 19,25-27)," in *Gesù Verità* (Turin: Marietti, 1973) 158–164 (and idem, "Das Wort Jesu 'Siehe deine Mutter,' und die Annahme der Mutter durch den Jünger (Joh 9,27b)" in *Neues Testament und Kirche: Festschrift R. Schnackenburg* [Freiburg–Basel–Vienna, 1974] 191–219); A. Sara, *Maria a Cana e presso la croce. Saggio di mariologia giovannea (Gv 2:1-12 e 19:25-27)* (Rome, 1978) 94–103. For a different interpretation of the same text, see J. Mateos and J. Barreto, *El Evangelio de Juan* (Madrid, 1979) 816–817: Mary represents the old Jewish community, which recognizes in the beloved disciple the new community of believers as her offspring and sphere of acceptance; thus, previously, R. Schnackenburg, *The Gospel According to St. John,* III (New York, 1980-82 [Ital. 1981]) 278–279.

We cannot treat the question exhaustively here. But I am impressed by the position of R. Brown, *The Gospel According to John,* Anchor Bible 29A (Garden City, N.Y., 1970) 924: though there is some evidence that already in the fourth century Mary at the foot of the cross was considered a figure of the Church, "this symbolic interpretation of Mary's role is quite distinct from the theory that Mary as an individual becomes the mother of all Christians." So I should think it exaggerated to see in this Johannine text "the establishment of the community of Jesus beneath the cross" (J. Blank, *The Gospel According to John,* III [New York, 1981] 92, along the line of G. Schürmann, "Jesu letzte Weisung, Joh 19,26-27," in *Sapienter ordinare. Fs. E. Kleneidam* [Leipzig, 1969] 13–28); this would be to base such an important conclusion solely on highly symbolic language (even more so than the "Bread of Life" in chapter 6).

13. Basically, the text of John 19:26-27 could be seen to have more theological than historiographical value, without desiring at all to detract from the richness of its meaning.

Actually, already in the archaic confession of faith reported in 1 Cor 15:3 ("He died for our sins according to the Scriptures"), and specifically in the plural "our," there are present in germ the later ecclesiological developments that see no more nor less in the Church than a community of the forgiven, of those reconciled with God by means of Christ's blood (see Eph 5:25-27) on the basis of faith in the cross (see Rom 3:21-26). But if it is on the cross that the fundamental event of the reconciliation of sinners with God took place, where else could they locate the origin of the community of sinners who received this grace?[14] The Church, then, is the pivot between the pre-paschal community of the disciples of the earthly Jesus and the Pentecostal community raised up by the Spirit of the Risen One. It purifies the former and prepares for the latter. As if to say, on the one hand, that the Church can achieve its own identity only by passing through the crucible of the cross and, on the other, that the Church would risk every kind of deviation if it entrusted itself to a Spirit that did not bear the features of the Risen One who had been crucified.

II. The "word of the cross," perennial origin and verification of the Church

What we have said thus far concerns the historical foundation of the Church. Of course, the historical level of which we speak is not the historiographical, as we have said; it refers rather to a unique event at one point of time, that of the cross, where Christ offered himself "once [for all]" (Heb 7:27). The cross of Christ is in this sense not repeatable, "since with a single oblation he has made those who are sanctified perfect for ever" (Heb 10:14). It has all at once generated the whole Church, or at least the mystery of it.

But the cross ever and again is at the origin of the Church, as its constant, repeatedly generating matrix or womb. And it is such in the form of the word. "The word of the cross is indeed folly for those who are being lost, but for us who are saved it is the power of God" (1 Cor 1:18). The first and fundamental way whereby the historical cross escapes a sterile remoteness in the past is by becoming a cross that is proclaimed. I find the statement of E. Käsemann most pertinent and stimulating: "The cross

---

14. I am aware that such language belongs more to Paul than to the school that derives from him, and that it is more Pauline than Johannine. But this gets to the root of things and elucidates the terms of the reply to the question. It would also be valuable to study the relationship between cross and baptism, which is the foundation of the Church in a special sense; the Pauline doctrine of baptism in particular makes it the hyphen between Christ and Church: see G. Delling, *Der Kreuzestod Jesu in der urchristlichen Verkündigung* (Göttingen, 1972) 29; and vol. 1, chap. 8, of the present work.

helps no one who does not hear the word of the cross and ground his faith on that."[15]

This means that if the Church is completely enclosed within the cross on Golgotha as in a mother's womb, it is still brought into the light of history generation after generation only by the proclamation of this pregnancy. This has been true from the beginning of Christianity: "When I came among you . . . I chose to know nothing among you but Jesus Christ, and him crucified" (1 Cor 2:1-2). And this must always be true, it must always be thus, unless we wish to establish the Church not on hearing and on the risk of its fragility, but upon the certainty (or over-confidence) of a vision that tends to impose the univocal, the externalistic, the triumphalistic by brute force.[16] The event of the cross, as we have said above, had no ecclesiastical character to it, and yet it is to the cross that the New Testament Church traces its initial existence, to a moment of supreme phenomenological powerlessness. In the same way, the "word of the cross" is paradoxically fragile, defenseless, and yet at the same time rich in possibility: it is "power." Like a seed (John 12:24).

And it is important to note that Paul chooses to confront the ecclesial divisions of the Corinthian community precisely with the "word of the cross," that is, by appealing to Christ crucified. He does not begin his argument with a simple paraenesis on the advantage of unity within the Church (this he will do in chapter 12) or on the need to give witness to non-believers (for this, 14:24-25). But in the first four chapters of the letter he challenges the problem of the divisions at Corinth with a clear and insistent appeal to the ultimate foundation of Christian identity, which is consequently the base of ecclesial identity: "Is Christ divided? Was Paul crucified for you?" (1:13). These are perhaps surprising questions. They seem not to address the specific situation but to be talking in a roundabout way. But for Paul, it must be understood that the cross, rather than standing at the periphery of Christian life, must be the heart of it at every

15. E. Käsemann, *Perspectives on Paul*, trans. M. Kohl (Philadelphia, 1971) 50. The recent book of H. Weder, *Der Kreuz Jesu bei Paulus. Ein Versuch über den Geschichtsbezug des christlichen Glaubens nachzudenken*, FRLANT 125 (Göttingen, 1981), is thoroughly motivated by an apologetic preoccupation and loses sight of Käsemann's important and stimulating theme of the link between the theology of the cross and the theology of the word, so much so that not only does the author never relate the cross to the Church, but when he mentions the value of the word, it is only to deny magic power and stress the historic dimension of the gospel (see 244; also 138 on 1 Cor 1:18: "in any case this is not a word that uses the cross as a symbol").

16. Note E. Käsemann, *Perspectives*, 51: "The theology of the Cross and the theology of the word belong together and are won or thrown away together. The person who sees has no need to hear, and the person who can no longer hear will inevitably want to see. According to Paul, faith is distinguished from superstition by whether one wants to hear or to see."

level. And this is the theme developed in 1 Cor 1:17-2:16, which we will now study.

For in every way, the important thing is that "the cross of Christ not be rendered empty" (1 Cor 1:17b). This concern acquires its full weight from the opposition set up with its contrary, "not with the wisdom of speech" (ibid.) And both alternatives are ways of describing both form and content in the enterprise of evangelization (1:17a).

Paul thus establishes an opposition between cross and wisdom that will be repeated in 2:1-2. Strictly speaking, he does not speak of a "wisdom of the cross." In his language this expression would mean an evaporation of the cross into ideology. Rather, according to his terminology the cross (but it would be better to personalize the expression by saying "the Crucified One") implies the concept but especially the reality of the "power of God" (1:21, 24, 30; 2:6, 7), and reveals it. But what characterizes the cross as such is "foolishness," μωρία (1:18, 21, 23, 25; 2:14) and "scandal/stumbling block," σκάνδαλον (1:23). So it would be more exact to say that the *foolishness of the cross* is the foundation of the Church.[17] Hence the usual expression "the wisdom of the cross" should be considered an abbreviation of "the wisdom of God revealed in the foolishness of the cross," for by itself it is in danger of losing the element of sharp dialectical contrast that Paul recognizes in the fact and in the message of the cross. And Luther is right in saying that God reveals himself *sub contraria specie*, "under a contrary appearance," since "the wisdom of God [is] hidden under the appearance of folly."[18] For Paul writes, "Since in God's wisdom the world did not know God through wisdom, God chose to save those who believe through the folly of the proclamation" (1:21), i.e., through the foolishness of the cross, since it is the cross that is the nucleus of the preaching. Therefore, the wisdom of God is revealed in the foolishness or scandal of the cross. And the cross gets its dimension of

17. We note that the Greek expression σοφία, "wisdom," occurs in the authentic Pauline letters nineteen times, sixteen of which are in 1 Cor 1:17-3:19; and *moria*, "foolishness," in the whole New Testament occurs only in 1 Cor 1:18, 21, 23; 2:14; 3:19—an obvious indication that these are central ideas in this section, which has at its base an ecclesiological preoccupation, and it must be considered in this light. On the idea of *dynamis*, see volume 1, chapter 10, of the present work, where each of the occurrences, in 1:19 and 24, is given a different modifying meaning (kerygmatic in v. 19, paschal in v. 24); however S. Vergulin, "La croce come potenza di Dio in 1 Cor 1:18.24," in the collection *La sapienza della croce oggi—I. La sapienza della croce nella rivelazione e nell'ecumenismo*, (Turin, 1976) 144-150, attributes a single kerygmatic significance to both occurrences (the proclamation of the cross as cause of the conversion and sanctification of believers).

18. *Sapientia Dei abscondita sub specie stultitiae. . . . Verbum Dei quoties venit, venit sub specie contraria menti nostrae* [the latter clause contains the phrase quoted in the text above: "Whenever God's Word comes, it comes under an appearance contrary to our expectations"—T.P.W.], WA 56:446-447, cited in B. Gherardini, *Theologia crucis. L'eredità di Lutero nell'evoluzione teologica della Riforma* (Rome: Edizioni Paoline, 1978) 39.

"power" only because behind it, yes within it, God is present in action (or perhaps better, "in passion/passively"). But this event, from the viewpoint of historical phenomenology, whether at Golgotha or at the moment of the preaching, always seems to be folly, and therefore disgrace (see Heb 12:2). But it is from this disgrace rather than from an act of power that the Church is born. And the word of the cross constantly repeats to the world and to the Church as well this same scandal, which never loses its force.

Numerous and subtle are the ways to give in to the temptation to move beyond this scandal or to soften or contain it. The first is to speak of the cross as a universal ethical law to which all human beings, including Jesus, are subject. In this case the final point of reference is not the cross of Jesus itself but an abstract, impersonal, and universally valid principle. But this forgets that in Paul the word "cross" *(σταυρός)* never has a general anthropological sense but is always exclusively Christological: there is no other cross than Christ's.[19]

A second way to temper the folly of the cross is to emphasize the Resurrection, and so present the sufferings of Jesus only as a transitory state, as if he lived that moment with the security of one who has an ace up his sleeve to use at the right moment, or as if another general law applied to him, the "per aspera ad astra" (the stars are reached through trials). But this is to underestimate the extreme seriousness of the drama of Calvary, both in the narrative texts of the gospels (from the agony in Gethsemane, to the last word on the cross) and in the kerygmatic-catechetical texts (which tend to distinguish the death suffered on the cross by Jesus from the act of the Resurrection attributed to God): the Risen One still remains indelibly marked with the cross and the wounds he received on it (see John 20:27).[20] And finally, the scandal of the cross can be eliminated by making it a *symbol* of power and victory in historical human society (or else a throne of glory for Jesus himself, according to a widespread iconography that substitutes splendid gold for the bare wood). But the death of Jesus is much more than a religious symbol, and also more than just an ethical example to imitate. And "when Paul talks of the 'folly' of

19. And so it is inconceivable that Paul would say of Christians that one must "take up one's own cross" (as we do read in Mark 8:34 and parallels, in a paraenetic sense; on the meaning of this evangelical *logion*, see R. Pesch, *Das Markusevangelium*, II, HThKNT [Freiburg-Basel-Vienna, 1977] 59–60).

20. See E. Käsemann, *Perspectives*, 56–57: the Risen One could have no face, save that of the Crucified One, since "only the Crucified One is risen, and today the dominion of the Risen One reaches where the Crucified One is served" [the quotations from Käsemann here follow the Italian edition quoted by Penna rather than the English edition—T.P.W.]; B. Rigaux, *Dieu l'a ressuscité* (Gembloux, 1973 [Italian: 1976]) 283–285.

the message of the crucified Jesus, he is therefore not speaking in riddles or using an abstract cipher. He is expressing the harsh experience of his missionary preaching and of the offense that it provoked."[21]

The Church, then, is invited to place itself before the cross, not just in order to understand the One who here reveals himself in such an extraordinary manner but to understand itself, for this is its point of origin. But what is the ecclesiological meaning of the "word of the cross"? We begin by noting that Paul never does an abstract or objective staurology or theology of the cross. His speech about the cross always requires a soteriological key, i.e., it must be seen in terms of its salvific fecundity, as we see especially in his rare allusions to the blood of Christ.[22] That is, he places himself and his hearers in a living and personal (or ecclesial) relationship with the cross, speaking about what the cross means for the purposes, the ends, of the new Christian life. And so he can also lament the existence and the deeds of "those who act as enemies of Christ's cross" (Phil 3:18). And although they must each be distinguished historically, they all certainly negate the salvific meaning of the cross[23] and, whether from a Jewish or a gnostic point of view, render it superfluous, of no use, precisely because scandalous. And hence the emergence of other conflicts within the Philippian Church, even though they are not so obvious as those of Corinth. But it is evident that the Apostle connects the understanding of the cross with a corresponding way of understanding the nature and the life of the Church. This brings about three consequences:

In the first place, the "word of the cross" acts as an eschatological discernment. If, in fact, it separates "those who are being lost" and "those who are being saved" (1 Cor 1:18), then it is a sign of contradiction and an anticipation of eschatological judgment: in the present reality, the *hic et nunc*, of the preaching of the cross and the response given to it, the radical differentiation already takes place as far as the final fortune of persons is concerned.[24] We can well apply to this what the author of Hebrews writes concerning the word of God: "sharper than a two-edged sword . . . and judging the feelings and thoughts of the heart" (Heb 4:12). What Paul says presents various implications for the Church. It is by accepting the cross of Christ that the Church becomes capable of standing with the

21. M. Hengel, *Crucifixion* (Philadelphia, 1977) 89.

22. See above, chap. 19; U. Vanni, "Il Sangue di Cristo in Paolo: realtà, simbolo, teologia," in F. Vattioni, ed., *Sangue ed antropologia biblica*, II (Rome, 1984) 689–736.

23. See H. Heriban, *Retto "phroneîn" e "kénōsis." Studio esegetico su Fil 2,1-5.6-11*, BSR 51 (Rome, 1983) 47–51; J. Gnilka, *the Epistle to the Philippians* (New York, 1971); *Der Brief an die Philipper*, HThKNT (Freiburg, 1968 [Italian, 1972]) 211–218 (Excurs 4: Die Philippischen Irrlehrer).

24. See K. Müller, "1 Kor 1:18-25. Die eschatologisch-kritische Funktion der Verkündigung des Kreuzes," BZ 10 (1966) 246–272.

saved; it is a community of the saved precisely because it is founded on the acceptance of the cross. Such an attitude, then, places the Church also in an eschatological situation; by adhering to the cross of Christ with faith, it shares in and lives by God's ultimate revelation of grace that is shown there. This is valuable discovery, which is often overlooked, as if the *eschaton* depends only on the Risen One as such. But the Risen One, through those who proclaim him, simply confronts people again with the "word of the cross"; one cannot help but note that "God's righteous-ness," i.e., his intervention restoring those who are alienated from him, is in Paul's theology actually revealed not by the resurrection but on the cross (see Rom 3:25), and likewise is revealed in the proclamation of the gospel (see Rom 1:15-17), which does nothing but re-present the cross of Christ from time to time in its ever intact, explosive power to save. That is why 1 Cor 1:18 associates the "power of God" with those who are being saved, whereas those who are being lost are associated with "foolishness." When one is lost, this is not an act of God's power; it is only a result of human folly that comes to be projected on the cross itself in the form of judgment. But God, in fact, affirms his power only positively, in the work-ing of salvation. And the Christian community is the sphere in which this power is displayed, especially from the acceptance of the cross in faith, which constitutes the entrance into the community of the saved. The whole Church, then, stands beneath the shadow of Christ's cross and is imprinted by the seal thereof. Such an eschatological situation removes the Church from the dimension of the world (in the negative apocalyptic sense of the word), to which it belongs no more. What Paul says of himself applies also to the Church: "Far be it from me to boast, except in the cross of our Lord Jesus Christ, through which the world is crucified to me and I to the world" (Gal 6:14).[25]

In the second place, the cross acts on the Church as a principle of unity and also of equalization of the members. Already the question expressed in 1 Cor 1:13a makes it clear that Christ is not divided. And this Christ is identified in the context by the cross. The same long speech of Paul in this first section of 1 Corinthians on the wisdom of God revealed in folly of the cross is all oriented toward the situation of creeping fragmentation

25. F. Mussner aptly comments (*Der Galaterbrief*, HThKNT IX [Freiburg-Basel-Vienna, 1981⁴] 414): "The use of κοσμος, "world," without an article indicates a very special type of world: the world of the flesh, the Law, sin, and death, which stands in opposition to the 'new creation' (6:15) and which has now been overcome by the latter. Christ's cross has dealt a mortal blow to the old world. And conversely the Apostle [where Mussner says "Apostle" we might also say "Church"] is "crucified" to the world, that is, dead—and this, once and for all (note the perfect εσταυρωται)"; see also Gal 2:19; 5:24.

within the Corinthian Church, threatening its communion. It is as if Paul wanted to say in these pages: Christ alone died on the cross for you, none other, and it is around this Christological uniqueness that your ecclesial plurality must gather together. If Christians do not unite themselves around the cross, they have not understood the only relevance it has, namely, to be the foundation. It is not without reason that Paul wrote a little further on: "No one can lay a foundation other than the one that is already laid, Jesus Christ" (3:11). And if we want to be faithful to the context, we must say that this foundation is none other than the Crucified Christ (2:2).[26] To avoid this reality is harmful to the Church. It would be like losing the compass, wandering lost, entrusting itself to any divisive, purely subjective hermeneutical choices; we would fall into a real ecclesiological schizophrenia, consisting in a tragic loss of identity. But although "all have sinned" (Rom 3:23; 5:12), Christ was given up for us (Rom 8:32), and so an earlier solidarity in sin yields to an even stronger solidarity in grace. This is the direction followed by Eph 2:14-16 and Rev 5:9f. examined above, which are concerned with the ecumenical effects of the cross. But there is another important aspect of this unity achieved (but always still called for). It is the essential equality among the participants. By its nature the cross does not establish any ecclesial class system—it even prohibits it. This is true of the ministry: "What is Apollo? What is Paul? [Only] ministers through whom you came to believe" (1 Cor 3:5). The cross does call forth ministry, but one that means service, not domination. This is also true in regard to the mystical: the distinction Paul draws between the "perfect/pneumatic" and the "psychic/carnal" in 1 Cor 2:6–3:3 refers not to two levels of Christian life within the Church; rather, "it is a matter of the contrasting conditions that actually exist concerning access to the understanding of the wisdom of God in Christ's

---

26. Unfortunately the commentators on 1 Corinthians generally (see C. K. Barrett, H. Conzelmann, Chr. Senft) do not grasp this aspect and fail to clarify in what sense Jesus Christ is the "foundation" (θεμέλιος) of the Church. But if in 2:2 Paul declares that he has not wanted to know anything else among the Corinthians "save Jesus Christ, and him crucified," and if then in 3:10 he claims to have laid the foundation among them (even if others have built on it), I should think it follows, indeed it must be concluded, that the foundation of the community is not just Jesus Christ in a general and more or less abstract sense, but rather "Jesus Christ, and him crucified." It is the same idea that reverberates (though in an accusatory tone) in Gal 3:1: "O foolish Galatians, who has deceived you, before whose eyes Jesus Christ was depicted crucified?" Here the image is different, the foundation becomes a προγραφή, a "public notification," which Chrysostom and Luther understood in the sense of "draw or paint," and which resonates in various current translations (C.E.I., RSV. . .); but in both instances (1 Corinthians and Galatians) it is a solemn initial act that leads to a continuing process. And Gal 3:1 clearly indicates that this beginning was brought about by the proclamation of Jesus Christ "crucified."

cross'';[27] Paul laments that at Corinth all are still "psychic" (3:1-3), and the expression "we (pneumatics)" refers not to the elite circle of apostles or a few Christians but rather simply to the Corinthian community as in union with Paul and considered in its actual pneumatic potential. In any case, all have equal need of the Spirit to perceive "the depths of God" (2:10) and discover that at their center, as pivotal point of God's plan of salvation, there is nothing other than the cross of Christ. The Church is actually made up of those who are granted to acknowledge this and who base their mutual communion on this.

And finally, the "word of the cross" constantly recalls to the historical Church its essential kenotic condition. If the foundation of the Church is Christ Crucified,[28] i.e., the One who, "being in the form of God . . . humbled himself, becoming obedient to death, even the death of the cross" (Phil 2:6a, 8), how can the Church consider "equality with God something to be grasped" (2:6b)? And if Christ "did not seek to please himself" (Rom 15:3; cf. Heb 12:2), how is it possible for the Church to find pleasure in a narcissistic contemplation of self? Of course, we do not want it to fall into a sort of eccelesiological masochism. But if one loves and gives oneself for others (see Gal 2:20; Eph 5:2, 25), this does not mean that one is inspired by a pathological complex of self-punishment; rather it is the pure, adult attainment of a love that in order to be fruitful knows something of the need to pass through the ecstasy of self-forgetfulness to dedicate self to the welfare of the other.

The life of the Church in history must be made up of this self-giving, forgetting its own presumed privileges: "We preach not ourselves but Jesus Christ the Lord; as for us, we are your servants for the love of Jesus" (2 Cor 4:5; cf. 1:24). The only real privilege is that noted above, whereby the Church today lives the *eschaton*, the final days, brought on by the cross of Christ. But it is a type of "life hidden with Christ in God" (Col 3:3).

---

27. U. Wilckens, "Das Kreuz Christi als die Tiefe der Weisheit Gottes. Zu 1. Kor 2,1-16," in L. De Lorenzi (ed.), *Paolo a una chiesa divisa (1 Cor 1-4)* (Rome, 1980) 43-81, then 81-108, cit. 57. See also chaps. 31 and 32 below.

28. It is worth noting that Paul never identifies Jesus Christ as "founder" (this would be *archēgos*, which, however, in the New Testament occurs only in Acts 3:15; 5:31; Heb 2:10; 12:2, but with a considerably greater theological density than "historical initiator"), but only as "foundation" *(θεμέλιος)*, as we have seen. This is not just a question of words. For a "founder" is one who at a specific moment in the past laid the basis of a movement or institution, which then can continue autonomously; but the "foundation" includes the idea of a constant, ever actual relationship between the base on which the building is founded and the building itself that is constructed on it and is constantly held up by the support that the former provides. Fortunately the ambiguous title of the book of C. H. Dodd, *The Founder of Christianity*, (London, 1970 [Italian: 1975]), is then explained in its fullest sense, though without giving much weight to the Pauline distinction; thus also R. Fabris, "Gesù Cristo come fondatore del cristianesimo," *Studia Missionalia* 33 (1984) 277-304.

So, if the Church chose to make a display of it and impose it authoritatively, it would finally be imposing only itself, betraying that cross from which it derives its identity.[29] To sum up, the Church is required to present itself to the world no more and no less than as Jesus was presented on the cross, and throughout his whole life (of which the cross was simply the consistent conclusion), *sub contraria specie*, "under the contrary appearance [to what would be expected]." Perhaps more study should be given to the (even ecclesiological) significance of the Pauline principle that the "power [of the Lord] is manifested in weakness" (2 Cor 12:9). In fact, "he was crucified through weakness but lives through God's power; and we also who are weak with him shall be alive with him through the power of God" (13:4). Note the verbs used by Paul in this text: for Christ he uses the past for the crucifixion and the present for his risen condition, whereas for the Christian community he uses the present to describe its condition of peril and weakness, and the future for the definitive affirmation of God's power on the Church's behalf.

The final proclamation of the Risen One is a function of that of the cross, and Jesus is raised up to help his community carry the cross of history with perseverance (see Matt 28:20). So the Church has no right to force the anticipation of God's future but is rather called to live its dedication to God and the world in faithfulness and love, again, no more and no less than Christ on the cross.[30]

29. In this regard we might recall the Matthean parable of the thistles (Matt 13:24-30). The impatience of the servants has, throughout history, all too often been that of certain ecclesiastical circles.

30. Essentially, the whole of Phil 2 addresses this lesson: to present the Christian community with the measure of Christ's behavior already enunciated in general terms in v. 5 ("Have the same attitude in you that Jesus Christ had"); on this passage see the excellent scholarly monograph of J. Heriban (cited above, n. 23).

Chapter 21

Paul's Attitude Toward the Old Testament

To be clear about it from the beginning, this chapter deals only with the seven Pauline letters whose authenticity is unquestioned (1 Thessalonians, 1–2 Corinthians, Galatians, Romans, Philippians, Philemon). As for the other letters, it is actually their use of the Old Testament that, in part, suggests their inauthenticity.[1]

I. Preliminaries

Paul's use of the Old Testament produces a complex problem that we cannot exhaust here, as is evident from the abundance of the bibliography on the issue.[2] To understand it, it may be useful to mention certain related questions that permit us at once to clarify some basic issues.

1. In 2 Thess 1:8-12 the heaping up in only five verses of Old Testament quotations or echoes (Isa 66:15; Jer 10:25; Ps 78:6; Isa 2:10, 19, 21; Pss 88:8; 67:36; Isa 49:3; 2:11, 17; 24:15; 66:5; Mal 1:11) contrasts with the very sparing use found throughout 1 Thessalonians. In Colossians, on the other hand, we are surprised by an almost total absence of the Old Testament, not only of explicit quotations but even of indirect use, if we except the wisdom substratum of the Christological hymn in 1:15-20 (cf. Wis 7:26; Prov 8:22ff.) and the fragmentary resonances of Isa 46:3 and Prov 2:3-4 is the text of 2:3 (cf. also Isa 29:13 in Col 2:22), since the allusion of 3:1 ("seated at the right hand of God") to Ps 110:1 is too vague, as are those of 3:10 ("according to the image of the One who created him") to Gen 1:26f., and of 4:1 to Lev 25:43, 53. Ephesians shows atypical usage of the Old Testament: in 4:8 the text of Ps 68:19 is introduced with a non-Pauline impersonal formula (διὸ λέγει, "and so it says"; also 5:14), while in 5:31 the long quotation from Gen 2:24 is not even introduced; also in 6:2 (reporting the commandment concerning father and mother from Exod 20:12; Deut 5:16) the Law is described as ἐπαγγελία, "promise," in contradiction to Pauline usage, which clearly contrasts the two concepts (see below). The three Pastorals hold only a few weak resonances of the Old Testament; only two quotations are introduced: one in 1 Tim 5:18 quotes Deut 25:4 ("You shall not muzzle the ox that treads out the grain"), but besides its being cited in a different context from 1 Cor 9:9, where it also occurs, the Greek text employs a different verb (in 1 Cor κημώσεις; in 1 Tim φιμώσεις, the verb used in the Septuagint); the other quotation is in Titus 1:12, which, however, cites a saying of the pagan philosopher Epimenides (described as a προφήτης!).

2. For a general bibliography, see H. Vollmer, *Die alttestamentlichen Zitate bei Paulus textkritisch und biblisch-theologisch gewürdigt* (Leipzig, 1895); C. Clemen, "Die Auffassung des

First. We can ask whether there are certain situations that tend to cause Paul to use the old Scriptures with special interest and intensity, or whether he is constantly using the Bible in his letters, finding it equally authoritative for all purposes. Now, we find that he actually does adjust himself to different situations (theological polemic, necessary pastoral intervention, careful apologetic reasoning), thus indicating that the Old Testament is not an absolute point of departure. It suffices to note the frequency and manner of use in various letters: 1 Thessalonians and Philippians are marked by a complete lack of direct quotations, with only a very sober use of allusions; in Philemon there is simply no quotation and no allusion; on the contrary, 1–2 Corinthians show an abundant use of the Old Testament, but without system, surely because of the disorganization of the themes treated.[3] It is especially in Galatians and Romans that we note a more organic use of the sacred texts, pivoting systematically on the theme

---

Alten Testaments bei Paulus," ThSK 75 (1902) 173–187; A. von Harnack, *Das Alte Testament in den paulinischen Briefen und in den paulinischen Gemeinden,* Sitzungber. der preuss. Akad. der Wissensch. 1928, XII (Berlin, 1928) 124–141; O Michel, *Paulus und seine Bibel,* BFChrTh II 18 (Gütersloh, 1929; Darmstadt, 1970); J. Bonsirven, "Saint Paul et l'Ancien Testament," NRT 65 (1938) 129–147; Ch. Masson, *Le Christ Jésus el l'Ancien Testament selon saint Paul,* Cahiers de la Fac. de Théol. de l'Univ. de Lausanne IX (Lausanne, 1941) 9–20; E. E. Ellis, *Paul's Use of the Old Testament* (Edinburgh, 1957 = Grand Rapids, 1981); J. Schmid, "Die alttestamentliche Zitate bei Paulus und die Theorie vom sensus plenior," BZ (NF) 3 (1959) 161–173; S. Amsler, *L'Ancien Testament dans l'Eglise* (Neuchâtel, 1960) 45–62; C. Dietzfelbinger, *Paulus und das Alte Testament. Die Hermeneutik des Paulus, untersucht an seiner Bedeutung der Gestalt Abrahams,* ThEx 95 (Munich, 1961); H. Lenard, "La lecture de l'Ancien Testament par Saint Paul," in *Studiorum Paulinorum Congressus Internationalis Catholicus 1961,* AB 18 (Rome, 1963) 207–215; S. del Paramo, "Las citas de los Salmos en S. Pablo," ibid., 229–241; J. Coppens, "Les arguments scripturaires et leur portée dans les lettres pauliniennes," ibid., 243–253; H. Ulonska, "Die Funktion der alttestamentlichen Zitate und Anspielungen in den paulinischen Briefen," ThLZ 90 (1965) 793f.; Ph. Vielhauer, "Paulus und das Alte Testament," in L. Abramowski and J.-F. Goeters, eds., *Studien zur Geschichte und Theologie der Reformation. Festschrift F. Bizer,* (Neukirchen, 1969) 33–62; R. Bring, "Paul and the Old Testament: A Study of the Ideas of Election, Faith and Law in Paul, with Special Reference to Romans 9:30–10:13," STh 25 (1971) 21–60; O. Michel, "Zum Thema: Paulus und seine Bibel," in H. Feld and J. Nolte, eds., *Wort Gottes in der Zeit. Festschrift K. H. Schelkle* (Düsseldorf, 1973) 114–126; A. T. Hanson, *Studies in Paul's Technique and Theology* (London, 1974) esp. chaps. 3, 5, 8, 9; J. Blank, "Erwägungen zum Schriftsverständnis des Paulus," in J. Friedrich, W. Pöhlmann, P. Stuhlmacher, eds., *Rechtfertigung. Festschrift E. Käsemann* (Tübingen, 1976) 37–56 (= *Paulus. Von Jesus zum Christentum* [Munich, 1982] 192–215); I. Dugandzi, *Das 'Ja' Gottes in Christus. Eine Studie zur Bedeutung des Alten Testaments für das Christusverstandnis des Paulus* (Würzburg, 1977); M. D. Hooker, "Beyond the Things That Are Written? Paul's Use of the Scripture," NTS 27 (1980–81) 295–309; G. Dautzenberg, "Paulus und das Alte Testament," BibKir 37 (1982) 21–27. Now see also M. Pesce, "Funzione e spazio dell'uso della Scrittura nell'attività apostolica paolina. Ipotesi di ricerca," Annali di Storia dell'Esegesi 1 (1984) 75–108.

3. In 1 Corinthians we count some nineteen passages dealing with the Old Testament, nine of which present direct quotations with a pertinent introduction; see F. S. Malan, "The Use of the Old Testament in 1 Corinthians," *Neotestamentica* 14 (1981) 134–170: according to this, the quotation from Job 5:12 in 1 Cor 3:19 is closer to the Hebrew text than to the LXX. In 2 Corinthians we count some forty Old Testament occurrences with five direct quotations.

of justification through faith and that of true descent from Abraham.[4] As we see, it is only in the four major letters that Paul really argues with Old Testament in hand; and only when he must confront Jewish or Jewish-Christian interlocutors does he do so in a more precise, careful manner.[5]

Second. Is it possible to distinguish certain recurrent spheres of interest, that is, thematic spheres in which to identify and group Paul's Old Testament quotations and allusions? One answer has been given by E. E. Ellis,[6] who lists some twenty *topoi* for which Paul goes back to the Old Testament. They range from the fall of Adam to the eschatological victory over death. Ellis then tries to synthesize these many themes, reducing them to five principal areas: faith and works (Rom 1:17; 4:3, 6-7, 17-18; 10:4ff.; Gal 3:6, 8-13, 16; 4:22-23); Jews and gentiles (Rom 9:7, 12-13, 15, 17, 25-29, 33; 10:16, 18-21; 11:3-4, 8ff., 24-25; 15:9ff., 21; Gal 3:8); ethic (Rom 12:19; 13:8; 14:11; 15:3; 1 Cor 6:16; 9:9; 10:7, 26; 2 Cor 6:16ff.; 8:15; 9:9; Gal 5:14, 31; 6:2-3); wisdom speech (Rom 11:24-25; 1 Cor 1:19; 1:31; 2:9, 16; 3:19); eschatology (1 Cor 15:27, 45, 54-55). Others have suggested different groupings.[7] But it is easy to see the subjectivity of such thematic divisions, and also of what little use they are. For with some themes the recourse to the Old Testament is crucial, while in others it is tangential. Such an approach would simply remain on the level of theological systems, which is certainly not the preoccupation that drives Paul. More pertinent and useful would be to identify the formal aspects under which Paul considers the Old Testament from his Christian and missionary viewpoint (see below).

Third. A useful problem is the investigation of what type of Old Testament text Paul recognized. And this is related to the question of his technique of reporting Old Testament passages. The great variety of his procedures has always been noted. They go from an extreme fidelity to the LXX text in Gal 4:27, which cites a long text from Isa 54:1 exactly to the letter, all the way to an extreme liberty, seen in a comparison of Deut 30:11-14 with Rom 10:6-8 (where we perhaps have an echo of the frag-

---

4. Galatians has seven direct quotations, Romans has as many as forty-two, plus seven cases of authentic reports without introduction.

5. This is not to say, as A. von Harnack would have it, that the Old Testament is useful to Paul only in his arguments against outsiders, and not for the edification of the Christian community (see below, "The Old Testament as Scripture" under "The Four Faces of the Old Testament").

6. *Paul's Use*, 116ff.

7. See, for instance, H. Conzelmann, *An Outline of the Theology of the New Testament* (New York, 1969 [Italian: 1972, 1991[4]]) 169, who proposes seven main themes: the Old Testament as prophecy (Rom 1:2; Gal 3:8); the Old Testament already reveals justification by faith (Rom 1:17); the reign of sin after Adam (Rom 5:12ff.); the call of the gentiles and Israel's reaction (Rom 9-11); the prefiguration of the sacraments (1 Cor 10:1-2); the teaching on eschatology (1 Cor 15); commandments "very rarely" (Rom 13:8-10; cf. 12:19f.).

mentary Palestinian Targum Jer II).[8] There seems to be no question that Paul worked on the basis of a Greek text: for instance, in 1 Cor 2:16 and Rom 11:34, Paul's Greek would be surprising (τίς γὰρ ἔγνω νοῦν κυρίου, "for who knows the *mind* of the Lord"), since the MT of Isa 40:13 has *rûaḥ yhwh*, "the *spirit* of the Lord"; except that just this passage is the only place where LXX translates *rûaḥ* as νοῦς (rather than πνεῦμα, θυμός, etc.), so Paul was evidently familiar with the Greek, which was the normative text for him.[9] The problem does remain, when he changes the LXX text (e.g., Exod 34:34 in 2 Cor 3:16), does he do so because the version he used had already changed the text, or is he quoting from memory with an inevitable margin of approximation, or is he deliberately changing the text, adapting it to his own hermeneutical context?[10] Probably all three sup-

8. See S. Lyonnet, "Saint Paul et l'exégèse juive de son temps. A propos de Rom 10,6-8," in *Mélanges bibliques rédigés en honneur de André Robert* (Tournai, 1957) 494–506; M. McNamara, *The New Testament and the Palestinian Targum to the Pentateuch*, AB 27 (Rome, 1966) 70–79. Meanwhile, A. T. Hanson, *Studies in Paul's Technique*, 148, maintains a bit too apologetically that Paul does not really alter the biblical text but uses a Greek translation of his own or an already existing tradition.

9. See H. Vollmer, *Die alttestamentlichen Zitate* (already in 1895) 10–11; O. Michel, *Paulus*, 68; "Zum Thema," 117–119. Another important case is Prov 3:4 LXX (καὶ προνοοῦ καλὰ ἐνώπιον Κυρίου καὶ ἀνθρώπων, "we take thought for the good before God and human beings"), which reverberates without citation formula in 2 Cor 8:21 (προνοοῦμεν γὰρ καλὰ οὐ μόνον ἐνώπιον Κυρίου ἀλλὰ καὶ ἐνώπιον ἀνθρώπων, "we take thought for the good, not only before God but also before human beings") and in Rom 12:17 (προνοούμενοι καλὰ ἐνώπιον πάντων ἀνθρώπων, "we take thought for the good before human beings"). But Prov 3:4 in MT is different "[you will find favor and] good sense before God and human beings." Here the MT noun *śēkel*, "sense," is read by the LXX as an imperative (qal *śᵉkol* or piel *śakkēl*: προνόου: "use sense/take thought"); see A. T. Hanson, *Paul's Technique*, 127–128.

10. According to E. E. Ellis, *Paul's Use*, 12 and 150–152, of ninety-three Old Testament texts in the entire Pauline corpus, fifty-one coincide substantially with the LXX, four are closer to the Hebrew, and thirty-eight diverge from both the Hebrew and every verifiable Greek text. But of the four texts considered closer to the MT, we omit one because it comes from the pastoral epistles (2 Tim 2:19 = Num 16:5); of a second one (Rom 11:35: ἢ τίς προέδωκεν αὐτῷ, καὶ ἀνταποδοθήσεται αὐτῷ, "Or who first gave to him, that something may be given in return?"), it is in fact not clear which passage it is quoting (according to Ellis, loc. cit., and E. Käsemann, *An die Römer*, ad loc., it would be Job 41:3; according to U. Wilkens, *Der Brief an die Römer*, ad loc., it would rather be Job 15:8; according to the critical edition of K. Aland, M. Black, etc., 3rd ed., it would be Job 41:11; but H. Schlier is probably right in *Der Römerbrief*, 347: "There is no prototype, either in the LXX or in the Hebrew text"). For a third quotation (in 2 Cor 8:15: ὁ τὸ πολὺ οὐκ ἐπλεόνασεν καὶ ὁ τὸ ὀλίγον οὐκ ἠλαττόνησεν, "One who [gathered] much did not have too much, and one who [gathered] little did not have too little"), which quotes Exod 16:18, it is hard to say whether it is closer to the MT (*uᵉlo' heᵉdîf hammarbeh uᵉhammam'ît lo' heḥsîr*, "And the one who did much did not have a surplus, and the one doing little did not lack") or to the LXX (οὐκ ἐπλεόνασεν ὁ τὸ πολύ, καὶ ὁ τὸ ἔλαττον οὐκ ἠλαττόνησεν, "The one who [gathered] much did not have too much, and one who [gathered] little did not have too little") [translator's note: the differences are subtle ones of lexicography and syntax—T.P.W.], so that the question remains open; only the fourth citation (1 Cor 3:19: ὁ δρασσόμενος τοὺς σοφοὺς ἐν τῇ πανουργίᾳ αὐτῶν, "Who catches the wise in their craftiness"), from Job 5:13, is certainly closer to the MT (*loqēd ḥăkamîm bᵉᶜormām*: literally, "who catches [the] wise in their cleverness") than to the LXX (ὁ καταλαμβα, "who seizes [the] wise in intelligence") because of the difference between the Greek verbs as well as the adverbial expression *bᵉᶜormām*, which is better expressed in Paul in the choice of the noun and use of the

positions are true from time to time, but we must decide text by text. As for the text in 2 Cor 3:16, I should think this represents the third possibility.[11]

Fourth. What is the relationship between Paul's exegetical method and that of his environment? As for the simple formulas of citation, these are quite varied, and parallels can be found, whether in Palestinian Judaism (cf. "as it is written" καθὼς γέγραπται with *ka'ăser kātûb* at Qumran in 1QS 8:14; CD 7:19; and the verb λέγει, "X says," referring to γραφή or νόμος, "Scripture" or "Law," or a person's name, with the rabbinic *we'ômēr*, "and X says," e.g., in *P. Abôt* 3:3, etc.),[12] or in Hellenistic Judaism (cf. the present "says," φησίν, only in 1 Cor 6:16 with Philo's *Abr.*, 31; 51; 71; 131; 273; and ὁ χρηματισμός of Rom 11:4 with Philo's χρησμός in *De praem.*, 95, in the sense of "oracle").

More problematic than the formulas is Paul's position with regard to the truly exegetical procedures of the rabbis, of Qumran, and of Philo. Already a contrast with these various spheres is the unique formula λέγει κύριος, "says the Lord" (1 Cor 14:21; Rom 12:19; cf. 14:11), which makes Paul's biblical quotations approach ancient prophetic style.[13] But similarity to rabbinic technique is undeniable,[14] as evidenced by the practice of a verbal exegesis like that of Gal 3:16 (concerning the "seed" of Abraham, in the singular)[15] and especially by the use of certain methodological principles such as *qal waḥomer* ("light and heavy," i.e., *a minore ad majus*, argument from lesser to greater: see 1 Cor 15:42-44; Rom 5:15, 17) and the *gezerāh šawāh* ("equal decision" or analogy, according to which one finds and compares two biblical passages that are somehow similar, to find the same point made in both; thus Gen 15:6 and Ps 31:1-2 LXX in Rom 4:3-8: the psalm has nothing to do with Genesis, but uses the same verb λογίζεσθαι, "recognizing," and so is used to interpret the passage about Abraham "recognizing righteousness" = "not recognizing sin").[16]

---

possessive pronoun. But can we exclude the possibility that Paul used a different Greek text from the one we know? Or that he quoted roughly from memory?

11. See C. K. Barrett, *A Commentary on the Second Epistle to the Corinthians* (London, 1973) 122; R. Bultmann, *The Second Letter to the Corinthians* (Minneapolis, 1985) 89.

12. We should note that Epictetus also uses the formula ὡς λέγει Πλάτων, "as Plato says": *Diatr.* I 28:4; III 24:99; IV 1:41, 73.

13. See E. E. Ellis, *Paul's Use*, 107–108; frequently the sayings of the Old Testament prophets are thus presented as God's word (e.g., Isa 1:2; Jer 2:2; Ezek 2:4; etc.).

14. See J. Bonsirven, *Exégèse rabbinique et exégèse paulinienne* (Paris, 1938); P. Bläser, "Schriftverwendung und Schrifterklärung im Rabbinentum und bei Paulus," ThQ 132 (1952) 152–169.

15. But a similar technique is also observable in Hellenistic Judaism: see H. Schlier, *Der Brief an die Galater*, ad loc.

16. But J. Jeremias, "Paul as Hillelite," in E. E. Ellis and M. Wilcox, eds., *Neotestamentica et Semitica. Studies in Honour of M. Black* (Edinburgh, 1969) 88–94, goes too far, making the Apostle a Hillelite.

But perhaps Paul is still closer to Qumran and the *pēšer* technique, not only, and not even so much, through a formula of introduction for quotations (see, for example, 1 QpHab 7:19; 8:1; 9:9; no Greek equivalent to the Hebrew *pisrô*, "Its interpretation:" is found in his letters, but the phrase "*τοῦτ' ἔστιν*" approaches it, in Rom 9:8; 10:6, 7, 8, immediately introducing reinterpretation of an Old Testament phrase), as rather through the fact that unlike rabbinism, Paul and Qumran alike interpret specific biblical texts in terms of their orientation to the future and their actual realization in the present (instructive is a comparison of the interpretation of the same prophetic text of Hab 2:4b in 1 QpHab 7:18–8:3 and in Gal 3:11; Rom 1:17).[17]

It is more difficult to pull together possible associations with the allegorical exegesis of Alexandrine Judaism. The Genesis passage that Paul explicitly calls *ἀλληγορούμενα*, "allegorized" (Gal 4:24), he actually treats more like what we would call typology (see below). In fact, a true allegory is not at all characteristic of Paul. Perhaps only in 1 Cor 9:10 (which quotes Deut 25:4: "you shall not muzzle the ox that treads out the grain") does it emerge with any clarity: the question, "Is God concerned about oxen? Or is he saying it about us?" sounds like the exegetical principles of Alexandrine Judaism.[18]

II. The autonomy of Christological faith

A question of decisive importance is the attempt to determine the fundamental hermeneutical principle that inspires Paul in his treatment of the Old Testament. This treatment is in complete agreement with the new Christian faith. But everything depends on recognizing that this faith is not based on the Old Testament but had its origin elsewhere, i.e., on the

17. Also the formula *ἰδοὺ νῦν*, "Behold, now," in 2 Cor 6:2 sets up a similar connection between the biblical text quoted (= Isa 49:8 LXX) and the Christian present. For characteristic of the *pēšer* is the prophetic-apocalyptic explanation of a Scripture passage. See especially J. Fitzmyer, "The Use of Explicit Old Testament Quotations in Qumran Literature and in the NT," NTS 7 (1960–61) 297–333; J. Carmignac, "Notes sur les Peshârim," RQ 3 (1962) 511–515; E. Jucci, "Il Pesher, un ponte fra il passato e il futuro," Henoch 8 (1986) 321–338.

18. Already at the beginning of the second century B.C., Aristobulus advised safeguarding "what is more fitting to God" *(θεοπρεπής)* in biblical interpretation (Eusebius, *Praep. ev.* 8:10:2); and the *Letter of Aristeas* 150 explained that God gave the prescriptions on the purity of animals "in a symbolic sense" *(τροπολογῶν)*; but it will be especially Philo in the midst of the first century A.D. who systematized the allegorical method, even if Philo writes of this Deut 25:4 only to emphasize the humaneness of the Mosaic Law (*Virt.* 145f.; but see *Spec. leg.* 1:260). On Paul's relationship to Hellenistic exegesis, see O. Michel, *Paulus*, 103–111; V. Nikiprowetzky, *Le commentaire de l'Écriture chez Philon d'Alexandrie. Son caractère et sa portée. Observations philologiques* (Leiden, 1977). But some allegorical reading is even practiced at Qumran, though rarely, as when the "well" of Num 21:18 is interpreted as meaning the Law, and the "staff" to dig it as its interpreter (in CD 6:3-4, 7).

basis of the Christ-event, and the experience thereof, and only secondarily does it turn to the Old Testament, to find its confirmation there. "The eschatological present . . . is the primary datum; the look back toward the promise is the integrating datum."[19]

On the road to Damascus a true "hermeneutical conversion" took place,[20] producing an authentic revolution in Paul's understanding of the ancient Scriptures. This is demonstrated by three important observations.

First. In the first place we note the almost absolute lack of scriptural proof in his letter regarding his Christology. We should especially note Rom 1:2-4 (". . . which he had promised through his prophets in holy Scripture") and 1 Cor 15:3-5 (with the phrase "according to the Scriptures" used twice, referring to the death and the resurrection of Jesus). But these passages are quite abstract, not recalling any specific text in detail, and simply go back to a pre-Pauline tradition. There are also two neighboring texts in Romans: 15:3 ("The insults of those who insult you have fallen on me" = Ps 68:10 LXX) and 15:12 (about the root of Jesse that will rule the nations = Isa 11:10 LXX), but we must note that these seem to appear in passing, in the paraenetic section concluding the letter. Also Joel 3:5 LXX ("whoever calls on the Lord's name will be saved") is interpreted Christologically in Rom 10:12-14 (cf. 1 Cor 1:2 and perhaps Phil 2:9, 11) especially in reference to the title χύριος, "Lord"; but the prophetic passage is quoted without any specific formula presenting it as a biblical proof; on the contrary, Paul simply makes Joel's words his own, already presupposing that the lordship of Jesus is an independent, presupposed fact. The Old Testament text, then, becomes only a literary embellishment.

The only biblical proof that is at all developed is in Gal 3:16 (cf. 3:28-29), where Paul refers to the singular τῷ σπέρματί σου, "to your seed," of Gen 13:15 (and 17:8; 22:18; 24:7) LXX; but the singular rather than collective interpretation of the "seed" of Abraham is already determined by Christological faith itself, so that it seems to be just a tendentious reading, a "Hilfskonstruktion":[21] for not only does it go against the literal sense of the biblical text, and against all Jewish interpretation of Genesis,[22] but neither does Paul ever repeat it when he refers to the same biblical passages in the next chapter, Gal 4:22-31, nor in Rom 4:13-17 or 9:6-9, where this σπέρμα, "seed," of Abraham always has a collective (Christian) dimension.

19. O. Michel, "Zum Thema," 115; cf. Ph. Vielhauer, "Paulus und," 43.

20. The happy phrase is by S. Amsler, *L'Ancien Testament*, 47, who compares the event to the Risen One's illumination of the two disciples at Emmaus (Luke 24:25-27).

21. Ph. Vielhauer, "Paulus und," 43.

22. See Strack-Billerbeck, III, 553.

But the text of 1 Cor 10:4 ("the rock was Christ," probably in the sense of the title ὁ Χριστός, "the Messiah"), is an exception *sui generis*, based on extrabiblical traditions (see note 57 below). Otherwise a characteristic of Paul is the absence of many Old Testament and Jewish titles typical of messianism and also of primitive Christianity: prophet, king, son of David, son of man, servant of Yahweh, chosen one, teacher, priest. Nor does Paul, surprisingly, ever cite a biblical proof to support Jesus's messianic role or to demonstrate his death and resurrection, though they are at the center of his gospel.[23] The only encounter of the Bible with the death of Christ in Paul is in Gal 3:13 ("It is written: Cursed is whoever is hanged on a tree": Deut 21:23 LXX retouched), but the biblical passage is here only a reminiscence to indicate Christ as being "made a curse for us," in a context that is not Christological but discussion at some length on the contrast between the works of the Law and faith. The same is true of the implicit Christological interpretation of the expression "rock to trip them and stumbling block" (a fusion of Isa 8:14 and 28:16) cited in Rom 9:33 not so much for its messianic dimension (especially since Paul is not speaking explicitly of Christ) as in reference to the believer's act of faith (Isa 28:16). As for 1 Cor 5:7 (καὶ γὰρ τὸ πάσχα ἡμῶν ἐτύθη Χριστός, "Christ our Pasch has been sacrificed"), it certainly resonates with the Old Testament phraseology of Exod 12:21 LXX (θύσατε τὸ πάσχα, "sacrifice the Pasch"; cf. Deut 16:2, 5, 6); but this is here purely for literary effect, and surely not as biblical proof.

Second. Concerning soteriology, Paul so much insists on the exclusive link of redemption and the forgiveness of sin with Christ and his death (e.g., 1 Cor 1:30; Gal 2:19-21; Rom 3:23-26; 5:8-10) that he forgets, or at least is completely silent about, the rich and complex Jewish expiatory system, not only in contemporaneous Judaism[24] but also as elaborated even in the Old Testament, consisting essentially of the sacrificial rites of the Jerusalem Temple, codified in Lev 1-7 and 16 (note also the principle of the love that "covers all transgressions": Prov 10:12; cf. Tob 12:9). In other words, he does not so much as pose the problem of the relationship of

23. Unlike the Paul of Acts (Acts 13:15-41; 17:3-4), who, however, reflects Lukan theology (cf. Luke 22:37; 24:44).

24. For example, the ancient *midraš Mek. Ex.* 20:7 enumerates four forms of expiation: repentance, the Day of Atonement, suffering, death. If this midras, dating as it does to the second century, and thus after the destruction of the Second Temple, does not list ritual sacrifices, we must remember that the apocryphal 4 Maccabees, which certainly precedes 70 A.D., mentions the expiatory value of the death of martyrs for the whole people (see 6:28-29; 17:21-22), and that in the first century A.D. there existed a baptismal movement, which offered the masses a baptism of forgiveness that dispensed with the various sacrificial liturgies of the Jerusalem Temple and assured access to salvation in simple forms possible to all (see Ch. Perrot, *Jésus et l'histoire* [Paris, 1979 (Italian: 1981)] 100-115).

the already existing ample expiatory doctrine and practice with the new Christian message that connects redemption only with the death of Christ on the cross.

Even if the Apostle alludes to this system (see Rom 3:25: ἱλαστήριον, "expiation"; 2 Cor 5:21: ἁμαρτίαν ἐποίησεν, "made him to be sin [= sin offering]"),[25] any such Old Testament material has been thoroughly Christologized; henceforth it is Jesus Christ who stands in the foreground, so much so as to absorb into himself what might be seen as a biblical background. This not only represents a real reinterpretation of the ancient material but rather leads him completely to ignore the means of expiation in Judaism, and thus to obliterate them totally (note also the theological insignificance of *t°šubâ*, μετάνοια, "repentance," in Paul). This does not happen polemically (as in Hebrews) but solely by ignoring the Jewish theme. It is as if Paul is so overwhelmed by the light of Christ and his death that he sees nothing else; all that the Old Testament (and contemporaneous Judaism) had developed concerning means of expiation is henceforth unexpectedly superseded and absorbed in Christ. This gives incontrovertible evidence of how Paul does not reach Christ through the Old Testament, but rather, if anything, returns to the Old Testament by beginning with the newness of the Christ-event, if we must not rather say that in soteriology the Christ-event distracts the Apostle from recourse to the Old Testament, and hence from mentioning it. As E. P. Sanders well expresses it, for Paul the solution even precedes the problem.[26]

Third. The new Christian reality seems to be so overpowering and self-sufficient that it leads Paul (and for that matter the other New Testament writers) to refer to the Old Testament only as needed, and to use it eclectically. While Qumran, Philo of Alexandria, and especially the rabbis all revere the Old Testament not only as a point of reference but as norm of faith and life, and undertake the composition of true biblical commentaries of some length, nothing like this happens among the New Testament writers. And yet if there was anyone who had more right to do so (that is, to write a *pēšer* or *midrāš* on a whole biblical book and not just part of one), this was Paul of Tarsus himself in view of his Pharisaic-

25. He does so too rarely, and then so vaguely that we cannot speak of quotations or even of definite allusions. On the Romans text, which may reflect Exod 25:17; Lev 16:15-16, see above, chap. 19. On 2 Corinthians, which may recall Isa 53:10-12 and perhaps Lev 4:1–5:13, see, e.g., P. Stuhlmacher, "Sühne oder Versöhnung?" in U. Luz and H. Weder, eds., *Die Mitte des Neuen Testaments. Festschrift E. Schweizer* (Göttingen, 1983) 291–316, 398.

26. See E. P. Sanders, *Paul and Palestinian Judaism* (London, 1977) 442; also his pp. 162–184, the discussion of the means of atonement in rabbinism: sacrificial rites, suffering, death, repentance (this latter always required as an element in the others, which are not adequate in themselves).

rabbinic training (see Phil 3:5; Acts 22:3). But there is none of this. In fact, these writers did not even make some sort of systematic collection of ancient biblical texts based on the new Christian faith, unlike Qumran, where some such thing is attested (4QFlor and 4QTest). There probably never was any such erudite exercise, at least not in the world of the Pauline community, and the contrary suppositions never rise above the level of pure hypothesis, apparently quite unsupported by the facts.[27] The Old Testament known to Paul does not seem to be mediated by supposed anthologies of texts, considering how original is the use he made of it; he knows it directly; and if certain biblical texts appear more than once in his letters (like Hab 2:4b in Gal 3:11; Rom 1:17), it is only because they are easily adapted to recurring theological themes (but note that the same prophetic passage will be quoted in Heb 10:38 in a different, moral perspective!)

In any case, we must recognize that the Old Testament discloses its true sense only "in Christ" (2 Cor 3:14; see below). And the reinterpretation of Deut 10:11-14 in Rom 10:6-8 offers the most obvious case of the new hermeneutical stance. But we could also cite 1 Cor 10:2 ("All were baptized in Moses in the cloud and the sea") and 3-4 ("All ate the same spiritual food and all drank the same spiritual drink"). In the first text Paul reads the data of the Exodus using the Christian baptismal formula (see Rom 6:3), especially since Exodus speaks of a cloud that preceded rather than enveloped the people (Exod 13:21), and the sea crossed dryshod, not by immersion (Exod 14:22). In the second text the strict parallelism of $\beta\varrho\tilde{\omega}\mu\alpha$ and $\pi\acute{o}\mu\alpha$, "food" and "drink," which as such has no precedent in the Old Testament, shows that Paul reasons on the basis of the elements of the eucharistic meal. But it is just these incongruities over against the Scriptures themselves that suggest with sufficient force that Paul reads the Old Testament on the basis of the Christian reality, projecting the new realities of faith on it.

Even so, Paul's attitude toward the Old Testament is complex and certainly not univocal. It assumes various forms, even with dialectic implications. In part the Old Testament is obsolete for Paul and must be refuted

---

27. Such theories have been constructed in England. J. R. Harris, *Testimonies*, I-II (Cambridge, 1916-20) concludes to the existence of isolated *testimonies* or "proof texts" (see the critiques of O. Michel, *Paulus*, 37-55; C. H. Dodd, *According to the Scriptures* [London, 1952] 24ff.); Dodd himself (p. 57) hypothesizes a collection of longer biblical texts ("textplots") especially of the prophets and psalms to interpret the kerygma (see the critique of A. C. Sundberg Jr., "On Testimonies," NT 3 [1959] 268ff.); see also M. Black, "The Christological Use of the Old Testament in the New Testament," NTS 18 (1971) 1-14; A. T. Hanson, *Paul's Technique*, 191-195. Another problem is determining whether the Pauline community was already using biblical texts that Paul then also appropriated: see D. A. Koch, "Beobachtungen zum christologischen Schriftgebrauch in der vorpaulinischen Gemeinden," ZNW 71 (1980) 174-191, on Isa 45:23; 28:16; 11:10; 59:20-21.

(Old Testament as Law); in part it is a foretelling, i.e., a preparation and hence validation in a positive sense (Old Testament as promise); in part it preserves the authority of inspired, divine books (Old Testament as Scripture); finally, and consequently, it furnishes Paul with an abundance of conceptual and lexical material that becomes compelling, an inescapable means of expression (Old Testament as language).[28] So we shall examine each of these four formal aspects one by one.

III. The four faces of the Old Testament

1) A striking treatment of the Old Testament by Paul is certainly that which considers it as "Law." But at once we must make a distinction. Sometimes Paul introduces a biblical quotation positively with this designation (e.g., 1 Cor 9:9: ἐν τῷ νόμῳ γέγραπται, "it stands written in the Law": Deut 25:4), even when the passage is prophetic (e.g., 1 Cor 14:21 on the missionary value of "tongues" = Isa 28:11 LXX quite revised), or sometimes he appeals to it to support a directive of his own (1 Cor 14:34 on the submission of women = Gen 3:16) or directly indicates to the recipients that the fulfillment of the Law is now possible (see Rom 8:4: ἵνα τὸ δικαίωμα τοῦ νόμου πληρωθῇ ἐν ἡμῖν, ". . . that the Law's just demands may be fulfilled in us") in the commandment of love (see Gal 5:14; Rom 13:9-10). A special case is Rom 3:31 ("Do we then abolish the Law through faith? Not at all! Rather, we *confirm the Law*, νόμον ἱστάνομεν"), where, while recognizing the semantic ambiguity of the idea, I think that νόμος, "Law," has not only the Jewish legal sense of the body of commandments but, given the context, also the more biblical sense of divine revelation.[29] Moreover, the "Law," νόμος, is called ἅγιος and πνευματικός, "holy and spiritual" (Rom 7:12a, 14; see 7:12b: "The commandment is holy, just, and good").[30]

---

28. The first three characteristics are found also in S. Amsler, *L'Ancien Testament*, 49–62, but with little development (especially the third). Meanwhile Grelot, *Sens chrétien de l'Ancien Testament* (Tournai, 1962²), distinguishes "history" (249–326) from "promise" (327–403). However, I should think that both dimensions are really contained in the latter, for the category of "history" is modern, not Pauline, but also because the "promise" must be understood not only of words but of events, so as to include these events. We must clearly state that to present the Old Testament "partly" as Law, "partly" as promise, "partly" as Scripture, and "partly" as language absolutely must not be understood in the sense of the *Letter of Ptolemy to Flora* (reported by Epiphanius, *Panar.* 33:3-7, esp. 5-6). The Valentinian Gnostic master perceived in the Old Testament (= "Pentateuch of Moses" 33:4; "Law of God" 33:5) a *material division* in three parts (one abrogated by the Savior, one perfected by him, and one to be read allegorically). We rather mean a simple *formal distinction*, justified primarily by a methodological necessity, except insofar as it concerns (at least partially) the Mosaic Law.

29. Already in 3:21 the expression "Law and prophets" almost attributes a sense of biblical canon to νόμος, "Law"; see Gal 4:21 as well. But this is shown decisively when immediately after, Paul tries to establish his theology of justification through faith *biblically*; see U. Wilckens, *Der Brief an die Römer*, EKK VI/I (1978) 249-250.

30. On the problem of "Law" in Paul, see chaps. 23 and 24 below.

But besides these positive ideas, Paul develops a whole polemic against the Law. We begin with a glaring omission for a rabbinically educated intellectual: at no place in his letters does he base the Christian moral life, the Christian *halakâ*, on any legal statute of the Old Testament. He does single out Lev 19:18 LXX (ἀγαπήσεις τὸν πλησίον σου ὡς σεαυτόν, "You shall love your neighbor as yourself," quoted in Gal 5:14; Rom 13:9) but interprets it in a new way, as a compendium of the whole Law, on the basis of a new hermeneutical principle, i.e., the "Law of Christ" (Gal 6:2; see 1 Cor 9:21).[31] So it is not so much question of a totally new reduction of the Law to a single command[32] as it is of putting the love displayed by Jesus Christ (Gal 2:20, etc.) and the behavior of Christians within the Holy Spirit (Gal 5:22) under the new normative principle that is both historical and mystical.

We at once see a disjunction between the new Christian theology and its Jewish matrix. And though we cannot here go back to some supposed rabbinic concept of an abolition of the Law in messianic times,[33] or an idea of a "Torah of the Messiah,"[34] still, the thesis of G. Scholem is important: according to him, Jewish messianism is in opposition to the Torah and to its written and oral tradition alike, at least what he calls "acute" or "active" in contrast to an "abstract" or purely theoretical messianism. The former type would be represented by Jesus of Nazareth and primi-

---

31. Another exception would seem to be Rom 12:20 with its citation of Prov 25:21-22a LXX (with only the variant of ψώμιζε for τρέφε, both meaning "feed"): "If your enemy be hungry, feed them; if thirsty, give them to drink; by doing so you will heap coals on their head"; and this *halakâ* is cited with two explicit quotation formulas in 12:19 ("'It is written,' 'Vengeance is mine, I shall repay,' says the Lord") with a free allusion to Deut 32:35; Prov 25:22b. But besides the looseness of the quotation, we should note certain things: the *halakâ* itself is drawn not from the Torah but from wisdom literature, and is introduced as authoritative only in a subordinate way through the formulas of v. 19, which actually directly address only God's self-vindication in judgment, which tends to forbid any human vengeance rather than urging help to one's enemies; finally, the works of mercy prescribed here under the Proverbs formulation are basically explained by the Gospel tradition of love of enemies (see Matt 5:38-42; 25:35-40; 1 Thess 5:15; 1 Pet 3:9) and even more in the light of the sole commandment of love of neighbor a little later enunciated in Rom 13:9 (which is, indeed, based more on the Torah of Lev 19:18 than on Jesus' words; but cf. Gal 6:2). See, for example, F.-J. Ortkemper, *Leben aus dem Glauben. Christliche Grundhaltungen nach Römer 12-13*, NA NF 14 (Munich, 1980) 106-124.

32. See, e.g., H. Hübner, *Law in Paul's Thought*, trans. J. Gerig (Edinburgh, 1984) 36-38, 83-87. On the whole question, see A. Nissen, *Gott und der Nächste im antiken Judentum*, WUNT 15 (Tübingen, 1974). However, this does abolish the norms concerning circumcision (see Gal 5:11-12), cult (Gal 4:10), and ritual diet (Gal 2:14).

33. See E. P. Sanders, *Palestinian Judaism*, 478, n. 22, and 479, n. 25; also P. Schäfer, "Die Torah der messianischen Zeit," ZNW 65 (1974) 32-36.

34. This expression appears late, in *Midr. Qoh.* 11:8, on the basis of which W. D. Davies (*Torah in the Messianic Age and/or the Age to Come*, JBL MS [Philadelphia, 1952] 91-92; *Paul and Rabbinic Judaism* [London, 1958²] 72-73) and H.-J. Schoeps, (*Paul* [Philadelphia, 1961 = Tübingen, 1959] 172-173) believed they could demonstrate that the Messiah would teach a new Law.

tive Christianity, but also Shabbatai Zevi in the seventeenth century, and the Sabbatianists. Paul, as an "interpreter of the post-messianic situation"[35] within Jewish messianism presents the case of a real crisis of the tradition such as will happen again with Sabbatianism:[36] in both cases there is the experience of redemption as a historical event, the end of the Law is proclaimed (in Sabbatianism leading to fanaticism and libertinism), and a new, messianic understanding of Scripture arises (thus, in Sabbatianism the apostasy of the Messiah is recognized as foretold in Scripture, something that no one had noticed before the actual apostasy of Shabbatai Zevi). As we see, certain comparisons can be made. The fact remains, however, that Shabbatai Zevi came much later, while the Judaism whence Christianity originated offers no parallels to the Pauline claim (unless we consider this claim itself to be an enormous, insupportable exception within Judaism itself).

We are, then, interested in the Pauline idea of the surpassing of the Law. On that matter we begin by recording an instance of downgrading of the Law in Gal 3. Verses 19-20 read: "[The Law] *was added* [προσετέθη] for transgressions, until the seed should come for whom the promise was made; and it was promulgated by angels through a mediator. But a mediator is not for one who is alone, but God is only One." It seems to me that A. Vanhoye has most helpfully illuminated this difficult text[37] by seeing the angels as the real givers of the Law, and the mediator as an (angelic) representative of them. Paul thus downgrades the Law to a level that is not really divine. It is not without reason that the statement is surrounded and emphasized with themes of diminution: the term "added" *(προσετέθη)*; the negative purpose of the gift "for transgressions" *(τῶν παραβάσεων χάριν)*;[38] the theme, in the context, of the Law's inability to give life (see 3:11-12:21); and the parallel motif of a curse associated with it (see 3:10, 13);[39] and finally that of the pedagogue (3:24), which unites the theme of

35. H.-J. Schoeps, *Paul*, 97.

36. See G. Scholem, "Die Krise der Tradition im jüdischen Messianismus," in his *Judaica*, III (Frankfurt a. M., 1973) 152-197, cited by J. Blank (n. 2 above) 201-206. Shabbatai Zevi lived between 1626 and 1676; in 1666, presented by the sultan with the choice between martyrdom and the acceptance of Islam, he chose the latter; one of his macarisms was: "Blessed is the one who permits the forbidden" (in J. Blank, 204). Concerning him, see the article "Shabbetai Zevi" in *Encyclopedia Judaica*, XIV (1971), cols. 1219-1254.

37. "Un médiateur des anges en Ga 3,19-20," *Biblica* 59 (1978) 403-411; the author appeals to Job 1:27; 2:1, 26-27, etc.; Acts 7:38, and maintains that the "mediator" was not Moses but an angel acting in the name of the other angels.

38. The final sense of χάριν, which I should think preferable to a causal sense, is based on parallel passages, Rom 4:15; 5:20; 7:8b-9 (against U. Wilckens, *Zur Entwicklung*, 171); thus also H. Hübner, *Law*, 26-34 (and the commentaries on Galatians by H. Schlier, H. D. Betz, G. Barbaglio).

39. See F. F. Bruce, "The Curse of the Law," in M. D. Hooker and S. G. Wilson, eds., *Paul and Paulinism: Essays in Honour of C. K. Barrett* (London, 1982) 27-36.

the transitory ("till Christ came") with that of severe constraint (3:23: "We were held in custody by the Law").

It's a short step from here to saying that the Law has finished its work for the Christian. And Paul does formulate an axiom in Rom 10:4 that evidently sums up his thought: "The end of the Law is Christ, for the justification of whoever believes" (τέλος γὰρ νόμου Χριστὸς εἰς δικαιοσύνην παντὶ τῷ πιστεύοντι). It is quite clear that τέλος, "end," here means "ending" rather than "purpose,"[40] but we must further clarify that the νόμος identifies Old Testament not as Sacred Scripture but as economy of salvation. A little earlier, in fact (in 9:31-32), Paul maintained that Israel, though pursuing a Law given for the sake of justice, has in fact not achieved it because they relied on works and not faith. And right after (in 10:6-8) he openly replaces the "commandment" (ἐντολή) of Deut 30:11ff. LXX (MT *miṣwāh*) with the person of Christ, and the "word" ῥῆμα of Deut 30:14 LXX (MT *dābār*) with "the word of faith": it is the connection of the two terms, Christ/faith, that brings about salvation (Rom 10:9). Clearly, henceforth on the one hand the word of precept is drained of power and replaced by Christ, while on the other "doing" (see Deut 30:12, 13, 14: ποιήσομεν [twice] and ποιεῖν) as a way of salvation gives place to "confessing" and "believing" (see Rom 10:9-10).

But before the Letter to the Romans, Paul had already shown an interest in the theme of the Law in 2 Cor 3:4-18, a passage that is really aimed not at Jewish-Christian opponents so much as at Judaism itself (see vv. 13, 14: "the children of Israel . . . until now").[41] Even though the word "Law" does not appear here, still Paul seems to be addressing just this reality, as we already see with the mention of the "tablets of stone" in v. 3 (see also v. 7) and the identification of "Moses" as the one that is read (v. 15). The whole passage is built on a series of antitheses that give it a very polemic tone. We summarize them here, juxtaposing the contrasts:

ink	Spirit of the living God
tablets of stone	tablets of the heart of flesh
old covenant	new covenant
letter	Spirit
kills	gives life
ministry of death	ministry of the Spirit

40. See the commentaries, esp. see A. Maillot, "Essai sur les citations vétérotestamentaires contenues dans Romains 9 à 11, ou comment se servir de la Torah pour montrer que le 'Christ est la fin de la Torah,' " EtThRel 57 (1982) 55-73; and above all, R. Badenas, *Christ the End of the Law. Romans 10,4 in Pauline Perspective* (Sheffield, 1986).

41. See E. Richard, "Polemics, Old Testament, and Theology: A Study of II Cor., III,1—IV,6," RB 88 (1981) 340-367; see vol. 1 of this work, chap. 16, V.

ministry of condemnation   ministry of justification
what is passing away   what remains

While acknowledging an element of "glory" in the Old Covenant (for the ministry of the gospel is credited only with a "greater glory": vv. 7-11), Paul still claims that it "kills" (v. 6), and emphasizes the verb καταρ-γεῖν, "abolish/annul" (vv. 7, 11, 13, 14), with repeated reference to the old economy. Its basic principle is identified as "letter," γράμμα (not γραφή, "scripture"!), i.e., a neutral principle, identified as dead Law that kills (cf. the juxtaposition of the two terms γράμμα and νόμος in Rom 2:27; 7:16). Moreover, the whole ancient system of salvation is for the first time labeled "old covenant" (παλαιὰ διαθήκη), and again we must note that this does not identify just the "Old Testament" in the literary sense, as we would understand in today's language. For Paul there was no opposition between Old and New Scriptures simply because there was no New Testament in a literary sense.

The "old dispensation," then, is the Old Testament not so much as book but rather as covenant,[42] and so as system of salvation founded by Moses; it is not without reason that the whole passage forms a sort of *midraš* on Exod 34:29-35 and on the veil that used to cover Moses's face. Of this veil we are told that ἐν Χριστῷ καταργεῖται, "in Christ it is abolished."[43] It is a decidedly strong verb. Elsewhere Paul uses it in explicit reference to the Law, "You *are estranged (κατηργήθητε)* from Christ, you who seek justification in the Law" (Gal 5:4); "But now we *have been liberated (κατηρ-γήθημεν)* from the Law, dying to what held us captive" (Rom 7:6). And if in Rom 3:31 Paul expressly excludes this (μὴ γένοιτο, "God forbid!"), it is because in that passage he attributes a different meaning to "Law," νόμος (see above). However, at various times he even uses the expression χωρὶς νόμου, "without the Law" (Rom 3:21, 28; 7:8, 9; cf. Phil 3:9).

This strongly critical attitude toward the Law is all the more surprising in view of the growing importance accorded to it in the Judaism of the time,[44] in all its expressions: wisdom (see Sir 24: identification with pre-existent wisdom); Qumran (see 1Qs 5:2, 21); Sadducees (see Fl. Josephus, *Ant.* 18:16); above all rabbinic (see, e.g., *P. Abôt* 6:2: identity of interests of Law and liberty); and even Hellenistic (see *Arist.* 139; 4 Macc 5:20; Philo *Vit. Mos.* 2:51-52: the Law coincides with the thought of eternal nature).

42. On this A. T. Hanson insists strongly, *Paul's Technique*, 138f.
43. For another translation, see R. Penna, *Lo Spirito di Cristo* (Brescia, 1976) 190, n. 8.
44. See the excellent synthesis of U. Luz, "Das Gesetz im Frühjudentum" in R. Smend and U. Luz, *Gesetz* (Stuttgart, 1981) 45–57. On the Law as cosmic order for salvation, see M. Limbeck, *Die Ordnung des Heils. Untersuchungen zum Gesetzverständnis des Frühjudentums* (Düsseldorf, 1971).

The only possible link with Pauline thought is in apocalyptic Judaism, represented especially (apart from the silence concerning the Law in the story of Moses in Ethiopian *Hen* 89:16, 37) in certain Qumran texts (e.g., 1QpHab 8:1-3: "Those who observe the Law of the House of Judah, whom God will deliver from the House of Judgment for their suffering and because of their faith in the Teacher of Righteousness"—G. Vermes, *The Dead Sea Scrolls in English* [Sheffield, 1987] 287), in 4 Esdr (see 3:20, 22: "Nor did you remove the evil heart from them that your Law might bear fruit in them . . . and their weakness became permanent . . .") and 2 Bar (see 54:19: "We are each Adam for ourselves"). We see here certain Pauline principles: a pessimistic vision of the universal human condition in this aeon (cf. Rom 5:12); the powerlessness of the Law to overcome it (Rom 8:3), even though the Law is good in itself; emphasis on a future salvation, based not on the Law but on an eschatological intervention (Rom 3:21).[45]

One thing is clear enough in this attitude of Paul's: he treats the Law negatively in polemic contexts, whether with Jewish Christians (as in Galatians and 2 Corinthians 11) or with Jews (2 Cor 3:4ff.), or with both Jews and Jewish Christians in their relations with gentiles or gentile Christians (as in Romans).[46] In all these cases the dialogue is always with persons who know the Old Testament and accord it (or are in danger of according it) a primary normative and salvific value that would deny Christ the primary, not to say exclusive, role in redemption. But Paul rejects the Law only as it would be antagonistic to Christ or substitute for him. If it claims to monopolize salvation, even though it be God's gift, it cannot stand up against Christ, and so must yield to him.[47]

Still, Paul readily recognizes aspects of preparation and prefiguration.

2) The Old Testament as ἐπαγγελία, "promise." The word is used by Paul only in a theological sense, practically always polemically to undermine the Law (in Gal 3:14, 16, 17, 18, 21, 29; 4:23, 28; Rom 4:13, 14, 16,

45. See U. Luz, op. cit., 56 and 98.

46. Concerning Paul's opponents, see G. Lüdemann, *Opposition to Paul in Jewish Christianity*, 64–109 (but the exposition is descriptive and the question of the Law is ignored; e.g., on Galatians see 97–103); and R. Penna, ed., *Antipaolinismo: reazioni a Paolo tra il I e II secolo*, RSB 2 (Bologna, 1989).

47. See E. P. Sanders, *Paul and Palestinian Judaism*, 550–551: "The Law is good, even *doing* the Law is good, but salvation is only by Christ; therefore the entire system represented by the Law is worthless for salvation. *It is the change of 'entire systems' which makes it unnecessary for him to speak about repentance or the grace of God shown in the giving of the [old] covenant*. These things fade into the background because of the surpassing glory of the new dispensation (II Cor 3.9f.). Paul was not trying accurately to represent Judaism on its own terms, nor need we suppose that he was ignorant on essential points. He simply saw the old dispensation as worthless in comparison with the new." See also the excellent book by the same author, *Paul, the Law, and the Jewish People* (Philadelphia, 1983 [Italian: 1989]).

20; 9:4, 8, 9; 15:8, and also 2 Cor 1:20; 7:1; the corresponding verb *ἐπαγ-γέλλεσθαι* in Gal 3:19; Rom 4:21). Only in Rom 1:2 do we read of the "gospel of God" that "was *announced beforehand (προεπηγγείλατο)* through his prophets in the sacred Scriptures"; and the same idea resonates in 3:21 concerning the "justice of God" that, though manifested apart from the Law, is still *"witnessed to (μαρτυρουμένη)* by the Law and prophets." So, according to Paul, the Christian reality does not represent a completely new beginning, nor is it only in opposition to what preceded it. On the contrary, the Old Testament already contained signals, orientations, anticipations that can be discovered there.

Here we must make a rudimentary but fundamental distinction. (But first we should note that hermeneutically we must understand the "promise" as forming a bridge, a kind of hyphen between the Old and New Testaments.) Now, the distinction is between texts and realities, the book and history. Paul does not actually think so much that the promise is contained in the Old Testament as a book as that it is present in the events it reports, and so has an existential, not just a verbal, dimension. Negatively this is shown by the simple fact that Paul never treats the Old Testament stories as real allegories like the Alexandrians.[48] Now he does write concerning the story of Hagar and Sarah in Gal 4:24: *ἅτινά ἐστιν ἀλ-ληγορούμενα,* "This is spoken allegorically." And Paul does seem in fact to allegorize the ancient vicissitudes of Abraham's family life, since he gives each element of the story a meaning different from its literal sense (two women = two covenants; two social conditions, slavery and liberty = the present Jerusalem and the heavenly Jerusalem; two sons = two opposing sets of descendants). But a fundamental difference from allegorical method stands out: the figures and events of Genesis are understood not as images used as ciphers for timeless moral truths, but rather as unrepeatable historical events that only become prefigurations and models for present situations. How eloquently he formulates it in 4:29: "Just as then . . . so now," *ὥσπερ τότε . . . ὄντως καὶ νῦν.*

The relationship, then, is not between a text and an abstract truth hidden in it, but between "then" and "now," past and present. This temporal dimension is decisive, comparing two historic moments, the first of which elucidates the second, is a kind of foretaste of the second. It is fair to say, then, that in this case "the 'allegory' is really an elaborate piece of typology."[49] The events of the old patriarchal story are considered pre-

48. As we have said, 1 Corinthian's treatment of Deut 25:4 is an exception, but this 25:4 is a legislative text, not a narrative one.

49. A. T. Hanson, *Paul's Technique,* 95; he quotes two clear statements on the subject, John Chrysostom (PG 61:662: "Paul improperly calls the type 'allegory' ") and Theodoret of Cyr

figurations of present realities, i.e., of the opposition today existing between the "Jerusalem here" (v. 25) and the "Jerusalem from above, which is our Mother" (v. 26), between the child according to the flesh and the child according to the Spirit (cf. v. 29), between the offspring of the slave and that of the free woman, who is the "child of the promise" (vv. 28, 31), i.e., between the Jewish Christians and the gentile Christians.[50]

All this, then, poses the question whether Paul avoids allegory and normally works on the Old Testament through typology. The answer cannot be completely negative, as we have already said; but neither can it be completely positive, if we give typology the technical meaning already defined in the patristic age.[51] For Paul, "Typology is not a hermeneutic method with specific rules of interpretation. It is a spiritual approach that looks forward to the consummation of salvation and recognizes the individual types of that consummation in redemptive history."[52]

A. T. Hanson makes a useful distinction between perfect types, which represent exact anticipations of New Testament figures, and dissimilar types, which do anticipate, but only by way of dissimilarity.[53] The *first kind* includes Abraham as believer (see Gal 3:6-9; Rom 4); Isaac as promised seed (Gal 3:16, 29; 4:23, 29, 31; and by contrast Ishmael as "son of the slave"); Pharaoh as the one who disobeys God (Rom 9:14-18); and we could add the paschal lamb (implied in the language of 1 Cor 5:7; cf. Exod 12:21) and especially the desert generation because of the dialectic of their

(PG 82:490: "He does not deny the historical story, but teaches what is prefigured in the story," τὰ ἐν τῇ ἱστορίᾳ προτυπωθέντα διδάσκει) 93–94. [In fact, Hanson cites only "Theodotus" (sic!), without PG reference; it is not clear whence Penna got his (correct) patristic references.— T.P.W.]. According to H.-J. Schoeps, *Paul*, 238, n. 3, the Pauline text "is sheer Hellenistic midrashic speculation," contrary to the rabbinic principle that no biblical word can lose its original meaning.

50. On this text, see esp. F. Pastor Ramos, "Alegoría o tipología en Gal 4:21-31," EstBibl 34 (1975) 113–119 (an example of strict Pauline typology); L. Gaston, "Israel's Enemies in Pauline Theology," NTS 28 (1982) 400–423. Among the commentaries, see especially F. Mussner, *Der Galaterbrief*, HThKNT IX (1974); and F. F. Bruce, *The Epistle to the Galatians* (Exeter, 1982) ad loc.

51. See L. Goppelt, *Typos. The Typological Interpretation of the Old Testament in the New*, trans. D. H. Madvig (Grand Rapids, Mich., 1982 [original: Gütersloh, 1939]) 127–152 (note 129: for Paul "the typology is more concerned with the Church than with the person of Christ"); idem, "Apokalyptik und Typologie bei Paulus," ThLZ 89 (1964) 321–344; idem, art. τύπος ["type"], TDNT 8:246–259. On the patristic age in particular, see B. De Margerie, *Introduzione alla storia dell'esegesi—I. I Padri greci e orientali* (Rome, 1983) 38–44 (= St. Justin; in *Dial.* 40:1; 42:4 he reveals a very broad conception of "type"; for him every single decree of Moses is a symbol and proclamation of what will take place in Christ), 95–98 (= Clement of Alexandria), 121–123 (= Origen); but the work fails to treat the *Letter of Barnabas* with its problematic typology.

52. L. Goppelt, *Typos*, 202; see 152: Paul regards it "not as a systematic exposition of Scripture, but as a spiritual approach that gives the Church basic guidance from Scripture here and now on concrete questions of faith and practice."

53. *Paul's Technique*, 151–158.

participation in the salvation event, but also their punishment by God (see 1 Cor 10:1-13). As we can see, none of these perfect types refers to Christ (except the paschal lamb, but the lamb is never referred to through a biblical citation), and thus Christ is not presented as part of the series.

The *second kind* includes Moses (whose typology as mediator belongs more to Hebrews than to Paul, who sees him in 2 Cor 3 as antitype of Christ, but not insofar as he radiates the Lord's glory but insofar as he hides it);[54] Jonah (implied in Rom 10:7 in "go down into the abyss," but to bring Christ back from the dead); and above all Adam (progenitor of death, whereas Christ is progenitor of a new life: 1 Cor 15:21-22; Rom 5:13-14). In Rom 5:14 Adam is called τύπος τοῦ μέλλοντος, "a type of what was to come," but by way of dissimilarity, in fact of opposition *in the same type of reality: in eodem genere.*[55] Moreover, that "type" *(τύπος)* is here used in the sense of temporal prefiguration is questionable. For actually we must recognize that Adam in Rom 7:11 is simply the image of the universal Human "I" (sinner), and so H. Conzelmann maintains that we are dealing with mythical rather than temporal patterns.[56] In any case, because of the developed contrast of Adam and Christ in the context, we can hardly help but recognize the almost technical sense of a typological hermeneutic, and attribute to the Greek word its concrete (etymological) meaning of "sign, impression, image" or even "pattern, mold," so that Adam becomes the negative anticipation, the shadow (see Col 2:17) of Christ, as it were.

1 Cor 10:6 is slightly different (ταῦτα δὲ τύποι ἡμῶν ἐγενήθησαν, "these things happened as types for us"), as is 10:11 (ταῦτα δὲ τυπικῶς συνέβαινεν ἐκείνοις, "these things happened to them by way of type"). At issue are happenings rather than persons; the context is paraenetic. Paul brings up the account of various events of the Exodus generation (participation in salvation, transgressions, punishment; see Exod 13:17-17:7; Num 11; 20:1-12; Ps 105:39; Wis 19:7) to urge the Corinthian Christians "not to desire

54. An embryonic "perfect type" concerning Moses could be seen in 1 Cor 10:2a ("All were baptized into Moses, πάντες εἰς τὸν Μωϋσῆν ἐβαπτίσθησαν), which seems to perceive in Moses an exact prefiguration of Christ as the one to whom one adheres personally and to whom one belongs by "baptism." But it is actually an inverted typology, since in speaking of Moses, Paul uses a Christian formula that has no correspondence in the Old Testament (see Rom 6:3: ὅσοι ἐβαπτίσθημεν εἰς Χριστὸν Ἰησοῦν, "all we who are baptized into Christ Jesus").

55. More properly, even though not Christologically, Heb 9:24 and 1 Pet 3:21 will use the expression "antitype" (ἀντίτυπον) to compare the heavenly sanctuary with the earthly, and baptism with the flood.

56. *Outline,* 170. Actually, A. T. Hanson, *Paul's Technique,* 152, admits that he is tempted to translate τύπος τοῦ μέλλοντος as "a warning for the future" (in an impersonal sense)! The anthropological sense of this μέλλοντος is supported by K Haacker, "Exegetische Probleme des Römerbriefs," NT 20 (1978) 1-21, 18; now see also D. Biju-Duval, "La traduzione di Rm 5,12-14," RivBibl 38 (1990) 353-373.

evil things as they desired them" (v. 6b), and so "let any who think they
are standing be on guard so as not to fall" (v. 12). Paul's primary purpose
is not to establish parallels between the Old Testament and the New as
such, nor to interpret the sacred writings in a Christian mode,[57] nor to
emphasize the existence of anticipation in the history of salvation, but to
warn the recipients against an undue confidence in the sacraments (baptism and Eucharist), as if these alone were enough for salvation. The purpose, then, is exhortative. Even so, it is true that Paul does seek to do
this by referring to examples derived from the Old Testament, which are
used to elucidate the present situation of the Corinthian community. A
certain typology can hardly be denied, especially because context implies
a comparison between the crossing of the Sea and baptism, the manna
and the Eucharist.[58] But "the typological system supports and reinforces
the paraenesis, showing that the present testing of Christians was already
determined beforehand. . . . The type is at the same time an example."[59]
True typology underlies the whole enterprise of the *relecture*, the hermeneutical "rereading" of the Old Testament and its general reference to

57. A clear exception is 1 Cor 10:4 ("they drank from a spiritual rock that followed them,
and the rock was Christ"), where Paul unites a rabbinic tradition (according to which the
rock struck by Moses [Num 20:11] would always have accompanied the Israelites in the desert:
see Strack-Billerbeck, III 407–408; E. E. Ellis, *Paul's Use*, 66–70) with a Judeo-Hellenistic speculation (according to which the rock itself would be identified with Wisdom or Word personified: see Philo, *Leg. alleg.* 2:86; *Det. pot. ins.* 118). But in 1 Cor 10:1-13 Paul's emphasis is not
on this Christological reality; he mentions it only in passing.

58. See the commentaries; there are few studies of the pericope: among the most recent,
see A. J. Bandstra, "Interpretation in 1 Corinthians 10:1-11," CalvTheolJourn 6 (1971) 5–21;
F. Hahn, "Teilhabe am Heil und Gefahr des Abfalls. Eine Auslegung von 1 Ko 10:1-22," in
L. De Lorenzi, ed., *Freedom and Love* (Rome, 1981) 149–171; Ch. Perrot, "Les examples du
désert (1 Cor 10:6-11)," NTS 29 (1983) 437–452.

59. Cf. Chr. Senft, *La première épître aux Corinthiens* (Neuchâtel, 1979) 130. L. Goppelt, in
TDNT 8:252, maintains that "the word takes on here for the first time the technical meaning
in which it is often used in [subsequent] Christian literature": (cf. n. 32: he recognizes that
"there seem to be no preparatory stages for the technical use of τύπος in Paul, which is not
attested before him"). H. Conzelmann, *1 Corinthians*, Hermeneia (Philadelphia, 1975) ad loc.,
more accurately claims, "Here, to be sure, we have not yet to do with the technical, hermeneutical use of the term, but with its moral sense"; thus also C. K. Barrett, *The First Epistle
to the Corinthians* (London, 1968, 1971²), who translates τύποι "as examples" and τυπικῶς
"by way of example." W. E. Orr and J. A. Walther, in their commentary in the Anchor Bible
(Garden City, N.Y., 1976), correctly maintain that what we have "is not paraenetic typology
but typological paraenesis" (ad loc.); and G. Barbaglio (*Le lettere di Paolo*, I [Rome, 1980] 416)
distinguishes, "We have a twofold sense of *typos*, anticipatory story and admonishing story."
Regarding 1 Cor 10:11, A. T. Hanson, *Paul's Technique*, 76, clearly distinguishes between why
these things happened as an admonition to Israel and why they were written for us (see also
p. 151: "the events of Israel's history had full reality for those who took part in them, but
were recorded for our benefit; they did not *take place* for our benefit, and Paul never says
they did"); but he does not take into account that v. 6 had said that the events themselves
are τύποι ἡμῶν, i.e., examples to warn *us*, already on the level of fact and not just of the written report. The distinction between Scripture and history is a modern one, and besides, Paul
is not speaking just of historical writing but of *sacred* Scripture.

the Christian community—and this is more than can be expressed by the mere words τύπος/τυπικῶς, which rather have a moral connotation (note this moral sense in Rom 6:17, Phil 3:17; 1 Thess 1:7.)

It is legitimate to ask at this point: What is Paul's general attitude toward the history of Israel reported in the Old Testament books? Is it promise, prefiguration, example? Does he recognize it as the basic authoritative document? How does he actually use it? Does he constantly refer to it? Does he consider it a unity? And what kind of continuity does he see there with the Christian event? Specifically, can we speak of a salvation history in Paul? These are appropriate questions, even if they probably reflect our modern intellectual sensitivities more than Paul's. We must note that the question of a salvation history in Paul has been a subject of scholarly dispute, especially in Germany during the sixties.[60] Against the fiercest opponents of a *heilsgeschichtlich* element in Paul's thought (R. Bultmann, G. Klein, G. Dietzfelbinger, H. Conzelmann) and against its most zealous supporters (J. Munck, O. Cullmann, W. G. Kümmel), other authors follow a more moderate path (L. Goppelt, U. Luz, E. Käsemann). With no pretensions of exhausting the issue here, we can establish certain fixed points to help us toward achieving a balanced judgment.

a) Especially in Romans and Galatians, Paul refers to various personages and events from the story of Israel, though never to anyone from later than the ninth century B.C. His preferences are in the stories of the First Ancestors (Abraham and Sarah, the sons Isaac and [the unnamed] Ishmael; Rebekah, Jacob, and Esau; see Gal 3; 4:21-31; Rom 4:9-10) and the events connected with the Exodus (Moses, the Pharaoh, the Law at Sinai, the excesses of the people in the desert; 1 Cor 10:1-13; 2 Cor 3; Gal 3; Rom 9–10); by way of exception he also notes Elijah and his dialogue with God (Rom 11:2-4).[61]

---

60. See J. Munck, *Paul and the Salvation of Mankind* (Richmond, 1959); G. Klein, "Röm 4 und die Idee der Heilsgeschichte," ETh 23 (1963) 424–447; idem, "Individualgeschichte und Weltgeschichte bei Paulus. Eine Interpretation ihres Verhältnisses im Galaterbrief," EvTh 24 (1964) 126–165; G. Dietzfelbinger, *Heilsgeschichte in Paulus?* (Munich, 1965); L. Goppelt, "Paulus und die Heilsgeschichte: Schlussfolgerungen aus Röm. IV und I. Kor. X,1-13," NTS 13 (1966) 31–42; O. Cullmann, *Salvation in History* (New York, 1967 [Italian: 1966]) 248–268; U. Luz, *Das Geschichtsverständnis des Paulus* (Munich, 1968); E. Käsemann, "Justification and Salvation History in the Epistle to the Romans," *Perspectives on Paul* (Philadelphia, 1971) 60–78; E. Güttgemanns, "Heilsgeschichte bei Paulus oder Dynamik des Evangeliums? Zur strukturellen Relevanz von Röm 9–11 für die Theologie des Römerbriefes" in his *Studia linguistica neotestamentica*, BETh 60 (Munich, 1971) 34–58; see also W. G. Kümmel, "Heilsgeschichte im NT," in J. Gnilka, ed., *Neues Testament und Kirche. Für R. Schnackenburg* (Freiburg–Basel–Vienna, 1974) 434–457.

61. Other personages (David, Isaiah, Hosea) are mentioned for their literary-theological rather than their historical value, therefore as sacred writers.

b) In particular, if we consider Abraham, we must note that his justification is not considered an atemporal model. For Paul is careful to observe that this took place "not after circumcision but before it" (Rom 4:10, a reference to the fact that circumcision is first mentioned in Gen 17:11, while in Gen 15:6 the faith of the Ancestor was already imputed as justice). The granting of the Law is likewise located in a historical sequence (see Gal 3:17-24). This means that Paul is sensitive to the historical dimensions of the events of divine revelation: these are not purely vertical interventions, but find their place precisely in relation to their horizontal succession.

c) For Paul, the principle that God is faithful to his promises is true: "The gifts and the call of God are *irrevocable* (ἀμεταμέλητα; cf. Ps 110:4 LXX)" (Rom 11:29; cf. 3:3-4: πίστις θεοῦ, "God's faithfulness"). And even though this idea is expressed especially in the context of the future and the certainty of Israel's salvation, it still presupposes the idea of an uninterrupted connection with the events of the past.

d) Even so, there is not a historical continuity between the Old Testament and the Christian event in the sense that it is not history as such that brings the various ages of salvation to maturity. For a rupture stands not only between the promises to Abraham and the Law of Moses but especially between the latter and the Christ-event. Nor does Paul sketch out a general picture of history as apocalyptic will do: he does not do so for world history nor even for that of Israel. Above any historical framework is God's judgment, beyond question, unfathomable (see Rom 11:33). Still, he never opposes the New Testament to the Old, as apocalyptic and even the rabbis will do with the idea of the two ages; the surpassing of the past is realized by God, but perceived only through faith (see Gal 2:20: "living in the flesh, I live in faith"). History is not an iron framework of the events of salvation, but only the place or dimension in which there takes place the revelation of the unpredictable εὐδοκία (gracious free choice) of God (and it is thus that we must interpret the "fullness of time" in Gal 4:4.)

e) Christ is the fulfillment of all that is awaited, and he reveals that the ancient hopes were oriented toward him. The typical Pauline principle in this sense is that "God's Son, Jesus Christ, was not 'yes and no,' but [only] 'yes' was in him. For *all God's promises (ὅσαι γὰρ ἐπαγγελίαι θεοῦ)* had their 'yes' in him" (2 Cor 1:19-20).[62] His reference to the Old Testa-

62. See I. Dugandzic̀, *Das 'Ja' Gottes in Christus* (n. 2 above); the author, who examines a series of Pauline texts, essentially maintains the dialectical conception of continuity and discontinuity in the Old Testament.

ment here prescinds from specific texts—it is general. Especially the idea of ἐπαγγελία, "promise," which Paul first uses here, seems to be original to Paul himself, since it has no real parallel in the Old Testament;[63] it expresses a clearly Christian and Christological interpretation of the old Scriptures in that he sees in them an internal dynamic that has not reached its goal. But again, Paul considers the "promises" not so much as a part of a verbal and atemporal Scripture as concrete and living events; in fact, he does not use the word "fulfill" to say that the Scriptures were completed (cf. Matthew on the other hand) but makes use of various unusual expressions such as "He became 'yes,'" ναὶ γέγονεν (in this passage) or "to confirm the promises," εἰς τὸ βεβαιῶσαι τὰς ἐπαγγελίας (Rom 15:8; 4:16) to indicate the accomplishment of the content. The point from which their fulfillment is observed is the salvation-historical "now," νῦν (see Rom 3:21, 26; 2 Cor 6:2) of the Christ-event.

f) Finally, if Christ is the one who realizes the promises, the Christian is heir on the basis not of Law but of the promise (see Gal 3:18; Rom 4:13-14). The expression "heir" (κληρονόμος) now becomes a term belonging to salvation history. For it raises the question who is integrated into this history of salvation that began with Abraham";[64] therefore this idea differs from the use of the term in the Old Testament (promise of the land, e.g., Gen 18:3) as well as in Judaism, both Palestinian (inheriting the age to come; see 4 Esdr 6:67) and Hellenistic (Philo Alex., *Div. rer. her.* 64; 68-70: "heir" has a spiritual-moral sense). Now, in Jesus Christ the blessing of Abraham has passed to the gentiles, and through faith we have received the spirit of the promise (see Gal 3:14). In this context even the concept of υἱοθεσία, of being children of God, acquires a dimension of salvation history (see 4:1-7). And especially in Romans 9–11 it seems evident that even justification by faith has a broad horizon in salvation history.[65] Hence even the anthropological aspect of the new Christian reality, Christian newness, is not an improvisation but is profoundly correlated to ancient plans and advance proclamations that are valid for Jew and gentile alike.

3) The Old Testament as γραφή, "Scripture." Paul considers the Old Testament positively, not just as a historic phase containing a promise.

63. See J. Schniewind and G. Friedrich, art. ἐπαγγέλλω, TDNT 1:579–581; in extrabiblical Judaism in general, "promise" refers to the reward for keeping the Law and its payment in the world to come.

64. W. Foerster, art. κληρονόμος, TDNT 3:785. See also R. Penna, *Lo Spirito di Cristo* (Brescia, 1976) 223f.

65. See U. Wilckens, *Der Brief an die Römer*, II, 182; and especially E. Käsemann, *Commentary on Romans* (Grand Rapids, Mich., 1980) 255–256, who denies that one must choose between justification by faith and history of salvation.

That is, the Old Testament is not just dynamically oriented toward the salvific event accomplished in Christ and experienced by the Christian. It also has a more general normative character in an objective and static kind of way, as a collection of sacred writings. Except for the already traditional generic formula of 1 Cor 15:3, 4 (κατὰ τὰς γραφάς, "according to the Scriptures"), Paul normally uses the singular γραφή, "Scripture" (seven times).[66] Actually, the Scripture is sometimes personified: not only in that it "says . . ." (see Rom 4:3; 9:17; 11:2, citing [in order] Gen 15:6; Exod 9:16; 1 Kgs 19:10, 14), but also because it *proclaimed beforehand* (see Gal 3:8: ἡ γραφὴ . . . προευηγγελίσατο) to Abraham the blessing of all the nations, and because it *imprisoned* (3:22: συνέκλεισεν ἡ γραφή) everything under sin. If we then compare this last text with the parallel in Rom 11:32 ("God imprisoned . . .," συνέκλεισεν ὁ θεός), we note that "God" and "Scripture" become equivalent, and so the latter is recognized as having a clearly divine authority; furthermore, we sometimes find an absolute λέγει, "it [he] says" (see Rom 15:10; 2 Cor 6:2; Gal 3:16), which can understand "God" as well as "Scripture" for subject (see Rom 9:25: ἐν τῷ Ὡσηὲ λέγει).

The same concept of normative authority is also present when Paul refers to the names of the sacred writers, even though each refers to only a part of Scripture; thus alongside the formula Μωϋσῆς γράφει/λέγει, "Moses writes/says" (Rom 10:5, 19), we encounter Δαυὶδ λέγει, "David says" (Rom 4:6; 11:9) and Ἡσαΐας λέγει, "Isaiah says" (Rom 10:16; 11:20-21; 15:12). The formula (καθὼς) γέγραπται, "(as) it is written," also indicated the final normative character recognized for Scripture.[67]

Of course, we do not know precisely what Paul thought of the biblical canon, but nevertheless the Scriptures must have nourished his mind and heart from his youth. Faith in Christ did not lead him to toss them in the "dustbin," as happens with other parts of the Jewish religious heritage (see Phil 3:5-8). The use he makes of the sacred books[68] shows that in cer-

---

66. The plural occurs again only among the pre- or post-Pauline passages of Rom 1:2 (with the only occurrence of the adjective ἁγίαι, "holy [Scriptures]"); 16:26; an exception is Rom 15:4 (διὰ τῆς παρακλήσεως τῶν γραφῶν, "through the consolation of the Scriptures"), where there is a global allusion to the Scriptures in a paraenetic context, without reference to any specific passage.

67. See the formulas at Qumran, *ka'ašer kātûb*, "as it is written" (1QS 8:14; CD 7:19); *kî' kēn katûb*, "for thus it is written" (1QS 5:15), and the like (note CD 1:13; 5:1-2). For the use of "Sacred Scripture(s)" in rabbinism and Hellenistic Judaism, see G. Schrenk, art. γραφή, TDNT 1:751–755; for the use of γέγραπται and γεγραμμένον, see ibid. 747–748 and 748–749. According to F. Mussner, *Der Galaterbrief*, 337 and 338, "Paul comes from rabbinic Judaism and that means: it is not history that is normative for him, not even the history of Israel, but Scripture . . . as something supra-temporal, stable, transcending history and independent of it"; but the author is quick to recognize that Paul does not ignore the importance of time (see p. 340).

68. According to the count of O. Michel, *Paulus und seine Bibel*, 10–13, of 87 citations of the Old Testament in the four main letters, 32 are from the Torah, 30 from the Nebi'im, and

tain central points of the Christian message recourse to them is necessary and decisive, or at least that it comes to him spontaneously. And there is actually no indication that Paul knows other so-called New Testament Scriptures, neither supplementary nor much less substitutive; nor, so far as we know, did Paul have any intention whatsoever to compose any such.[69]

We must also consider the typical Pauline distinction between γραφή and γράμμα, "Scripture" and "letter." While the former is always used in its positive sense as a synonym for divine revelation, the latter always connotes the negative aspect of written norm that would regulate moral behavior and ultimately determine the outcome of human salvation. For Paul, then, γράμμα, "letter," is a polemical concept, since it appears contextually in antithesis to πνεῦμα, "spirit" (see Rom 2:27, 29; 7:6; 2 Cor 3:6, 7) and so is identified with the "old" (παλαιότητι γράμματος: Rom 7:6), the "external" (see 2 Cor 3:7), death (2 Cor 3:6).[70] But in that case, at least an implied antithesis also exists between γραφή and γράμμα. The γράμμα,

---

24 from the Ketubim; the single most frequently quoted book is Isaiah (21 times), followed by Psalms (19 times). Of the Torah, the book most cited is Genesis (11 times), followed by Deuteronomy (10 times): "It is perfectly clear that next to the Book of Isaiah and the Psalter, Genesis and Deuteronomy determined the personal piety and the missionary work of the Apostle" (p. 11); see also A. T. Hanson, *Paul's Technique*, 171–172. On the importance of the prophets in ancient Synagogue worship, see Ch. Perrot, *La lecture de la Bible dans la Synagogue. Les anciennes lectures palestiniennes du Shabbat et des fêtes* (Hildesheim, 1973). And of course the only complete book of the Old Testament discovered at Qumran is precisely a scroll of Isaiah.

69. The following observation of Ph. Vielhauer, "Paulus und," 56–57, is quite stimulating: "[Besides the Old Testament] we must also note the Jewish and Hellenistic context. If Paul . . . can present his doctrine of justification without regard to the Old Testament and can develop his proclamation of the saving act of God in Christ even in pagan-Hellenistic categories, we must then ask if the Old Testament has not been pushed onto the same level as elements of popular philosophy and ideas of mystery religion and Gnosticism accepted by Paul." It is of course true that Paul does take up apocryphal elements of Judaism (see 1 Cor 10:4; note 54 above) and is not insensible to elements of popular philosophy (see 2 Cor 4:16-18). "But Paul would answer the question in the negative . . .; for him the Old Testament is *the* divine authority and gives legitimacy to the proclamation of Christ" (p. 57). And still it is true that for Paul "the Old Testament is not a final authority. . . . Paul always already knows what he has to say and does not derive it from the Old Testament" (p. 51). We might add that it is precisely this fact that opens the way for him to use support from the broad cultural context.

70. "Any sacred text, even of the Old Testament, is cause of 'death' when it comes to be interpreted and used simply as 'written norm' " (G. Schrenk, "γραφη," col. 674). This means that the γράμμα is not simply equivalent to "letter," "physical written word"; in fact, the contrasting word, "spirit," is simply the cipher for all that is new about Christian salvation, identifies a whole economy as its determining principle, and cannot be reduced to some elusive spiritual sense characteristic of the Alexandrian biblical hermeneutic (Prat and Allo say much the same thing.) See E. E. Ellis, *Paul's Use*, 25–28; E. Kamlah, "Buchstabe und Geist. Die Bedeutung dieser Antithese für die alttestamentliche Exegese des Apostels Paulus," ETh 14 (1954) 276–282; I Dugandzič, *Das 'Ja' Gottes in Christus*, 88–97; J. Kremer, " 'Denn der Buchstabe tötet, der Geist aber macht lebendig.' Methodologische und hermeneutische Erwägungen zu 2 Kor 3,6b," in J. Zmijewski and E. Nellessen, *Begegnung mit dem Wort. Festschrift H. Zimmermann* (Bonn, 1980) 219–250.

"letter," is similar to the νόμος, "Law." And the γραφή, "Scripture," is as much superior to the former as to the latter. It is never contrasted as such with any component of the New Covenant.

We could say that for Paul the Old Testament is γραφή not so much in itself but to the extent that it "promises" the New (see Rom 1:2: προεπηγ-γείλατο . . . ἐν γραφαῖς ἁγίαις) and "announces the good news in advance" (see Gal 3:8: ἡ γραφή . . . προευηγγελίσατο). In this sense there is continuity between the old and the new; and in this sense Paul sets the Scriptures free from their exclusive connection with Judaism, rises above the idea of the private property of the Jews, and makes them an ecumenical heritage for circumcised and uncircumcised alike (see Rom 3:20-30; 10:12), raising them to the level of universal significance, in which even those who at first were not beloved as God's people (see Rom 9:25, citing Hos 2:25) can now recognize themselves: even gentiles, then, can say that herein *Sua res agitur*, it addressed their affairs. Even today the Scriptures speak to us, for us, "whom God called not only from the Jews but from the gentiles" (Rom 9:24). Paul repeats it more than once: "These things were written *(ἐγράφη)* as a warning to us" (1 Cor 10:11); "It was written *(ἐγράφη)* not only for him [Abraham] that 'it was imputed to him,' but for us as well" (Rom 4:23-24); "Indeed, all that was written beforehand *(προεγράφη)* was written for our instruction, that we might have hope through perseverance and *through the encouragement of the Scriptures*, διὰ τῆς παρακλήσεως τῶν γραφῶν" (Rom 15:4).

The Old Testament remains a primary source of light and power on the Christian's path, an indispensable point of reference. And even though it is inappropriate to derive a hermeneutical rule for faith and Christian life from the problematic formula of 1 Cor 4:6 (μὴ ὑπὲρ ἃ γέγραπται, "nothing beyond what is written"),[71] still, it is clear that Paul does not consider the Old Testament to be superseded as "Scripture." Nor does he even deny the glory of Moses, as we have seen. The Old Testament as Scripture is not in opposition to the gospel; its function is, rather, supportive of the gospel.[72] Of course, this places it in a position subordinate to the

71. See the commentaries, and especially M. D. Hooker, "Beyond the Things That Are Written," NTS 10 (1963) 127–132 (maintains that Paul refers to the Old Testament citations in 3:19-20 = Job 5:12-13 and Ps 93:11, but C. K. Barrett, ad loc., rightly objects that it is not evident in what way one must not "go beyond" these two simple biblical references); A. Legault, " 'Beyond the Things Which Are Written' (1 Cor 4,6)," NTS 18 (1972) 227–231 (maintains that the phrase is the gloss of a corrector who wanted to re-insert in the text the μή omitted by the previous copyist); but J. Weiss, ad loc. (1910⁸), had already identified this solution as "almost a jest"); the clause is actually "unverständlich," unintelligible (H. Conzelmann, ad loc.), and so it would hardly be honest to build a theological or hermeneutical principle on it.

72. Paul uses various expressions: πρὸς νουθεσίαν ἡμῶν, "for our instruction" (1 Cor 10:11); δι' ἡμᾶς, "for us" (Rom 4:24); εἰς τὴν ἡμετέραν διδασκαλίαν, "for our instruction" (Rom 15:4). The three different prepositions indicate that there can be different ways to express the same basic truth about the relationship between the Old Testament and the new Christian situation.

gospel. As we have already said, the Christian faith of Paul and of the baptized flows not from the Old Testament Scriptures but from the Risen Lord and from his Spirit (see Gal 3:2-5), from whom it derives its nourishment and its support. But behind him are the Scriptures, which may not be the point of departure but are a fulcrum, as it were, certainly a point to take into account, the historical-theological reality that predates the Christ-event and in that sense is the most authoritative reality.

Not to credit such characteristics to the Old Testament would mean to open oneself to Marcionism. And A. von Harnack, whose huge monograph on Marcion was no accident, did try to dissociate Paul completely from the Old Testament, actually attributing to the Apostle too critical an attitude toward the old Scriptures and developing an antithesis between *Geistesreligion* and *Buchreligion*, "religion of the Spirit" and "religion of the Book."[73] This he does on the one hand by emphasizing to the utmost Paul's silence on the Old Testament in the "minor letters," and on the other hand by disqualifying the Old Testament where it *is* present in the four major letters, making the opposition between "Law" and "gospel" dominant, to the exclusive advantage of the latter. The partiality of this conception has from time to time been taken up again since him,[74] but in fact has been criticized by practically all. Still, we cannot help but commend him for having brought out the difference in Paul's use of the ancient Scriptures depending on the different audiences addressed in his letters and the different approaches to the issues.

But rather than a judgment of Paul's devaluation of the Old Testament, this ought to lead to a study of his evolution in this matter. For we can recognize that by having to deal with the conditions imposed on him in contending with Jewish Christian opponents and their arguments, Paul's attitude toward justification and law evolved. Then all the more so must some such maturation have developed not only in his use of the Old Testament but in his judgment of its value. Moreover, it is worth noting that it is precisely in the four major letters, where the polemic against the Old Testament as "Law" (νόμος) is enkindled, that Paul also develops his contrasting positive evaluation of it as ἐπαγγελία, "promise." This indicates

---

73. See A. von Harnack, *Das Alte Testament*, 140: it is only when addressing Jewish Christians that Paul appeals to the Old Testament. The immense interest in the Old, found already by the end of the first century in 1 Clement, along with the considerable space already found in Romans, would seem to indicate that the Christian community of Rome was at the time of Paul already tending toward a religion of the Book (139-140). See also Harnack, *Marcion: The Gospel of the Alien God* (Durham, N.C., 1990 [orig. Leipzig, 1921]) 123: the great error that Marcion is fighting in the *pseudoapostoli et Judaici evangelizatores* is that they have put the new wine in old skins, have transformed the gospel into the Old Testament, have united Law and gospel together.

74. See H. Ulonska (note 2 above), who puts even greater emphasis on the opposition between gospel and Scripture.

that right in the heat of theological conflict Paul was able to maintain—or even to develop—a judicious distinction that preserves the Old Testament even in its role as "Scripture" and thus passes it on to the later Church.[75]

4) The Old Testament as language, or better, a linguistic medium. In addition to any direct disquisition on the theoretical value Paul attributes to the Old Testament, it is useful to determine how much he depends on it on the practical, concrete level, for his vocabulary and phraseology, and hence much of his conceptualization—even when he does not acknowledge the dependence. It is true that a considerable part of his language finds contact with Old Testament vocabulary or conceptions only with difficulty or partially (we need only think of expressions like "body of Christ," "in Christ," "adoption as children" in a personal sense, "parousia," "freedom," etc.). But another part that is at least as considerable coincides with and certainly derives from the Old Testament heritage.[76]

Naturally, here we will only consider the terms and phrases that are not introduced and so identified by a citation formula, but are simply part of normal Pauline speech, with nothing to separate them from their context. It is here that we can actually touch with our hands the extent to which the Old Testament language (of the Septuagint!) nourishes Paul's mind and his expression. Such a study must be done in both groups of Pauline letters. In the major ones, where the use of the Old Testament is abundant, we can verify the presence of the Old Testament even outside and independent of the quotations; but in the other three letters, where there are no quotations at all, the evidence may be even more instructive.

a) From the major letters we will present only a few cases purely by way of example: θύειν τὸ πάσχα, "kill the passover [lamb]" in 1 Cor 5:7 (= Exod 12:21); τοῦ κυρίου ἡ γῆ καὶ τὸ πλήρωμα αὐτῆς, "The earth is the Lord's, and its fullness" in 1 Cor 10:26 (= Ps 24:1); φάγωμεν καὶ πίωμεν, αὔριον γὰρ ἀποθνῄσκομεν, "Let us eat and drink, for tomorrow we die" in 1 Cor 15:32 (= Isa 22:13); ἐκ σκότους φῶς λάμψει, "Light shall shine forth from darkness" in 2 Cor 4:6 (cf. Gen 1:3); ἐκ κοιλίας μητρός μου, "from my mother's

75. Still, Paul is far from the apologetic use of the Old Testament that is to be displayed from the second century on, already in 2 Pet 1:19-21; Barn. 1:7; Justin, 1 Apol. 381. "Here polemic and apologetic preoccupations progressively lead the biblical argumentation toward a function of proof" (S. Amsler, *L'Ancien Testament,* 76). On the other hand, it is worth noting the almost total absence of the Old Testament in writings like the *Didache* (only one citation in 14:3 = Mal 1:11), the seven letters of Ignatius of Antioch (which have only two γέγραπται ["it is written"] of no great significance, Ad Eph. 5:3 = Prov 3:4 = 1 Pet 5:5; and Ad Magn. 12 = Prov 8:17), and the Past Herm (nothing from Old Testament!).

76. A certain amount of research on this issue was already attempted by H. Vollmer, *Die Alttestamentlichen Zitate,* 12-13, to prove Paul's dependence on the Septuagint.

womb," in Gal 1:15 (= Isa 49:1); τοῖς φύσει μὴ οὖσιν θεοῖς, "who are not gods by nature," in Gal 4:8 (cf. 2 Chron 13:9; Jer 2:11); περιτομὴ καρδίας, "circumcision of the heart," in Rom 2:29 (= Deut 30:6); τοῦ ἰδίου υἱοῦ οὐκ ἐφείσατο, "spared not his only Son," in Rom 8:32 (see Gen 22:16). The same thing is true of "Spirit of God," "first fruits," "God's wrath," "good will/favor," etc.[77]

Specifically, we can demonstrate that the familiar and frequently used lexical family "δικ-" ("just," "justify," "righteousness," etc.) is only very rarely found in explicit Old Testament quotations, and so its use in Pauline texts may actually begin before and independently of any citation. Thus, the verb δικαιοῦν/δικαιοῦσθαι, "justify," only after repeated use in 1 Corinthians (4:4; 6:11), Galatians (2:16 [twice], 17; 3:8, 11, 24; 5:4), and Romans (2:13), is first found in a biblical citation in Rom 3:4 (ὅπως ἂν δικαιωθῇς ἐν τοῖς λόγοις σου, "that you may be justified in your words" = Ps 51:6 [4]), and then in a resonance of Ps 143:2 in Rom 3:20. The adjective δίκαιος, "righteous," first appears in Paul with the citation of Hab 2:4b in Gal 3:11, repeated in Rom 1:17 (the adjective is used again in Rom 2:13; 5:7, 19, while in 3:10 it recalls Qoh 7:20 and in 3:26 describes God). Finally the noun δικαιοσύνη first appears in a biblical citation in 2 Cor 9:9 (= Ps 111:9) after having already been used in 1 Cor 1:30; 2 Cor 3:9; 5:21; 6:7, 14; but it then becomes a major theme in Galatians and Romans with the decisive citation of Gen 15:6 (in Gal 3:6 and Rom 4:3, 9; but in Galatians the term is used four times, and in Romans alone thirty-three times). I should think one would be justified in concluding that Paul's use of this specific word depends not on the few Old Testament passages he cites, but on a much broader lexical background that fits general Old Testament usages better than it does the extrabiblical Jewish milieu.[78] The Apostle's theology, then, is based not just on explicit citations but on a much broader biblical language, even if this may be mediated and conditioned by intertestamental Judaism.

b) Now in the other authentic letters (in practice 1 Thessalonians and Philippians, since Philemon contains no Old Testament allusions) it is important to note how Paul, despite all, makes indirect use of the Old Testament, though without ever citing it. We restrict ourselves here to 1 Thessalonians. A recent German study of the question of the presence

77. Note also the case of Prov 3:4 in 2 Cor 8:21; Rom 12:17 (note 9 above).
78. On the use of ṣᵉdaqâ-δικαιοσύνη, "righteousness," in the Old Testament see, for instance, K. Kertelge, *"Rechtfertigung" bei Paulus*, NA NF 3 (Münster, 1967) 15–24 (on Judaism: 24–25); E. P. Sanders, *Paul and Palestinian Judaism*, 305–310, 407–408, 494; J. Vella, *La giustificazione forense di Dio* (Brescia, 1964); J. Reumann, *"Righteousness" in the New Testament* (Philadelphia, 1982) 12–22.

of tradition in this letter dedicates a page[79] to the words and concepts derived from the Judaic Greek of the Septuagint, citing only expressions present in the first chapter of the letter: χάρις ὑμῖν καὶ εἰρήνη, "peace to you and love" (1:1); ἀγάπη, "love" (1:3); εὐαγγέλιον, "good news" (1:5), πίστις-πιστεύειν, "faith, believe" (1:3, 7, 8); ἡ ὀργὴ ἡ ἐρχομένη, "the wrath to come" (1:10). In addition, we list here eleven more expressions scattered throughout 1 Thessalonians that can only be traced to the Old Testament.

1:9: θεῷ ζῶντι καὶ ἀληθινῷ, "living and true God" (the two adjectives are found separately but both modifying "God": "living" in Ps 41:3; 2 Kgs 19:4, 16; Est 6:13; Tob 13:1; "true" in 2 Chron 15:3; Ps 85:15; Isa 65:15).

3:13: μετὰ πάντων τῶν ἁγίων αὐτοῦ, "with all his holy ones" (see Zech 14:5: καὶ πάντες οἱ ἅγιοι μετ' αὐτοῦ, "and all his holy ones with him").

4:5: τὰ ἔθνη τὰ μὴ εἰδότα τὸν θεόν, "the nations that know not God" (see Jer 10:25: ἔθνη τὰ μὴ εἰδότα σε, "the nations that know you not"; Ps 78:6 has the synonym γινώσκοντα).

4:6: ἔκδικος κύριος, "the Lord is an avenger" (see Ps 93:1 LXX: ὁ θεὸς ἐκδικήσεων κύριος, "God is Lord of vengeance"; similar formulas in Num 33:4 and passim; Sir 5:3).

4:8: τὸν θεὸν τὸν καὶ διδόντα τὸ πνεῦμα αὐτοῦ τὸ ἅγιον εἰς ὑμᾶς, "God, who gave you his holy Spirit" (see Ezek 37:14: δώσω τὸ πνεῦμά μου εἰς ὑμᾶς, "I will give you my spirit"; Ezek 36:27: ἐν ὑμῖν, "in you").

5:3: ὅταν λέγωσιν, Εἰρήνη καὶ ἀσφάλεια, "when they say 'peace and security' " (see Jer 6:14: καὶ λέγοντες Εἰρήνη, εἰρήνη, "and saying, 'Peace, peace' " = Ezek 13:10).

5:3: αἰφνίδιος αὐτοῖς . . . ὄλεθρος, "sudden destruction on them" (see Wis 17:14: αἰφνίδιος αὐτοῖς . . . φόβος, "sudden fear on them").

5:3: ὥσπερ ἡ ὠδὶν τῇ ἐν γαστρὶ ἐχούσῃ, "like labor pain on one with child" (see Isa 13:8: καὶ ὠδῖνες αὐτοὺς ἕξουσιν ὡς γυναικὸς τικτούσης, "And labor pains will take hold of them like a woman giving birth").

5:8: ἐνδυσάμενοι θώρακα πίστεως καὶ ἀγάπης καὶ περικεφαλαίαν ἐλπίδα σωτηρίας, "putting on the breastplate of faith and love, and the hope of salvation as helmet" (probably conflating two sayings: Isa 59:17: καὶ ἐνδύσατο δικαιοσύνην ὡς θώρακα καὶ περιέθετο περικεφαλαίαν σωτηρίου, "and he will be clothed with justice like a breastplate and covered himself with the helmet of salvation," and Job 2:9a LXX: προσδεχόμενος τὴν ἐλπίδα τῆς σωτηρίας μου, "donning the hope of my salvation").

---

79. T. Holtz, "Traditionen im 1 Thessalonicherbrief," in U. Luz and H. Weder, eds., *Die Mitte des Neuen Testaments. Festschrift E. Schweizer* (Göttingen, 1983) 55–78, 96.

5:14: παραμυθεῖσθε τοὺς ὀλιγοψύχους . . ., μακροθυμεῖτε πρὸς πάντας, "Encourage the fainthearted, be forbearing toward all" (see Isa 57:15: καὶ ὀλιγοψύχοις διδοὺς μακροθυμίαν [said of God] "and grant forbearance to the fainthearted"; see also Prov 14:29).

5:22: ἀπὸ παντὸς εἴδους πονηροῦ ἀπέχεσθε, "abstain from every sort of evil" (see Job 1:1, 8: ἀπεχόμενος ἀπὸ παντὸς πονηροῦ πράγματος, "abstaining from every evil deed").

Two more possible Old Testament derivations could be added, for conceptual rather than lexical analogies: θεοδίδακτοί ἐστε, "You are taught by God," in 4:9 (see Jer 38:34 LXX = 31:34 MT) and τὸ πνεῦμα μὴ σβέννυτε, "Quench not the Spirit," in 5:19 (cf. Num 11:26-29).

It is evident that in this letter (and in Philippians as well), Paul had no need to take proof texts from the Old Testament to demonstrate specific theses. The letter is quite familiar in tone. Even the more doctrinal section on the relationship between the living and the dead at the time of the parousia (4:13-18) had no matter that required reference to the Old Testament; rather, he here speaks of "the Lord's word" (4:15: ἐν λόγῳ κυρίου), which in any case refers to the Christian (if not the Jesus) tradition. Still, as we have shown, Paul cannot help frequently expressing himself with Old Testament language, which shows how much he depended on it and esteemed it. Whether the recipients were capable of perceiving this or whether this use should be relativized as being historically conditioned by Paul's pre-Christian formation are quite different questions.

Chapter 22

Justification by Faith in Paul and James

The contrast between Paul and James on justification has become a classical theme in exegetical and theological discussion since Martin Luther. While his judgment of James may be dramatic and oversimplified, at least it is unambiguous, and even amusing, as when he describes the work as a "letter of straw" because lacking in any evangelical content, or when he declares that one or the other time he would have used it to light the stove![1] The same is true when he considers the mutual relationship between the two writers: "Many folks sweat a lot to reconcile James with Paul. . . . It's a matter of rival claims *(pugnantia):* faith justifies, faith does not justify. Whoever can reconcile the two can have my academic hat and call me a lunatic."[2] And yet, in the commentary on Romans Luther had held a more harmonizing position: "When Saint James and the Apostle [Paul] maintain that one is justified by works, they are resisting the false understanding of those who claimed that faith sufficed without its own works, *fidem sine operibus suis sufficere putabant.*"[3] Calvin also argued in this line, actually the first opinion expressed by the Reformer, maintaining that James demanded "a justice that was shown through deeds," with no intention of directly treating the doctrine of gratuitous justification.[4]

Even today, in Protestant circles, where the problem seems to be more acutely felt than among Catholics and is treated with more precision, certain exegetes are more inclined to accept the corrective contribution of

1. See the preface to the *Septemberbibel* (21 September 1522) at the end, and *Tischreden,* 5:382.
2. *Tischreden,* 3:253 (spring, 1533).
3. Luther continues: "Now, the Apostle does not say that faith justifies without its own works . . ., but that faith justifies without the works of the Law. So justification requires not the works of the Law but living faith, which accomplishes its own works *(viva fides, quae sua opera operatur)"*—(*Lectures on Romans,* on 3:19-20 [Philadelphia, 1961]) 101–102.
4. See *Institution de la religion chrétienne,* III:17:11-12, and the preface to the commentary on James's epistle (C.R. LV 381).

James to a somewhat deviant Paulinism,[5] while others resolutely insist on an irreconcilable opposition between James and Paul himself.[6]

Here we want to reexamine the question as a whole, trying to shed more light at least on some aspects.

I. A subject that originates with Paul

In his polemic James has in mind a subject that began with Paul. I find it inadequate to explain the position of James by reference only to a supposed Jewish-Christian tradition.[7] Even less can we trace it back to Judaism. Abraham's faith (Gen 15:6) and his loyalty when tested (Gen 22), which are brought together in Jas 2:21-23 (but reversed in order to show that the justification of the Ancestor is a consequence of his obedience in the sacrifice of his son), are found used in the same way in 1 Macc 2:52 ("Was Abraham not found faithful in his temptation, and was it not credited to him for justice?") But the problem of a justification by faith alone never existed before Paul. Judaism distinguishes the two but never separates them, and especially never opposes the two elements; if anything, it emphasizes works. Let us look at some significant passages taken from authors of quite different theological perspectives.

In the apocalyptic 4 Esdras we read, for example: the wicked "did not have faith, nor did they accomplish works" (7:24); whoever will be saved can be so "by their works and by faith" *(per opera sua et fidem)*: 9:7; the just are those "who have works and faith *(opera et fidem)* in the Mighty One" (13:23); also 7:25; 8:33, 35. *Ap. Bar.* 14:12 speaks of a "reserve of works" with the Lord that reassures the just.

In Mishnaic rabbinism, *Pirqê Abôt* likewise witnesses to a distinct preference for works: "For those who have more works than wisdom, their wis-

5. Thus M. Lackmann, *Sola fide. Eine exegetische Studie über Jak. 2* (Gütersloh, 1949); G. Eichholz, *Jakobus und Paulus. Ein Beitrag zum Problem des Kanons* (Munich, 1953); J. Jeremias, "Paul and James," ExpT 66 (1954-55) 368-371; E. Lohse, "Glaube und Werke—zur Theologie des Jakobusbriefes," ZNW 48 (1957) 1-22; W. Schmithals, *Paul and James*, trans. D. M. Barton (Naperville, Ill., 1965); U. Luck, "Der Jakobusbrief und die Theologie des Paulus," ThGl 61 (1971) 161-179; W. Nicol, "Faith and Works in the Letter of James," *Neotestamentica* 9 (1975) 7-24.
6. Thus in particular E. Käsemann, "Begründet der ntl. Kanon die Einheit der Kirche?" in idem, (ed.), *Das Neue Testament als Kanon* (Göttingen, 1970) 124-135, 140; also R. Bultmann, *Theology of the New Testament*, trans. Kendrick Grobel, 2 vols. (New York, 1951-55) and H. Conzelmann, *An Outline of the Theology of the New Testament* (New York, 1969), completely ignore James (the former has only one citation in its index [referring to I, 131], and irrelevant at that; see Conzelmann, 295); also V. Subilia, *La giustificazione per fede* (Brescia, 1976), mostly emphasizes the opposition (45-47). Finally, see T. Lorenzen, "Faith without Works does not count before God! James 2:14-26," ExpT 89 (1978) 231-233.
7. See R. Fabris, *Lettera di Giacomo e Prima Lettera di Pietro* (Bologna, 1980) 85; G. Marconi, *La lettera di Giacomo* (Rome, 1990) 16-17. But see W. Pratscher, *Der Herrenbrüder Jakobus und die Jakobustradition*, FRLANT 139 (Göttingen, 1987).

dom will last; but those who have more wisdom than works, their wisdom does not last" (3:9: Rabbi Hanina ben Dossa); "Without doctrine there is no good behavior, and without good behavior there is no doctrine" (3:17: Rabbi Eleazar ben Azaria).

The apologetic writing of Flavius Josephus, *Contra Apionem*, gives us a Judaism that thoroughly reconciles the two: "Our lawgiver . . . requires works that correspond to the words" (2:169: τὰ ἔργα . . . σύμφωνα τοῖς λόγοις); "He correlated both these things . . . and did not allow the words of the Law to go undone" (2:173: λόγον ἄπρακτον); "To have on the one hand one and the same idea of God, and on the other not to separate it from life and behavior, produces a beautiful harmony in a person's character" (2:179: καλλίστην . . . συμφωνίαν ἀποτελεῖ).

Hellenistic Judaism in the wisdom tradition also combines the two aspects: Philo of Alexandria (*Praem. poen.* 79) and the apocryphal *Testament of Job* (4:2) both present the theme of the synthesis between "hearing" and "doing," with the same terminology (ἀκοή/πράξις) that recalls Deut 5:27 (cf. Exod 19:8; 24:3).

And on this basis we can better understand certain Synoptic passages and certain sayings of Jesus on the union of "hearing" and "doing" (see Matt 7:21, 24; Luke 8:21). The perspective, or better the heritage, of these passages has definitely got a Jewish sound. Even the saying, the logion of Matt 23:3 ("they say, but they do not do"), rather than alluding to a situation within the Christian community, has all the flavor of a Jewish polemic confrontation, as is actually attested in rabbinic tradition.[8]

James, then, fits perfectly into this theological background both because he is careful to keep faith and works together and because he is inclined to emphasize works more. This conceptual arrangement was brusquely disturbed by Paul (who must have seemed to be like the Luther of the time) and by the typical disjunction he introduced between faith and works. But Paul's thought, which was ultimately quite balanced, was distorted by undetached accusers, as Paul himself attests: "we are slandered, and some say that we urge doing evil that good may result" (Rom 3:8; see vol. 1, chap. 7, of this work).

Whether James is aware of these accusations (intentional or simply myopic) by outsiders of Paul's circle or refers to a false interpretation on the part of Paul's disciples, he is reacting to a precisely pseudo-Pauline position, explicable only by tracing it to Paul's own theology. And with this position he makes no attempt to reach a true accommodation, unless I perceive a slight loophole in the μόνον, "faith *alone*," in 2:24.

8. See Strack-Billerbeck, I 910–911: but actually the distinction between theory and practice is not developed as a theme; the texts dealing with the issue are few and are linked to specific circumstances.

II. The vocabulary

An examination of the vocabulary belonging to our theme is basic to an understanding of the semantic world of the two authors. But we must begin with an observation, obvious as it may be: In the brief Letter of James, we can hardly expect a frequency of vocabulary at all like that of the extensive Pauline correspondence. And even though in Paul the theme of justification really occurs only in Galatians, Romans, and Philippians 3, the length of James is in no way comparable to the sum of these works. Consequently, much more important than a simple statistical comparison will be the attempt to understand the context of the terms, their various associations, and especially their differing connotations in each author. We are about to consider four different groups of ideas from the point of view of James.

a) The vocabulary of "justification." In James there is simply no use of the two terms for "justification," δικαίωσις (twice in Romans) and δικαίωμα (five times in Romans); even the adjective δίκαιος, "just" (six times in Galatians and Romans) occurs only twice in James (5:6, 16) and has no particularly theological sense.

The noun δικαιοσύνη in James is found only three times (compared with four times in Galatians and thirty-two times in Romans): 1:20 ("Human anger does not produce God's justice": given the contrast with "anger," the term could seem to be limited to a moral concept, but some sort of theological element is involved, as indicated by a kind of synonymous parallelism with the "word implanted" in the following v. 21; even so, the context is paraenetic); 2:23 ("was accredited to him as justice": is a citation of Gen 15:6; more literal than that of Rom 4:9, which adds the subject "faith," πίστις, to the Septuagint text, but even so, our text follows the reference to Gen 22:2, 9, in light of which it gets a distinctively different sense from its Pauline meaning); 3:18 ("A fruit of justice is being sown in peace": the genitive can be understood as subjective, and then the phrase means that "justice makes peace fruitful"; but the idea is not defined any more closely, while the immediate sapiential-paraenetic context dominates everything).

We see, then, that not only does James not make a thematic point of the subject, but he retains the concrete Jewish meaning for the term "justice," as found, for instance, in Prov 10:2; Sir 3:30; *Abôt* 2:7; Matt 5:20; 6:1. As for the verb δικαιοῦν, "justify," it does recur three times in James (twenty-four times in Paul), and always in the form of a set phrase, preceded by ἐξ ἔργων, "by works" (said of Abraham: 2:21; Rahab: 2:25; of human beings in general: 2:24). This positive combination with "works" is altogether un-Pauline (see below).

b) The vocabulary of "works" is quite varied in James. Besides the verb ἐργάζεσθαι, "to work" (1:20: "work justice"; 2:9: "work sin") and the noun ἐργάτης (5:4 = "laborers"), the main emphasis is on the noun ἔργον, "work" (recurring fifteen times, actually more than in Galatians and Romans together, where it is found only thirteen times!). Almost all its use is within the pericope 2:14-26 (twelve times), which is thus confirmed as the passage most concerned with our subject. Moreover, the derived verb συνεργεῖν appears in 2:22, with "faith" as its subject!

There are also the nouns ποιητής, "doer," present four times in James (1:22, 23, 25; 4:11), while found only once in Paul (Rom 2:13, but as an almost perfect parallel to Jas 1:22; see below: 4a), and ποίησις, "doing," in Jas 1:25 ("not the hearer . . . but the doer will be blessed in the doing"), the only instance of the expression, a *hapax legomenon* in the whole New Testament.

Finally we mention the "law," νόμος, which occurs ten times in James (thirty-two times in Galatians and seventy-four times in Romans), the first three of which are modified by an expression of nobility (1:25; 2:8, 12). It is important to note that James never connects the "law" with the problematic of justification or even with "works." This is quite different from Paul's practice (see Gal 2:16; 3:2, 5, 10; Rom 3:20, 28), for whom works are precisely called for or inspired by the Law. We get the impression that James does not attach a technical meaning to it, at least not in reference to the Torah; rather, he means either the simple Old Testament commandment of love (thus F. Mussner)[9] or else the Christian gospel in its ethical implications (thus R. Fabris).[10] It is significant that while Paul uses the term "law" much more than James does, the latter prefers the expression "works," which in consequence he uses much more often than Paul. The most immediate conclusion from this is that the concern of James is not speculative but pastoral and practical.

c) The vocabulary of "faith." The term πίστις, "faith," in James (sixteen times; Paul: seventeen times in Galatians, thirty-seven in Romans) occurs almost only in the pericope 2:14-26 (twelve times), exactly like the "works," a strict correlation with which is therefore evident. The relationship between the two terms is, if not antithetical, at least strongly dialectical; the other occurrences are in 1:3, 6; 2:1, 5. What is important to note here is that the object is never specified. The only exception is the genitive construction of 2:1: "the faith of our Lord Jesus Christ of glory," an expression that might be described as more heavy than solemn, but

---

9. = Lev 19:18: F. Mussner, *Der Jakobusbrief*, HThKNT (Freiburg–Basel–Vienna, 1981⁴) 124.
10. R. Fabris, *Legge della libertà in Giacomo* (Brescia, 1977).

in any case in a paraenetic context (in opposition to ''acceptance of persons'' [partiality]). Otherwise the term is never modified, as if to express an abstract conception. This is confirmed by the only occurrence of the verb πιστεύω, ''believe'' (2:19), the object of which is the existence of only one God, and which describes an action attributed to the ''demons''!

d) The vocabulary of ''sin.'' Besides the frequency of the word ἁμαρτία, ''sin'' (seven times in James, three in Galatians, fifty-one in Romans),[11] it is very helpful to compare and contrast the way this vocabulary is employed in two texts of Paul and James that have a considerable parallel character. We here present them synoptically structured according to their logical order:

Romans 7:7-11	James 1:15
ὁ νόμος, ''the Law'' (vv. 7, 9);	
ἡ ἐντολή, ''the commandment'' (8, 9, 10, 11)	
ἡ ἁμαρτία, ''sin'' (7, 8, 9, 11)	ἡ ἐπιθυμία συλλαβοῦσα τίκτει, ''Desire, having conceived bears
ἡ ἐπιθυμία, ''desire'' (7, 8)	ἁμαρτίαν, ἡ δὲ ἁμαρτία . . ., ἀποκύει ''sin, and sin brings forth
ὁ θάνατος, ''death'' (10; cf. 11)	θάνατον, ''death.''

The succession of these concepts in Paul and in James alike is meant causally, like a chain reaction: each is the effect of what precedes and the cause of what follows. But in this regard we must be clear about two things. First, while in Paul the first link of the chain is the ''Law''/''commandment,'' and to this is linked the whole series of negative effects in order (''sin,'' ''desire,'' ''death''; see 1 Cor 15:56), in James, on the other hand, we hear nothing of this component: there the first element in the series is ''desire,'' that is, an anthropological factor. Second, we must particularly note the inversion of the roles of ''sin'' and ''desire.'' In Paul sin is personified, and precedes the movement of human desire, but rather brings it about, as a kind of power exerting its evil influence; but for James it is human desire that ''conceives and bears'' sin, which here seems to be a single act that can be traced back precisely to desire or creaturely inclination (see v. 14: ''Each person is tempted by their own desire''), a conception that is easily explicable on the basis of rabbinism, with its speculation on the *yêṣer* [inclination] in the human heart.[12] All this will be of

---

11. See also ἁμαρτωλός, ''sinner,'' in Jas 4:8; 5:20; and παραβάτης, ''transgressor,'' in Jas 2:9.

12. See Strack-Billerbeck, IV:466-483 (Excursus 19: ''Der gute und der böse Trieb''); the theory is that in the human person the *yêṣer hārāʿ* is older than the *yêṣer ṭôb*: ''The evil inclina-

great utility in recognizing the differing origins of the thought of Paul and of James (see below 3c).

III. Divergences Between James and Paul

a) A simple lexical study already gives rise to some important observations.

First. In James the primary role attributed to "works" leaps out at us (thirteen out of fifteen times we read the plural ἔργα); this is where the whole accent falls. We conclude, however, that the reference is not to works of the Mosaic Law, not only from the fact that "works" are never associated with νόμος, "Law," but also from the definition of θρησκεῖα ("cult, religious practice") in 1:27, where not a single allusion is made to the Temple or the Law, but only an appeal for social love and avoiding conformity to the world, both exteriorly and interiorly. Paul, on the other hand, brings up the question of νόμος as principle of salvation, and works as fundamentally those commanded by the Law.[13]

Second. As for "faith," though it is true that James takes it for granted, it is also true that he never makes it specific, never attributes a specific content to it, much less a specifically Christian content. For it is quite possible that the possessive of 2:1 ("the faith *of* our Lord Jesus Christ") should be understood not as an objective genitive (faith *in* the Lord), but rather with at least a suggestion of a possessive genitive (the faith *that belongs to* our Lord, i.e., faith in the "God [who] has chosen those who are poor": 2:5). And it does remain true of James that "not even once, in such a long sermon, does he recall the passion, the resurrection, and the Spirit of Christ."[14] Whereas in Paul one simply cannot miss the Christological and paschal content of faith (see Gal 2:20; Rom 4:24-25; 10:9; etc.), repeatedly identified as a personal relationship through the prepositions (indifferently translated "in" in English) ἐπί, εἰς, ἐν, (in particular the expression in Rom 4:5, πιστεύειν ἐπὶ τὸν δικαιοῦντα, is unimaginable coming from the pen of James).

---

tion is thirteen years older than the good inclination; the former grows little by little with a person from the mother's womb. . . . After thirteen years the good impulse is born" (*Abot di Rabbi Natan* 16; see J. Goldin, *The Fathers According to Rabbi Nathan*, Yale Judaica Series X [New Haven, 1955] 38 = Version A; see also A. J. Saldarini, S.J., *The Fathers According to Rabbi Nathan. Version B*, Stud. in Jud. in Late Ant. [Leiden, 1975] esp. p. 115, n. 16).

13. On the concept of "Law," see chapter 23 below.

14. As already noted by Luther, who continues: "But the office of a true apostle is to preach the passion, the resurrection, and the mission of Christ, and to lay the foundation of faith in him" (preface to the *Septemberbibel*, in which we also find the declaration of the criterion or "touchstone" for what is or is not "apostolic," i.e., to speak of Christ and announce the forgiveness of sins; on the whole text, see F. Mussner, *Jakobusbrief*, 42-44).

Third. With regard to the real idea of "justification" itself, we cannot miss the absolute novelty of James's language, ἐξ ἔργων δικαιοῦσθαι, "to be justified by works," associating two concepts considered irreconcilable in a Pauline perspective. It is, of course, important to note that James never says ἐξ ἔργων νόμου, "by works of the Law," and thus by working a different semantic region from Paul's seems to be avoiding direct confrontation. And yet we find two opposing beatitudes: while James "beatifies" the one who actively performs works (1:25: "will be blessed in one's works"), Paul in contrast cites Ps 32:1-2 to proclaim "blessed the one to whom the Lord imputes no sin" (Rom 4:8), i.e., in context, "the one who does not work" (note 4:5: τῷ δὲ μὴ ἐργαζομένῳ, πιστεύοντι δέ . . ., "the one who does not work, but believes," a contrasting of working and believing).

Now with regard to James, we must note the final limiting, concessive, and tentative phrase of 2:24: "One is justified by works, *and not by faith alone*" *(καὶ οὐκ ἐκ πίστεως μόνον).* This "not . . . alone" seems to—and actually does—leave room for Paul and Paulinism; works are not an absolute, there is not an either-or between faith and works. Still, we must note that this recognition of the role of faith occurs unexpectedly and remains isolated, and is, moreover, expressed negatively. It is as if this is the least James can get by with, as if he is forced to admit the part due to "faith."

This seems also to be the sense of the preceding v. 22 (βλέπεις ὅτι ἡ πίστις συνήργει τοῖς ἔργοις αὐτοῦ καὶ ἐκ τῶν ἔργων ἡ πίστις ἐτελειώθη, "you see that faith works together with his works, and that by the works faith is perfected"), where the contextual reference is to Abraham, but to his works rather than his faith (v. 21; in contrast to Paul in Rom 4:3, 9, 22; Gal 3:6). Thus James says not "*his* faith" but just "faith" (thus retaining an impersonal broadness, a principle that has no substance unless incarnated in works), whereas he specifies "works," τοῖς ἔργοις, with the pronoun "his," αὐτοῦ. The grammatical subject of the phrase is faith, but the logical subject is "works," repeated in the center of a lovely chiasmus (as if to say, "It is with works that faith cooperates"). And even the two verbs, συνήργει and ἐτελειώθη emphasize the inseparability of the two components: of course, no works without faith, but especially no faith without works. F. Mussner and R. Fabris[15] note that it is a question of "living" faith. But we can hardly claim that W. Schrage is wrong in saying that James "attacks Paul himself by including works in justification, thus corrupting it in a nomistic direction";[16] perhaps this should be said with more nuance,

---

15. *Jakobusbrief,* 146, *Lettera di Giacomo e,* 81–82.
16. In H. Balz and W. Schrage, *Die "Katholischen" Briefe,* NTD (Göttingen and Zurich, 1973 [Italian: 1978]) 36.

but it is true that James never directly connects the verb δικαιοῦσθαι, "justify," with πίστις, "faith," as Paul does in the famous axiom of Rom 3:28. For James the vocabulary of justification refers not to the first event of salvation (faith/baptism) but to the second (that of lived witness). Thus the two authors intend quite different things by the same word.

b) The personal experience of the two authors, and its implications. Here we distinguish three levels.

First: conversion. In Paul the fact of conversion had quite astonishing resonances (whether this depends on the objective character of the Damascus event or on the personal sensitivity of the subjective recipient, or both). On the theological level these effects are translated into very dialectical terms of opposition, either/or alternatives (see Phil 3:7: "gain"/"loss"; 3:8: "knowledge of Christ Jesus"/"rubbish"; Gal 2:21: "Law"/"Christ" = Rom 10:4). The pattern, then, fits in with the typical phenomenon of Pauline antitheses. And to the shock of conversion (see Gal 2:20: "I live, but now no longer I") is now added the unprecedented missionary responsibility among the gentiles (see Gal 1:16; 2:7), which, perhaps because of roots in his youthful encounter with Stephen and his group, led him to attitudes that are at least partly anti-Mosaic, and to a transcendence of the Law-centered order of Judaism (see Gal 5:11: "If I still preach circumcision . . . the scandal of the cross is rendered harmless").

On the other hand, for the author of James (whether or not the work is written by James himself),[17] the passage to Christianity must have taken place smoothly and painlessly, with the simple transfer of a great heritage of ideas from one vessel to another—indeed more as if the two vessels already communicated. For his perspective is clearly Jewish-Christian (note 1:1: "To the twelve tribes of the diaspora")[18] and in all probability the recipients of the letter were also Jewish Christians.

Second: Christology. It was actually with regard to the Letter of James that Luther enunciated the principle of "apostolicity" (canonicity) of the New Testament writings, namely, "whether they promote Christ or not" (*Ob sie Christum treyben odder nit).*[19] Now, it is well known that James's Christology is fuzzy, almost within the danger zone. Except for the epistle's

17. An early date (= James, brother of the Lord, died at Jerusalem in A.D. 62: see Fl. Josephus, *Ant.* XX:200; Eusebius, *Hist. Eccl.* II:23:4-18) might be suggested by the existence of a false interpretation of Paulinism during the life of the Apostle, as Paul himself attests in Rom 3:8.

18. Already Luther, in the preface to the *Septemberbibel,* actually advanced the hypothesis that the author was simply Jewish. Today the Christian character of the letter is generally recognized, even though it must still be justified (see the introductions and commentaries).

19. See note 14 above. In the same preface Luther explains himself: "What does not teach Christ is not apostolic, even if it were taught by Peter or Paul; but whatever preaches Christ is apostolic, even if it were Judas, Annas, or Herod that taught it."

introductory formula (1:1: "James, servant of God and of the Lord Jesus Christ"), we glimpse it only in a text already cited, 2:1: "My brothers, do not mix the faith of our Lord Jesus Christ of glory with favoritism." Even so, there is a distinction we must not ignore. For Paul, we know, is completely overwhelmed by the figure of the risen Christ, the glorious Lord, whom he has "seen" (1 Cor 9:1; 15:8; cf. 2 Cor 4:6), and so barely touches on the phase of the earthly, pre-Easter Christ, in whom he is not really interested, since he has, in a sense, something more (see 1 Cor 5:16-17). It is precisely the Risen One in the role of his personal mystery, so that Christ in person becomes the epicenter of the whole system of his thought (see Phil 3:7-12).[20]

With James it is much different. There is, of course, practically no paschal Christology in him—not in the form of attribution (the twofold κύριος of 1:1; 2:1 is only formulaic), much less in any soteriological form. Even so, there is a different type of Christology, almost hidden, that consists in the reproduction of the ethical teaching of the historic Jesus, but without any direct citation. We have no intention of making an analysis of this matter, which has in any case already been done.[21] But the many links that can be found between James and the Sermon on the Mount (Matthew 5-7) argue for a Christological perspective that is certainly not Pauline, but is not for that reason nonexistent. James's Christology is at the service of ethic, something that might have irritated Paul. But even so, what we have is a case of two different ways of approaching Christ, something that illustrates the theme of "unity and diversity in the New Testament."

Third: the character of the treatment of justification. Only once does Paul deal with this matter in an autobiographical, and thus personalized, setting—in Phil 3, but this is scarcely more than a framework and is on the point of exploding simply from the force of the theological content that fills it. In Galatians and Romans a speculative-systematic interest comes to the fore (though in the autobiographical passage of Gal 1-2 the theme becomes explicit only with 2:16ff.) Paul is interested in a radical and theoretical contrast between the way of salvation presented by the gospel message and that which belongs to a certain Jewish understanding centered on the Law.[22]

---

20. For a reduction of all the Pauline thought to the Damascus event (but in somewhat forced terms), see S. Kim, *The Origin of Paul's Gospel*, WUNT II 4 (Tübingen, 1981); better, C. Dietzfelbinger, *Die Berufung des Paulus als Ursprung seiner Theologie*, WMANT 58 (Neukirchen-Vluyn, 1985).

21. See F. Mussner, *Jakobusbrief*, 74-79.

22. E. P. Sanders, *Paul and Palestinian Judaism: A Comparison of Patterns of Religion* (London, 1977), has correctly called attention to the fact that first-century Judaism was much less legalistic than what Paul seems to suppose and actually combats. Still, he has not completely avoided

But James, on the other hand, is speaking on another level: he writes as a pastor, a preacher, who is more interested in a certain concrete situation of the community he is addressing in his letter. They are in danger of a cooling down in their way of life, and of flight—a kind of refuge in a purely verbal, sterile ideology. This demanded a decisive intervention in order to stimulate "good conduct" (καλῆς ἀναστοφῆς: 3:13) that recalls the exhortation of Matt 5:16: "that they may see *your good works (ὑμῶν τὰ καλὰ ἔργα)* and give glory to your Father in heaven."[23]

c) The theological and cultural matrix of each. We shall compare the two New Testament writers, tracing the thought of each back to its source. By doing so, we will see that in Christian circles they are the heirs and representatives of two cultural streams that were already different in Jewish tradition. We will begin with James.

James, according to all evidence, follows the path of the wisdom tradition. This is true in two different ways. First, he shares the doctrine that one becomes wise through the experience of suffering and through perseverance in trials (Jas 1:2-6; cf. Prov 3:11-12; Jdt 8:25-27; Philo Alex., *De Abr.* 52-59; Heb 12:2). In the second place, and above all, he teaches that one becomes wise through the keeping of the Law. James actually makes use of certain wisdom expressions (σοφία, "wisdom": 1:5; 3:13, 15, 17; σοφὸς καὶ ἐπιστήμων, "wise and understanding"; 3:13: τέλειος, "perfect," five times). What is characteristic of these is their occurrence in contexts that are not speculative but are concerned with the duties of daily life (note 3:13: τὰ ἔργα αὐτοῦ, "his works"). Specifically, James follows the tradition of Jesus ben Sirach, the author most often cited in his text.[24]

Jesus ben Sirach taught precisely the achievement of wisdom through the practice of the Law, not to speak of the identification of wisdom with

---

the risk of slighting aspects of Judaism and of Paulinism alike; see the reviews of N. A. Dahl and S. Sandmel in RSR 4 (1978) 153–160; J. Neusner in HistRel 18 (1978) 177–191; W. Horbury in ExpT 90 (1979) 116–118; J. Murphy-O'Connor in RB 85 (1978) 122–126. Also by E. P. Sanders see "Paul's Attitude Toward the Jewish People," USQR 33 (1978) 175–187. Also: M. Barth, "St. Paul—A Good Jew," Horizons in Biblical Theology 1 (1979) 7–45.

23. From a literary point of view and considering expository technique, we could illustrate the relationship between Paul and James with the example of the Alexandrian Jewish writers Philo and Pseudo-Phocylides. Contemporaries though they were, they reveal a considerable difference of style, literary range, and loftiness of thought. While the former is engaged in lofty philosophical and theological discourse, the latter is just as much concerned about concrete ethical behavior; and while the one proceeds with remarkably organic logic, the other has not the least systematic interest. See E. Fry, *The Testing of Faith: A Study of the Structure of the Book of James*, BibTrans 29 (1978) 427–435; J.-L. Blondel, "Le fondement théologique de la parénèse dans l'épître de Jacques," RTP 29 (1979) 141–152.

24. One can confirm this simply by noting the references in the margins of the critical editions of Merk or Nestle-Aland. Along with Sirach, the author prefers Psalms, followed by Proverbs.

Law. A few texts will document what I am saying: "If you want wisdom, keep the commandments; then the Lord will give you it" (Sir 1:23-24); "One who is faithful to the Law will also gain wisdom" (15:1b); "All wisdom is fear of God, and in all wisdom there is the *doing of the Law, ποίησις νόμου*" (19:18); "Better one of limited intelligence with fear of God than one who is very intelligent but violates the Law" (19:21; see *Abôt* 3:9: see above, I); "If one observes the Law, one controls one's instincts; the result of fear of the Lord is wisdom" (Sir 21:11); "A wise person does not despise the Law, but the hypocrite is like a ship in a storm;[25] the prudent person trusts in the Law, finding the Law trustworthy as an oracle" (33:2-3).

This type of attitude affirms a typical form of anthropological and moral optimism that exalts the Law as the only means of achieving wisdom, and also exalts the human capacity to put it into practice: "If you want, you will keep the commandments, and faithfulness depends on your good will" (15:15). Regardless of the problematic translation of the last clause,[26] the fact remains that in the Greek text, the decision for obedience is termed πίστις, "faith,"[27] with a semantic use of the term such as suggests a polemic about the possibility of human freedom."[28]

James also displays this sapiential nomism, which presupposes and supports the human capacity to fulfill the Law, or at least does not question this capacity as Paul does. James simply takes it for granted. And it is in this perspective that faith is explained. "In James [faith] is subordinated to reason. And so the author cannot understand the 'sola fide.' If faith amounts to the perfection of wisdom, then it is obvious that faith can be brought to completion only through works (2:22). It is proper to wisdom to act, to be recognized by its actions and to be justified by its works; note Matt 11:19; *καὶ ἐδικαιώθη ἡ σοφία ἀπὸ τῶν ἔργων αὐτῆς*, 'and wisdom is justified by its deeds.' "[29]

And it is, then, in this context that we understand the apologetic preoccupation of Jas 1:13-15 ("Let no one who is tempted say, 'I am being tempted by God'; for God tempts no one to evil"; v. 14: "Each one is

---

25. Cf. the image of the controlling of the boat in Jas 3:4.

26. The translation above depends on that of the Italian Episcopal Conference; but M. Hengel translates: "and to act faithfully is to do God's will" (*Judaism and Hellenism*, trans. J. Bowden, I [Philadelphia, 1974] 140; meanwhile G. L. Prato, following the Hebrew, translates thus: "and it is wise to do its [the Commandment's] will" (*Il problema della teodicea in Ben Sira*, AB 65 [Rome, 1975] 214; 221-222).

27. See M. Hengel, *Judaism and Hellenism*, 140.

28. "One is given the impression that in the Jerusalem of Ben Sirach—whether as a continuation to the thought of Qoheleth . . . or under the influence of determinist astrology—the freedom of man, and thus the foundation of obedience to the Law was denied" (ibid.).

29. U. Luck, "Der Jakobusbrief und . . .," 175.

tempted by their own desire [ἐπιθυμία]"). Here James is only reproducing a theme of Sir 15:11-17 (v. 12: "Do not say, 'He has led me astray'; for he has no need of a sinner"; v. 14: "From the beginning he created human beings, and left them in the power of their own *will* = διαβούλιον = *yēṣer*"). This clear separation of responsibility is found frequently in Philo of Alexandria as well.[30] It tends to reinforce the full liberty of the human person in the choice between good and evil. In this view only one conclusion can be drawn: the human person is not only obliged to observe the Law given by God's good will, but is also capable of doing so in full autonomy, being created capable of choosing the good (see Sir 17:6-7: "[God] filled them with knowledge and understanding, and showed them the good and the evil; he put his eye in their hearts").

This particular wisdom tradition, in conclusion, does not perceive, or at least does not emphasize, an inward brokenness inherent to the human person. The only means of salvation is the Law, which manifests its own validity in the good works performed. It is orthopraxy that makes a person "God's friend" (Jas 2:23; *Abôt* 6:1). James would probably subscribe completely to the words of *Abôt* 6:1, that the study of the Law makes a person "capable of being just, pious, honest, faithful; it separates one from sin and associates one with good actions, and brings one from him [God] counsel, wisdom, prudence, and fortitude." The preoccupation with praxis, which is also somewhat externalistic, is actually confirmed in Jas 4:17: "One who knows how to do good [εἰδότι οὖν καλὸν ποιεῖν; not: 'knows *what is* good'] and does not do it, sins."

Paul, in the Christian sphere, is an exponent of a different tendency of Judaism in sharp contrast with the preceding. "Paul finally clearly formulated a drama of Jewish thought deriving from the contradictory co-existence of certain elements in its ideology that had become firmly embedded in the consciousness of the Jewish people: on the one hand, God's omnipotence, emphasized ever more through the centuries, which governs history as well as nature,[31] and on the other hand, absolute human liberty, which is a basic presupposition in order to have salvation through the Law."[32]

---

30. See *Conf. ling.* 180: "God is the author only of what is good, and absolutely no evil can be imputed to him" (in the context evil is attributed to "inferior beings": 179; to "angels": 182); see also *Opif.* 75; *Agr.* 129; *Det. pot.* 122; etc.

31. See Exod 7:3: "I shall harden Pharaoh's heart"; above all Isa 45:7: "I form light and darkness, *I make the good and I create the evil*" ('*ośeh šalôm ûbôrēh ra*ʿ = ὁ ποιῶν εἰρήνην καὶ κτίζων κακά).

32. P. Sacchi, "Appunti per una storia della crisi della Legge nel Giudaismo del tempo di Gesù," BibOr 12 (1970) 199–211, 199–200.

Actually, in the background of the Pauline theology concerning the relationship between faith and works is a broader problem that had been disturbing Judaism for centuries: the problem of the relationship between human liberty and God's liberty, or put in broader terms, the problem of the origin of evil, and thus of the origin of salvation.[33] It is no accident that when Flavius Josephus presents the three principal Jewish sects, it is on the basis of their solution of the relationship between human freedom and God's action that he describes them. The Sadducees make it impossible for God to do any kind of evil whatsoever, and locate good and evil only in the power and decision of human beings.[34] The Essenes attribute everything to God, since for them "nothing happens to human beings apart from what destiny has established."[35] The Pharisees seem to have an intermediate position ("They maintain that acting justly or otherwise depends mostly on the human person"),[36] but in the event resolve the question in favor of human moral freedom (note R. Akiba: "All is provided; free will is granted . . . all comes about according to the quantity of action," said of the relationship between good and evil deeds.)[37]

Turning to Paul, we do note clear wisdom elements in his understanding of the Law (it is "holy and just and good": Rom 7:12; "spiritual": 7:14; is summarized in the love of neighbor: 13:10; Gal 5:14; Paul recognizes its δικαίωμα: Rom 8:4; also compare the climax based on trials in Jas 1:2-4 with its parallel in Rom 5:3-5). But this is not really his favorite instrument. For him, the Law cannot save (Gal 2:16, 21); justification is a free gift of God (Rom 3:28); there is an opposition between Law and promise (Gal 3:18; Rom 4:14). God is all-powerful and chooses whom he wills (see Rom 9:11-12, 16, 18; 11:33-36). For Paul, it is absolutely impossible to think that God has made or makes his choices on the basis of works (see Rom 4:2-6). For the Apostle, there is "another law" that acts in the human being, and this is not the Law of God (Rom 7:23). For him, one

33. See M. Hengel, *Judaism and Hellenism*, 140ff.; G. Segalla, "Il problema della volontà libera nell'apocalittica ebraica e nei 'Testamenti dei Dodici Patriarchi,'" Divus Thomas 88 (1967) 108–116; B. J. Malina, "Some Observations on the Origin of Sin in Judaism and St. Paul," CBQ 31 (1969) 18–34; L. Wächter, "Die unterschiedliche Haltung der Pharisäer, Sadduzäer und Essener zur Heimarmene nach dem Bericht des Josephus," ZRG 21 (1969) 97–114; M. J. Fiedler, "Δικαιοσύνη in der Diaspora-jüdischen und intertestamentarischen Literatur," JSJ 1 (1970) 120–143; P. Sacchi, "Retribuzione e giudizio fra ebraismo e cristianesimo," RivStLettRel 9 (1973) 407–420; idem, "Introduzione generale," Apocrifi dell'Antico Testamento, I (Turin, 1981) 11–50.
34. *Bell.* II 164.
35. *Ant.* VIII 5; XIII 172.
36. *Bell.* II 162–163.
37. *Abôt* 3:15; see TB *Nid.* 16b: Rabbi Hanina ben Papa (ca. 300) tells that an angel stationed at each conception determines various qualities of the one to be born, but not the good or bad that this person will do.

is not fully free to do the good even if one wants to (Rom 7:13ff.). And thus salvation cannot come from the Law or from its observance, from works: since the origin of sin does not reside in the human will alone (since "sin" already "dwells in" the person, ἐνοικοῦσα ἐν ἐμοὶ ἁμαρτία: Rom 7:17), by way of parallel, and in consequence of this, salvation does not come from the practice of the Law, as if this were obvious, with no problems (of a moral and theological nature). Alone before God, the human person is "impious," ἀσεβής (Rom 4:5); a "sinner," ἁμαρτωλός (Rom 5:8); an "enemy," ἐχθρός (Rom 5:10); "unfortunate," ταλαίπωρος (Rom 7:24); and liberation from such a situation cannot come from the Law and its works because the Law is seen rather as that which identifies sin, if it does not actually instigate it (see Rom 3:20; 5:20; 7:7; Gal 3:19), and also because the works themselves, or better the failure regarding any one, is a source of malediction (see Gal 3:10 = Deut 27:26). And there is no doubt that such a position, with its markedly pessimistic coloring, diverges from, even contrasts with, that of James, who has much more confidence in human possibilities with regard to the Law.

At this point we may ask whether such a problematic arose in Paul only with his conversion, or do its roots reach into a previous tradition? Actually, we read in Qoh 7:20: "On earth there is no one so just as to do only good and not to sin"; and in Ps 143:2: "No one that lives is just before God" (cited in Rom 3:20). And here we must remember the description of the Essenes by Flavius Josephus that we have already cited. Actually, at Qumran, along with an exaltation of the Law as practical rule of life (see 1QS 5:2.21; 8:22; 1QSa 1:11, we find two other complementary statements. On the one hand, the people of Qumran maintain that human nature is impure. The idea is typically apocalyptic in origin: evil consists not just in transgression, since it already actually exists in the person.[38] According to the Teacher of Righteousness, the human person is a "construction (a structure) of sin" (1QH 1:22: *mbnh hht'h*; the whole text reads as follows: "a totality of ignorance and a fountain of impurity, a furnace of iniquity and a structure of sin, a perverse spirit; see 13:14-16a), "and in sin, since being in the womb" (4:29-30); and it goes on: "how can a creature of clay be righteous?" (12:32; cf. 4:30: "I know that righteousness does not belong to the human person"; 15:12-13: "one's own life

---

38. On the origin of evil according to apocalyptic, see D. S. Russell, *The Method and Message of Jewish Apocalyptic* (Philadelphia, 1964) 249–254. A fundamental role in the development of this theme is represented in the so-called "Book of the Vigilant" (= *Ethiopian Henoch* 6–36), the beginning of the composition of which P. Sacchi dates to the fifth century B.C. (see *Apocrifi dell'Antico Testamento*, I:438–442); on its conception of evil, see P. Sacchi, *L'apocalittica giudaica e la sua storia*, BCR 55 (Brescia, 1990) 31–153.

is not in the control of the flesh''), while God has ''created the righteous and the wicked'' (4:38: *ky 'th br'th ṣdyq wrs'*), and ''All the works of justice belong to the Most High'' (4:31: *l'l 'lywn kwl m'śy ṣdqh;* see 1:9; 15:13).[39]

But to free oneself from this situation the Law is not enough; something more is wanted that only the sect possesses. This ''extra'' consists in two elements. First of all, in a supplement to revelation that is characteristic of the sect and is hidden from outsiders (see 1QS 9:17; 1QH 4:10). Specifically, the author of the Hodayôt is aware of possessing a new interpretation of the Law which is not of human origin and which has the power to save (see 1QH 5:11-12). In fact, one who refuses to enter the community or does not reach its upper level will not be purified by all the water of the sea and ''will not be righteous'' (1QS 3:3: *lw yṣdq;* cf. 3:7). P. Sacchi well notes, ''Here the word 'righteous' now has a new meaning in Judaism; henceforth it means 'justified,' because such justice no longer derives from the observance of the Law, even if it does not exclude this.''[40] Moreover, in pHab 8:1-3 we read concerning ''those who keep the Law in the house of Judah,'' that ''God will save them from judgment *(mbyt hmśpt)* for what they have suffered and for faith in the Teacher of Righteousness *('mwnh bmwrh hṣdq).*'' It is evident that for the authors and also the readers of these texts, salvation derives not only from having practiced the Law—which therefore clearly undergoes a devaluation. And finally, the author of 1QS 10:11 says to God, ''You are my righteousness *l'l 'wmrh ṣdqy'';* and this *sḏqh* surely does not come from the Law, but from a loving pretemporal election by God himself (see 1QS 3:26-27). ''I rely upon your grace and the fullness of your mercy; since you expiate guilt and purify us of crime through your justice'' (1QH 4:36-37: *bṣdqtkh*)!

This accounts for the religious-cultural milieu in which the basic problem of Paul's theology originates: How is it possible to be righteous before God? And at the same time we clearly perceive the divergence from the viewpoint of James. While James writes that ''faith without works is dead'' (2:26: ἡ πίστις χωρὶς ἔργων νεκρά ἐστιν), Paul does use a very similar terminology but writes in glaring contrast, ''Without the Law sin is dead'' (Rom 7:8: χωρὶς γὰρ νόμου ἁμαρτία νεκρά)! For Paul, it is sin that lives with the Law, while for James it is faith that lives with works (even though we must obviously remain aware of the nuances of vocabulary; see above).

---

39. Among the apocrypha, see *Eth. Hen.* 81:5; 4 Esdr 7:46; 8:35-36; for rabbinism, see Strack-Billerbeck, III 156–157.

40. ''Introduzione generale,'' *Apocrifi dell'A.T.,* I:32. See also J. Becker, *Das Heil Gottes. Heils- und Sündenbegriffe in den Qumrantexten und im Neuen Testament,* SUNT 3 (Göttingen, 1964).

IV. Convergences Between Paul and James

There are two fundamental convergences, corresponding to the relationship of each writer with the other.

a) Agreement of Paul with James: the value of works. There is one text in Paul that sounds surprisingly parallel to the principle of James:

Jas 1:22: "Become doers of the word, and not hearers only" *(γίνεσθε δὲ ποιηταὶ λόγου καὶ μὴ μόνον ἀκροαταί).*

Rom 2:13: "For it is not the hearers of the Law that are righteous before God, but the doers of the Law will be justified" *(οὐ γὰρ οἱ ἀκροαταὶ νόμου δίκαιοι παρὰ θεῷ, ἀλλ' οἱ ποιηταὶ νόμου δικαιωθήσονται).*

There are, of course, certain differences between the two sayings: νόμος, "Law," in Romans, λόγος, "word," in James (but note 1:25: ἔργον, "work"; 4:11: ποιητὴς νόμου, "doer of the law"); language of (eschatological) justification in Paul, language of illusory or actual happiness in James (see 1:23-25); moreover, the μὴ μόνον, "not only," of James leaves more room for the value of hearing than does the Pauline text.

But these sayings do have in common the same positive evaluation of action, against any philosophy of passivity (with the same descriptive nouns, ποιηταί/ἀκροαταί, "doers/hearers," even though reversed). And it is important to note that the Pauline sentence, which has an Old Testament and Jewish character in content as well as in form (see I above), appears in a part of Romans dealing with the attitude of the Jew regarding the Law (even though the Apostle then provocatively extends the principle to the gentiles in vv. 14-15). At any rate, we should note that Paul *accepts* the principle of the value of works, or better, the principle of working. At least he respects it in Judaism, does not contest its truth, even recognizes the possibility that a person could be thus justified (note the passive representing the Deity as subject). Nor is there a contradiction to the antithetical principle in the well-known text of Rom 3:28. Actually, "the righteousness ἐκ πίστεως [by faith], which Paul proclaims as gospel, does not *as such* abrogate righteousness ἐξ ἔργων νόμου [by works of the Law]. The opposition between the two (which he does maintain in 10:5f.) consists only in the fact that *sinners* should not expect any justification on the basis of the *Law, precisely because* the Law promises life only to the righteous who have practiced it (10:5; see Gal 3:12). . . . But the saying of 2:13, with which all Jews would agree, turns against them, because Paul confronts them with their actual concrete behavior (2:1). Though the Law is a sign of election over against the gentiles, in fact it does not help the

Jew who sins."[41] The Law "serves only to justify the righteous, not sinners."[42]

So for Paul it is not the keeping of the Law that is sin but its transgression; by way of parallel, only the observance of the Law is reason for justification, not simply boasting about possessing it (as Paul maintains throughout Rom 2). Against the Bultmannian thesis of "works" as "sin,"[43] U. Wilckens rightly indicates that in Paul it is not the work in itself that is subject to condemnation but the sinful work that contrasts with the Law, and that thus "there is a justice in the execution of the Law, and the one who fulfills the Law will be recognized as just in the final judgment."[44] Finally, the boast of the Jews (see Rom 2:17: "You glory in God"; 2:23: "You glory in the Law") is concerned with their privilege in the history of salvation, not egotistically with a justice obtained before God by means of their own work;[45] but for Paul it is a boasting that is not sufficient (see Rom 2:25: "If you are a transgressor of the Law, your circumcision becomes uncircumcision"!).

It is true that "Protestant theology" (and I might say also a certain recent Catholic hermeneutic) "has considered Judaism a 'Leistungsreligion [religion of performance],' that finds its ultimate expression in human self-affirmation. Bultmann has tried to show that the glorying (Sich-Rühmen) of the Jew is glorification of self (Selbst-Ruhm). But the Jew glories not in self but in the Law, in the wisdom that is not actually one's own wisdom but the reality and efficacy of the power and the glory of God in oneself. The Jew glories in God."[46]

All in all, there are four claims of Paul of which we should be aware: first, that the Jew glories not in self but in the divine election; second, that this is not enough, and does no good if the Jew does not become a real observer of the Law; third, that the actual observance of the Law can obtain justification; fourth, that even so, in fact everyone is a sinner, and hence in that case the Law no longer helps but condemns one.

41. U. Wilckens, *Der Brief an die Römer*, I, EKK VI/I (Zurich–Einsiedeln–Cologne–Neukirchen Vluyn, 1978) 132–133.
42. Ibid., 175.
43. See R. Bultmann, *Theology of the New Testament*, I (New York, 1951) 264: "The human endeavor to gain one's own salvation by means of fulfilling the Law only leads one into sin, indeed it is itself basically already sin."
44. U. Wilckens, *Römer*, 145.
45. Ibid., 177.
46. U. Luck, "Der Jakobusbrief und . . .," 169. This author, but even more so the commentary of U. Wilckens on Romans and the fundamental study of E. P. Sanders cited above (see note 22), represents a kind of U-turn of recent Protestantism in judging the value of the Judaism contemporaneous with the New Testament, and consequently also in the evaluation of Paul's antinomistic polemic.

In summary, I should say that the difference between Paul and James in this matter is that James accepts the first three in full, only substituting "Christian" for "Jew," while Paul is more dialectical and integrates them, emphasizing the radical newness of the revelation of God's righteousness in connection with the oblation of Christ on the one hand and human faith on the other. And actually, one of Paul's claims, the fourth one just listed, goes completely beyond the perspective of James; this is the claim that despite the possibility of justification inhering in the Law, in fact everyone is a sinner (note Rom 3:9: "in fact, Jews and Greeks alike, all are under sin"). "The Law is not unfulfillable, but unfulfilled: thus its actual function is only that of a mirror, in which on the basis of one's own works one recognizes oneself to be a sinner."[47] "For through the Law comes awareness of sin" (Rom 3:20b).[48]

Paul does retain the fundamental value of doing, even under the regime of grace and faith. For this we need only refer to all the paraenetic sections in the Pauline correspondence with their typical relationship between indicative and imperative,[49] and to the principle enunciated in Gal 5:6: "In Christ Jesus neither circumcision nor uncircumcision has any value, *but faith working through love*, ἀλλὰ πίστις δι᾽ ἀγάπης ἐνεργουμένη" (see Gal 6:10).

Both Paul and James, however, place not only human behavior in general (Rom 2:12-16) but also specifically Christian behavior on the eschatological horizon of the final judgment, which also for Paul is based on what each "has done" (2 Cor 5:10; cf. 11:15; Rom 14:10; Eph 6:8; cf. James 1:12; 2:12-13; 5:3). This is an idea which causes no problem in the perspective of James, since the decisive judgment comes "on the basis of works," ἐξ ἔργων (2:20, 24, 25), but which does present a problem in Paul's perspective. On this, after noting that we are talking about occurrences in or next to paraenetic contexts, the least we can say is that the "judgment anticipated places the Christian with his behavior in ultimate accountability, which he can now, as justified sinner, in fact recognize precisely

47. U. Wilckens, *Römer*, 179. This author had already expressed himself clearly with his contribution, "Was heisst bei Paulus: 'Aus Werken des Gesetzes wird kein Mensch gerecht'?" in the collection *Rechtfertigung im neuzeitlichen Lebenzusammenhang* (Gütersloh, 1974) 77–106 (polemic against R. Bultmann: 103–106). According to Wilckens, only the sinful work, i.e., that contrary to the Law, is harmful to one who *in fact* turns out to be a sinner, so that sin comes to consciousness not only with the faith in the gospel but already with the proper function of the Law; and even the Christian is actually called to fulfill the Law (see Rom 8:3-4) that is summed up in the commandment of love (Rom 13:8-10; Gal 5:14; cf. 1 Cor 13).

48. Compare the related saying of Epicurus, though meant on a psychological and pedagogical level: "The beginning of salvation is awareness of sin" (*Initium salutis notitia peccati*, in L. A. Seneca, *Ep.* 28:9).

49. On this last issue, see now L. Álvarez Verdes, *El imperativo cristiano en San Pablo. La tensión indicativo-imperativo en Rom 6. Análisis estructural* (Rome, 1980).

because in faith he knows that every inadequate work is removed by the atoning death of Christ'';[50] cf. Rom 5:9-10; 6:5.

b) Agreement of James with Paul: the foundational value of ''the implanted word.'' Two verses of Jas 1, while separated from each other, provide a single consistent theological thematic conception and would best be read consecutively: ''By his will [God] has brought us into being with a word of truth, to be the first fruits of his creation. . . . So, putting aside all uncleanness and the abundance of wickedness, with meekness accept the implanted word that can save your souls'' (1:18, 21). We see here certain concepts of powerful theological validity that bring the passage close to the typical Pauline thematic.

God freely brings into being *(βουληθεὶς ἀπεκύεσεν)*; even if the word is *hapax legomenon* in the New Testament, we can't help but think of the Pauline passages in which the free initiative of God is announced in bringing about what is totally new, or the Christian reality, expressed in concepts like ''purpose'' *(πρόθεσις)*, ''good pleasure'' *(εὐδοκία)*, ''election'' *(ἐκλογή)*: see Rom 8:29-30; 9:11; Eph 1:4-11 *(κατὰ τὴν βουλὴν τοῦ θελήματος αὐτοῦ,* ''according to the counsel of his will'').

The ''word of truth'' is a Pauline expression (2 Cor 6:7; Col 1:5; Eph 1:13; 2 Tim 2:15) and indicates the proclamation of the gospel in preaching.[51]

The ''first fruits of creation.'' The term ἀπαρχή in the New Testament can be said to be exclusively Pauline (except Rev 14:4): Rom 8:23; 11:16; 16:5; 1 Cor 15:20; 16:15; (2 Thess 2:13). The closest text would be 2 Thess 2:13 (''God has chosen you as first fruits (?) for salvation, and has called you by means of our gospel'') if it were not textually problematic (is it ἀπαρχή or ἀπ' ἀρχῆς, ''first fruits'' or ''from the beginning''?). Still closer is Philo of Alexandria, *De spec. leg.* 4:180: the Jewish people was ''assigned to the Creator and Father as a kind of human 'first fruits' *(τις ἀπαρχή)* of the whole human race'' (see *Ex. R.* 15:6). The term encompasses the ideas of originality, beginning, and delight.

The ''putting aside'' of ''all uncleanness'' (see 1 Pet 3:21: βάπτισμα, οὐ σαρκὸς ἀπόθεσις ῥύπου): in ''Pauline'' speech the verb ἀποτίθεσθαι not only

---

50. U. Wilckens, *Römer*, 146. On the subject of the coming judgment and justification, see esp. E. Synofzik, *Die Gerichts- und Vergeltungsaussagen bei Paulus. Eine traditionsgeschichtliche Untersuchung*, GThA 8 (Göttingen, 1977). See also K. Kertelge, ''*Rechtfertigung''* bei Paulus (Münster in Westphalia, 1967 [Italian: 1991]) 256 (''of no constitutive significance''); K. P. Donfried, ''Justification and Last Judgment in Paul,'' Int 30 (1976) 140–152; M. Wolter, *Rechtfertigung und zukünftiges Heil. Untersuchungen zu Röm. 5,1-11* (Berlin, 1978). Also R. Pregeant, ''Grace and Recompense. Reflections on a Pauline Paradox,'' JAAR 47 (1979) 73–96.

51. The sense of ''creative word of God'' (F. Mussner, *Der Jakobusbrief*, 94) is unacceptable; in Colossians and Ephesians the identification of the gospel is explicit.

is always associated, as in James, with negative moral values but often occurs in baptismal contexts (Eph 4:22, 25; Col 3:8; cf. Rom 13:12; 1 Pet 2:1). It is clear enough that the passage of James also refers to the first moment of Christian life (aorist participle ἀποθέμενοι, "having put aside"!).

The ἔμφυτος λόγος, "implanted word": the expression is *hapax legomenon* (as such it might recall the similar *hapax* σύμφυτοι of Rom 6:5. But the perspective is different: there it is the Christians who are "implanted" in the atoning death of Christ). It is explained on the basis of two traditions: a Jewish tradition that refers to the Law or to wisdom (see Qoh 12:11; 4 Esdr 9:31-33; *Syr. Bar.* 32:1; 51:3); and a Christian tradition referring to the word of preaching, whether by Jesus or by the Apostles (see the parable of the sower in Mark 4:15; Luke 8:6, 8, and the Pauline image in 1 Cor 3:6; 4:15b; see also 1 Thess 2:13; Col 3:16). In the context the expression "implanted word" is the "word of truth" of the previous v. 18, an expression that in Eph 1:13 is directly linked to "hear." We are, then, doubtless talking about preaching that was heard by the recipients of the letter. This preaching, along with baptism, has, as it were, sowed them and given them new life (see Gal 3:2b: "Is it by the works of the Law that you received the Spirit or by the hearing of faith?").[52]

The salvific power of the word *(τὸν δυνάμενον σῶσαι)* is contextually related to the "first fruits" of v. 18: the word produces its first fruits (see Isa 55:11). Like Paul, James too attributes to it an intrinsic dynamism oriented toward salvation (see 1 Thess 2:13: λόγον θεοῦ, ὃς καὶ ἐνεργεῖται ἐν ὑμῖν, "the word that is also active in you"; 1 Cor 15:1-2: τὸ εὐαγγέλιον . . . δι' οὗ καὶ σῴζεσθε, "the gospel . . . by which you are saved"). Still, we must not gloss over the fact that James's conception of salvation is precisely associated with works, as implied in the question of 2:14: "How can faith save such a one?" the understood response to which is clearly negative. Still, "for an overall judgment of the theology of James it is most important to note that he ascribes a saving power to the 'word' as well as to 'works.' "[53] But James does not emphasize this theme; for him it is enough to have mentioned it.

V. Conclusion

There is no need to repeat the classic harmonizing solution formulated by Saint Augustine ("The one speaks of works that precede faith, the other

52. The text of James 4:5 (τὸ πνεῦμα ὃ κατῴκισεν ἐν ἡμῖν: God "made the spirit dwell in us") would fit splendidly in this thematic environment if the word "spirit" here had the strong sense of "divine Spirit"; but in the context it can only mean creaturely "human spirit" (see the commentaries of F. Mussner, W. Schrage, R. Fabris).
53. F. Mussner, *Der Jakobusbrief*, 103.

of those that follow it")[54] and since repeated to satiety. This is so obviously right that even Luther accepts it, so that he even, perhaps uncon-
sciously, re-echoes James himself when he writes, "If works do not follow,
it is certain that this faith of Christ does not dwell in our hearts but is
dead";[55] "It is impossible for faith to exist without many and great unceasing works";[56] "Faith without works is null and vain . . . a fanatical
abstraction, pure emptiness, a dream of the heart; it is false and does not
justify";[57] even though over it all we hear the clearly Pauline principle:
"We are not made just by acting but being just, we do just things."[58]

What we must here note, I believe, is the accuracy of E. Käsemann's
contention: he describes the Pauline doctrine of justification by faith, somewhat enigmatically indeed, as a "fighting doctrine." It "does not retain
its true character if its antitheses are softened or abolished—a process which
is already at work in the pastoral epistles. It is paralyzed if its attacking
spear-head is blunted and for that reason it is only seldom that it has been
able to determine theology and the Church."[59] But the terms "fighting"
and "antithesis" demand explanation: with whom and in what sense?
It is surely not just a question of ancient history, referring to Paul's anti-
Jewish polemic, much less of ecclesiology, simply as an instrument of conflict between Christian confessions. Much more, the Pauline teaching is
a "fighting doctrine" *against* the constantly recurring presumptions of
human persons (and sometimes structures) before God, and *in favor* of
the sovereign will of God himself; a "fighting doctrine" of every prodigal son against the self-sufficiency of every self-styled older brother—what
I mean to say is: a doctrine of absolutely unmotivated, disarming grace,
which absolves the wicked person who believes, and condemns the self-
sufficient worthy.

This "polemic" dimension of Pauline justification is rooted, of course,
in the story of his sharp confrontation with the Pharisaic and, to some
extent, the Qumran Judaism of his time. But this should not lead us to
relativize it,[60] but at least in Christian circles the same is true of the other
side. James is also very polemical. Even though he seems to bring about
an interweaving of opposites, this actually ends up overbalanced on the

54. *De diversis quaestionibus LXXXIII* (PL 40:89).
55. WA (= *D. M. Luthers Werke. Kritische Gesamtausgabe* [Weimar, 1883 . . .]) XXXIX/I, 44–45.
Thesis 30; after the translation of V. Subilia, *La giustificazione per fede* (Brescia, 1976) 200.
56. WA VII, 231 (Subilia, 201).
57. WA XL/I, 266 (V. Subilia, 201).
58. *In Rm*, 224 (the phrase recalls the Scholastic axiom *Operari sequitur esse:* "doing follows
being").
59. E. Käsemann, *Perspectives on Paul*, trans. M. Kohl (Philadelphia, 1971) 71.
60. As does K. Stendahl, *The Apostle Paul and the Introspective Conscience of the West*, HThR
56 (1963) 199–215.

side of "works"; no harmonious synthesis is proposed. Nor does the New Testament give witness to any third position that tries to arbitrate between Paul and James.

Without trying to engage in systematic dogmatics, as long as we remain only in the New Testament environment, when we compare Paul and James they may not be opposites, but they are certainly very different, at least on the level of language. While Paul would surely have agreed with the contention that faith without works is dead (Jas 2:17-26), he would never have accepted the thesis that one is justified on the basis of one's works (2:24; against Rom 3:28), even though James intends it as a "second" justification.

Perhaps their mutual agreement can be found only if we rise above the restricted field of the conflict between the language of faith and works, and consider a more vast theological horizon, that is, God in God's own self. From God, according to James, "comes every good gift (δόσις) and every perfect gift (δώρημα)" (Jas 1:17a; cf, 1:5; 3:17), a sentence that has every appearance of an aphorism. With this, Paul would have agreed, since he also speaks of justification with terms meaning "gift," δώρημα and χάρισμα (Rom 5:16ab, 17) and of an ἐπιτέλεσις, "completion," by God of the "good work done by him" (Phil 1:6). "So it is not so much a question of moving the emphasis from works to faith alone . . ., but putting the emphasis on God without reservation, on God alone, who comes to occupy the central and exclusive place."[61] This theoarchism is the minimal basis, but actually very broad (and perhaps a bit vague), on which faith and works find their correlative, legitimate place.

The relationship between Paul and James, then, constitutes one of the typical cases, if not the most typical, of the theme "unity and diversity in the New Testament." It would seem to emphasize diversity more than unity, but we should realize that "unity" does not mean uniformity, and that "diversity" is not the same as opposition. As we have indicated above (see IIIc and also IId), the two sacred writers were bearers and witnesses within Christianity of differing theological emphases that were already to be found in the Jewish environment from which they both came. And so we ought first, perhaps, to study the phenomenon of "unity and diversity in Judaism" (especially before A.D. 70) in order adequately to grasp the New Testament phenomenon, which in part reflects the Judaic reality. And at least we can recognize that the canonization of the works of both Paul and James represents an invitation to the Church of all times not to restrict to one dimension her own reflection on the "manifold wisdom of God" (Eph 3:10).

61. V. Subilia, *La giustificazione*, 349.

Chapter 23

The Problem of the Law in Paul's Letters

The subject to which we dedicate this study has always been felt to be a fundamental factor in the elaboration of what constitutes the central nucleus of Christian identity. This is true from Origen's commentary on Romans, through the crucial moment of Luther's reform, to our present days, in which there seems to prevail in Catholic teaching a markedly ethical approach to the understanding of the gospel at the sacrifice of its original dimension of grace and freedom. With this we also immediately recognize the importance of the issue—and of its clarification—an issue that presents two major problems: the one is the seriousness of the question at hand, concerned as it is with a fundamental reality of Christian revelation and also with the awareness that Christians must have of this revelation in order correctly to shape their spiritual lives; the other is the objective difficulty of ascertaining all the aspects of the problem in the writings of Paul, who represents the principal source of reflection on this issue. Within the New Testament he is the author who most argues the question, and yet he never seems to have arrived at a clarification that will fully satisfy our thirst for the "clear and distinct ideas" demanded by our Aristotelian and Cartesian heritage.

In the last few years the subject has undergone specialized research in a number of valuable monographs, which have revived more discussion than greets most issues and have contributed to restoring an ancient chapter of Christian theology to contemporary urgency.[1] One thing is cer-

---

1. These are the principal works: H. Hübner, *Law in Paul's Thought*, trans. J. Gerig (Edinburgh, 1984); E. P. Sanders, *Paul and Palestinian Judaism: A Comparison of Patterns of Religion* (Philadelphia, 1977, 1984²); idem, *Paul, the Law, and the Jewish People* (Philadelphia, 1983); H. Räisänen, *Paul and the Law*, WUNT 29 (Tübingen, 1983); idem, *The Torah and Christ: Essays in German and English on the Problem of the Law in Early Christianity* (Helsinki, 1986); E. J. Schnabel, *Law and Wisdom from Ben Sira to Paul: A Tradition Historical Enquiry into the Relation of Law, Wisdom, and Ethics*, WUNT 2.16 (Tübingen, 1985); L. Gaston, *Paul and the Torah* (Vancouver,

tain and should be confirmed at once: among all the New Testament writers, Paul is the one who sets the agenda, so that the Christian cannot adequately consider the problem of the Law without dealing seriously with Paul and his writings. We can confirm this with a simple statistical observation about the occurrence of the term νόμος, "Law," and its role in context. Of 193 occurrences in the New Testament, 116 are found in the seven authentic letters of Paul (104 of which are in Galatians and Romans alone!); and there are besides other synonymous terms found in him alone, such as ἐντολή, "commandment" (9 times), and γράμμα, "letter" (6 times). Moreover, in the other authors the occurrence of the word νόμος, "Law," either is not connected with a specific discussion of the theme (thus in Gospels and Acts, 50 times, normally meaning the Scriptures) or is simply evaluated in positive terms (thus 10 times in James), or is treated polemically but from a different perspective (thus in Hebrews, 14 times, but never in connection with sin or justification, but rather as the cultic arrangement understood as a "shadow" of the new Christological reality). From this we conclude that it is only in Paul that the "Law" is perceived as a problematic issue on the anthropological and soteriological level, and so can be treated from the viewpoint of an inevitable confrontation with the basic components of Christian reflection (Christ, Spirit, justification, works, faith, sin, flesh, freedom) and of the moral life in general.

In what follows we will examine certain aspects of the question. These are meant not to exhaust the subject but to bring into focus certain factors that are anything but secondary.

I. The main difficulty

To recognize the specific difficulties of an argument means already to run a good part of the distance to be traveled, or at least some part of way—besides confirming oneself in a fruitful attitude of Socratic humility. Now, there are in Paul many aspects that make the subject difficult.

The first is the wide variety of meanings of this term νόμος: now as Scripture or Pentateuch (e.g., 1 Cor 9:8, 9), now as natural law (Rom 2:14-15),

1987); J. S. Marino, *Saint Paul and the Law: Toward a Concept of Church Law* (Rome, 1988); R. Liebers, *Das Gesetz als Evangelium. Untersuchungen zur Gesetzkritik des Paulus*, AThANT 75 (Zurich, 1989); B. L. Martin, *Christ and the Law in Paul*, NT Suppl. 62 (Leiden 1989). A balance in the debate, besides O. Kuss, "Nomos bei Paulus," MThZ 17 (1966) 177–210, has recently been proposed by D. J. Moo, "Paul and the Law in the Last Ten Years," ScottJourTheol 40 (1987) 287–307, and by S. Westerholm, *Israel's Law and the Church's Faith: Paul and His Recent Interpreters* (Grand Rapids, Mich., 1988), who, however, do not consider the abundant production of articles in specialized reviews, not to mention certain major commentaries on Galatians and Romans, and the last four monographs named above. While some of the important monographs have been translated into Italian, Italian research on the subject is unfortunately missing.

now in a general sense as a rule or conformity to a principle (Rom 7:21), now occurring in abstract genitival expressions (like "law of faith" in Rom 3:27, or "law of sin" in Rom 7:23 or "law of the Spirit" in Rom 8:2, where it is not immediately evident whether we have a true genitive of specification or simply an epexegetical genitive), now as "law of Christ" (in Gal 6:2), and finally and especially as Sinaitic or Mosaic Law—but then sometimes judged negatively (1 Cor 15:56), sometimes positively (Rom 7:12).

A second difficulty comes from the frequently polemical contexts in which Paul discusses the problem (especially in Galatians), so that here we can ask just when is Paul expressing a reasoned stance, that is, one that is not conditioned by paradox or hyperbole, but as part of his stable and irrevocable theological property.[2]

A third question, connected with the previous one, concerns the possibility of an evolution undergone by Paul on the subject: Was his position on the Law as opposed to justification by faith completely clear at the moment of his conversion on the road to Damascus?[3] Or, as others would have it, did it force itself on him only little by little during his missionary ministry and especially on the occasion of the crisis of the Churches of Galilee?[4] Or finally, should we actually speak of a personal crisis of Paul even before his conversion?[5]

2. Note that actually within the Protestant circles questions are surprisingly raised against the most classical Lutheran tradition from P. Wernle (*Beginnings of Christianity*, trans. G. A. Bienemann, I [London, 1903–1904] 309–310), and W. Wrede (*Paul* [Boston, 1908; original: Tübingen, 1907²] 122–124), on through A. Schweitzer (*The Mysticism of Paul the Apostle*, trans. W. Montgomery [New York, 1968 = ca. 1931] 219–226) and W. D. Davies (*Paul and Rabbinic Judaism* [London 1952²] 221–222), and finally E. P. Sanders (*Paul and Palestinian Judaism* [Philadelphia, 1977] 502–508). Paul's teaching against the works of the Law and the parallel teaching of justification by faith alone are considered only "one of his most disastrous creations" (Wernle) or at most a "Kampflehre," or polemical doctrine (Wrede), a "Nebenkrater," or subsidiary crater ("which has formed within the rim of the main crater—the mystical doctrine of redemption through the being-in-Christ": Schweitzer), one metaphor among many (Davies) and at least an aspect secondary to the more important topic of participation in the life of Christ (Sanders). For a reaffirmation of the classical position, see H. Hübner, "Pauli Theologiae Proprium," NTS 26 (1980) 455–473; H. W. Boers, "The Foundations of Paul's Thought: A Methodological Investigation. The Problem of the Coherent Center of Paul's Thought," STh 42 (1988) 55–68.
3. Thus S. Kim, *The Origin of Paul's Gospel*, WUNT 2.4 (Tübingen, 1981) 269ff.; Chr. Dietzfelbinger, *Die Berufung des Paulus als Ursprung seiner Theologie*, WMANT 58 (Neukirchen-Vluyn, 1985) esp. 90ff.; see also T. L. Donaldson, "Zealot and Convert: The Origin of Paul's Christ-Torah Antithesis," CBQ 51 (1989) 655–682.
4. Thus G. Strecker, "Befreiung und Rechtfertigung. Zur Stellung der Rechtfertigungslehre in der Theologie des Paulus," in J. Friedrich et al. (eds.), *Rechtfertigung. Festschrift E. Käsemann* (Tübingen, 1976) 479ff.; G. Howard, *Paul: Crisis in Galatia. A Study in Early Christian Theology*, SNTS MS 35 (Cambridge, 1979); U. Schnelle, *Wandlungen im paulinischen Denken*, SB 137 (Stuttgart, 1989) 71–76; but H. Räisänen, *Paul and the Law*, 256–263, thinks rather of the incident between Paul and Peter in Antioch (Gal 2:11-14).
5. This is hard to determine. Rom 7:7-25 would seem to indicate that this is so, but this is extremely doubtful simply because the passage is not found in an autobiographical context, and because the contrary is stated in Phil 3:5-6 (but note the intermediate solution of

A fourth difficulty, which derives in turn from the third, concerns the final stage of Paul's thought on the issue, which does not seem to have reached a final maturation: Romans itself (which according to the hypothesis distinguishing the authentic letters ought to be the last written by Paul) contains apparently contradictory statements (e.g., 3:20 and 7:12), which indicate that Paul, while developing certain stable and irrevocable elements (like the uselessness of the Law in the process of justification, the proclamation of Christ as its alternative, and the fundamental principle of Christian liberty), had not clarified even for himself other, no less important aspects of the question (like the inward nature of the Law in relation to its origin, and its precise role and value with regard to the moral life of the Christian).[6]

A fifth difficulty comes from dispassionate comparison, based directly on the sources, between Paul's conception and that of contemporaneous Judaism with regard to the Jewish Law. While the Apostle would seem to see therein a purely legalistic principle of justification through works, the Judaism of the period did not understand it in such terms but subordinated it to the free divine election, which was considered the sole principle of entry into the people of the alliance, so that it would seem that Paul has distorted for his own purposes a reality meant quite differently by his coreligionists at the time.[7]

II. Hermeneutical approaches

Historically there have been many different ways of evaluating the Law according to the Pauline viewpoint. We have here a clear example of what since H. G. Gadamer has been called the "Wirkungsgeschichte," i.e., the history of the interpretation of a biblical passage or motif over the centuries.

A first attitude is the totally negative one of the *Jewish Christians*, already witnessed in the first century in the Letter of James[8] and then de-

---

G. Theissen, *Psychological Aspects of Pauline Theology*, [Edinburgh, 1983] 177–265). But it would be quite another thing to investigate whether in contemporaneous Hellenistic Judaism there were antilegalistic tendencies to explain the development of Paul's attitude—at least in part (see a documentation in H. Räisänen, *Paul and the Law*, 33–41, 234–236).

6. H. Räisänen, *Paul and the Law*, emphasizes this aspect especially, speaking of unresolved tensions (p. 14) and taking Paul's intuition (= faith in Christ) more seriously than his unsuccessful rationalizations (pp. 268–269).

7. We are indebted to E. P. Sanders for these very valuable historical insights in his *Paul and Palestinian Judaism* (= *Paolo e il giudaismo palestinese* [Brescia, 1986]: note the ample presentation I made of it in *Osservatore Romano*, 11 Dec. 1986, p. 7); see below. Actually, Paul does not distort the Jewish concept of the Law; rather, he criticizes it as reducing the Torah only to "law," neglecting the typical Jewish combination of Torah as covenant, Torah as promise, and Torah as gospel (see R. Liebers, *Das Gesetz als Evangelium*, e.g., 229–236 on Gal 3:15-22).

8. See chapter 22 above; W. Pratscher, *Der Herrenbruder Jakobus und die Jakobustradition*, FRLANT 139 (Göttingen, 1987) 213–214.

veloped by the successive more or less orthodox currents of the first centuries. Paul's position (perhaps distorted?) is seen as dangerous and in need at least of correction (see Jas 2:24: "One is justified by works and not by faith alone," against Rom 3:28), or even as a clear sign of apostasy: "Those who are called Ebionites reject Paul, saying that he is an apostate from the Law; . . . they have themselves circumcised and keep the customs of the Law and the Jewish manner of living."[9] In these circles evidently they "considered strict observance of the Mosaic law indispensable, since they believed that faith in Christ with a life conformed to this faith was not sufficient to save them."[10] We probably find such a conviction astonishing; and yet this hermeneutic is not Jewish,[11] but rather Christian (Jewish Christian), an expression of a pluralism we find hard to accept, accustomed as we are to a uniform interpretation.

A second attitude is attested by the great Alexandrian *Origen*, in his *Commentary* on Romans (which is the very first commentary on a Pauline letter).[12] Anti-Gnostic and anti-Marcionite, he tends to protect the Mosaic Law from any negative interpretation, claiming that Paul was speaking of natural law: if sin existed before Moses, the Law that provoked it or that revealed it must have been different from that of Moses, namely, the natural law (see his commentary, 7:7-13). Origen establishes a philological criterion, that νόμος with the article would indicate the Law of Moses, while without the article it would indicate the natural law (see 3:21: 944A-B). But the criterion is unreliable, since it does not always hold (e.g., 2:14-15 concerning the gentiles uses νόμος with the article, but right after that 2:17 concerning the Jew uses the word without the article).[13]

---

9. Irenaeus of Lyons, *Adv. haer.* 1:26:2; cf. Eusebius of Caesarea, *Hist. eccl.* 4:29:2 and 5. Also the so-called Pseudo-Clementines witness the most vigorous possible rejection of Paul among Jewish Christians, actually describing him as "adversary," "enemy," "impostor," sower of "a doctrine contrary to the Law"; see G. Barbaglio, *Paolo di Tarso e le origini cristiane* (Assisi, 1985) 390–; L. Cirillo, "L'antipaolinismo delle Pseudoclementine," in R. Penna, ed., *Antipaolinismo: Reazioni a Paolo tra il I e II secolo*, RSB 2 (Bologna, 1989) 121–137.

10. Eusebius of Caesarea, *Hist. eccl.* 3:27:2.

11. A Jewish hermeneutic can assume two opposite attitudes: either Paul is considered an irreconcilable traitor (see the ancient *Toledôt Yeshu*, according to which a certain Eliahu separated the rebels of the community of Israel: "To them he suggested 'laws that were not good' [Ezek 20:25], he did it for the good of Israel; and the Nazarenes call him Paulus": after the translation of R. Di Segni, *Il Vangelo del Ghetto* [Rome, 1985] 64), or else reabsorb him irenically into Jewish tradition as if there were no problem (A. Chouraqui, *Jésus et Paul, fils d'Israël* [Aubonne, 1988], who, however, bases himself primarily on the Acts of the Apostles); more realistic is a recognition of his greatness but also his distance (S. Sandmel, *The Genius of Paul* [New York, 1959]; A. F. Segal, *Paul the Convert: The Apostolate and Apostasy of Saul the Pharisee* [New Haven, Conn.–London, 1990]).

12. See now the excellent Italian translation, Origen, *Commento alla lettera ai Romani*, introduction, translation and notes by F. Cocchini, I-II (Marietti: Casale Monferato, 1985); cf. I, XX–XXIII.

13. P. Bläser, *Das Gesetz bei Paulus* (Münster, 1941) 1–23, demonstrated that the presence or absence of the article before νόμος indicates no semantic distinction.

A third attitude consists in making a distinction in the Mosaic Law (which is regularly Paul's subject) between *moral precepts* and *ceremonial precepts* (note the distinction already in Justin, *Dial.* 44:2; Irenaeus, *Adv. haer.* 4:15:1; 4:16:2): Paul's negative judgment would refer only to the latter, while the former would be left alone. Thus Saint Thomas, who clearly declares, "The New Law does not invalidate the observance of the Old Law except for the ceremonial matters,"[14] elsewhere explaining (commenting on Rom 3:31) that Christian faith does confirm the Law, but in the sense that the ceremonial precepts must be seen as figurative, and so have already been fulfilled in Christ, while the moral precepts (perpetually valid) are confirmed in that grace helps to fulfill them.[15] Now, it is true that in the Judaism of Paul's time we must probably distinguish Hellenistic Judaism, where a certain allegorization of the ritual components of the Law is attested,[16] and rabbinic Judaism, which admitted no exception;[17] but in either case the Law is considered indivisible (after all, even Philo compares the two components to the body and the soul, which together form one entity). And even though Paul, when giving examples of legal precepts in his argument refers only to circumcision, feasts (Sabbath), and dietary regulations (Galatians), still he always speaks of the "Law" in its entirety, of "the whole Law" (Gal 5:3, 14; see 1 Cor 7:19), and the only specific commandment he quotes in a critical way, "Thou shalt not covet" (Rom 7:7), is actually not ceremonial (whether the allusion is to Exod 20:17 or Gen 3:1-6).[18] In any case, Paul is talking not about the observance of the Law as such but about the deeper process of justification, which stands behind any actual practice. Actually it would be well worthwhile to study to what extent such a distinction depends on a "Pauline" reading of the Letter to the Hebrews, where νόμος does actually refer only to the old cultic order (see Heb 7:12, 16, 19; 10:1); but there the perspective is quite different from that of the Apostle.

A fourth attitude consists in judging the Law (in Saint Paul's thought) as having an *educative, pedagogical function*. This interpretation (already attested in Hellenistic Judaism)[19] could be said to be traditional in Christianity, and can be traced at least from John Chrysostom to Thomas

14. Sum. Th., I-II, q. 107, a. 2 ad primum; the whole issue is treated at length in qq. 98–108.

15. *Super Epistolas S. Pauli lectura*, ed. R. Cai, I (Marietti, 1953) 56, n. 321.

16. Thus the "allegorists" mentioned by Philo of Alexandria, *Migr. Abr.* 89-93.

17. See the documentation of E. E. Urbach, *The Sages: Their Concepts and Beliefs*, I (Jerusalem, 1975) 360–365; E. P. Sanders, *Paul and Palestinian Judaism*, 111–114, and the observations of H. Räisänen, *Paul and the Law*, 23–28.

18. Recently J. Becker, *Paul: Apostle to the Gentiles* (Louisville, 1973) 393, hypothesizes that such a distinction may have existed in the Church of Antioch (but that Paul did not make it his own), while others think of the circle of Stephen (see Acts 6–7).

19. See G. Bertram, art. παιδεύω in TDNT 5:612–616.

Aquinas, Martin Luther, Calvin, and certain moderns.[20] This is based especially on Gal 3:24 ("The Law was our παιδαγωγός to Christ"), as well as certain passages like Rom 3:20; 7:24; 10:4, and understands the role of the Law in one of two ways: either positively, in that it was to educate people gradually to cause them to grow and to lead them to Christ as a final crowning of every moral life; or negatively, in that it was to infuse the awareness of sin and bring our trust in works to crisis, thus arousing the desire for grace. This type of interpretation has in fact been abandoned today in Catholic and Protestant circles alike on the basis of a more accurate exegesis of the context of Gal 3:24[21] and a more thoroughly documented comparative research of the figure of the pedagogue in antiquity, and specifically on his extremely severe function connected with a child's minority.[22]

A fifth position is typical of *Martin Luther.* He understands the Law and the works done in its name as something wholly negative; as he describes Paul's doctrine in *De servo arbitrio* ("The free will even in human beings who are excellent as to the Law, justice, wisdom, were they endowed with every virtue, is something impious, deviant, and worthy of God's wrath")[23] and in the commentaries on Romans and Galatians: his conclusion is that the person under the Law and without God's grace is always a sinner, since the works resulting from it are done only for fear of punishment or for selfish interest,[24] so that commenting on Gal 3:10 he actually maintains that the observance of the commandments is nothing but "idolatry and blasphemy" because it violates the first commandment! Certain other great Lutheran theologians of our century follow this line: R. Bultmann, according to whom *"man's effort to achieve his salvation by keeping the Law* . . . *in the end is already sin,'"*[25] and E. Käsemann, who says that "the law in fact throws a person back upon himself and therefore into the existing world of anxiety about oneself, self-confidence and unceasing self-assurance . . . it is the mark and power of the world which

20. See the authors cited by H. Schlier, *Der Brief an die Galater* (Göttingen, 1971 [Italian: 1965]) 169–170 at 3:24.

21. Besides the commentary of Schlier noted above, see those of F. Mussner, *Der Galaterbrief* (Freiburg–Basel–Vienna, 1974 [Italian: 1987]) and B. Corsani, *La lettera ai Galati* (Genoa: Marietti, 1990).

22. See esp. D. J. Lull, " 'The Law Was Our Pedagogue': A Study in Galatians 3:19-25," JBL 105 (1986) 481–498; N. H. Young, "*Paidagogos:* The Social Setting of a Pauline Metaphor," NT 29 (1987) 150–176.

23. See *D. M. Luthers Werke. Kritische Gesamtausgabe,* vol. 18 (Weimar, 1908) 758; cf. 743 and 772.

24. See ibid., vol. 56 (Weimar, 1938) 102, 248, 12; and the translation of G. Pani, *Martin Lutero. Lezioni sulla Lettera ai Romani* (1515–1516), I:177–178.

25. R. Bultmann, *Theology of the New Testament* (New York, 1951-55) 264 (emphasis his).

does not believe even in its religiousness."[26] In this perspective, then, the Law provokes the person only to acts of pride (cf. the Pauline term καύχη-σις, "boasting"), of self-realization, and hence of self-exaltation before God (= merit). This interpretation has an apparently opposite inversion, according to which the Law, rather than giving one matter for the pursuit of self-sufficiency, leads one to failure and despair, since it leads one actually to touch with the hand one's inability ever to keep it completely (see Rom 7:7-25). But actually these are only two sides to the same understanding of the data.

A sixth attitude, which goes beyond the previous one and is also found in Protestant circles, actually considers very seriously the Pauline idea of "boasting" that has its basis in the Law. But this boasting is concerned not with the actual observance of the Law but *simply with the possession of the Law* itself, which is understood in itself as a basis and expression of a privileged status. The boasting, then, takes place not before God as a presumptuous self-affirmation based on one's own moral superiority, but before the gentiles as a proud title to exclusive privilege for Israel, which sees in this the guarantee of their own secure election. Thus the attention is shifted from the individual and moral (and somewhat psychologizing) level to the religious-institutional sphere. It is actually a Protestant like E. P. Sanders who attacked the caricaturing presentation of the Jewish Law especially characteristic of classic Lutheranism, which considered Judaism as a legalistic religion of a mere justice based on the calculation of works.[27] Paul's polemic against the Law, then, must be seen from the point of view of salvation history rather than anthropology, for in Judaism also the observance of the Law is based on the supposition of the free grace of God,[28] and it is certainly not to this that Paul takes exception, but only to the fact that the Law keeps Israel from perceiving the new manifestation of God's merciful will in Jesus Christ.[29] This position has

---

26. *Commentary on Romans* (Grand Rapids, Mich., 1980) 102 (on 3:27-28).

27. See *Paul and Palestinian Judaism*, 58–59: the work of certain classic Protestants (F. Weber, W. Bousset, P. Billerbeck, R. Bultmann), who helped to spread an idea of Judaism as a religion of self-redemption, "is based on massive perversion and misunderstanding of the material," and therefore that vision must be destroyed. The position of Bultmann is explicitly refuted by the commentary of the illustrious Lutheran exegete U. Wilckens, *Der Brief an die Römer*, I, EKK VI/1 (Zurich–Neukirchen, 1978) 145; see also F. Watson, *Paul, Judaism and the Gentiles: A Sociological Approach*, SNTS MS 56 (Cambridge, 1986) 1–18 (note p. 18: "The process of 'de-Lutheranizing' Paul is already well under way"); R. Liebers, *Das Gesetz als Evangelium*, 238 (Bultmann's interpretation "does not correspond to Paul's statements").

28. See the lovely and significant rabbinic parable in Midrash *Mek. Ex.* 20, reported in R. Penna, *L'ambiente storico-culturale delle origini cristiane. Una documentazione ragionata* (Bologna: Dehoniane, 1991³) 48.

29. "Paul regarded zeal for the law itself as a good thing (Rom 10:2; Phil 3:6). What is wrong with it is not that it implies petty obedience and minimization of important matters, not that it results in the tabulation of merit points before God, but *that it is not worth anything*

been criticized by some as too irenic an interpretation of Paul's relationship to Judaism (in both, it is not the Law but divine election that determines entry into the covenant community, while the works of the Law would be only a condition for "staying in"),[30] for the critics claim that Paul's negative attitude toward the Law is based on the total framework of his thought rather than on limited comparisons;[31] in any case, the contribution of the proponents to our understanding of the Judaism of Paul's time is beyond question.[32]

A seventh hermeneutical position we want to mention maintains that the theme of the Law in Paul undergoes *a semantic dislocation between Galatians and Romans:* while the former presents Christ as the end of the Law as a reality of salvation history, the latter would see him only as the end of the carnal abuse of the Law (so that the vision of Bultmann could be justified on the basis of Romans but not of Galatians).[33] The more positive vision in Romans would represent a rehabilitation of the Law in comparison to Galatians—and all the more so if the expression of Rom 3:27, "the Law of faith," were actually meant to allude to the Torah as seen by the eyes of faith! But apart from this last indefensible exegetical opinion,[34] Hübner's thesis is based on the dating of Galatians as chronologically the first of Paul's letters, thus leaving time for a long enough lapse to justify the progress claimed. But this is a last resort.[35] Now, we do not mean by this to deny that there is a change of tone between the two letters; but this is due rather to the different circumstances and purpose, as well as a reduction of the level of polemic.[36]

---

in comparison with being in Christ (Phil 3:4-11). The fundamental critique of the Law is that following the Law does not result in being found in Christ" (E. P. Sanders, *Paul and Palestinian Judaism*, 550). J. D. G. Dunn also argues in essentially the same direction, "Works of the Law and the Curse of the Law (Galatians 3.10-14)," NTS 31 (1985) 523–542, speaking correctly of the Law as a "boundary marker" of which Israel boasts; still it seems a bit much to me to say that "the curse which was removed therefore by Christ's death was the curse . . . of a wrong understanding of the Law" (p. 536), since Paul does not in fact call for a *different* observance of the Law!

30. See especially R. H. Gundry, "Grace, Works, and Staying Saved in Paul," *Bib* 66 (1985) 1–38: Paul rejected Judaism and Jewish Christianity because he was convinced not only that God had revealed his Son to him but also that works-righteousness was at the heart of Judaism and Judeo-Christianity.

31. See H. Weder, "Gesetz und Sünde. Gedanken zu einem qualitativen Sprung im Denken des Paulus," NTS 31 (1985) 357–376, 358 ("Paul opposes a conception that links grace and Law together": p. 372, n. 7); and the monograph of R. Liebers (see note 1 above).

32. The only really "legalistic" ancient document is the apocalyptic 4 Esdras: see E. P. Sanders, *Paul and Palestinian Judaism*, 409–418.

33. Thus H. Hübner, *Law* (cited in n. 1 above).

34. See H. Räisänen, *Paul and the Law*, 50–52 and 170–171.

35. See the criticisms by S. Westerholm in *Svensk Exegetische Arsbok* 44 (1979) 194–199; H. Räisänen, *Paul and the Law*, 8–9; E. P. Sanders, *Paul, the Law*, 148–149.

36. See also U. Wilckens, "Zur Entwicklung des paulinischen Gesetzesverständnis," NTS 28 (1982) 154–190; U. Schnelle, *Wandlungen*, 54–71.

In the eighth and final place we note the prominent attitude[37] that considers the Law as *good in itself, but incapable of redeeming,* for it can only indicate God's will for people and outline the sanctions for transgressions, but is simply incapable of justifying the transgressor, i.e., the sinner, so that "the Law, which should have brought life, brought death" (Rom 7:10), not because by its nature it tends to produce death, but because by being violated it reveals the sin in me that actually does lead to death (see Rom 6:23a, 7:8b). This reasoning (even if the Pauline concept of sin requires better definition, see vol. 1, chap. 8, III) is especially faithful to Paul, even because it recognizes that for him the Law was observed by Israel precisely in view of justification (see Rom 9:31) and that from the Jewish point of view "it is not those who hear the Law that are just before God, but those who keep the Law will be justified" (Rom 2:13). Still, there are certain questions that build on this basic position. Is the goodness of the Law really radical, in that it comes from God (as Rom 7:12, 14 would suggest), or is it secondary because it was given only by the angels (thus Gal 3:19-21)? And does the "curse" that Paul attributes to the Law (see Rom 4:15; Gal 3:10) derive only from the fact that it is impossible for a person to keep the whole Law,[38] or is it the Law as such that is considered radically powerless and incapable of justifying?[39] And then, does the redemption accomplished by God in Jesus Christ only help one to observe the Law fully (even if we consider it all included in the commandment of love), as one could not have done without grace, or has it so fundamentally surpassed legalistic categories that the decisive relationship between God and us is no longer determined by anything like an ethical observance?[40]

37. Today essentially held in common by Catholics and Protestants alike; note the most recent monograph by R. Liebers, *Das Gesetz als Evangelium,* 237–244.

38. Thus H. Räisänen, *Paul and the Law,* 94ff., comments on Gal 3:10: the weakness is in the human person. See also J. Lambrecht, "Gesetzesverständnis bei Paulus," in K. Kertelge, ed., *Das Gesetz im Neuen Testament,* QD 108 (Freiburg-Basel-Vienna, 1986) 88–127, esp. 113–116.

39. Thus E. P. Sanders, *Paul, the Law,* 19–27, commenting on the same text: the weakness is in the Law itself. Paul's declaration about the justifying intent is made only with regard to Israel and from Israel's point of view, but Paul knows that in Christ God excludes from the Law any possibility of justification (see Gal 3:21-22). Therefore there is no justification for the position of K. Snodgrass, "Spheres of Influence: A Possible Solution to the Problem of Paul and the Law," JSNT 32 (1988) 93–113, which claims that the Law is negative only in the sphere of sin, while it is positively valid for life in the sphere of Christ, the Spirit, and faith.

40. A good answer to this question maintaining the second alternative would be obtained by an adequate exegetical examination of Rom 8:4 with reference to τὸ δικαίωμα τοῦ νόμου (which the Italian Episcopal Conference version translates generically "the justice of the law"); although we cannot undertake this here, see the study of L. A. Keck, "The Law and 'the Law of Sin and Death' (Rom 8:1-4): Reflections on the Spirit and Ethics in Saint Paul," in J. L. Crenshaw and S. Sandmel, eds., *The Divine Helmsman: Studies on God's Control of Human Events. Presented to L. H. Silberman* (New York, 1980) 41–57; and also the commentary of E. Käsemann, ad loc.

An adequate response to each of these questions would require more than these few pages. But just formulating them is no small help toward clearing the field of the clouds of confusion, thus clarifying what is at issue and indicating the actual paths open to research.

III. Some important clarifications

Unable here to exhaust the problems inherent in the Pauline theme of the Law, and especially unable to reply to all the questions it raises, we will only try to suggest a solution to some of its basic aspects.

1) In the first place we identify *the fundamental meaning Paul attributes to the Law*. What is important is to recognize that he is not preparing some kind of abstract presentation of human self-justification, as if the Law were simply the objective aggregation of all human desire for self-affirmation. There are, it is true, two passages that seem especially to indicate something of the sort: Rom 2:14-15 and Rom 4:4-5. The first even attributes to the gentiles the possibility of accomplishing what the law requires, so that the underlying Hellenistic concept of the *nomos agraphos* ("unwritten law" or "law written in the hearts") seems to lead Paul's discourse on to such a level of universality that religious distinctions are lost sight of. But actually, when we consider the context, these affirmations are made only to decrease the absolute importance of the Mosaic Law, and to say that God is impartial to gentiles and to Jews alike, so that these latter can boast no special privilege (see Rom 1:18–2:29).[41]

The second passage reasons about the execution of the works of the law as a basis of claims for the one who observes it—almost by way of contract—over against God, who thus becomes debtor to the human person. This likewise seems to enunciate a generally valid principle that would include any moral claim and any type of religious relationship between human beings and God, thus reducing the law to nothing but a temptation to overconfidence. But actually, it is again the context that provides the corrective reading lenses: Paul is speaking of the pure faith of Abraham, who was, after all, justified by this faith rather than through the keeping of the Law, which had not yet been given (see Rom 4:1-22). Once again the reference is to the Mosaic Law.

Hence, the Pauline polemic against the Law must be seen historically in relation to the Judaism of the time, in which the Torah had become so much an absolute as to be identified with the wisdom of God (see Sir 24:21, 30-31; Bar 3:32–4:4) and with the universal order of all creation (*Eth. Henoch*

41. See vol. 1, chap. 6, and more generally chap. 4.

81:1-2; *Jub.* 3:10, 31; 4:5, etc.): when this was done it is not just that the Law became wisdom, but especially that wisdom became contained within the Law.[42] Therefore Paul, except for the passages where νόμος refers to the Pentateuch or to Scripture in general, normally means to speak of the Mosaic Law, which, though on one hand it is the gift of God's grace to Israel and the incarnation of his salvific will (see Rom 2:20), on the other hand is made up of a set of prescriptions that are to be kept and are not to be broken (note the verbs ποιεῖν, "do"; φυλάσσειν, "keep"; ἐργάζειν, "work"; πράσσειν, "do").

The objection could be made: Does not such a historical approach to Paul's idea deprive it of a universal meaning that does belong to it? And what significance does such a reading have for us? These are, of course, two questions.

a) The Pauline problematic constantly keeps alive in the Christian's consciousness the question of our relationship to Judaism. The confrontation of Christians with what Israel still thinks of the Mosaic Law has contributed greatly to a constant rediscovery of their identity, from the first controversies (with Jesus, Stephen, and Paul) to the present time.

b) The problem of the Law, even if considered historically, still gives rise to healthy scandal and provokes a twofold clarification (1) of the nature of sin (and so of the unredeemed human situation, and in this sense what Paul says of the Law cannot help but be paradigmatic of a condition that is not limited to Judaism), and (2) of the depth of God's grace, which in Christ most generously grants that forgiveness of sins (and of sin!) that the Law, and any law, neither could nor can offer.

2) *The Law of Moses and Christ.* The Jewish conception of the mediating and saving function of the Torah is rejected by Paul not because he considers the Law weak and imperfect, but because he recognizes that henceforth the definitive revelation of the "righteousness of God," i.e., of the merciful restoration of the right relationship for human beings with God, took place in Jesus Christ, and especially in his death on the cross. The Apostle's point of departure is not a reflection on the defects of the Law and anguish that comes from one's failure to fulfill it.

Rather, Paul begins with his own encounter with Christ, and with the way in which Christ has literally turned upside down all previous values. "What was for me an advantage, has become a loss for me because of Christ" (Phil 3:7); and the Law was surely the "advantage" par excel-

---

42. See especially M. Limbeck, *Die Ordnung des Heils. Untersuchungen zum Gesetzesverständnis des Frühjudentums* (Düsseldorf, 1971); and also E. J. Schnabel, *Law and Wisdom*, with bibliography.

lence, i.e., what the Pharisee Saul considered the greatest privilege he had. So if the Law has expired in Paul's eyes, it is not through some internal collapse of its values but by the new arrival from outside of something (indeed, of someone) that was greater than it. No one has emphasized this aspect more than E. P. Sanders, synthesizing it perfectly in the phrase that for Paul "the solution preceded the problem."[43] To speak exactly, we should say that Paul is developing a Christology rather than a Toralogy. Were it not for the encounter with Christ, there would be no criticism of the Law. Only the contemplation of Christ and of the event that took place in him is capable of causing the function of the Law to be obscured and to expire, however "holy the Law" may be, "and holy and just and good the commandment" (Rom 7:12). In Christ there is something more, which the Law never counted on and with which God himself wanted to prevail over the age of minority and the time of servitude (see Gal 4:1-6). Henceforth "the end of the Law is Christ, that righteousness may be given to whoever believes" (Rom 10:4).

What Judaism sees in the Law, Paul sees in Christ. This means that the ancient Jewish conception of the Law is taken up and preserved, with the sole difference that henceforth it is transferred to Christ.[44] So now the universal access of the peoples to God no longer passes through the Law but through Christ, our new "wisdom from God, justification, sanctification, and redemption" (1 Cor 1:30), so that we can no longer glory in the Law but only in Christ (see Gal 6:14). Attachment to a code or to any demanding word of God that at any moment may become a "dead letter" (see 2 Cor 3:6; Rom 7:6) is now replaced by attachment to a living

43. See *Paul and Palestinian Judaism*, 442–447 [Penna quotes the title of a section from the Italian edition; in the original English the title is "The solution as preceding the problem"— T.P.W.]; also, *Paul, the Law*, 149–154; T. L. Donaldson, "Zealot and Convert," 667–668. Most recently F. Thielman, *From Plight to Solution: A Jewish Framework for Understanding Paul's View of the Law in Galatians and Romans*, NT Suppl. 61 (Leiden, 1989), while appearing to declare the contrary in the title, actually tries only to establish a parallel between the Jewish conception of what will become of the Law in Israel (in the *eschaton* God will liberate his people both from sin and from the Law's condemnation for sinners) and Paul's concept of what has become of the Law for humanity (since the *eschaton* has already begun, God has already freed humanity from both.) Actually, Sanders' epigram should basically be applied to Paul's personal experience, and not so much to the judgment Paul makes of the situation of humanity without Christ, for example in Rom 1:18–3:20. There a pattern is at work that was already Jewish, and especially typical of the apocalyptic vision of history and of the world (with clear biblical links). All that Paul does is to attribute to Christ (and scandalously to his cross) as actually taking place, what Judaism expected only from the eschatological future. We should add, though, that the Christian attitude is parallel to a Jewish pattern that is at least partly valid for the present, i.e., as Israel by adhering to the Torah separates itself from the lost situation of the gentiles, from whom it keeps its distance, Christians likewise by adhering to Christ acquire a new way of judging the world (with which—to add to the scandal—Israel itself is now identified insofar as it opposes the gospel).

44. See the following chapter 24.

and life-giving person in the gift of communion with him. Hence passages like Rom 1:18–2:29 (which quickly traces a dark picture of the objective human condition of distress and sin, which are not overcome by clinging to the Law) and Rom 7:7-25 (which sketches the picture of a subjective situation of internal anguish and the frustrating experience of powerlessness under the external principle of the Law) flowed from Paul's pen on the basis not of a socio-religious or psycho-religious analysis of the human person, but on the basis of his attitude of radical faith in Christ, derived from the experience of Christ's hitherto unimagined and utterly incomparable meaning for humankind: before him not only does the whole appearance of Jewish Law and Greek wisdom change, but the whole poverty and emptiness of the human condition without Christ is laid bare.

Now, even a pagan like Ovid can acknowledge that he sees the better and approves it, but even so follows the worse:[45] but in his case the problem precedes the solution and simply remains without any solution! But the personal experience of Paul (which could also be the case with every Christian) shows how one can be perfectly satisfied with oneself and the values that fill one's life (see Phil 3:5-6: ''. . . Hebrew of Hebrews; as for the Law, a Pharisee; as for zeal, persecuting the Churches; as for the righteousness coming from the Law, blameless''), and still it is possible to discover something one could not have imagined that totally overturns these values because it is unexpectedly discovered to be greater and more noble, even though these had previously seemed worthy of total dedication. This is how Christ surpasses the Law, simply by what he is and what God has done in him. He is great in himself, not through the deficiencies of the Law. For these are not even perceived apart from him (note Deut 4:32: ''Was there ever anything like this?'') Christ is not just a fixer—he does not just take care of human inadequacies, filling up the the voids. He also can add more to what is already presumed to be full. And it is only his overflowing presence that shows up otherwise unsuspected deficiencies. The time of the Law is past only because he has appeared; and prescinding from the Law, with him the ''new creation'' is possible.

3) Even so, Paul *devotes some quite substantial passages of his letters to exhorting Christians,* calling for specific behavior from them (e.g., Rom 12–13), apparently demanding of them (at least this can be the first impression) what had been imposed by the very Mosaic Law he has criticized (besides the passage cited, see almost all of 1 Corinthians and also 2 Cor 12:20–13:10; Gal 5:16–6:10; Phil 2:1-5, 12-18; 3:15ff.; etc.) Is he bring-

45. Ovid, *Metamorph.* 7:17ff.; note other similar material from antiquity in G. Theissen, *Psychological Aspects,* 212–219.

ing back through the window what he had thrown out the door? On this question we must make three important observations.

First of all, we must note that paraenesis and hence moral duty have an absolutely necessary place and function in Christian life, provided they remain in their proper function. There is a text in Paul that has a validity similar to that of a first principle in philosophy: "In Christ Jesus what counts is not circumcision or uncircumcision, but faith working through love" (Gal 5:6). Then faith standing alone is not acceptable. Still, faith remains the basis, the point of departure, the indication of the key at the beginning of a musical staff, without which nothing makes sense. But just for this reason it must support and even stimulate corresponding outward behavior. Not that faith derives from the works of love, since "one is not justified by works of the Law, but only through faith in Jesus Christ" (Gal 2:16); on the contrary, faith must show its fruitfulness and produce works that befit it, so that James can write: "Faith without works is dead" (Jas 2:26), i.e., sterile, being without fruit. It is in view of this that Luther himself (something too often forgotten by Catholic controversialists in the past) can openly declare: "When I exalt faith and reject the works of unbelief, they accuse me of forbidding good works, whereas I should actually like to teach the true good works of faith," since faith without works is a "fanatic abstraction, a pure vanity and a dream of the heart."[46] Therefore Christians, while deriving their deepest identity from a purely gratuitous act of grace done by God in Christ, still manifest this identity in a life lived in working taught by a demanding love (of which 1 Cor 13 is the hymn of praise). Just as there cannot be a love that can be called Christian if it is not anchored in and instigated by faith in Christ, so there cannot be a full and vital faith if it is not externalized, made somehow visible and efficacious in the daily responsibility of love.[47]

But in the second place, an important observation leads us to ascertain that *Paul never bases his paraenesis on the text of the Torah.* This is surprising if we consider Paul's Pharisaic education and the whole cultural setting that explains the normal rabbinic practice. There is not a passage in his letters where he bases the Christian *halakah* on any legal regulation of the

46. See these citations and others in V. Subilia, *La giustificazione per fede* (Brescia: Paideia, 1976) 198–201.

47. Still, we must always remember what Saint Thomas Aquinas has to say about Rom 4:5: "[Paul] shows how the outward reward is related to faith, saying, 'To one who does not work,' that is, outward works, e.g., because there is no time to work, as in the case of one who dies immediately after being baptized (*sicut patet in baptizato statim mortuo*), 'but believes in the One who justifies the ungodly,' i.e., God, 'that person's faith,' i.e., alone without outward works, 'will be counted for righteousness,' so that through this, this person will be called just and receive the reward of righteousness as if they had actually done the works of justice" (*Super epistolas S. Pauli*, ed. Cai., I, 59, n. 330).

Old Testament. The sole exception would seem to be Lev 19:18 ("You shall love your neighbor as yourself"), echoed in Gal 5:14; Rom 13:9. But this is interpreted in an original way, as a summary of the whole law, and especially because it acquires its real value not just as a "scriptural" norm but from the fact that it is subject to a new hermeneutical principle, which is the love of Christ, who "loved me, and gave himself up for me" (Gal 2:20; cf. Rom 8:32).[48] This does not mean that the Old Testament loses its value as Scripture *(γραφή)*, which he keeps substantially intact (despite Marcion), but it does lose its authority as Law *(νόμος)*, so that the frequent use of biblical passages (especially drawn from the wisdom books!) that Paul does make in his paraenetic sections actually functions only for vivid expression, or at most as commentary, but is not really the basis of his ethical instruction.[49]

In the third place, we should note that *Paul presents his moral instructions as exhortation rather than law.* Legal terminology is absent from the paraenesis; his recommendations, even if pressing (note 2 Cor 13:2: "When I come again I shall not pardon"!), are never identified with any of the terms that the Septuagint had used to translate the abundant legal-prescriptive vocabulary of the Hebrew Scriptures: νόμος, νόμιμος, πρόσταγμα, ἐπιταγή, διάταξις, σύνταξις, δίκη, ἐνδίκησις, δικαίωμα, κελεύειν ("law, precept," etc.). All these expressions, which at least traditionally express legal imposition, are absent from Paul's paraenesis. At times he makes use of the verbs meaning "order/direct," παραγγέλλειν (1 Thess 4:2, 11; 1 Cor 7:10; 11:17); and διατάσσειν (1 Cor 7:17; 11:34; 16:1); and "judge," κρίνειν (1 Cor 5:3 only); and of the noun ἐντολή, "command" (1 Cor 14:37 only). But besides being rare (and also they are all in two of the oldest letters, 1 Thessalonians and 1 Corinthians, but never in Galatians or Romans, which actually develop the problem of the Law!), the expressions represent the normal exercise of apostolic authority, "which the Lord has given me to build up and not to destroy" (2 Cor 10:8; 13:10), which he can also renounce (note Phlm 8-9: "Though I have in Christ full liberty to command you to do what you must, I would rather appeal to you for love's sake") and which in any case he means to exercise in anything but an inquisitorial

48. See chap. 21 above. However, it is not appropriate to speak, as J. S. Marino does, *Saint Paul and the Law,* of a "law of love" (pp. 35–64 *passim*) that would have "canonical implications" (see pp. 238–275), since not only does Paul himself not use such terms (see below), but, as Marino recognizes, "his norms are not based upon the Law, but on the faith in Jesus Christ" (p. 295).

49. This is basically the understanding of W. Schrage, *The Ethics of the New Testament* (Philadelphia, ca. 1988 [Göttingen, 1982]) 201–207; and especially A. Lindemann, "Die Biblischen Toragebote und die paulinische Ethik," in *Studien zum Text und zur Ethik des Neuen Testaments,* ed. W. Schrage (Berlin, 1986) 242–265. In the light of this, the position of E. J. Schnabel, *Law and Wisdom,* 313–314, requires slight modification.

way (note 2 Cor 1:24: "Not that we lord it over your faith, rather, we are fellow-workers in your joy").[50]

Paul, rather, is satisfied to ἐρωτᾶν, "ask/beseech" (1 Thess 4:1; 5:12; Phil 4:3); but above all he prefers to "exhort" παρακαλεῖν, a word he uses some twenty times in his authentic letters (first person active, singular or plural), and which more than any other expresses not an imposition but the pastoral solicitude that takes well into account the responsible dignity of the Christian adults to whom it is addressed.[51] The fact is that Paul takes up not the attitude of legislator toward the Christians of his Churches but that of father (1 Cor 4:14-15; 2 Cor 6:13; Gal 4:19; 1 Thess 2:11) and even of mother (1 Thess 2:7). Their reciprocal relationship is expressed not in juridical but in familial terms: he regularly addresses the recipients as ἀδελφοί, "brethren," or τέκνα, "children." Such a situation neither could nor can be typified as the impersonal coldness of a legal order, not even if it is presented as God's will, since "against such things there is no law" (Gal 5:23). Actually, Gal 6:2 does speak of the "law of Christ" (see also 1 Cor 9:21), which is fulfilled by carrying one another's burdens; but this is a very special text, which would require a more extensive treatment to show that this does not really contradict the thesis we have presented.[52]

4) To conclude, we will only succeed in detaching ourselves from a legalistic reading of Paul if we come to understand that according to him

---

50. On this question see J. H. Schütz, *Paul and the Anatomy of Apostolic Authority*, SNTS MS 26 (Cambridge, 1975); and above all B. Holmberg, *Paul and Power: The Structure of Authority in the Primitive Church as Reflected in the Pauline Epistles*, CB NTS 11 (Lund, 1978) 82–88, which among the verbs of authority also includes some occurrences of the verb λέγω, "I say" (Rom 12:3; 1 Cor 7:12; Gal 5:2) and θέλω, "I want" (Rom 16:19; 1 Cor 7:32; 10:20; 11:3).

51. Note the foundational monograph of C. J. Bjerkelund, *Parakalô* (Oslo, 1967). Also H. Schlier, "Die Eigenart der christlichen Mahnung nach dem Apostel Paulus," *Besinnung auf das Neue Testament* (Freiburg–Basel–Vienna, 1964 [Italian: 1969]) 340–357 (this study is not among the selections from this volume in *The Relevance of the New Testament* [New York, 1968]); J. J. H. McDonald, *Kerygma and Didache*, SNTS MS 37 (Cambridge, 1980), esp. chap. 3.

52. Actually this text can be interpreted in four different ways. (1) The "law of Christ" is simply the Law of Moses, in that now it is only in Christ that the observance is possible (thus A. Van Dülmen, *Die Theologie des Gesetzes bei Paulus*, SBM 5 [Stuttgart, 1968], 67–68). (2) The "law of Christ" in opposition to the Law of Moses, it is the "law of the Messiah" and is identified with the authoritative code of the words of Jesus, such as the Sermon on the Mount (thus C. H. Dodd, "*Ennomos Christoû*," in *Studia Paulina, in honorem J. de Zwaan* [Haarlem, 1953] 96–110). (3) The "law of Christ" in practice is reduced to the commandment of mutual love given by Jesus, which is formulated most clearly in John 13:34 and also in Mark 12:31 (this is the most common thesis: see, for example, the commentary of F. Mussner). (4) Finally, it is possible to read in the expression "law of Christ" either a purely metaphorical and hence generic value for the word νόμος, so as to understand it as "the way of life characteristic of the Church of Christ" (thus H. Räisänen, *Paul and the Law*, 80–82), or simply an epexegetical genitive, so as to understand it as "Christ as the Law" of the Christian (thus O. Hofius, "Das Gesetz des Mose und das Gesetz Christi," ZThK 80 [1983] 262–286; R. B. Hays, "Christology and Ethics in Galatians: The Law of Christ," CBQ 49 [1987] 268–290). This fourth position seems best to me.

henceforth *the primary, fundamental reality for the Christian is liberty*, not Law. "Christ has set us free so that we may be free" (Gal 5:1). "The law of the Spirit that gives life in Christ Jesus has freed you from the law of sin and death" (Rom 8:2). "And where the Spirit of the Lord is, there is freedom" (2 Cor 3:17). Christians are not "children of a slave, but of a free woman" (Gal 4:31) and the whole allegory of the descent of the two sons of Abraham (Gal 4:21-31). But the freedom of which Paul speaks is not just an interior, spiritual freedom from the metaphysical realities of sin/flesh/death but also an outward historical and religious freedom from the Law of Moses: "You who seek justification in the Law are severed from Christ, you have fallen from grace" (Gal 5:4; see 2:21).[53] It is precisely this Pauline vindication of freedom that the Jewish Christian wing of the earliest Christian Church well understood, so that they accused Paul of apostasy (see above); thus he can rightly be described as the Apostle of freedom.[54]

But we must be very precise.[55] Freedom for Paul is not so much the counterpoint to Law; rather, freedom finds its precise antithesis nowhere else but in sin, which represents its complete negation. Law and sin, while placed in opposition, together make up the two poles of a self-enclosed system; they are indivisibly dependent one on the other. This system is overcome only by Christ, who represents the real alternative to νόμος (i.e., law) and ἀνομία (i.e., sin) alike. Christ puts an end both to the Law (cf. Rom 10:4) and to the sin linked to it (cf. Rom 7:24–8:2). And liberty is connected to him alone and to his Spirit. But this is defined not negatively as an abrogation of the Law but positively as an eschatological good that

53. This theme is developed especially in Galatians: see C. K. Barrett, *Freedom and Obligation: A Study of the Epistle to the Galatians* (London, 1985); and especially I. Herman, *Liberi in Cristo. Saggi Esegetici sulla libertà dalla Legge nella Lettera ai Galati*, SPAA 27 (Rome, 1986).
54. Note that the lexical family ἐλευθ-, "free-" (adjective, noun, and verb), is used by Paul some thirty out of forty-four occurrences in the whole New Testament (while in the whole vast text of the Old Testament it is present only thirty-three times!)
55. Among the studies of freedom in Paul, see the most recent monograph by S. Vollenweider, *Freiheit als neue Schöpfung. Eine Untersuchung zur Eleutheria bei Paulus und in seiner Umwelt*, FRLANT 147 (Göttingen, 1989) with bibliography. The author (arguing against F. St. Jones, *"Freiheit" in den Briefen des Apostels Paulus*, GThA 34, [Göttingen, 1987]) correctly maintains that Paul's message about freedom and the Law is central to his theology, and that it not only has forerunners in pre-Pauline Christianity but has its true historical anticipations (not its origin, which is in the Christ-event) in Greek philosophy, where, unlike in Judaism, there already was controversy about νόμος with a characteristic contrast between the written and the unwritten law. But I should maintain that we must specify that there is at least one aspect to Paul's criticism of the Law that has no Greek precedent, the connection between Law and sin (Rom 7:23; 1 Cor 15:46): as Chrysippus puts it so well, "The law is no accomplice to its transgression, just as the gods are no accomplice to impiety" (SVF II 326:35). For this thematic sphere we must identify an apocalyptic matrix, which (admittedly in general terms) actually was treated by S. Vollenweider himself, "Zeit und Gesetz. Erwägungen zur Bedeutung apokalyptischer Denkformen bei Paulus," ThZ 44 (1988) 97–116.

brings about the new human being—it is not an absence but an acquisition. It stands beyond nomism and antinomism alike. It is a category of a completely different genus, understandable on a different level, touching the ontological and the metahistorical: that of the *eschaton*, where "they need no longer teach one another" (Jer 31:34), since love is the measure of all (cf. 1 Cor 13.) The freedom of the Christian is measured not by the Law but by Jesus Christ. It is not a lack but a fullness. It is precisely the offer here and now of such liberty that represents the kernel of the gospel according to Paul. The announcement and the proposal of this gospel does make this truly "good news," such as the imposition of a commandment to observe with works could not be. It is gospel not because it demands but because it gives: and the gift is freedom.

Even so, precisely because Christian freedom takes place existentially in *agape* (cf. Gal 5:13-14), this places the Christian in a new condition of servitude, paradoxically. Actually, the Christian is free only in order to love more and better. For the Christian, to "stand fast" (Gal 5:1) means to stand "with fixed feet, remaining in freedom" (Thomas Aquinas, *Ad Galatas*, 277). But if it is true that the "condition of standing is freedom," it is also true that "the way of standing is through love" (Saint Thomas, ibid., 299, 301). Now, nothing is more demanding than love; the word used by Paul, δουλεύειν (Gal 5:13), means not just "serve" but rather "serve as a slave," since it alludes more to a state than to a function: "A slave is one who, putting aside what is useful to self, adapts to the needs of the other" (Saint Thomas, ibid., 302). Hence the Christian lives and experiences in self this antinomy of freedom and slavery. In fact, "a Christian is a free lord over everything, and is subject to no one; a Christian is a voluntary servant in everything, and subject to everyone" (M. Luther, *De libertate christiana* 1).

This is why no one has more liberty than the Christian, and no one takes fewer liberties. Thus there is reinstated an ascetic exigency that is more rigorous than that demanded by the Torah, precisely because it is not a question of norms given by a ready-made code. The Christian lives, so to speak, "without a net," with the only principle being love, which has no real measure ("Though free from everyone, I make myself a slave to everyone": 1 Cor 9:19).[56] The fact is that instead of a written law the

---

56. This does not exhaust all there is to to say about Paul's moral paraenesis, i.e., about Pauline ethic (for a methodological discussion about this, see chapter 25 below, and G. Segalla, *Introduzione all'etica biblica del Nuovo Testamento. Problemi e storia*, BB 2 [Brescia, 1989] 193–225). The problems concern the question of criteria, content, cultural conditioning, and hence the permanent validity of such an ethic. For us now, it is enough to emphasize that what is specific to Christian morality according to Paul does not consist in the observance only of the Torah, nor even of the natural law as such (even though elements of them both can sur-

Christian has as the only norm of reference Christ himself, who, when I was still a sinner (see Rom 5:6-8), "loved me and gave himself up for me" (Gal 2:20). He and his cross are the real surpassing of the Law. He and his cross are, then, the true law of the Christian.

---

vive, e.g., the Decalogue), but in a Christological criterion that by its nature is essentially open to needs and cultural situations that are not predetermined (whereby even the Torah can be reduced to one element of tradition like others): what is important is adherence to Christ. By analogy, note the similar important distinction made by Moses Maimonides concerning the gentiles: everyone who accepts the seven [Noachic] commandments [the Noachic commandments: prohibition of blasphemy, idolatry, adultery, murder, stealing, eating meat cut from a living animal, and the injunction to set up courts] and observes them carefully is one of the righteous of the nations of the world. . . . But he must accept and observe them on the ground that the Holy One, blessed be he, commanded them. . . . But if he practices them on the basis of his own rational considerations, he is not . . . one of the righteous of the nations of the world, but one of their sages" (cited by L. Gaston, *Paul and the Torah* [Vancouver, 1987] 23–24; see *b. Sanh.* 56a, *Ber.R.* 34:8; to *Av.Z.* 8:4)! Analogously, Christians are called to transfigure their own ethos thoroughly, whatever becomes of its contents, in the light of being in Christ; otherwise it is simply not truly Christian.

Chapter 24

Dissolution and Restoration
of the Relationship of Law and Wisdom in Paul

Preliminaries

1) *Status quaestionis*. The two basic Jewish treasures "Law" and "Wisdom," *torah/νόμος*, and *ḥokmah/σοφία*, with reference to Paul's perspective, have been the object of many studies. The former has enjoyed the greater attention, to be sure, doubtless because of its higher profile, the earliest studies dating to the 1870s.[1] The latter comes to the attention of Paulinists with a study by H. Windisch in 1914.[2] Bibliographies of each for later years can be found in recent studies.[3] But what has not been adequately studied is the relationship between the two elements, not so much on the level of canonical and extra-canonical Jewish theology (where publications are not lacking), but rather in the area of Pauline theology. An attempt to fill the present void has been made in E. J. Schnabel's 1985 book.[4] He has certainly produced a work of great breadth, which approaches Paul by way of ben Sira, with the unquestionable merit of

1. See the large bibliography, current up to 1960, in H. Schlier, *Der Brief an die Galater* (Göttingen, 1972) 176–177, n. 2: dating to the late nineteenth century are works by A. Zahn, R. Tilling, E. Grafe, Sieffert; also, see above, in the previous chapter, n. 1.

2. H. Windisch, "Die göttliche Weisheit der Juden und die paulinische Christologie," in *Neutestamentliche Studien. Festschrift G. Heinrici*, ed. A. Deissmann (Leipzig, 1914) 220–234; according to the author, "essential traits of the Pauline Christ derive from Jewish wisdom" (221); "The pre-existing Christ of the New Testament, especially for Paul, is the divine wisdom of the Jews" (232), but while 1 Henoch, Wisdom, and Philo set other hypostases alongside Wisdom (Spirit, *Logos*, Soul of the World), Paul is more simple, concentrating everything in Christ (see 233–234).

3. Esp. E. J. Schnabel, *Law and Wisdom from Ben Sira to Paul: A Tradition Historical Enquiry into Relation of Law, Wisdom, and Ethics*, WUNT 2:16 (Tübingen, 1985): Law: 264–271; Wisdom: 237–240.

4. See the preceding note. Also M. D. Ryan, "The Acts of Religious Identification in Ben Sirach and Paul," *Drew Gateway* 54 (1983) 4–16 (unexamined).

presenting Paul's thought against the great backdrop of Judaism from the second century B.C. to the first century A.D. Schnabel's work is very rich in data, with minute analysis, though perhaps a bit like a dry catalogue; however, it is based on certain methodological tenets that I cannot say I share.[5] So in this study I plan to exclude Colossians from the list of authentic Pauline letters, even though by doing so I am cutting off material that certainly belongs to the Christian "sophiology" of the first century. Consequently, I am here limiting myself to the so-called *Hauptbriefe* (1–2 Corinthians, Galatians, Romans).

2) I take for granted the cultural background of the Jewish world with regard to our subject. Judaism, from which Paul comes and in which he moves, is characterized by an identification between Law and wisdom, which at least since ben Sira in the second century B.C. endowed Israel's patrimony of ideas and practice with certain important new factors, which we will briefly recall:

a) The Torah acquired the universal and divine dimensions of wisdom, becoming an absolute from which one could not withdraw without violating the cosmic order itself.[6]

b) Wisdom in turn has adopted the lineaments and specific contents of Jewish Law, so that from ben Sira on, *ḥakām*, "wise," and *sofēr*, "scribe," become equivalent and superimposed, so that Judaism tends to become more and more a religion of the book.[7]

c) Because of this irreversible function on the theoretical, intellectual level, the concrete life of the pious Jew will be considered wise insofar as it strictly conforms to the Law, and correlatively the observance of the Law will confer the only possible dimension of wisdom;[8] indeed, what Prov 3–4 says about the necessity of acquiring wisdom and walking in it

5. For example, historically Schnabel considers Galatians the first letter written by Paul and thinks of Colossians as authentic (see p. 235, n. 47); hermeneutically he is perhaps a little hasty and too direct in identifying wisdom with Christ (see p. 262). Furthermore, he attributes to Paul an unacceptable conception of Israel's attitude toward the Law, as having "degenerated into *gramma*, 'letter' " (pp. 292–293, along the line of H. Hübner); also, he extends the identification to the sphere of Pauline ethic, whereas Paul never uses the vocabulary of Law in a paraenetic context; and above all, he does not notice that the relationship between Law and wisdom, while indeed dissolved by Paul, was restored by him on a higher level.

6. See M. Limbeck, *Die Ordnung des Heils. Untersuchungen zum Gesetzverständnis des Frühjudentums* (Düsseldorf, 1971), which documents this claim on the basis of Qumran; for rabbinism, see briefly A. Cohen, *Il Talmud* (Bari, 1984 = 1935) 170.

7. See M. Küchler, *Frühjüdische Weisheitstraditionen. Zum Fortgang weisheitlichen Denkens im Bereich des frühjüdischen Jahweglaubens*, OBO 26 (Freiburg Schw.–Göttingen, 1979) esp. 33–61; E. J. Schnabel, *Law and Wisdom*, 63–69 (Excursus 1: The Identity and History of the Sopherim).

8. This is seen even in martyrdom, for 4 Macc 7:7 lauds the old man Eleazar as "a man in harmony with the Law, and a philosopher of a divine existence," since he dies for the Law, which he calls παιδευτής, "educational" (see 5:34; 6:27).

with perseverance, an anonymous rabbi of the first century A.D., whom the *Pirqê Abôt* calls "son of Bag-Bag," attributes to the Law alone, admonishing, "Keep turning it over, everything is in it; meditate on it, grow old and and be consumed in it; and do not depart from it, for there is nothing better for you than this" (*m. Ab.* 5:21; after the translation of V. Castiglioni).

Now, Paul comes from this world, which by equating Law with wisdom had defined itself by a specific cultural enterprise, with enormous consequences that make the daring anti-conformist position he espouses all the more unthinkable.

I. Crisis of the "nomos"

This is surely not the place to discuss the whole Pauline conception of the νόμος. Moreover, this has been done repeatedly in recent years from various points of view.[9] The fact is that Paul's thought on the issue is complex and probably never did reach a true logical maturity, as H. Räisänen maintains, enthusiastically emphasizing the tensions and contradictions.[10]

Still, for our purposes I should think that we could observe and emphasize certain points.

1) In the first place, we can determine from his letters that the identification of Law with wisdom was well known to Paul. We deduce this basically from three different texts in Romans.

In Rom 2:14-15, in the context of God's impartiality between Jews and gentiles, and hence the uselessness of boasting about possessing the written Law if it is not observed, Paul proposes the principle that before God and from the Jewish point of view it is not the hearers of the Law that are justified but those who observe it. He illustrates this with the example of the gentiles, who "do not have the Law, but by nature do what belongs to the Law" (2:14), thus showing that they have "what the Law demands written in their hearts, with their consciences bearing witness for them" (2:15). That the Hellenistic ethical theme of the νόμος ἄγραφος is echoed here is recognized by some commentators.[11] But I should also like to call attention to possible wisdom elements in this conception. For

9. See at least the studies of H. Hübner, 1977, 1982³; E. P. Sanders, 1977 and 1983; H. Räisänen, 1983; R. H. Gundry in Bib 66 (1985) 1–38; H. Weder, in NTS 31 (1985) 357–376. See the preceding chapter.
10. See H. Räisänen, *Paul and the Law*, WUNT 29 (Tübingen, 1983) 10–15; but his theory of *secondary rationalization* (201) seems to me to outstrip his premises.
11. See C. E. B. Cranfield, *The Epistle to the Romans*, I, ICC (Edinburgh, 1982 [= 1975]), 160; U. Wilckens, *Der Brief an die Römer (Röm 1–5)* I, EKK VI/I (Zurich–Neukirchen, 1978) 133–135. On Hellenism see R. Hirzel, *Agraphos Nomos*, (New York, 1979 [= reprint: Leipzig, 1900]).

example, it surely means something that the terms φύσις, "nature," and συνείδησις, "conscience," occur in the Greek of the Septuagint only in writings of a sapiential character.[12] And this lexical observation corresponds well to the universalistic conception of Jewish wisdom in the Hellenistic era, according to which Wisdom has "held dominion over every people and nation" (Sir 24:6 [10]; cf. 1:9-10); and it is also ben Sira who speaks of the νόμος ζωῆς given to every person (17:11). The Law, then, is a universally valid form of wisdom.[13] And while Philo of Alexandria maintains that the "person submitting to the Law" (νόμιμος ἀνήρ) is, as such, a citizen of the world, since the actions of such a person are conformed "to the will of nature" (πρὸς τὸ βούλημα τῆς φύσεως: Opif. 3; cf. Abr. 276), Paul declares inversely—but equivalently—that one who conforms to nature thereby accomplishes "what belongs to the Law," τὰ τοῦ νόμου (Rom 2:14).[14]

In Rom 2:17-24, pursuing the subject of the inappropriateness of the dichotomy of Israel's boasting about the Law but not observing it, Paul describes the Jew as one who has τὴν μόρφωσιν τῆς γνώσεως καὶ τῆς ἀληθείας ἐν τῷ νόμῳ (2:20c),[15] i.e., the one who has in the Law the "actual embodiment[16] of absolute knowledge and truth." This definition of νόμος clearly implies its identification with wisdom, even with divine wisdom, since it incorporates "knowledge and truth" absolutely, without any further specification. It is as if to say that "God's wisdom, which is truth pure and simple," and as such the source of knowledge, "has assumed a recognizable form in the Torah."[17] The background of this declaration is found in texts like Sir 24:22; Bar 4:1. And the Jewish self-understanding, which Paul here describes, of being "guide to the blind, light to those in darkness, teacher of the ignorant, master of children" (2:19-20ab), is es-

---

12. The former: Wis 7:20; 13:1; 19:20; 3 Macc 3:29; 4 Macc 1:20; 5:7, 8, 25; 13:27; 15:13, 25; 16:3. The latter: Qoh 10:20; Wis 17:11; Sir 42:18.

13. See G. L. Prato, *Il problema della teodicea in Ben Sira*, AB 65 (Rome, 1975) 282-283; J. Marböck, "Gesetz und Weisheit. Zum Verständnis des Gesetzes bei Jesus ben Sira," BZ (NF) 20 (1976) 1-21.

14. We understand the modifier in this passage φύσει, "by nature," in a technical sense, and not in an attenuated sense of the simple adverb "spontaneously" (as E. Käsemann, and H. Schlier would have it). In fact, the context clearly contrasts the written and unwritten law. See also A. Sacchi, "La legge naturale nella lettera ai Romani," in *Fondamenti biblici della teologia morale. Atti della XXII Settimana Biblica* (Brescia, 1973) 375-389 (on page 387 he defines φύσις as "structure of the human being").

15. This is the only text cited by Schnabel in *Law and Wisdom*, 232-234, to demonstrate Paul's familiarity with the Jewish correlation of Law and wisdom.

16. The translation of μόρφωσις as "Verkörperung/embodiment" depends on J. Behm in ThWNT 4:762 = TDNT 4:754; accepted by H. Schlier (HThKNT VI:81: the Italian translation in CTNT 6:152 has "incarnazione," a bit excessive) and C. E. B. Cranfield (1:136: "embodiment") and RSV, JB; this is preferable to "Ausprägung" (Käsemann, *An die Römer*, HNT 8a (Tübingen, 1980⁴) 64 (English edition: "shape," p. 68), or "Urgestalt" (U. Wilckens, 1:146) or simply "expression" (BJ and C.E.I.).

17. See Schnabel, *Law and Wisdom*, 233.

sentially all of a wisdom character, based on the fact of possessing the Law and being able to teach it.[18] It is even not impossible that in this description Paul reflects autobiographically his own self-understanding as a perfect Pharisee before what happened at Damascus (see Gal 1:14; Phil 3:5-6).

Another text showing Paul's acquaintance with the identification of Law and wisdom is found in Rom 7:12, 14, 16. Actually, we have here the only explicitly positive descriptions Paul wrote of the Law. He describes it as "holy," ἅγιος (7:12a); "spiritual," πνευματικός (7:14); "beautiful," καλός (7:16). In the commentaries I find no referral of this vocabulary to a wisdom background. And yet we must note that in the Greek of the LXX such expressions are used only of wisdom. Thus we read in Wis 7:22: ἔστιν γὰρ ἐν αὐτῇ πνεῦμα νοερόν, ἅγιον, "in her is a perceptive and *holy spirit*," and in Prov 3:17: αἱ ὁδοὶ αὐτῆς ὁδοὶ καλαί, "Her ways are beautiful" (cf. Sir 46:10). What sapiential literature says of wisdom, Paul says of the Law, a clear sign that certain laudatory descriptions could pass indifferently from one to the other because of their recognized equivalence. And that Paul attributes to the "Law" (νόμος) a greatness that goes beyond the precepts is indicated by the fact that in the same text he distinguishes it from the ἐντολή, "commandments," which he describes only as ἁγία καὶ δικαία καὶ ἀγαθή (7:12b). Thus he distinguishes the Law in general from the specific commandments; and yet, again, among the adjectives, while the first is a repetition of 7:12a (holy), and the second is never applied to the Law by Paul,[19] the third belongs to the sphere of wisdom, since we read in Prov 4:2a: δῶρον γὰρ ἀγαθὸν δωροῦμαι ὑμῖν, "I give you a good gift" which is referred to both παιδεία, "instruction," and νόμος, "Law," as synonyms.[20]

2) What we have just said certainly associates Paul with the Jewish background concerning the identification of Law with wisdom. Still, he never develops this theme systematically. Indeed, we find only fragments, splinters as it were, of the Jewish idea, enough to show this as the historical matrix of the Apostle's thought. But where these fragments appear they look for all the world merely like concessions made at the beginning of the argument only to set up an affirmation of the opposite, or at least to present a powerful contrast.

---

18. See the documentation cited by Schnabel, *Law and Wisdom*, 234.

19. While Paul never uses for the Law the adjective δίκαιος, which has more of a juridic than of a sapiential connotation, he does speak of a νόμος δικαιοσύνης, "Law of justice" (Rom 9:31), and "justice" is often associated with wisdom in Prov 1:3; 2:9, 20; 3:16a; 8:8, 20; 16:5.

20. But *m. Ab.* 6:3 will refer it to the Law alone, since in citing Prov 4:2 it says, "Now, the good is none other than the Torah.''

Actually it is something quite other that Paul develops systematically: not the veneration of the Law raised to the rank of divine wisdom, but a scandalous recasting of this—scandalous from the viewpoint of traditional, orthodox Judaism, which saw precisely the Torah as the supreme good granted by God to Israel, which, according to Simon the Just already in the second century B.C., was considered "one of the three things on which the world rests" (*m. Ab* 1:2: along with the cult and acts of loving kindness).[21] Therefore, according to the opinion of R. Joseph (disciple of R. Aqiba and master of R. Judah the Prince), "Who dishonors the Torah will, in fact, be dishonored by the human race" (*m. Ab.* 4:6). And yet, the amazing historical fact is that Saul of Tarsus, once the zealous disciple of Rabbi Gamaliel I (see Acts 22:3), who in *m. Sot.* 9:15 is described as the "honor of the Law,"[22] could end up beating such heterodox paths.[23]

Concretely, Paul's radical re-evaluation of the νόμος can be understood on three levels:

a) The first and most persistent is that of *direct* and even heavy-handed *polemic*. The Law is precipitously reduced to δύναμις τῆς ἁμαρτίας, "power of sin" (1 Cor 15:56; see Gal 3:19; Rom 5:13, 20; 7:8-11, 13), to a ministry of "malediction" rather than "justification" (Gal 3:10-13, 21-22), to a "pedagogue," who holds his subjects in a state of servitude and minority (see Gal 3:23-25; 4:1-5), to a source of awareness of sin (Rom 3:20; 7:7) and that which provokes God's wrath (Rom 4:15). We have here a rank scandal, unacceptable to any of the various elements of Second Temple Judaism.[24] For, while in this period we can find some traces of apparent antinomism,[25] faith in the divine origin and hence divine nature of the

21. On the extraordinary elevation of the Torah in Judaism, besides Schnabel, *Law and Wisdom*, 8–226, see also U. Luz in R. Smend and U. Luz, *Gesetz*, Urban-Taschenbücher 1015 (Stuttgart, 1981) 45–57; specifically on rabbinism, see J. Neusner, *Torah: From Scroll to Symbol in Formative Judaism* (Philadelphia, 1985).

22. See W. Bacher, *Die Agada der Tannaiten*, I (Strassburg, 1903) 12–13, 21; E. E. Urbach, *The Sages, Their Concepts and Beliefs* (Jerusalem, 1975) 252, 410.

23. According to the *Toledôt Yešû*, Paul was actually commissioned by the Wise of Israel definitively to separate those who did not observe the Law fully from the people of Israel, by giving them "laws that were not good" (= Ezek 20:25): see R. Di Segni, *Il Vangelo del Ghetto* (Rome, 1985) 63–64. Apart from this fanciful reconstruction, the problem remains to understand how Paul could historically reach his unique conception of the Law; see the presentation and discussion of seven different possibilities in Räisänen, *Paul and the Law*, 229–263.

24. In the search for possible analogies between Paul's concept of Law and the Jewish environment, Räisänen, *Paul and the Law*, 33–41, 92–93, 120–127, 157–161, 179–181, 236–245, reaches negative results, while noting certain limited contacts (like the "allegorists" mentioned by Philo, *Migr. Abr.* 89-93, or with the concept of sin in 1QH [but note E. P. Sanders, 1977, 281] and to some extent in 4 Esdr 3:20-22).

25. In Ps.-Phocylides, *Sent.*, there is never a mention of Israel or the Law or any specific precept, but rather a common Hellenistic type of ethic; in Ps-Philo, LAB 16:1, Korah opposes the Law of Moses concerning the fringes on garments, speaking of an "insufferable law";

Torah is a common, unalterable reality, even within Hellenistic Judaism (see *Arist.* 31; *Syb. Or.* 3:719-720; Philo Alex., *Dec.* 15; Flavius Josephus, *C.Ap.* 1:60). Paul withdraws from this unison chorus in the most jarring manner conceivable both by raising doubts about the divine origin of the Law (esp. in Gal 3:19) and by debasing its function with regard to sin, presenting it as not just causing an awareness of sin (Rom 3:20; 7:7), but as an occasion for committing sin (see 1 Cor 15:56; Gal 3:19; Rom 5:13, 20; 7:8-11, 13).

Several authors have, it is true, tried to perceive in the genitive phrases νόμου πίστεως, "Law of faith" (Rom 3:27), and νόμος τοῦ πνεύματος τῆς ζωῆς, "Law of the spirit of life" (Rom 8:2), a favorable evaluation of Jewish Law by Paul, which would understand it positively from the point of view of faith and of the vivifying Spirit, in opposition to a distorted understanding as law of works.[26] But I think that exegetical reasons including a study of Paul's ideas will not allow such an interpretation,[27] so that in these two

---

in Flavius Josephus, *Ant.* 4:146, Zambrias rebels against Moses, who, speaking under the pretext of God and of laws, is supposed to have imposed slavery on the people ("taking from us the sweetness of life and self-determination, things that befit free persons who have no master"); also *m. Sanh.* 10:1 refers to those who declare that "the Torah was not revealed by God," who will be denied a share in the world to come.

26. See esp. H. Hübner, *Law in Paul's Thought* (Edinburgh, 1984), and the commentaries of C. E. B. Cranfield and U. Wilckens.

27. See especially H. Räisänen, "Das 'Gesetz des Glaubens' (Rom 3.27) und das 'Gesetz des Geistes' (Rom 8.2)," NTS 26 (1979) 101-117; *Paul and the Law*, 50-52; E. P. Sanders, "Paul, the Law, and the Jewish People" (Philadelphia, 1983) 15 (n. 26), 33, 116 (n. 14); and the commentaries of S. Lyonnet, E. Käsemann, H. Schlier. The two expressions certainly should be understood as epexegetical, or else νόμος should be understood in a general sense as "principle" for the following reasons: (1) the two expressions have no parallel in Hellenistic Judaism, and hence there are no examples of contrast between law reduced to works and law vivified by faith and the spirit; (2) Paul never calls for a *new way* of putting the Mosaic Law into practice, something that would mean a relapse into nomism rather than an escape from it; it is true that in Rom 8:4 he speaks of the δικαίωμα τοῦ νόμου [lit. "justice of the law," but note, for example, the RSV: "just requirement of the law"— T.P.W.] as valid for Christians, but even if this is actually to be understood with reference to moral behavior (surely not to the cultic-ritual precepts of the Torah), even the proponents allow that this is summarized in the commandment of love (see Rom 13:8-10; Gal 5:14; 6:2: see Wilckens in EKK VI/2: 128-129) or is inspired by the interior principle of the Holy Spirit (see Jer 31:31-34: see Hübner, *Law*, 146-147), unless we perceive a reference to the same Spirit in us (see L. A. Keck, "The Law and the 'Law of Sin and Death' [Rom 8:1-4]: Reflections on the Spirit and Ethics in Paul," in J. L. Crenshaw and S. Sandmel, eds., *The Divine Helmsman: Studies on God's Control of Human Events, Presented to Lou Silberman* [New York, 1980] 41-57); (3) the νόμος ἁμαρτίας, "law of sin," of Rom 7:23 would then also have to refer to the Mosaic Law, something that is contextually improbable (see the following note); (4) the use of νόμος in the general sense of "principle" is attested in Wis 2:11 in close connection with the use of the same term in the direct sense of "law" (note other cases identified by Räisänen, *Paul and the Law*, 50-51, n. 34); (5) the epistolary units Rom 1:18-3:20 and 3:21-5:21 are structurally contrasted in the articulation of the letter, and this literary fact implies a clear opposition between νόμος/ἔργα, "Law/works," on the one side and πίστις/χάρις, "faith/grace," on the other, rather than some sort of relative scale between them.

texts it is best to understand νόμος generically as "principle," "arrange-ment," thus leaving the symmetrical contrast with the νόμος τῆς ἁμαρτίας καὶ τοῦ θανάτου clear (Rom 8:2b; cf. 7:23), by referring to sin insofar as it has become a dominating principle or law.[27bis]

Granting this, I do not think we can speak simply of an *abrogation of the Law* by Paul, as H. Räisänen tends to do.[28] He is right in insisting that Paul's criticism of the Law refers to the νόμος in its entirety and as such, and not just as a carnal degeneration thereof on the part of Judaism;[29] Paul actually simply opposes the Torah to the promise and faith (see Gal 3:19-29), not as a different degree of what can justify but as an alternative. But it is also true that Paul never uses such strong language as Heb 8:13 ("By saying 'new covenant,' God has declared the former one obsolete; now, what is old and antiquated *is close to vanishing,* ἐγγὺς ἀφανισμοῦ"). Paul never speaks explicitly of an abrogation of the Law; and both the καταργεῖται, "is removed," of 2 Cor 3:14 and the κατέλυσα, "tore down," of Gal 2:18, understood in context, either do not refer to the Law or actually have a limited application.[30]

In fact, it is important to note that when the Apostle uses the verbs ἀποθνῄσκειν and καταργεῖν in reference to the Law, he never makes the νόμος the subject, but rather human beings, represented by an "I" or "we" or "you": "I died to the Law" (Gal 2:19; cf. Rom 6:10); "You have been put to death as for the Law" (Rom 7:4); "Now we are released from the Law, having died to what held us bound" (Rom 7:6). It is as if he did not have the courage to pronounce the Law's death sentence. Actually this is also explained by the fact that Paul's polemic is not against Juda-ism as such but against Jewish Christianity, therefore not against those who adhere to the Law alone (indeed, from this viewpoint see Rom 2) but against anyone who claims to make it coexist with faith in Christ (thus Galatians).[31] As Wilckens says, he champions not the *abrogatio legis* but

27bis. Even Hübner, *Law,* 145, senses the difficulty of understanding Rom 7:23 as refer-ring to the Torah, and admits the possibility of explaining the "law of sin" not as a perver-sion of the Torah but as the sinful principle of the human person.

28. See *Paul and the Law,* 42-50, 200; "Galatians 2.16 and Paul's Break with Judaism," NTS 31 (1985) 543-553.

29. Against C. E. B. Cranfield, "St. Paul and the Law," ScottJourTheol 14 (1964) 43-68; Hübner, *Law,* 137-149; and also Schnabel, *Law and Wisdom,* 282, 284, 292-295.

30. On the first text see vol. 1, chap. 16, note 46; on the second see F. Mussner, *Der Galater-brief,* HThKNT IX (Freiburg-Basel-Vienna, 1981⁴ [1974]) 178 (the object is the neuter plural ἅ . . . ταῦτα, "what [I tore down]," referring either to specific legal prohibitions like the ritual dietary regulations or the Law itself—but considered insofar as it was a dividing wall placed between Jews and gentiles as in Eph 2:14).

31. From this point of view, Paul is the exact mirror of Judaism, which tends not to criticize Christians as such, but only insofar as they join their faith with the Torah (Jewish Christians!): R. Di Segni, *Il Vangelo del Ghetto,* 204-207.

the *abrogatio servitudinis sub lege:* not the abrogation of the Law but the abrogation of slavery under the Law:[32] still, not from the subjective viewpoint of service to a misunderstood Law (as if it would be possible to maintain it if Law were rightly understood), but rather from the objective point of view of a decisive liberation from slavery to the Law as such, i.e., the Law as principle of justification. And if in Rom 3:31 Paul denies that he wants to abrogate it, and rather declares its validity *(νόμον ἱστάνομεν)*, he is moved not so much by a spasm of orthodoxy as by the conviction that *"the Law in its role as witness to righteousness by faith is established in the apostolic preaching of justification by faith as Rom 4 (Gen 15:6) clearly shows."*[33]

In any case, the Law in Paul obviously completely loses the centrality that traditional Judaism attributed to it, in part on the basis of its close association with the divine hypostasis of Wisdom.

b) The import of Paul's re-evaluation of the Torah is seen also in its *reduction to the single commandment of love.* This happens in Gal 5:14 and in Rom 13:8-10. The attribution πᾶς, "all," in Gal 5:14 (ὁ γὰρ πᾶς νόμος, "the whole Law"; cf. Rom 13:9: ἔι τις ἑτέρα ἐντολή, "if there is any other commandment") indicates the Law in its totality, considered as a whole, almost as an abstract principle, but not different from the Law of Moses (cf. Gal 5:3: ὅλον τὸν νόμον, "the entire Law").[34] What Paul means to say is not that the Torah participates in the commandment of love in every one of its precepts. In fact, especially in Gal 2:11-5:12 he polemicizes against at least three specific provisions of the Law (concerning circumcision, Sabbath, and dietary laws).[35] And the deliberate rejection of any one of the commandments of the Law according to the later rabbinic formulation (and the earlier period gives no evidence of distinctions) also meant the rejection of the God who gave it.[36] But what the Apostle teaches is a radical reduction of the Law to the commandment of love, to which nothing in Judaism is comparable. It is true that the love of neighbor has its place of honor already in ben Sira, and especially in the *Testaments of the Twelve Patriarchs,* the author of which seems to have recognized the need to find some sort of unity in the Law; but, as P. Sacchi writes, "He does not unite

---

32. U. Wilckens, *Der Brief an die Römer,* II, EKK VI/2:71.

33. C. Th. Rhyne, *Faith Establishes the Law,* SBL DS 55 (Chico, Calif., 1981) 117f. (author's emphasis); see other interpretations by Hübner, *Law,* 141–142; Räisänen, *Paul and the Law,* 69–71.

34. Hübner, *Law,* 36–38, understands "the whole Law" of Gal 5:14 as meaning something different from "the entire Law" of Gal 5:3 (the former, the Law as understood by Christians; the latter, the Mosaic Law as such; the awkward distinction is made to determine how it is that in Rom 13:8-10 Paul does require the observance of the Mosaic Law; see Hübner, 83–84). For a critique see Sanders, *Paul, the Law,* 96–97; Räisänen, *Paul and the Law,* 27, n. 72.

35. See Sanders, *Paul, the Law,* 100–105.

36. See Sanders, *Paul, the Law,* 103, 118, n. 32.

but simplifies,'' so that there remains a ''zeal for the Law that can even lead to violence,'' and ''to pardon offenses is acceptable insofar as the offense is something personal, but never insofar as it is transgression of the Law.''[37]

But Paul explicitly refers to the command of Lev 19:18: ''You shall love your neighbor as yourself,'' and in this he sees the unifying synthesis of the whole Torah. Even the rabbinic commentary *Sifra Lev.* 19:18 preserves a saying of R. Aqibah on this text: ''This is a great principle of the Torah,'' *zh kll gdwl btwrh*.[38] But it is evident that the Rabbi still considered all the precepts and prohibitions of the Law valid; indeed, it is only ''within the Torah'' *(btwrh)* that he emphasizes the special value of Lev 19:18, whereas Paul uses the verbs πληροῦν, ''fulfill'' (Gal 5:14; Rom 13:8; cf. 13:10), and ἀνακεφαλαιοῦσθαι, ''be summed up'' (Rom 13:9), to express a *reductio ad unum*, a reduction of the whole Law to one element.[39] As F. Mussner correctly puts it, ''This 'fulfillment' is anything but a renewal of the Law, which would be an admission by Paul of the 'other gospel' of his opponents; rather, it is a more than obvious critique of this 'other gospel,' since it radically reduces the provisions of the whole law to the commandment of love. . . . The whole emphasis is on the phrase 'in one word' *(ἐν ἑνὶ λόγῳ).*''[40] Paul's intent, then, is not to identify a central core within the Law, one important commandment on which somehow to hang all the rest.[41] On the contrary, he ignores everything else to concentrate on agape, as if to say that where this one commandment is fulfilled, the Torah in its entirety is fulfilled.

c) In this direction another observation can be made, that Paul seems actually to substitute ''another Law, that of Christ'' for the Law of Moses. Thus we read in 1 Cor 9:21 that he has behaved ''with those without the Law like one without the Law, yet not being without the law but ἔννομος Χριστοῦ, *within the law of Christ*''; and in Gal 6:2 he exhorts the addres-

---

37. P. Sacchi, *Apocrifi dell'Antico Testamento*, I (Turin, 1981) 744–747. See also *Aristeas*, 227 and 229.

38. See Strack-Billerbeck, I, 357 and 907.

39. On the value attributed to Lev 19 by the rabbis, see *Sifra Lev.* 19:18: ''Most of the principles of the Torah are contained in this section'' (repeated in *Lev. R.* 24:5).

40. Mussner, *Der Galaterbrief*, 369–370. The Jewish Christians did not approach this kind of simplification, and as late as the third century Rabbi Simon ben Laqish says in their favor that ''they were as full of commandments as a pomegranate'' (cited in B. Bagatti, *Alle origini della Chiesa I. Le comunità giudeo-cristiane* [Città del Vaticano, 1981] 113; see *b. Sanhed.* 37a).

41. See the enumeration of various attempts of the kind by the rabbis in A. Nissen, *Gott und der Nächste im antiken Judentum. Untersuchungen zum Doppelgebot der Liebe*, WUNT 19 (Tübingen, 1974) 389–415; E. P. Sanders, *Paul and Palestinian Judaism: A Comparison of Patterns of Religion* (London, 1977) 112–114 (Hillel's Golden Rule; justice in business; the Decalogue, and specifically the reduction of the 613 commandments to only one in *b. Mak.* 23b–24a).

sees: "Carry one another's burdens, and thus you will fulfill τὸν νόμον τοῦ Χριστοῦ, the law of Christ." Here we cannot do a detailed exegesis of the texts. Nevertheless, among the possible interpretations,[42] I judge that we must accept the proposal of those who give the word νόμος not the technical sense of a "code of precepts," as if corresponding to the "Law of Moses," but an "attenuated sense, as it were metaphorical, very much as in Rom 2:27 and 8:2."[43]

In 1 Cor 9:21 Paul means to say essentially that although he declares himself ἄνομος with the ἄνομοι, "without law" along with "those who are without law," he is not, however, separated from God's will, which now has to do with Christ. Hence, ἔννομος Χριστοῦ, "within the law of Christ," signifies dependence on Christ: not on a will of his that is codified (against Dodd), but on his economy of salvation in general.[44]

Similarly, Gal 6:2 occurs just after the Apostle has strongly emphasized "the fruit of the Spirit" (5:22) in Christian life, and after declaring that "against such things there is no law," as if to say that typical Christian behavior does not depend on an external law of any sort, since "if we live by the Spirit we also walk in the Spirit" (5:25). Paul goes on to invite the Galatians to deal gently with sinners, calling them back to the right way (6:1); thus they bear one another's burdens and fulfill "the law of Christ" (6:2). Here the approach is not to contrast two different laws, that of Christ and that of Moses; the latter is not even named, and when it was mentioned in the preceding chapters 3 and 4, there was no mention of any law of Christ. Once again the perspective is general. It is a question of not just one command of Christ (actually, in 5:14 the commandment of love is not even attributed to him), but of Christ himself in the entirety of his life, his word, and his death; in a certain sense it is Christ himself understood as law for the Christian (see below, III), in a personal, existential, and hence "mystical" sense.[45]

42. For the present state of the question, see Räisänen, *Paul and the Law*, 77–82.

43. Räisänen, *Paul and the Law*, 80. Mussner rightly observes, *Der Galaterbrief*, 399, that "in the syntagma τὸν νόμον τοῦ Χριστοῦ ['the law of Christ'] the element carrying emphasis and the significance is the genitive ['of Christ']: only through this does the nomen regens [i.e., 'law'] receive its semantic value, which is totally different from that of the syntagma 'Law of Moses.' "

44. See Chr. Senft, *La première épître de Saint Paul aux Corinthiens*, CNT VII (Neuchâtel-Paris, 1979) 124: "To live under Christ's law is to live under grace, which does make demands, but with an obligation that derives from the liberty that grace gives." We can specify that given the context to be ἔννομος Χριστοῦ implies also an "imitation of Christ," in the sense of not practicing favoritism, but, like Christ, accepting the just and sinners (Jews and gentiles) with equal loving devotion (see Luke 15:1-2).

45. Such an interpretation is approached by E. Bammel, "Νόμος Χριστοῦ," StEv 3 (1964) 120–128; H. Schürmann, "Das Gesetz des Christus (Gal 6,2)," in J. Gnilka, ed., *Neues Testament und Kirche. Festschrift R. Schnackenburg* (Freiburg, 1974) 282–300; O. Hofius, "Das Gesetz des Mose und das Gesetz Christi," ZThK 80 (1983) 262–286.

Thus, the only times Paul applies the term νόμος as clearly belonging to Christ, he gives it a meaning that, with regard to the Law of Moses, is more attenuated but also more technical. In each case, too, the Torah is clearly surpassed as a norm of life; in some way, then, the Torah is replaced, not along the same line in some homogeneous way, but with a discontinuity of content. But the point of these observations will become apparent in the third section of this chapter.

In conclusion, as a result of this study we maintain that Paul so undermines the authority of the Torah that what remains of its wisdom connotation is simply not enough to preserve the typical Jewish understanding of its dignity as absolute and definitive revelation of God's will concerning human life and the whole cosmos,[46] if not yet as the personification of God's creative intelligence.[47] The *nomos* as such is for Paul no longer the expression of the divine wisdom.

II. Permanence of "wisdom"

In contrast to Paul's discourse about the νόμος, what he says of σοφία is never polemic, except when he is contrasting the "wisdom of this world" with the "wisdom of God" (1 Cor 2:6-7). But the σοφία θεοῦ is always evaluated positively. However, we must note on the other hand that unlike the extensive treatment of the Law by Paul, his treatment of wisdom is limited and sometimes enigmatic.[48] This fact creates a problem: Why on earth did Paul not further exploit a concept of this sort, which perhaps

46. The statement in 1 Cor 7:19b that what is important is the τήρησις ἐντολῶν θεοῦ, "the keeping of God's commandments," sounds paradoxical after what has just been said, that "circumcision does not count and uncircumcision does not count" (7:19a); now, circumcision is actually one of the most important of God's commandments, and yet here it is being reduced to something indifferent. So rather than attributing a continuing legalistic conception to the text, which will then be transcended in Galatians (thus J. W. Drane, "Tradition, Law and Ethics in Pauline Theology," NT 16 [1974] 167–178, 170ff., approved by Räisänen, *Paul and the Law*, 68), we should take careful note of the context and see in both religious conditions, of Judaism and paganism (symbolized by circumcision and physical integrity respectively), the normal locus of Christian life, the acceptable sphere in which to observe the norms of the new existence (see Senft, *La première épître*, 97).

47. The conception of a pre-existence of the Torah is rabbinic: see G. Schimanowski, *Weisheit und Messias. Die jüdischen Voraussetzungen der urchristlichen Präexistenzchristologie*, WUNT 2:17 (Tübingen, 1985) 216ff. In later developments of the Kabbalah, the Torah will be directly identified with God himself: see G. Scholem, "The Meaning of the Torah in Jewish Mysticism," in *On the Kabbala and Its Symoblism* (New York, 1964 [Italian: 1980]) 32–86.

48. As already said, we exclude Col 1:15-20, which belongs to a probably inauthentic letter, even if chronologically close to Paul's dates; on this text see S. Lyonnet, "Ruolo cosmico di Cristo in Col 1,15ss alla luce del ruolo cosmico della Tora nel giudaismo," in *La Cristologia in San Paolo. Atti della XXIII Settimana Biblica* (Brescia, 1976) 57–79; and especially J.-N. Aletti, *Colossiens 1,15-20. Genre et exégèse du texte. Fonction de la thématique sapientielle*, AB 91 (Rome, 1981).

would have been more appropriate for a new theological synthesis, while at the same time remaining anchored in tradition?

We shall try to answer with all due precautions in an attempt to develop a hypothesis: Paul did not do a real exploitation of the wisdom theme precisely because of the strict linkage at his time between Hokmah and Torah, so that one reality carried the other with it; he wanted to avoid the danger of bringing about a restoration of the Law along with wisdom.

But let us proceed systematically. Paul's wisdom discourse, insofar as it can be described, develops on two levels: Christological and paraenetic. Let us briefly examine each of these aspects.

1) It is in Christology that the wisdom influence is most evident, despite the scarcity of texts.[49] These are found mostly in 1 Corinthians; and it is significant that Paul first makes a positive discourse on wisdom before making a negative treatise on the Law (in the later Galatians and Romans). The fact that he dealt with wisdom alone suggests at least a lesser interest in the Law, which at the time was considered the other face of wisdom.

a) In 1 Cor 1:17–3:20 we have the main concentration of explicit wisdom vocabulary in Paul. Suffice it to say that of the forty-four occurrences of the terms σοφία/σοφός, "wisdom/wise," in all the Pauline epistles, twenty-eight are found in these pages alone. Leaving aside the numerous questions posed to exegetes by these pages (see the commentaries), we restrict ourselves to noting certain basic components.

Today it is generally maintained that the discourse on wisdom in these chapters is not just a concession to the cultural context of the Corinthians (possibly Gnosticizing), but also reflects a specific theological dimension of Paul himself, whose treatment is expository as well as polemic.[50] Specifically, there is plenty of evidence for a wisdom-apocalyptic background (recalling themes from 1 Henoch, Daniel, Qumran), consisting in a sav-

---

49. Except for the denial by A. van Roon, "The Relation Between Christ and the Wisdom of God According to Paul," NT 16 (1974) 207–239, such an influence is generally noted and accepted: see J. D. G. Dunn, *Christology in the Making: An Inquiry into the Origins of the Doctrine of the Incarnation* (London, 1980) 176ff. ("Christ and Wisdom in Paul," including Col 1:15-20).

50. Even U. Wilckens, who in *Weisheit und Torheit. Eine exegetisch-religionsgeschichtliche Untersuchung zu 1. Kor. 1 und 2*, BHTh 26 (Tübingen, 1959) was of the opposite opinion, has corrected himself in "Das Kreuz Christi als die Tiefe der Weisheit Gottes. Zu 1. Kor. 2,1-16," in L. De Lorenzi, ed., *Paolo a una chiesa divisa (1 Cor 1–4)* (Rome, 1980) 43–81. See also B. A. Pearson, "Hellenistic-Jewish Wisdom Speculation and Paul," in R. L. Wilken, ed., *Aspects of Wisdom in Judaism and Early Christianity* (Notre Dame–London, 1975) 43–66; J. A. Davis, *Wisdom and Spirit: An Investigation of 1 Corinthians 1.18–3.20 Against the Background of Jewish Sapiential Traditions in the Greco-Roman Period* (Lanhan, Md., 1984: not examined).

ing plan of God, first hidden and then revealed, in the opposition to two alternative wisdoms (that of God and that of the world), and in emphasis on the Spirit as the sapiential means of revelation.[51]

But what Paul calls "the Wisdom of God in mystery," θεοῦ σοφίαν ἐν μυστηρίῳ (2:7), is not a generic plan of salvation of indeterminate historical-eschatological dimensions like "the mysteries of prudence" at Qumran (1QpHab 7:14: *rāzê 'ormātô*). Actually, in the context this wisdom is Christ himself insofar as he is the Crucified One (see 1:23; 2:1-2).[52] Here we have a fusion of the specifically Christian kerygma and certain apocalyptic-wisdom traditions of Judaism, to the point that it is said of Christ that he ἐγενήθη σοφία ἡμῖν ἀπὸ θεοῦ, "became Wisdom for us from God" (1:30; cf. 1:23-24: "We announce Christ crucified . . . the power of God and the Wisdom of God"). The identification is daring but unsatisfying at the same time. Daring, because God's wisdom is coterminous no longer with the venerable Torah received by Moses on Mount Sinai, but scandalously with a demagogue executed on a cross.[53] Unsatisfying because, as Windisch had already noted, there is here no explicit allusion to the decisive chapters Prov 8; ben Sir 24; Wis 7;[54] and so the identification of Christ as Wisdom is not so much in the sense of his personal pre-existence as in the sense that in him the "verborgene Weisheit," the hidden wisdom, is revealed, as both content of faith and measure of life. The viewpoint is functional and soteriological rather than ontological.

Paul has a twofold intention: (1) to acknowledge in the gospel a wisdom component, though derived by metonymy from the fact that its primary content, Christ himself, is wisdom—by revelation and hence as a gift of God, rather than by autonomous human acquisition (thus already in the wisdom books, where wisdom is not of human origin: see Job 28; Sir 1:5-6; Prov 2:1-6; Bar 3:14-38);[55] (2) to recall the Corinthian Church to

---

51. See R. Scroggs, "Paul: Σοφός and Πνευματικός," NTS 14 (1967–68) 33–35; R. R. Hamerton-Kelly, *Pre-Existence, Wisdom, and the Son of Man: A Study of the Idea of Pre-Existence in the New Testament*, SNTS MS 21 (Cambridge, 1973) 114–115, 192; G. Schimanowski, *Weisheit und Messias*, 315–316; but A. Feuillet, *Le Christ sagesse de Dieu d'après les épîtres pauliniennes* (Paris, 1966) 25–57, makes no reference to apocalyptic conceptions. On the "wisdom of the apocalyptics," see M. Küchler, *Frühjüdische Weisheitstraditionen*, 62–113 and 561.

52. See R. Penna, *Il 'mysterion' paolino. Traiettoria e cosituzione*, RivBibl Supplimento 10 (Brescia, 1978) 56–58.

53. See M. Hengel, *The Son of God. The Origin of Christology and the History of Jewish-Hellenistic Religion* (London, 1976 [Italian: 1984]) 74.

54. See H. Windisch, "Die göttliche Weisheit," 227, who notes that the first Christian author to call Christ "Wisdom" in connection with Prov 8:22-23 is Justin, *Dial.* 61 and 129; but his explanation that Paul would have wanted to avoid giving the *Kyrios* a feminine title (227, 234) is less than convincing.

55. Note the typology of wisdom ("hidden," "nearby," "disappearing") in B. L. Mack, *Logos und Sophia. Untersuchungen zur Weisheitstheologie in hellenistischen Judentum*, SUNT 10 (Göttingen, 1973) 21–33.

community comportment, centered not on the attribution of an inappropriate wisdom-scholastic role to the preachers, but on the primacy of the cross of Christ as unexpected expression of the one wisdom of God above all parties.[56]

It is not without reason that Paul goes beyond the simple identification of Christ as θεοῦ σοφία, "God's wisdom" (1:24), and defines him as σοφία ἡμῖν ἀπὸ θεοῦ, "Wisdom for us from God" 1:30, with the "for us" being so essential that he continues with three more attributes in apposition: δικαιοσύνη τε καὶ ἁγιασμὸς καὶ ἀπολύτρωσις, "justice and holiness and atonement." And the citation of the sense of Jer 9:23 in 1 Cor 1:31 ("that, as it is written, Let one who glories glory in the Lord") surely takes the preceding verse, Jer 9:22 into account: μὴ καυχάσθω ὁ σοφὸς ἐν τῇ σοφίᾳ αὐτοῦ, "Let not the wise glory in their wisdom." So Paul's intention is not speculative but practical and pastoral, characterized by a fruitful linkage to reflection on the kerygma. If we wanted to compare this to the evolution of the Israelite concept of wisdom,[57] we should have to say that Paul is moving on a simple level of instruction for Christian life, and not yet in terms of a hypostatization of Christ as Wisdom in itself.[58]

b) 1 Cor 8:6 provides a bipartite confession of faith ("For us there is only one God, the Father, from whom are all things, and we are for him, and only one Lord, Jesus Christ, through whom are all things, and we are through him"), which is interesting in many ways.[59] We will examine two complementary aspects.

In the first place, we note that the formula clearly breaks the monotheistic confession of the Shema', since the declaration of Deut 6:4 LXX, κύριος ὁ θεὸς ἡμῶν κύριος εἷς ἐστιν, "The Lord our God is one Lord," is partially contradicted, and at least separated in two in 1 Cor 8:6: ἡμῖν εἷς θεὸς ὁ πατήρ

---

56. See H. Schlier, "Kerygma und Sophia" in *Zeit der Kirche* (Freiburg, 1956 [Italian: 1965]) 220: "In the obedience of faith not only does the self-reliance that goes with works of the Law disappear . . . but also the self-reliance that goes with the wisdom that claims to give light and foundations to my world"; while the Christians of Galatia did not want righteousness as pure gift, those of Corinth did not want wisdom as pure gift.

57. Cf. H. H. Schmid, *Wesen und Geschichte der Weisheit. Eine Untersuchung zur altorientalischen und Israelitischen Weisheitsliteratur*, BZAW Beihefte 101 (Berlin, 1966) 144ff.; M. Küchler, *Frühjüdische Weisheitstraditionen*, passim.

58. See H. Conzelmann, "Paulus und die Weisheit," NTS 12 (1965–66) 231–244, 237; B. A. Pearson, "Hellenistic-Jewish Wisdom," 148 (Paul is writing against a sort of "wisdom mysticism").

59. It is disputed whether the formula is a citation of a pre-Pauline confession (thus commonly) or whether a creation of Paul (thus Dunn, *Christology*, 179). In favor of the first hypothesis is the consideration that if it were original with Paul, "the verse says much more about God and Christ than the context would require" (W. Thüsing, *Per Christum in Deum. Studien zur Verhältnis von Christozentrik und Theozentrik in den paulinischen Hauptbriefen*, NA NF 1 [Münster i. W., 1965] 225); at most we can concede to Feuillet, *Le Christ sagesse de Dieu*, 79, that Paul adapted an earlier confession.

. . . *καὶ εἷς κύριος Ἰησοῦς Χριστός*, "For us there is one God, the Father . . . and one Lord, Jesus Christ."[60] This may be motivated in the context by the double polemic opposition to the *θεοὶ πολλοὶ καὶ κύριοι πολλοί*, "many gods and many lords" (8:5), that the pagans of Corinth distinguished; but Christological faith is certainly determinative as well, expressing itself in antinomic terms as a declaration of equality but simultaneously of dependence toward God.[61]

In the second place, but above all, we should note that here we have the only authentic statement of Paul on Christ's mediating function in creation.[62] It is just this attribution of such a creative function to Christ that best explains the binary formulation of the confession of faith. Actually, Jewish wisdom tradition had long since been recognizing for *Ḥokmah-Sophia* such a role in the creation of the world.[63] Thus in the LXX we read in Prov 3:19: "God founded the earth *with wisdom* [*τῇ σοφίᾳ*], he prepared the heavens *with intelligence* [*ἐν φρονήσει*]" (notice the presence of the Greek article in the first of the two adverbial phrases); see also especially Prov 8:22-31 and Wis 8:4; 9:2, 9. The Palestinian TgN renders Gen 1:1 thus: "From the beginning the Word of YHWH with Wisdom created and completed the heavens and the earth." The apocryphal *Slavic Henoch* 30:8 has God say, "The sixth day I ordered my wisdom to create the human on the basis of seven constituents."[64] And Philo of Alexandria writes of honoring "as a father the One who generated the world [*πατέρα μὲν τὸν γεννήσαντα τὸν κόσμον*], and as a mother Wisdom, by which the universe was completed [*μητέρα δὲ τὴν σοφίαν, δι᾽ ἧς ἀπετελέσθε τὸ πᾶν*]" (see also *Fug.* 109). This type of comparative distinction in Philo, as heir to and expression of a long tradition, is what we find in Paul. Now, in place of the title "mother" he puts "Lord," and in place of the personification of "wisdom" he puts "Jesus Christ." But the function of each is the same: the expressions "by whom," the feminine *δι᾽ ἧς* in Philo and the masculine *δι᾽ οὗ* in Paul, correspond exactly. So for Paul (and perhaps already for such early Christians as may have provided Paul with this confession of

60. See Dunn, *Christology*, 180.

61. See V. H. Neufeld, *The Earliest Christian Confessions*, NTTS V (Leiden, 1963) 65–66; M. Hengel, *The Son of God*, 13–14; G. Segalla, *La cristologia del Nuovo Testamento*, SB 71 (Brescia, 1985) 129.

62. See above, note 48.

63. See H. Hegermann, *Die Vorstellung vom Schöpfungsmittler im hellenistischen Jüdentum und Urchristentum*, TU 82 (Berlin, 1961) (only on Philo of Alexandria); R. A. Horsley, "The Background of the Confessional Formula in 1 Kor. 8.6," ZNW 69 (1978) 130–135 (only on the Hellenistic environment).

64. I.e., "the flesh from the earth, the blood from the dew, the eyes from the sun, the bones from the earth, the intelligence from the agility of the angels and from the clouds, the veins and hair from the grass of the earth, the soul from my breath and from the wind."

faith), Jesus Christ is identified with Wisdom in her role as mediator in the creation of the world and of humanity.

It is true that such a surprising article of faith is never further developed (except in the later hymn of Col 1:15-20);[65] but precisely because it is rare, but also so daring, it indicates a Christological understanding that was probably fundamental for the Apostle.[66] And it is a wisdom Christology, which necessarily implies the idea of pre-existence. I do not see how one could deny this conclusion on the specious grounds that here Paul would be making a statement about the present Lordship of Christ.[67] The undeniable presence of wisdom language (admitted even by Dunn) cannot be diminished by Paul's intent to associate a soteriological mediation of Christ with his cosmic mediation. To τὰ πάντα, "all things," he adds both καὶ ἡμεῖς εἰς αὐτόν, "and we are for him," and καὶ ἡμεῖς δι᾿ αὐτοῦ, "and we are through him"; but the mediating function of Christ in the first place concerns "all things." But also, the wisdom literature attributes to Wisdom not only a cosmic but also a historic function, with regard to the leading and educating of the people of Israel and its leaders (see especially Sir 44–51; Wis 10–19). Thus the Christian community as well comes into existence and lives δι᾿ αὐτοῦ, "through him [Christ]," for "[people] were saved through wisdom," τῇ σοφίᾳ ἐσώθησαν (Wis 9:18).

It is precisely this emphasis on mediation that prevents us from thinking of Paul's thought here as violating the monotheism of Israel's faith: the Christological confession no more infringes on it than does the Jewish conception of wisdom, even though Wis 9:4 identifies it as πάρεδρος, "sitting beside," God, and Philo of Alexandria makes it "mother" alongside God as "father."[68] The theocentrism in these cases remains absolute; and in the confession of faith in 1 Cor 8:6 the phrase εἰς αὐτόν, "for him," is referred to God alone, thus making God the point of orientation, the unique and total final goal of all human and Christian events,[69] just as the wisdom communicated to Israel had the sole purpose of making known God's will as the fountain of life (see Prov 8:35; Bar 3:36–4:4). Therefore, even though Paul does not here identify Christ explicitly as the σοφία θεοῦ, "wisdom of God," before the creation of the world,[70] there can be no doubt

65. Besides, the context did not permit it. Paul's intention was to demonstrate the indifference of the Christian with regard to every type of food, even to that which had been offered to idols; he is, therefore, primarily moved by pastoral, not Christological, concerns.

66. Note the comparable observation of J. Jervell, *Imago Dei. Gen. 1:26ff. im Spätjudentum, in der Gnosis und in den paulinischen Briefen*, FRLANT 76 (Göttingen, 1960) 171.

67. Thus Dunn, *Christology*, 181–182; but see the critique of Schnabel, *Law and Wisdom*, 245.

68. For the various epithets of Wisdom in Philo, see Mack, *Logos und Sophia*, part 2.

69. See Thüsing, *Per Christum in Deum*, 257–258; see also below, chap. 28.

70. Aletti, *Colossiens 1,15-20*, 176, rightly stresses the fact that "though never calling the pre-existing Christ σοφία or σοφία θεοῦ ['wisdom' or 'God's wisdom'], the Pauline letters . . .

that implicitly he thinks of him with the wisdom categories of pre-existence and of an instrumental participation in creation itself.

Rather, we must specify that such functions describe Christ precisely as wisdom more than as Law. It is true that later, on the basis of the identification between wisdom and Law, the cosmological functions of the former were attributed to the latter. This takes place in the rabbinic literature, which henceforth more rarely reflects on Ḥokmah, "Wisdom," as such, and rather emphasizes the Torah, applying to it the traditional wisdom categories. In the Mishnah (*m. Av.* 3:14) R. Aqibah is among the first to attribute to the Torah a cosmological role of mediation in creation: "Dear to God were the Israelites . . . for to them was given the tool wherewith the world was created [*šntn lhm kly šbw nbr' h'wlm*], according to the text that says (Prov 4:4!), 'A good teaching I gave you; my Law abandon not.' " In this passage the statement about the Law-wisdom entails another one concerning Israel, since "by being granted the pre-cosmic instrument of creation, the Torah, the whole people is taken from the very beginning into a divine plan of special election."[71] The thematic perspective is similar to that of the Pauline text 1 Cor 8:6, and given the lack of an express identification of Christ with σοφία, one could question whether in the background of the Christological confession of faith there does not stand the personification of law rather than that of wisdom. But I should think the latter to be more probable on historical grounds (the privileged emphasis on the Torah is later), literary grounds (the association and distinction between Torah and divine wisdom is already found in Hellenistic Judaism), and linguistic grounds (while Paul at least in 1 Cor 1:24, 30 refers to Christ as "wisdom of God," he never does explicitly describe him as *nomos*; see below).

c) Other texts would have to be considered to give the full picture of Paul's wisdom Christology. Here we mention only in passing 1 Cor 10:4; 2 Cor 4:4b; Gal 4:4; Rom 8:3; Phil 2:6-7, where various themes are intertwined: the saving function of Christ in the story of the Exodus (1 Cor 10:4); his identification as image of God (2 Cor 4:4b); his mission from on high (Gal 4:4; Rom 8:3); his pre-historic divine condition (Phil 2:6-7).[72] But in all these passages there is a common denominator, the conception of pre-

---

remain in line with the tradition of the wisdom books, which never considered wisdom to be either God or equal to God, even though coming from God."

71. Schimanowski, *Weisheit und Messias*, 218: for commentary on the text relative to other texts with bibliography, see Schimanowski, 216–221, 283–284.

72. For these texts we refer to the commentaries; also see Feuillet, *Le Christ sagesse de Dieu*, 87–161; Hamerton-Kelly, *Pre-Existence*, 103–168; Dunn, *Christology*, 183–184; Schnabel, *Law and Wisdom*, 240–255; Schimanowski, *Weisheit und Messias*, 320–336.

existence, which is explained only on the basis of the use of Jewish categories concerning the personification of divine Wisdom and its functions.[73] Therefore, as Hengel rightly observes, the scandal originally aroused among the Jewish ranks by the Christian proclamation "was not so much grounded on the teaching of the pre-existent Son of God . . . but on the christologically motivated abrogation of the Law."[74]

2) The Jewish wisdom tradition survives in Paul not only on the level of theological speculation but in moral instruction for the concrete life of the addressees. Unfortunately specific studies have not yet been done in this area.[75] But it was with regard to the paraenesis that Polycarp already spoke of the σοφία τοῦ μακαρίου καὶ ἐνδόξου Παύλου, "wisdom of the blessed and glorious Paul" (*ad Phil.* 3:2). The Apostle certainly was himself a wisdom teacher, and in many ways he follows the line of the ancient masters. As such, he invites Christians to be σοφοὺς . . . εἰς τὸ ἀγαθόν, "wise as to the good" (Rom 16:19; cf. Sir 18:8 [7]), and to take care to do good before God and others—this last an exhortation deriving from Prov 3:4 LXX, repeated (without indicating source) in 2 Cor 8:21 and Rom 12:17.[76] But all the paraenetic sections of his letters show Paul as a teacher of life.[77] And it would also be valuable to study the wisdom background, concerning the teacher-disciple relationship, in those texts where Paul declares himself to have become father of the Christians of his Churches (see 1 Cor 4:14-15; Gal 4:19; Phlm 10);[78] at least what is clear is that Paul's role as father is associated not with baptism but with the proclamation of the word.

---

73. See in particular E. Schweizer, "Zur Herkunft der Präexistenzvorstellung bei Paulus," in *Neotestamentica* (Zurich, 1963) 105–109; H. Merklein, "Zur Entstehung der urchristlicken Aussage vom präexistenten Sohn Gottes," in G. Dautzenburg, ed., *Zur Geschichte des Urchristentums*, QD 87 (Freiburg i.B., 1979) 33–62; Hengel, *The Son of God*, 66–77. On the preexistence of a messianic figure already in pre-rabbinic Judaism, see Schimanowski, *Weisheit und Messias*, 107–205: LXX (Mic 5; Pss 110 and 72); Book of the Parables (1 Hen 37-71); 4 Esdr 12:32; *Syb.Or.* 5:414-415; *Ass.Mos.* 1:12-14.

74. Hengel, *The Son of God*, 74; but better than "abrogation" would be the term "discrediting."

75. At most, only very general works are available; see, for instance, F. Festorazzi, "Originalità della morale cristiana secondo San Paolo," in L. De Lorenzi, ed., *Dimensions de la vie chrétienne (Rm 12-13)* (Rome, 1979) 237–256, 243: "If we can indicate where it originates . . . I believe we must have recourse to popular Greek philosophy, or even more broadly and more directly to the typical tradition of Jewish wisdom literature based on the broadest and most diverse experience possible"; W. Schrage, *The Ethics of the New Testament*, trans. D. Green (Philadelphia, ca. 1988) 205.

76. See above, chap. 21, n. 9.

77. On the use of paraenesis in both the Greco-Roman and Jewish worlds, see briefly J. I. H. McDonald, *Kerygma and Didache: The Articulation and Structure of the Earliest Christian Message*, SNTS MS 37 (Cambridge, 1980) 69–79.

78. Unfortunately the study of D. von Allmen, *La famille de Dieu. La symbolique familiale dans le Paulinisme*, OBO 41 (Fribourg–Göttingen, 1981), does not so much as mention this, and the commentaries also leave much to be desired.

I certainly do not intend here to do an exposition of the methods, motifs, and contents of the Pauline ethic.[79] I should only like to try to sample three different approaches to the question: one exegetical, one thematic, and one methodological.

a) Romans 12:9-21 is a typical paraenetic passage, which we can describe as sapiential in character. Even though the literary framework recalls the robustness and fluidity of the diatribe,[80] it is generally admitted that Paul is to a certain extent using traditional material, since Daube demonstrated the dependence of the imperative sense of the participles here upon Semitic forms of moral instruction.[81] The section comes to a head in vv. 19b-20 with the citation of two biblical texts, Deut 32:35 ("Vengeance is mine, it is I who shall repay") and Prov 25:21-22 ("If your enemy is hungry, provide food, or if thirsty, give a drink: for by doing so you will pour burning coals on the person's head"), which taken together provide the logical foundation of the whole pericope. As Michel perceptively notes, "The authoritative word of Deut 32:35 gives its weightiness to the attached wisdom saying, while the latter gives to the former a precise positive orientation."[82]

But there are still more observations to make. First: the invitation to leave vengeance to God itself belongs to wisdom literature (see Prov 20:22; Sir 28:1; Test. Gad 6; 1QS 10:17-18; CD 9:2-5). Second: the reasoning of the whole text is devoted to the necessity of benevolence and compassion toward the neighbor; and already Sir 27:30–28:7 treats the same theme in a most humane fashion. Third: certain formal characteristics (the presence of two other references to the Book of Proverbs [see Prov 3:7 in v. 16 and Prov 3:4 in v. 17]; the use of the technique of parallelism, a similar somewhat disorganized accumulation of various exhortations) locate our section securely enough within the wisdom tradition.

---

79. See the good general view in Schnabel, *Law and Wisdom*, 299–342, with discussion of the positions of various authors, and large bibliography; the author very clearly distinguishes between "foundational motivations" (Christological, salvation-historical, Pneumatological, ecclesiological, eschatological), "binding norms" in the line of law (the Word of God, the words of Jesus, the dicta of the Apostle, the orders of creation) and "guiding criteria" in the line of wisdom (the existing orders, the Spirit, love, reason and discernment, conscience).

80. See R. Bultmann, *Der Stil der paulinischen Predigt und die kynisch-stoische Diatribe*, FRLANT 13 (Göttingen, 1910) 75–76; S. K. Stowers, *The Diatribe and Paul's Letter to the Romans*, SBL DS 57 (Chico, Calif., 1981) passim.

81. D. Daube, "Participle and Imperative in 1 Peter," in E. G. Selwyn, *The First Epistle of St. Peter* (London, 1955) 467–488. Less demonstrable is that Paul should have personally reworked an existing Semitic code, as Ch. H. Talbert would have it, "Tradition and Redaction in Romans XII, 9-21," NTS 16 (1969–70) 83–94.

82. O. Michel, *Der Brief an die Römer*, Meyer Kommentar (Göttingen, 1960⁴) 310.

b) Among the various possible motivations in Pauline ethic there is also that of the order of creation, deriving from a certain universalism and optimism that is typical of a specific wisdom tradition. Wis 11:24 proclaims openly: "You love all that exists and despise nothing of what you have created; had you hated something, you would not have created it . . ., O Lord, lover of life" (cf. 1:13-14). The same idea underlies those passages that sing the beauty of the created as expression of wisdom (see Job 38-39; Prov 8:22-31) or say that the Lord "has poured it on all his works" (Sir 1:7).

Paul echoes this vision in certain statements of expansive consciousness, as in 1 Cor 10:26 ("The earth is the Lord's, and all that is in it" = Ps 24:1, cited in the context of food offered to idols and the related moral dilemmas) or in Rom 14:14 ("Nothing is unclean in itself"; this principle recognizes a limitation in reference only to the conscience of another Christian, but not to the things in themselves.)[83] And it is surprising to note that this optimistic view of the world coexists with Paul's pessimistic conception of sin as a destructive power greater than the individual, universal, and inevitable. Evidently his apocalyptic self has not destroyed the sage; the one speaks in a soteriological, the other in a paraenetic perspective. And it is as if he wanted to say that one carries a component of corruption in oneself, but with a cosmological context that is good, that "is subject to futility not of its own will" (Rom 8:20).[84] Moreover, Paul's attitude toward work (see 1 Thessalonians) and marriage (1 Cor 7) and the state (Rom 13:1-7) shows that even the basic structures of society have for him a foundation based on the divine ordering of creation itself.[85] Not to mention here the concept of "conscience," which Paul shares with Greek tradition.[86]

83. The same principle, with a similar limitation, occurs again in Rom 14:20; and in the translation of the text, U. Wilckens, *Der Brief an die Römer* III, EKK VI/3 (Zurich–Neukirchen, 1982) 95, n. 470, rightly takes issue with C. K. Barrett, *The Epistle to the Romans*, Black's NT (London, 1971 = 1957), who translates Rom 14:20b: "All things are clean, but they cause evil to the man . . .," and proposes instead: "Zwar ist alles rein. Doch, schlimm ist es für einen Menschen . . . ("All is indeed clean. But it is bad for anyone to . . .").

84. Concerning this last passage, see the good exegesis of H. Schlier, *Der Römerbrief*, HThKNT (Freiburg–Basel–Vienna, 1977 [Italian: 1982]) 260–262, concerning the difference between ματαιότης and φθορά, "futility" and "corruption"; and the comment of C. E. B. Cranfield, *The Epistle to the Romans*, II, ICC (Edinburgh, 1975) 414: "We may think of the whole magnificent theatre of the universe together with all its splendid properties, and all the chorus of sub-human life, created to glorify God but unable to do so fully, so long as man the chief actor in the drama of God's praise fails to contribute his rational part."

85. See T. Holtz, "Zur Frage der inhaltlichen Weisungen bei Paulus," ThLZ 106 (1981) 385–400; Schrage, *Ethics*, 203.

86. See the excellent monograph of H.-J. Eckstein, *Der Begriff Syneidesis bei Paulus. Eine neutestamentlich-exegetische Untersuchung zum "Gewissensbegriff,"* WUNT 2:10 (Tübingen, 1983).

c) As for Paul's paraenetic methodology, let us ascertain Paul's characteristic use of Scripture. That he often finds a basis for his exhortations by a citation of a biblical text is a fact.[87] But it is not enough to say that the Old Testament remains an authoritative model for Christian *ethos*, or that it is normative a priori as revelation of God and not just for its reference to Christ.[88] We must distinguish between a theological and a paraenetic use of the Old Testament. It is still striking that an intellectual of Pharisaic formation like Paul (with the exception of Lev 19:18 in Gal 5:14; Rom 13:9; see above) never bases the Christian *halakah* on any legal provision of the Old Testament.[89] And where that does seem to happen, as in 1 Cor 5:13 (where Deut 13:6 LXX is cited: "drive the wicked person out from among you"), the Torah text is added as one more thing at the end of the treatment of the case, and then not in its original sense, which demanded death of the guilty one by stoning; in 1 Cor 9:8-9 (which quotes Deut 25:4: "You shall not muzzle the ox that treads out the grain"), the cited text is watered down to a merely metaphorical meaning.[90]

We make two short observations about the originality of Paul in this area. In the first place, Paul emphasizes wisdom or prophetic texts over legal ones, and Rom 12:9-21, examined above, may be paradigmatic of this.[91] Moreover, from the lexical point of view, we note that Paul's paraenesis is never termed νόμος, "law," or even ἐντολή, "commandment." He prefers to use terms like διατάσσειν, "command" (only in 1 Cor 7:17; 11:34; 16:1); νουθετεῖν, "admonish" (1 Cor 4:14); παραμυθεῖσθαι, "encourage" (1 Thess 2:12); and especially παρακαλεῖν, which indicates "a challenge that admonishes, a plea that incites, and an encouraging, almost comforting address."[92]

Thus, Paul is a sage who gives instruction, by no means a legislator who wants to give a definitive form to his communities; and his instructions

---

87. See, for example, an enumeration of citations in W. Schrage, *Die konkreten Einzelgebote in der paulinischen Paränese* (Gütersloh, 1961) 223 and note 205.

88. Thus Schnabel, *Law and Wisdom*, 313 and 314.

89. See above, chap. 23, III, 3.

90. In 1 Cor 14:34 we find a generic appeal to the νόμος, "Law," to say that for women "it is not appropriate to speak, but they should be submissive, as the Law also says"; commentators generally refer to Gen 3:16, but for want of an explicit citation, "Law" could also here mean Jewish custom as a whole (but for those who consider 1 Cor 14:33b-36 an interpolation, like Conzelmann and Senft, the problem no longer exists).

91. Unfortunately, as far as I can determine there are no specific studies on the issue.

92. H. Schlier, "Die Eigenart der christlichen Mahnung nach dem Apostel Paulus," *Besinnung auf das Neue Testament*, Exegetische Aufsätze und Vorträge (Freiburg–Basel–Vienna, 1964) 340–357, 341; see also C. J. Bjerkelund, *Parakalô. Form, Function und Sinn der parakalô-Sätze in den paulinischen Briefen*, BThN 1 (Oslo, 1967) 112–113. Regarding παρακαλειν above, in the LXX out of about 120 occurrences, it is found only 4 times in legal texts (Exod 15:13; Deut 3:28; 13:6; 32:36).

are illuminated not by the absolute of the Torah but by faith in Christ,[93] who has become for us what the Law is in Judaism, i.e., "wisdom, righteousness, sanctification, and redemption" (1 Cor 1:30).

III. Reconstructing the relationship

As we have seen, the Jewish pattern law/wisdom underwent a sharp rupture at Paul's hands. In its traditional terms it no longer functions. Still, while he makes a clear enough polemical discourse against the salvific power of the Law, the same cannot be said of wisdom, even though wisdom as such can hardly be said to fill in the space left by the deposing of the *nomos*. Still, it is certain that Paul destroyed an equation that had become fundamental in the Judaism of the time as a basis of self-identification and boasting. Moreover, he is interfering—seriously—precisely with that member of the equation, i.e., the Law, which had previously been considered the eternal and inalienable glory of Israel (see Bar 4:1-3) and which was actually to become through rabbinism a substitute for priesthood and royalty (see *m. Ab.* 6:6). It is difficult for us as twentieth-century gentile Christians adequately to judge the actual importance of this cultural undertaking of Paul's. But the fact that five times he received from his Jewish coreligionists the prescribed "forty lashes minus one" (2 Cor 11:24; cf. Deut 25:1-3; *m. Mak.* 3:10) does indicate the gravity of his way of thinking in the eyes of the Synagogue,[94] which considered it absolutely punishable for a Jew not just to behave like one without the Law for those without the Law (cf. 1 Cor 9:21), but openly to preach the uselessness of the Law for salvation (see Gal 2:16; 3:21-22; 5:4).

From a strictly Jewish point of view, Paul would have been considered wise only if he had adhered fully to the Torah, according to the principle of ben Sira, "One who is faithful to the Law will also obtain wisdom," ὁ ἐγκρατὴς τοῦ νόμου καταλήμψεται αὐτήν (Sir 15:1b LXX).[95] Paul could hardly be called ἐγκρατὴς τοῦ νόμου, and so could not have achieved wisdom.

---

93. See P. Grech, "Christological Motives in Pauline Ethics," in L. De Lorenzi, ed., *Paul de Tarse, apôtre de notre temps* (Rome, 1979) 541-558; S. Zedda, *Relativo e assoluto nella morale di San Paolo*, BCR 43 (Brescia, 1984) 33-34.

94. See Sanders, *Paul, the Law*, 191-192, who, however, rightly notes that the punishment inflicted on Paul by the synagogue authorities gives us to understand that despite everything the latter did consider his movement as being *within* Judaism ("Punishment implies inclusion," 192).

95. Translation after the C.E.I; the JB translates more precisely, "Whoever grasps the Law will obtain wisdom." The text probably refers not to the Jew in general but to the scribe (cf. Jer 2:8); in any case, the Law stands in parallelism with the "fear of the Lord" (Sir 15:1a) and in 15:1b an indestructible association is proclaimed between Law and wisdom.

Still, as we have seen, if wisdom is no longer to be identified with the Law, it is that Paul has established an identification of wisdom with Christ. Therefore we can affirm in the form of a thesis: For Paul it is Christ who occupies the space left open by the Law, and so the Jewish equation is reconstructed as "Christ/wisdom." The restatement of the pattern assumes a functional substitution between the Law and Christ in the sense that what used to be true of the Law is now true of Christ. And in fact this is the case. Now, it is true that Schnabel holds that "Paul never correlates Christ and Law. . . . whereas Christ is described in terms of wisdom, Christ is not described in terms of Torah."[96] But this is only partly true. Actually, if by "correlation" we mean a relationship between Christ and a new Torah proposed for people to obey, then we certainly cannot speak of Christ as a legislator. But it is one thing to speak of Christ as giver of Torah, and quite another thing to speak of him personally as the substitute for the Torah, even if he is never explicitly identified as such.

But actually, a sentence like Gal 2:21 ("If justification comes from the Law, Christ died in vain") sets up an alternative relationship, a mirror image between the Law and Christ: henceforth the latter cancels the function of the former.[97] Where the Law prevails as absolute salvific revelation of God, there is no room for Christ, and likewise, if Christ is to be the decisive point of soteriological encounter between God and humanity, then the Law must give way. As Sanders writes, Paul tends to think in black and white terms;[98] and one of the great antitheses consists in the alternative poles of Law/Christ.

But we must explain. According to Paul, Christ does not just exclude the Law but takes its place. He is henceforth for the Christian what the Law is for the Jew. Let us be perfectly clear: Paul does not deny that for the Jew the Law is and continues to be "a Law of righteousness" (Rom 9:31a: νόμον δικαιοσύνης).[99] But he accuses Israel of not having reached what the Law intends (Rom 9:31b), that is, justification itself, which is possible

---

96. Schnabel, *Law and Wisdom*, 298.

97. A different problem is to determine whether Christ justifies because the Law cannot do so, or whether the Law does not justify because henceforth it is Christ who is to do so. The first alternative assumes a negative experience of the human condition, while the second begins only with the consideration of the exclusive salvific function of Christ. The second possibility is forcefully affirmed by Sanders, *Paul and Palestinian Judaism*, 439–440; *Paul, the Law*, 150–151 (this position excludes any essential anthropological analysis of Rom 7; see ibid. 77). The former is in fact the opinion of G. Theissen, *Psychological Aspects of Pauline Theology*, trans. J. P. Galvin (Edinburgh, 1987) 177–265, according to whom Rom 7 reflects the personal experience of Paul on the ambiguity of the Law. I am inclined to subscribe to the position of Theissen, for whom the "I" of chapter 7 "combines personal and typical traits" (ibid., 201).

98. *Paul, the Law*, 70.

99. See Wilckens, *Der Brief an die Römer*, III, 212, n. 944.

only by accepting through faith the revelation of God's righteousness, which, apart from the Law, is now accomplished in Christ.

This is where the famous Rom 10:4 comes in. For our present interests, we can ignore the highly disputed question whether τέλος, "end," here means "purpose" or "termination."[100] The important thing to note is the Christological affirmation. Whether Christ is considered the purpose of the Law or its termination, one thing is clear: henceforth it is he who takes the place of the Law as cause of justification.[101] Actually, the following vv. 5-6 set up a clear opposition between the δικαιοσύνη ἐκ νόμου, "righteousness by the Law" and that "by faith," ἐκ πίστεως, representing two distinct economies of salvation;[102] and, as if to demonstrate its newness, the formulation of the second member of the contrast can vary according to the context: the "faith" of v. 6a can become "word of faith" in v. 8 or simply "Christ" in vv. 6b, 7.

To explain his conception, Paul in Rom 10:6-8 reports the words of Deut 30:11-14[103] with considerable liberty, interpreting it with the exegetical technique of the *pēšer*.[104] The grammatical subject of Deut 30:11 is "the commandment" of God (MT: *hammiṣwāh*; LXX: ἡ ἐντολή), of which it is said that it is not too high or too far away to be able to know and do it. Now, both the questions about "going up to heaven" and "crossing the sea" (which in Romans becomes "descending into the abyss") are given an added explanation by Paul, the former, τοῦτ᾽ ἔστιν Χριστὸν καταγαγεῖν, "that is, to bring Christ down" (v. 6b), the latter, τοῦτ᾽ ἔστιν Χριστὸν ἐκ νεκρῶν ἀναγαγεῖν, "that is, to bring Christ up from the dead" (v. 7). According to the Apostle, then, God's commandment now takes the name of Christ, i.e., the latter replaces the former. It is now not the Law but Christ that is "near" in the proclamation of the kerygma; and "the word" (MT: *haddābār*; LXX: τὸ ῥῆμα), which in the biblical text of Deut 30:14 was a

---

100. For the present state of the question, see Wilckens, *Der Brief an die Römer*, II, 221–224; Räisänen, *Paul and the Law*, 53–56; see also C. Th. Rhyne, " 'Nomos Dikaiosynēs' and the Meaning of Romans 10:4," *CBQ* 47 (1985) 486–499; and especially R. Badenas, *Christ the End of the Law. Romans 10,4 in Pauline Perspective*, JSNT Supplement Series 10 (Sheffield, 1986).

101. "The discussion whether we should translate 'end' or 'goal' sets up a false alternative. Christ is the *termination* of the Law . . . since he anticipates its goal and incorporates the goal in his own person" (F. Siegert, *Argumentation bei Paulus, gezeigt an Röm 9–11*, WUNT 34 [Tübingen, 1985] 149, n. 5).

102. Against any denial of the contrast between vv. 5 and 6, see Räisänen, *Paul and the Law*, 54–55, notes 56–57.

103. The biblical passage reads: ¹¹For this commandment that I am giving you this day is not too wonderful for you, nor is it remote. ¹²It is not in the heavens, that you should say, "Who will go up to the heavens for us to get it for us and let us hear it, that we may do it?" ¹³Nor is it across the sea, that you should say, "Who will cross the sea for us to get it for us and let us hear it, that we may do it?" ¹⁴For the word is very close to you, in your mouth and in your heart [LXX adds *and in your hands*], that you should do it.

104. The formula τοῦτ᾽ ἔστιν, "that is . . .," is analogous to the *pisrô ʻal* in 1QpHab.

synonym of "commandment," is now explained in a new way by Paul: τοῦτ' ἔστιν τὸ ῥῆμα τῆς πίστεως, "this is the word of faith" (v. 8), thus establishing an essential correlation between Christ and faith.

Schnabel, however, insistently argues[105] that Paul describes Christ not in terms of Law but of wisdom, since contemporaneous Jewish interpretation of the deuteronomic text is predominantly sapiential: he refers to Bar 3:29-30; and to seven passages of Philo, *Post.* 84-85; *Mut.* 236-238; *Praem.* 80; *Prob.* 68; *Virt.* 183; *Somn.* 2:180; *Spec. leg.* 1:301. He even claims that "There are no early examples [before Paul] for the application of this passage to the Torah."[106] Now, it is true that we have clear and explicit interpretation of the biblical text in the sense of the Law only in the Palestinian Targum TgN to Deut 30:12-13.[107] But we must make three observations.

1) Though the Targum is redactionally late, this does not exclude the possibility that at least some of its contents are very old.[108] And specifically in TgN we must notice the interesting affinity between its paraphrase of Deut 30:12-13 and Rom 10:6-7; in fact, they both translate the text about ascending to heaven literally, but both offer the same paraphrase to "go across the sea," with the novel phrase "go down into the abyss," referring to the ἄβυσσος of Jonah 2:6.[109] It is possible, then, that TgN with its orientation to the Torah represents the background of the Pauline passage.[110]

2) The biblical text as such deals only with the Torah; indeed, the grammatical subject of Deut 30:11, "the commandment," or "this commandment," is nothing but an allusion to v. 10, which speaks of "his commandments and his decrees written in this book of the Law," and so simply stands for "Law." Now, while the Israelite sages sometimes represent wisdom as inaccessible (see above), Deut 30:11-14 means rather to say that the Law is within reach of everyone.[111] And even according to the vocabu-

---

105. *Law and Wisdom,* 247-249; 292, n. 319; 298, n. 340.

106. Schnabel, *Law and Wisdom,* 249.

107. This is the text: [12] The Law is not in heaven, that you should have to say, "Ah, if we had someone like Moses the prophet who could go up to heaven, he would get it for us and let us hear the commandments that we might do them!" [13]Nor is the Law beyond the Great Sea, that you should have to say, "Ah, if we had someone like Jonah the prophet who could go down in the depth of the Great Sea, he would bring it back up and would let us hear its commandments that we might do them!" (see R. Le Déaut, *Targum du Pentateuch. IV. Deutéronome,* Sources Chrétiennes 271 [Paris, 1980] 248).

108. In general, see A. D. York, "The Dating of Targumic Literature," JSJ 5 (1974) 49-62; specifically TgN already, according to its editor, A. Díez Macho, would probably be of pre-Christian material (cf. Le Déaut, *Introduction à la littérature targumique* [Rome, 1966] 118-119).

109. See M. McNamara, *The New Testament and the Palestinian Targum to the Pentateuch,* AB 27 (Rome, 1966) 76 and 75.

110. See S. Lyonnet, "S. Paul et l'exégèse juive de son temps," in *Mélanges A. Robert* (Paris, 1957) 494-506; M. Black, "The Christological Use of the Old Testament in the New Testament," NTS 18 (1971-72) 1-14, 19.

111. Cf. P. Buis and J. Leclercq, *Le Deutéronome,* SB (Paris, 1963) 187; A. Penna, *Deuteronomio* (Turin, 1976) 242.

lary it is clear that the Pauline text is a reworking of Deut 30:11-14 LXX, and not of Bar 3:29-30, as can easily be ascertained by comparing the three passages synoptically. Therefore, "where the Old Testament text speaks of Law, Paul on principle speaks of Christ."[112]

3) This Pauline elaboration of Deut 30:11-14 in Rom 10:6-8 appears in a context that is not properly sapiential, but is a partly polemic reflection on the supposed salvific value of the Law. In fact, the axiom guiding Paul's reasoning is formulated in 10:4: Τέλος γὰρ νόμου Χριστός . . ., "The end of the Law is Christ for the justification of whoever believes."[113] It is true that the exposition moves indifferently from Χριστός, "Christ" (10:6b, 7), to τὸ ῥῆμα τῆς πίστεως, "the word of faith" (10:8), to ῥῆμα Χριστοῦ, "the word of Christ" (10:17); but the person of Christ always remains at the center as the alternative to the Law, and this is confirmed by the anthropological contrast between "doing" (ποιεῖν: 10:5 = Lev 18:5) and "believing/confessing" (πιστεύειν/ὁμολογεῖν: 10:4b, 9-10). Paul means that Christ, just like Torah for Judaism, is a gift, yes the greatest gift given by God to his people, and that this gift is completely at our disposal in the word of proclamation. But if in Judaism salvation comes about through the actual observance of the Torah, in Christianity it comes by adhering to the Lord in faith, for Jew and Greek alike (see 10:12-13). But the function in each case is the same.[114]

We can, then, conclude by saying that Christ's overcoming of the Law takes place not simply through exclusion, as though the one element were unrelated to the other, but by substitution, that is, by transfer of soteriological functions from the one to the other. Paul actually compares this passage from adherence to the Law to adherence to Christ to what takes place when a woman's first spouse dies and she is free to unite with another (Rom 7:1-6). Thus the Christian passes to Christ to the extent that one dies to the Law; it is like a change of spouse, not in some naive sense, as if one were as good as the other; indeed, the second is better than the first, but still in a formal sense actualizes the same concept of partner and master, and carries out the same life-giving functions.[115]

Basically, I think we can say that Paul would never have criticized the Law had he not come to adhere to Christ and to interpret Christ's new salvific role as he did. But that means that the Law deserved criticism not

---

112. Michel, *Der Brief an die Römer*, 257; see Schlier, *Der Römerbrief*, 311: "Christ replaces the exhortation of the Torah"; U. Wilckens, II 225; A. Maillot, *L'épître aux Romains* (Paris-Geneva, 1984) 272; H. Hübner, *Gottes Ich und Israel. Zum Schriftgebrauch des Paulus in Römer 9-11*, FRLANT 136 (Göttingen, 1984) 86-87.

113. See Sanders, *Paul, the Law*, 36-43.

114. See also the commentary of C. E. B. Cranfield, II, 524-525.

115. Although elsewhere Paul speaks of "sin" and "flesh" instead of Law, and of "grace" and "Spirit" instead of Christ, still despite the inevitable shades of difference, he repeats the same pattern, i.e., overcoming by substitution.

so much in itself but because it could not hold its own in comparison with Christ and with the possibilities laid open to all by his death. Sanders is right when he writes that we have here simply a change in the "total type" or "entire systems" of religion,[116] whatever we choose to call them.[117] But the dimensions in each case (that of the Law and that of Jesus Christ) correspond, considering the notable difference between mute obedience and vital participation. After all, for the baptized, Christ becomes the norm of one's life; and in him *somehow* the characteristic Jewish principle of a single and absolute means of salvation lives again; indeed there is reason to hypothesize that without the Jewish categories of Law and wisdom, Pauline Christology would not even have been possible, for in large part it is just on these presuppositions that Paul's thought must be explained.[118]

So henceforth Christ takes the place of the νόμος, and as such is identified with σοφία. It is in Christ that God's wisdom has now found its dwelling; and in him, as a disciple of the Apostle has written, one can find "all the treasures of wisdom and knowledge hidden" (Col 2:3).

116. Sanders, *Paul and Palestinian Judaism*, 548, 550; cf. 552: "This is what Paul finds wrong in Judaism: it is not Christianity"! But see note 97 above.

117. Sanders, *Paul and Palestinian Judaism*, 236 and 549, calls the one "covenantal nomism" and the other "participationist eschatology"; but his thesis, that the difference between Paul and Judaism would stand only in the general "pattern of religion" and not in some antithesis between grace and works, has been severely criticized by R. H. Gundry, "Grace, Works, and Staying Saved in Paul," Bib 66 (1985) 1–38.

118. See Hengel, *The Son of God*, 104–105.

Chapter 25

Problems of Pauline Morality:
The Present State of the Question

The scholarly investigation of Pauline moral doctrine considered as an independent issue is something that was first begun only toward the middle of the nineteenth century with a study by the German Ernesti.[1] The complexity of the issue is shown by the great variety not only of methods used but of solutions achieved in the past hundred odd years.[2] Among the issues that must be considered are literary criticism,[3] the relationship of Pauline morality to his theology in the strict sense, acculturation, and hermeneutic.

Here we consider five specific and particularly characteristic problems, around which the current discussion as well as that of the past can coalesce: I. cultural indebtedness; II. relationship to the teaching of Jesus; III. the problem of the Law; IV. the tension between the indicative and the imperative; V. hermeneutics.

I. Cultural indebtedness

Apparently it was H. Weinel[4] who first noted that Paul's concrete moral demands were not completely original; he spoke of ethical sanctions of

1. H. R. Ernesti, "Die Ethik des Apostels Paulus in ihren Grundzügen dargestellt" (Göttingen, 1868).
2. The most recent monograph to have appeared [at the time this study was prepared, i.e., 1973—T.P.W.] is by the American V. P. Furnish, *Theology and Ethics in Paul* (Nashville, 1968: with bibliography). For later works see G. Segalla, *Introduzione all'etica biblica del Nuovo Testamento. Problemi e storia*, BB 2 (Brescia, 1989) 193–225.
3. See, for example, the study of G. H. Bahr, "The Subscriptions in the Pauline Letters," JBL (1968) 27–41, according to whom, for all effects, we should consider "Pauline" only the moral-paraenetic sections of the Apostle's correspondence. Paul, then, would be not the first Christian theologian but the first great ethics teacher! I believe, however, that such a conclusion cannot be accepted lying down, without further study of the literary and thematic links between the kerygmatic and ethical parts of the Pauline letters.
4. *St. Paul, the Man and His Work* (New York, 1906).

Jewish character and also of requirements of Hellenistic origin. But he failed to develop his remarks in any depth.

The succeeding discussion, then, divided the field between supporters of the one or the other cultural background. On one side, it was M. Dibelius[5] and M. E. Andrews[6] who emphasized the fact that Pauline paraenesis Christianizes various matters from the Greek world. On the other side, M. S. Enslin[7] and W. D. Davies[8] set the discussion of Pauline moral thought against the (unfortunately exclusive) background of Judaism.

Here we shall briefly verify some points of contact between Paul and his twofold environment.

1) *Old Testament and Judaism*

a) Old Testament: its use in paraenesis is extensive.[9] Some examples among many: 1 Thess 4:6 (= Ps 93:1-2); Gal 5:14 (= Lev 19:18); Rom 12:16 (= Prov 3:7 LXX); etc. But we should note: its use is never casuistic in the rabbinic sense; the Old Testament appears in paraenetic contexts not as a real "source" of moral precepts but as a theological basis in a deeper sense.

b) Apocrypha: the contacts are rather rare. But we can note Rom 12:21 (= *Test. Ben.* 4:3) and 1 Cor 7:29-31 (= 4 Esdr 16:42-45).[10]

c) Rabbinism: the similarities have been exaggerated by W. D. Davies, cited above (but see the following section). But at least the sequence of participles with imperative value in Rom 12:9ff. seems explicable in terms of Tannaitic Hebrew.[11]

2) *The Hellenistic Greek world*

It does not seem possible to speak of true "sources" for Pauline moral doctrine in the Greek cultural world, despite repeated attempts by J. R.

5. *Urchristentum und Kultur* (Heidelberg, 1928); "Das christliche Leben (Eph. 4,17–6,9)," ThBl 9 (1930) 341–342; *Botschaft und Geschichte (Gesammelte Aufsätze),* II (Tübingen, 1956) esp. 1–13.

6. *The Ethical Teaching of Saint Paul. A Study in Origin* (Chapel Hill, N. C., 1934).

7. *The Ethics of Paul* (New York–London, 1930).

8. *Paul and Rabbinic Judaism: Some Rabbinic Elements in Pauline Theology* (London, 1955[2]) esp. 111–146.

9. See O. Michel, *Paulus und seine Bibel* (Gütersloh, 1929); E. E. Ellis, *Paul's Use of the Old Testament* (London, 1957); H. Ulonska, "Die Funktion der alttestamentlichen Zitate und Anspielung in den paulinischen Briefen," ThLZ 90 (1965) 793–794.

10. For this last case see W. Schrage, "Die Stellung zur Welt bei Paulus, Epiktet und in der Apokalyptik. Ein Beitrag zu 1. Kor 7,29-31," ZThK 61 (1964) 125–154.

11. Thus D. Daube, "Participle and Imperative in 1 Peter," in E. Selwyn, *The First Epistle of Peter* (1947[2]) 467–488. Against him, in maintaining a Hellenistic background (papyri) see A. Salom, "The Imperatival use of the Participle in the New Testament," ABR 11 (1963) 41–42.

Harris to identify them.[12] This does not mean, however, that Paul was impervious to this culture; actually his work attests to the absorption through osmosis of numerous elements which, though they cannot be reduced to verified "sources," still attest to the considerable diffusion of a certain culture (stoicism in practice) as well as the considerable extent of his openness to it.[13]

It is thus clear that *Popularphilosophie* influences Pauline vocabulary and style. Nor is it just a matter of the diatribe form (as in 1 Cor 3:16; 15:35; Rom 3:1-8; 6:16; 9:19, etc.), but also of certain typically Stoic vocabulary (τὸ ἀνῆκον, "duty": Phlm 8; προσφιλής, εὔφημος, ἀρετή, ἔπαινος, "lovely, gracious, excellence, laudable": Phil 4:8), as well as certain images of human life such as warfare (2 Cor 10:3ff.) or athletic competition (1 Cor 9:25). We could further cite the allusion to God who is τὰ πάντα ἐν πᾶσιν, "the all in all" (see the commentaries) and the concepts of ἐλευθερία, "freedom"; ἀυτάρκεια, "self-sufficiency";[14] and of the human person as "temple of God."[15] We must also note the concept of συνείδησις, "conscience" (1 Cor 8:7ff.; 10:25ff.; 2 Cor 1:12; 4:2; 5:11; Rom 2:15; 9:1; 13:5)[16] and of "natural law."[17] Finally, there are the easily recognized catalogues of vices (1 Thess 4:1-8; Gal 5:19-21; Rom 1:29ff.) and virtues (Gal 5:22-23; Phil 4:8).[18]

But in all these instances we have only material that has been selectively assimilated and integrated in an already Christian context.[19]

---

12. He published a series of articles on the subject from time to time in *Expository Times* from 1912 to 1924: on Epimenides (= Tit 1:12), Euripides (Acts 21:39), Pindar (2 Tim 2:7). Aristophanes (Col 2:18, 23), Aeschylus (Phil 4:4).

13. "The mantle of the Greek orator does hang on Paul's shoulders, but he has no feel for artistic draping, and the lines of his foreign figure show up everywhere" (R. Bultmann, *Der Stil der paulinischen Predigt und die kynisch-stoische Diatribe* [Göttingen, 1910]) 108; see also idem, "Das religiöse Moment in der ethischen Unterweisung des Epiktet und das Neue Testament" ZNW 13 (1912) 97–110; 177–191; *Primitive Christianity in Its Contemporary setting*, trans. R. H. Fuller (New York, 1969 [Italian: 1964]) 121–205. Also, A. Schlatter, "Paulus und das Griechentum" in *Das Paulusbild in der neueren deutschen Forschung* (Darmstadt, 1964) 98–112; M. Pohlenz, "Paulus und die Stoa," ibid., 522–564; J. N. Sevenster, *Paul and Seneca*, (Leiden, 1961).

14. See K. Niederwimmer, *Der Begriff der Freiheit im Neuen Testament* (Berlin, 1966); D. Nestle, *Eleutheria. Studien zum Wesen der Freiheit bei den Griechen und im Neuen Testament. I: Die Griechen* (Tübingen, 1967).

15. The concept recurs in Poseidonius, Seneca, Epictetus, Sextus Pythagoricus: see J. Hausleiter, "Deus internus," in *Reallexikon für Antike und Christentum*, III, 1967 (cited by P. Rossano, "Paul et le pluralisme théologique," in *Parole et Mission* 56 [1971] 209–218).

16. See C. A. Pierce, *Conscience in the New Testament* (London, 1955); J. Stelzenberger, *Syneidesis im Neuen Testament* (Paderborn, 1961).

17. See G. Bornkamm, "Gesetz und Natur," in *Studien zu Antike und Christentum (Gesammelte Aufsätze)*, II (Munich, 1959) 93–118. But on this matter please also note the recent Pontifical Biblical Institute doctoral thesis (1971) of A. Sacchi, who after analysis of Rom 2:12-16, denies an idea of "natural" law there.

18. See A. Vögtle, *Die Tugend- und Lasterkataloge im Neuen Testament* (Münster, 1936); S. Wibbing, *Die Tugend- und Lasterkataloge im Neuen Testament* (Berlin, 1959).

19. See V. P. Furnish, *Theology and Ethics*, 81–92.

II. The relationship to Jesus' teaching

In few cases do we see exegetes in greater disaccord than on this subject. But we would do well to doubt the extreme positions, whether the attempt to find almost a thousand parallels between the Synoptics and the Pauline letters,[20] or the belief that Paul "seriously distorts" the teaching of Jesus.[21]

For greater clarity we divide the question into three parts.

1) *Quotations and allusions to sayings of Jesus*

Only eight passages seem to present convincing parallels to the Synoptics: 1 Thess 5:2, 13, 15; Rom 12:14, 17; 13:7; 14:13, 14; to which paraenetic texts we can add the Lord's supper in 1 Cor 11:23ff.)

Then there are a few Pauline themes that offer some kind of connection with words more or less attested as those of Jesus: 1 Thess 4:15 (the parousia); 1 Cor 7:10 (divorce); 9:14 (support of the Apostle); 14:37 (instructions on the relations between the prophets and the "spiritual").

We can at least summarily conclude from this that Paul seems to have had some familiarity with Jesus' ethical teaching. But it is surprising how little use he makes of it (even less than for the Old Testament). Paul never speaks of Jesus as "teacher" or of Christians as "disciples." And in citing or alluding to sayings of Jesus, he always uses the post-Easter title of κύριος, "Lord"; this indicates that he is not so much interested in the *ipsissima verba*, the very words of Jesus as such, as in their actual presence in the community context of the life of faith in the Risen One.[22]

2) *The "law of Christ"*

The expression is found literally in Gal 6:2; and to this we must add the adjectival expression, ἔννομος Χριστοῦ, "under the Law of Christ," in 1 Cor 9:21. What law is meant? According to C. H. Dodd,[23] Paul is refer-

---

20. As attempted by A. Resch, *Der Paulinismus und die Logia Jesu in ihrem gegenseitigen Verhältnis untersucht* (Leipzig, 1904). In this line see also C. A. A. Scott, *New Testament Ethics: An Introduction* (1930).

21. J. Knox, *The Ethics of Jesus in the Teaching of the Church* (New York, 1961) 75.

22. On the general problem of the relationship between Paul and Jesus, see V. P. Furnish, "The Jesus-Paul Debate: From Baur to Bultmann," BJRL 47 (1965) 342ff.; J. Blank, *Paulus und Jesus. Eine theologische Grundlegung* (Munich, 1968).

23. "The Ethics of the Pauline Epistles," in *The Evolution of Ethics*, ed. E. H. Sneath (New Haven, 1927) 293ff.; *The Ethics of the New Testament* (1952); somewhat differently in "The Primitive Christian Catechism and the Sayings of Jesus," in *New Testament Essays: Studies in Memory of Th. W. Manson*, ed. A. J. B. Higgins (Manchester, 1959) 106ff.

ring to "a new Torah," the nucleus of which would be a group of sayings of the historical Jesus. Meanwhile, W. D. Davies (*Paul and Rabbinic Judaism*, 144–145) speaks of a "Christian *Halakah*."[24]

But the two contexts seem to treat the real meaning of Christian freedom in the context of the commandment of love, and so the expression under consideration must be considered on this semantic level: "law of Christ" = law of love.[25] Nor can one argue against this on the basis of a concept of a "new law" (in conrast to the old Torah); actually this expression is not Pauline, though attested and developed from the second century (*Barn*. 2:6, *Hermas*, Sim. V 6:3; VIII 3:2).

3) *The imitation of Christ*

The texts are the following: 1 Thess 1:6-7; 2:14; 1 Cor 4:16-17; 11:1; Phil 3:5; 3:17; moreover there are the texts with εἰκών.

There is agreement that in Paul the Synoptic vocabulary about "following" (ἀκολουθέω) and "disciple" (μαθητής) gives way to that of "imitating" (μιμέομαι) and "imitator" (μιμητής).

But there are at least three interpretations of this phenomenon; or better, while explaining the lexical difference on the basis of the new Hellenistic environment, the authors disagree on the meaning to attribute to the idea of "imitation":

a) some understand the imitation as a copying of various characteristic traits of the earthly Jesus (material sense);[26]

b) others reduce it to obedience to God's will, pure and simple, as Jesus did in his whole life (formal sense);[27]

c) finally, "imitation" is understood as a process of almost mystical conformation to the Lord on the part of the Christian, who experiences a profound interior transformation (mystical sense).[28]

---

24. See *Torah in the Messianic Age and/or the Age to Come*, JBL Monograph Series 7 (1952); he therefore translates the text of Gal 6:2 as "the Torah of the Messiah," basing this on the (rather late!) passage in *Midr. Qoh.* 11:8. See also R. M. Longenecker, *Paul, Apostle of Liberty* (New York–London, 1964).

25. In basic agreement with: W. Gutbrod, TDNT 4:1076; W. Schrage, *Die konkreten Einzelgebote in der paulinischen Paränese* (Gütersloh, 1961) 99–100, 250; V. P. Furnish, *Theology and Ethics in Paul*, 64–65. See also above, chap. 23, note 52.

26. See W. D. Davies, "Ethics in the New Testament," in *The Interpreter's Dictionary of the Bible*, E–J, 167ff.; W. P. De Boer, *The Imitation of Paul: An Exegetical Study* (Kampen, 1962); more balanced is A. Schulz, *Nachfolgen und Nachahmen. Studien über das Verhältnis der neutestamentlichen Jüngerschaft zur urchristlichen Vorbildethik* (Munich, 1962).

27. Thus W. Michaelis, in TDNT 4:668–669; less so, E. Lohse, "Nachfolge Christi," RGG IV (Tübingen, 1960¹) cols. 1286–1287; V. P. Furnish, *Theology and Ethics in Paul*, 223.

28. See, for instance, E. J. Tinsley, *The Imitation of God in Christ* (London, 1960); H. D. Betz, *Nachfolge und Nachahmung Jesu Christi im NT* (Tübingen, 1967).

III. The meaning of the Law

We must here distinguish between the Pauline attitude toward the specifically Jewish Law on the one hand, and on the other the value he attributes to many exhortations contained in the paraenetic sections of his letters.

1) *Paul and the Jewish Law*

Paul's antithetical statements about the Law are well known: it is identified now as an instrument of sin (see Gal 3:19; Rom 7:5), now as holy and spiritual (see Rom 7:12, 14), again identified with the Old Testament itself (as in Rom 3:31).[29] But here we can ask whether Christ has surpassed it only in its anti-salvific effects, while keeping it "intact as expression of God's will."[30] Such a way of seeing things seems imprecise, if not worse, and requires at least the division we have proposed, the second part of which we shall now examine.

2) *Paul and Christian Paraenesis*

The basic problem is the apparent contradiction into which Paul seems to fall. On the one hand, he constantly proclaims the inward liberty that the Christian has now attained (see 2 Cor 3: Gal 5; Rom 7, etc.);[31] but on the other hand we have the numerous paraenetic sections in his letters, where he goes on at length with exhortations, commands, admonitions, requirements. How can the two attitudes be reconciled? From the end of the nineteenth century to the present there have been two opposing tendencies, with a third alternative attempting a conciliation.

a) A first way of clarifying the question, beginning with P. Wernle[32] and continues at least until E. H. Wahlstrom,[33] identifies Pauline theology as characterized by "enthusiasm": the Christian is completely freed

29. See, for example, H. Schlier, "Excurs. Die Problematik des Gesetzes bei Paulus," *Der Brief an die Galater* (Göttingen, 1971) 176-188. Especially see chapter 23 above.

30. Thus A. van Dülmen, *Die Theologie des Gesetzes bei Paulus* (Stuttgart, 1968) 218 (moreover, the author dedicates a useful appendix, 231-257, to the examination of typical positions regarding our problem). For a different understanding, see P. Stuhlmacher, " 'The End of the Law.' On the Origin and Beginnings of Pauline Theology," *Reconciliation, Law, and Righteousness* (Philadelphia, 1986 [= ZThK 67 (1970) 14-39]) 134-154.

31. "The dominant motif of the Pauline credo is not provided by the *Kyrie eleison*, but by the *Alleluia!*" wrote H. Jacoby, *Neutestamentliche Ethik* (Königsberg, 1899) 327.

32. *Der Christ und die Sünde bei Paulus* (Freiburg-Leipzig, 1897); see also A. Schweitzer, *The Mysticism of St. Paul the Apostle* (New York, 1968 = ca. 1931).

33. *The New Life in Christ* (Philadelphia, 1950); see also J. T. Cleland, *The Religious Ethics of Saint Paul* (unpublished dissertation: New York, 1954).

from sin, being no longer of this world, and therefore not subject to any law, all law being now superfluous; being in Christ and having the Holy Spirit, the Christian "has no need of any moral code." Now, the paraenetic sections of the epistles still remain a problem but are absorbed in a proclamation of faith (Wernle) or else are considered valid for the old person, not for the new (Wahlstrom). Such an interpretation is pneumatic.

b) A solution that at least tends toward the nomistic is represented by M. Goguel[34] and J. Murray:[35] the Law, at least the Christian law, retains a decisive value; it is only in theory that Paul maintains the Christian to be led by the Spirit, but in practice he returns to various preceptive attitudes; he is willing to speak of a nomistic principle, or directly of instructions and commandments as a norm for human behavior. The kerygmatic parts of the epistles, then, essentially become in a certain sense subordinated to the moral parts, or at most put on the same level.

c) A rather more balanced attempt has been made by various writers especially in recent years.[36] Paul's solution is freedom not from all law but from slavery to it; therefore the Law is superseded as *Heilsweg*, as "way of salvation," but not as *Lebensnorm*, "norm of life" (thus Schrage). "The permanent function of the commandment is that it keeps the Christian within God's will, giving content and orientation to freedom" (Wendland; he does speak of the "imperatives of grace"); Law and freedom thus find their higher reconciliation in love, which is the law of Christ (Lopez).

But all this leads us to what can be considered the central problem of Pauline ethic, which we shall now consider.

IV. The relationship between indicative and imperative

The Pauline reality consists in the fact that Paul at various times, even within the same text, links the basic aspects of Christian life either with the indicative mode of the verb to designate its new and already effective reality (e.g., 2 Cor 1:1: Christians are holy), or with the imperative mode

34. *The Primitive Church* (New York, 1964); but see already C. H. Dodd, "The Ethics of the Pauline Epistles" (1927); *Gospel and Law* (Cambridge, 1951 [Italian: 1968]).

35. *Principles of Conduct: Aspects of Biblical Ethics* (Grand Rapids, Mich., 1957); but see already W. D. Davies, *Paul and Rabbinic Judaism.*

36. [I.e. when the study was written—T.P.W.] See, for example, L. Nieder, *Die Motive der religiös-sittlichen Paränese in den paulinischen Gemeindebriefen. Ein Beitrag zur paulinischen Ethik* (Munich, 1956); W. Schrage, *Die konkreten Einzelgebote in der paulinischen Paränese. Ein Beitrag zur neutestamentlichen Ethik* (Gütersloh, 1961); S. Lyonnet, *St. Paul: Liberty and Law* (Rome, 1963); E. Jüngel, "Erwägungen zur Grundlegung der evangelischen Ethik im Anschluss an die Theologie des Paulus," ZThK 63 (1966) 379-396; O. Merk, *Handeln aus Glauben. Die Motivierung der paulinischen Ethik* (Hamburg, 1968: with bibliography); H. D. Wendland, *Ethik des Neuen Testaments. Eine Einführung* (Göttingen, 1970) esp. 55-59; L. Lopez, "Ley y libertad en san Pablo," *Studium* 10 (1970) esp. 53-82.

of the verb to indicate an enduring exigency of appropriate moral behavior (e.g., 1 Thess 4:3). The principal passages are the following: 1 Thess 5:5-6; 1 Cor 5:7; Gal 5:25; Gal 3:27 compared with Rom 13:14; and also Rom 6 (esp. vv. 11-12); Phil 2:12-13; Col 3:3-5. These individual texts must be seen in connection with the relationship between the kerygmatic (indicative) and paraenetic (imperative) parts, especially of the major letters. As can be easily recognized, the question is not just grammatical or literary, but a highly theological problem that involves the whole of Paul's conception of what Christian life is and how it is related to the mystery of salvation.[37]

The discussion of this question revolves around three basic interpretations.

1) *A relationship of contradiction*, more or less marked, which is then resolved in different ways. (a) A compromise is postulated within Paul himself between his ideal picture and the reality of the various Christian communities: the Christian is saved only "in principle," so that the main emphasis falls on the imperative.[38] (b) Or else all the emphasis is on the indicative (see above, Wernle). (c) Or some kind of progress is seen, beginning with "justification" that has already taken place, to reach the "sanctification" that is still to be achieved.[39]

2) *A relationship of antinomy* (co-existence of opposite poles, the combination of which is decisively resolved on the vital level of Christian existence). This seems to be the most satisfactory solution, since it does not diminish but actually affirms the mysterious aspect of Christian life. The first formulation is found in R. Bultmann[40] and then, it would seem, commonly in subsequent writers.[41] We dare not diminish or emphasize either one to the advantage or disadvantage of the other; the imperative is based

37. See R. Schnackenberg, *Moral Teaching of the New Testament* (London, 1965 [Italian: 1971²]) 268-277; H. Ridderbos, *Paul, an Outline of His Theology* (Grand Rapids, Mich., 1975) 253ff.

38. Thus A. Juncker, *Die Ethik des Apostels Paulus*, I-II (Halle, 1904-19); somewhat in this direction (= pastoral aspect, understanding the Pauline paraenesis as a concession to the human weakness of Christians) see the Catholic K. Benz, *Die Ethik des Apostels Paulus* (Freiburg, 1912).

39. See the works cited above by Ernesti, Jacoby, Goguel; thus D. E. H. Whitely, *The Theology of Saint Paul* (Oxford, 1964), esp. 208; it could also be attributed to a diffuse way of preaching. See E. Gaugler, "Die Heiligung in der Ethik des Apostels Paulus," JKZ NF 15 (1925) 100-120; K. Stadler, *Das Werk des Geistes in der Heiligung bei Paulus* (Zurich, 1962).

40. "Das Problem der Ethik bei Paulus," ZNW 23 (1924) 123-140 (= *Das Paulusbild in der neuen deutschen Forschung*, ed. K. H. Rengstorf [Darmstadt, 1969²] 179-199).

41. See, for example, H. Schlier, "Indicatif und imperatif bei Paulus," in *Der Brief an die Galater* (Göttingen, 1971) 264-267; W. G. Kümmel, *The Theology of the New Testament According to Its Major Witnesses* (Nashville, 1973) 224-228; J. Murphy-O'Connor, "Pauline Morality: The Human Options," *Doctrine and Life* 21 (1971) 3-16; "The Contemporary Value of Pauline Moral Imperatives," ibid., 59-71; H. Conzelmann, *Outline of New Testament Theology* (London, 1969).

on the indicative and proceeds from it. Moral behavior gets its value as a consequence or fruit of the new existence ("Become what you are!"); it is a kind of paradox, a moral antinomy between the already and the not yet.

3) *A third attempt at a solution*, which seems problematic to me, is that of V. P. Furnish: "The Pauline imperative is not just the result of the indicative, but fully integral to it. . . . For Paul, obedience is neither preliminary to the new life (as its condition) nor secondary to it (as its result and eventual fulfillment). Obedience is *constitutive* of the new life."[42] The author does thus rehabilitate the imperative, but seems to me to risk a kind of "moral Eutychianism," excessively emphasizing obedience to the detriment of the salvific Event.[43] The author could be correct only if he understood the indicative in the sense of a pure possibility offered to the Christian,[44] but this understanding is in stark contrast to Pauline theology.

V. The hermeneutic problem

We limit ourselves here to the roughest sketch because in our treatment we have chosen to limit ourselves to the most general and basic questions of Paul's moral doctrine, prescinding from the specific and particular aspects of moral content[45] with which moral hermeneutic really ought to be concerned.

The point of departure for the problematic seems to be indicated by the previously cited 1924 article of R. Bultmann (see note 40), where he writes, "The moral imperative for [the justified] has no new content, and their behavior differs from [non-believers] only in that it bears the imprint

42. *Theology and Ethics in Paul*, 225–226.
43. Furnish would not be able to explain the case of the Christian who "does not have time to work, as with the person who dies immediately after being baptized" (Saint Thomas, *In epist. ad Rom.* 4:5). Nor does he recognize the value of the paraenetic *oûn*, "therefore," by denying the distinction between kerygma and didaché (98–111); see W. Nauck, "Das *oûn*-paräneticum," ZNW 49 (1958) 134f.
44. As R. Bultmann seems to mean it in *The New Testament and Mythology* (Philadelphia, 1984 [Italian: 1970]) 20.
45. Such are, for instance, Paul's attitude toward the State: see E. Käsemann, "Röm 13,1–7 in unserer Generation," ZThK 56 (1959) 316–376; W. Affeldt, "Die weltliche Gewalt in der Paulus-Exegese" (Göttingen, 1969: a historical study); or toward marriage and sexuality: see E. Kähler, *Die Frau in den paulinischen Briefen* (Zurich, 1960); P.-H. Menoud, "Saint Paul et la femme," RTP 19 (1969) 318–330. Then there is the issue of slavery: see F. Lyall, "Roman Law in the Writings of Paul—The Slave and the Freedman," NTS 17 (1970) 73–79, and also the catalogues of vices and virtues (see above), the *Haustafeln* (tables of domestic rules), etc. Nor, finally, can the influence of eschatological expectation on Paul's moral doctrine be neglected: see H. D. Wendland, "Ethik und Eschatologie in der Theologie des Paulus," NKZ 41 (1930) 757–783; 793–811; G. Hierzenberger, *Weltbewertung bei Paulus nach 1 Kor 7:29-31. Eine exegetisch-kerygmatische Studie* (Düsseldorf, 1967).

of obedience" (p. 138); therefore "the continuity between the 'old person' and the 'new person' is not ruptured as in Hellenistic mystery religion" (p. 137). While this second statement is clearly partisan in a Lutheran
sense, and as such is not difficult to refute,[46] still, his first statement, while
needing some nuances, seems quite worthwhile to me. It presents the
problem of the "historicity" of morality,[47] of its acculturation, i.e., where
the ethic would be understood as a variable element compared with the
constant element of the kerygma. So, must we speak of a form (the message) that transforms a constantly changing matter (the ethic)? Or would
it not be possible to establish among the various Pauline paraeneses (and
those of the Bible in general) a certain element of moral conduct that would
be absolutely incompatible with the gospel, and on the other hand some
element that must always be retained as valid and indispensable? At the
present time it would seem that these problems have not yet been adequately solved from a strictly biblical perspective:[48] this is perhaps because
hermeneutic as such is not for the biblical scholar alone (nor for the dog-
matician or the moralist), but should be considered the work of the whole
ecclesial community, since it involves not just an aspect of scientific research but especially the existential level of all Christians.

In one's moral behavior, however, as a Christian one cannot dispense
with one criterion, which seems to be as important in concrete life as is
the transcendent principle in philosophy, namely, the "attempt to learn
what is God's will" (Rom 12:2; cf. Eph 5:10, 17), especially since this was
the formative principle of Jesus' whole life (cf. John 4:34). But perhaps
because this is such a formal element, this has further need for other principles, the identification of which would have to be a constant hermeneutical preoccupation.[49] We can also agree with Furnish on the centrality of

46. Note already in the same year and the same review the reply of another Lutheran:
H. Windisch, "Das Problem des paulinischen Imperativs," ZNW 23 (1924) 265–281, defend-
ing such a destruction of continuity between the old and the new person as to require a qualitative change in the believer, even on the level of visible experience.

47. See A. Grabner-Haider, "Zur Geschichtlichkeit der Moral (Biblische Bemerkungen),"
Catholica 22 (1968) 262–270. It seems a normal law of salvation history to adapt to the environment: from Abraham, who follows the custom of the time concerning union with a slave,
to Saint Paul, who urges obedience to the brutal Roman state and is not impatient to destroy
the social institution of slavery.

48. Whereas the hermeneutic in the strictly moral field would seem to be more advanced:
simply for information see J. Fuchs, *Esiste una morale cristiana?* (Brescia, 1970) [and now,
Christian Morality: The Word Becomes Flesh (Dublin–Washington, 1987) esp. 1–101—T.P.W.].

49. I consider too minimalist the position of V. P. Furnish, *Theology and Ethics in Paul*, 227–237,
who rejects not just the "spontaneous" but the law code, the teachings and example of Jesus,
not to mention the very Holy Spirit; positively, he reduces everything to agape joined to
"discernment" (the αἴσθησις of Phil 1:9), and that as practiced in a communal (one's neighbor) and situational context (p. 237: "that is finally . . . a matter of 'insight' into the given
situation").

agape,[50] but provided we link it to its basic theological principles, which he neglects in an almost unpardonable manner. Actually, if love is the "most excellent way" (1 Cor 12:31b), we cannot forget that it is the first "fruit of the Spirit" (Gal 5:22) and that one must therefore study the connections between moral doctrine and pneumatology.[51] And the Spirit, of course, has essential Christological implications, so that "one who has not the Spirit of Christ does not belong to him" (Rom 8:9). Actually, then, the ultimate linkage of the Christian's ethical behavior cannot but be Christological.[52] Only in the light of these principles—if ever—would it be possible to speak of a "discernment" done by the Christian in a communitarian and situational context (see note 49).

50. See also H. Schlier, "Uber die Liebe," *Zeit der Kirche* (Freiburg, 1956) 186–193; and above all the works of C. Spicq, *Agapè. Prolégomènes à une étude de théologie néotestamentaire* (Louvain, 1955); *Agape in the New Testament*, I–III (St. Louis, 1963–); "La morale néotestamentaire: morale chrétienne et morale de la charité," in *Neotestamentica et Patristica: Freundesgabe O. Cullmann* (Leiden, 1962) 228–239; "La morale paulinienne," in *Morale chrétienne et requêtes contemporaines* (1954) 47–70; *Théologie morale du Nouveau Testament*, I–II (Paris, 1965; but observe the restrictive note in vol. I, 10, note 1).

51. See the previously cited K. Stadler (n. 39); also: W. Pfister, *Das Leben im Geist nach Paulus. Der Geist als Anfang und Vollendung des christlichen Daseins* (Fribourg, Switz., 1963).

52. See G. Staffelbach, *Die Vereinigung mit Christus als Prinzip der Moral bei Paulus*, Diss. Theol. Freiburg i. Uechtl (1932); G. Friedrich, "Christus, Einheit und Norm der Christen. Das Grundmotiv des 1. Korintherbriefs," *Kerygma und Dogmatik* 9 (1963) 235–258; E. Lohse, "Christologie und Ethik im Kolosserbrief," in *Apophoreta. Festschrift E. Haenchen* (Berlin, 1964) 156–168; R. Baumann, *Mitte und Norm des Christlichen (1 Kor. 1,1–3,4)* (Münster, 1968); finally, O. Merk, op. cit., see note 36.

Chapter 26

Christianity and Secularity/Laicity in Saint Paul: Remarks

Preliminaries

Paul exists and carries out his work within a twofold tradition, where the theme of the secular (and the lay)[a] was very much alive and had unique characteristics.

This is true first of all in Judaism. Here we must note two levels. On the one hand, the doctrine of creation radically desacralizes the world and earthly realities, setting forth a basically secular view of the whole cosmos (as distinguished from pagan Greco-Roman tradition, which considered all cosmic reality to be an epiphany of a divine force). On the other hand, on the social-religious level there is between priests and laity a clear distinction which is not just functional (as in paganism) but actually tribal (note the tribe of Levi), and which is surrounded by extensive discourse on the clean and unclean.

In the second place, pre-Pauline Christianity was already engaged in distancing itself from Jewish regulations concerning certain aspects of social life (such as purity concerning diet and certain human relations and the sacredness of certain times like the Sabbath and the place of the Jerusalem Temple). This had taken place in two stages: first with Jesus, who did not belong to the social institution of the priesthood (note Heb 7:14; 8:4) and repeatedly showed freedom with regard to laws of purity (e.g., Mark 7); then with Stephen and companions, who showed a critical atti-

a. Following normal Italian usage, Penna uses the terms *laicità* and *laico* to refer to the "secular" (as distinguished from the sacred) and the "lay" (as distinguished from the priestly). Though the concepts are regularly distinguished in English with "lay" always referring to persons, their affinity is obvious in that a priesthood is evidently a sacred institution. In this chapter the terms "secular" and "secularity" will generally be used, but where the context requires, "lay" and (God forgive me) "laicity" appear.—T.P.W., translator.

tude toward the Temple understood as a human-constructed dwelling of God's presence among human beings (see Acts 6–7).

In its relationship to Judaism, then, Christianity had taken up the first conception of secularity, the general one of the total profaneness of the world, which is no longer seen as a manifestation of the divine but is demythologized and understood in its diversity. But Christianity did not follow Judaism in distinguishing and separating a group of persons devoted to sacrificial worship from the rest of the community of secular lay persons.

Historically, Christianity considered itself heir not to the Temple but to the Synagogue, where to preside at cult (centered on the word) it was not necessary to be a priest; a recognized awareness of the Law as God's word sufficed. This Christian characteristic began with Jesus, for on the one hand he was not qualified to act as a priest in the Temple but could (and did—see Luke 4:16-30) take a leading role in Synagogue worship, and on the other hand, when he called his disciples and even the Twelve he assigned them duties of evangelization and pastoral care rather than priestly duties (see Matt 10; Mark 3:14-15; Luke 22:19; Acts 1:8).

In the New Testament writings not only is the Christian community never described as priests and laity, but none of its members is ever described in such a way as to suggest this duality. In the New Covenant there is only one priest, Jesus Christ (see Hebrews), and he is so in an absolutely different way, and all the baptized are in various ways and at the same time objects of and participants in Jesus' unique mediatorial function (see 1 Pet 2; Rev 1:6; 5:10; 20:6).

And Paul is a primary witness to this uniqueness of Christianity. He even contributes to its character with certain fruitful personal contributions, which we now intend to treat under two headings.

I. Christian secularity, based on the salvific event, and constitutive of the community of the baptized.

1) *The salvific event.* More than anywhere else, in the first chapters of Romans Paul well indicates that God grants his grace to all persons without distinction, regardless of any religious or cultural condition. Indeed, "there is no partiality with God" (Rom 2:11; cf. Gal 2:6; Eph 6:9), literally, "God does not look at anyone's face," i.e., does not make an exception of anyone.

In Rom 1–5 Paul espouses two theses that seem to be expressed in contrasting terms but in substance are complementary. The first is that human persons are equal in sin (see 1:18–3:20). "Jews and Greeks are all under the dominion of sin" (3:9); "There is none that is just, not even one" (3:10 = Ps 14:3); "There is no distinction: all have sinned, and all are deprived of God's glory" (3:22b-23); "All have sinned" (5:12). The second is that all human persons are also equals in justification (see 3:21–5:21). "All . . . are justified free of cost by his grace" (3:24); "For there is only one God, who by faith will justify the circumcised and by faith the uncircumcised as well" (3:30); "If by the fall of one, all die, all the more God's grace . . . is poured out abundantly on all" (5:15).

Therefore, before God no one can take advantage of any special privilege, whether personal or institutional. In the first place, there is no claim to personal privilege based on works, that is, on strict observance of the Law. "No one will be justified before him on the basis of works of the Law" (3:20), since these only obscure the purity of God's grace and lead one to boast about one's own moral achievements, like the Pharisee of the parable (see Luke 18:9-14); and Paul himself, who in his pre-Christian existence was "a Pharisee as to the Law . . . without reproach as to the righteousness deriving from the Law" (Phil 3:5-6), after his encounter with Christ considered all these things a "loss" (Phil 3:7, 8) and "garbage" (Phil 3:8), thus turning his scale of values completely upside down.

In the second place, even a supposed institutional privilege with which to protect oneself is worth nothing. Jeremiah already had warned against confidence in the Temple of the Lord as a guarantee of salvation (Jer 7:4); and yet it was typical of Israel to celebrate the Torah as its own boast and as a cause for prideful distinction from other peoples (note Bar 4:4: "Blessed are we, O Israel, for to us has been revealed what is pleasing to God").

Well, Paul irreverently dismantles this presumption; and of the Law, which he knows to be the "expression of wisdom and truth" (Rom 2:20) for the Jew, he says without mincing words that "through this [comes only] awareness of sin" (3:20) and that through it God's "anger is provoked" (4:15; cf. Gal 3:10, 19).

Paul, then, brings about a complete leveling of human persons before God, not only in the condition of sin, please note, but also in that of redemption. Essentially, it is justification purely by faith that becomes the primary factor of a radical equalization. "Where then is the boasting? It is excluded. By what law? That of works? No, but by the law of faith!" (Rom 3:27). Faith, then, is the new law, the new saving principle of the Christian, of all Christians. And to believe is to recognize oneself as recipient of God's grace in Christ, in an act that makes all indistinguishably alike and and makes us actually recognize that we are all together "only one in Christ Jesus" (Gal 3:28). By its nature the cross of Christ, far from separating different groups within the Christian community, closely joins all the baptized together around itself, all on the same level. Thus none, in the light of the cross, are distinguished as priests and laity; rather they find themselves all as laity before the only priest, who is Jesus.

2) *Nature of the "ekklesia" and its functions.* The Church, as community of baptized believers, is one homogeneous whole of men and women who are redeemed, that is, justified, and who humbly and joyously submit themselves to the grace of God revealed in the blood of Christ. Let us be more precise.

a) The Church is a community entirely of "saints by their calling" (Rom 1:7), in the sense of Saint Augustine's comment: "It is not that they are called because they are holy, but that they have become holy because they were called" (PL 35:2093). The Greek expression Paul uses for the Romans, $\varkappa\lambda\eta\tau o\tilde{\iota}\varsigma$ $\dot{\alpha}\gamma\acute{\iota}o\iota\varsigma$, is the same as that used for the Corinthians in 1 Cor 1:2, but here in this latter text the Italian C.E.I. translates "chiamati ad essere santi (called to be holy),"[b] erroneously conferring a moral meaning to the holiness of the Christian, which in reality rather has a primarily ontological dimension. (N.B.: In fact, according to Greek grammar the verbal adjective has two forms: one ending in -$\tau o\varsigma$, as in our case, which indicates a state in relation to an action actually accomplished or only potentially so; only the ending in -$\tau\varepsilon o\varsigma$ indicates the need for an action still to be completed, thus corresponding to the Latin gerundive.)

It is the grace of God that, just by being received, constitutes Christians in this new condition: "You have been washed, you have been sanctified, you have been justified in the name of the Lord Jesus Christ and in the Spirit of our God" (1 Cor 6:11). This is a reality so true, objective, and concrete that Paul identifies the baptized as "a new creation" (2 Cor 5:17; Gal 6:15), a daring expression that Judaism reserved for the eschatological era of the new heavens and new earth. And it is most interesting, indeed surprising, to note that Paul attributes the description "holy by calling" to the Christians of Corinth already at the beginning of the first letter (cf. ibid., also: "sanctified in Christ Jesus") and that, as we discover as we read the rest of the letter, this description is applied to members of a church wracked by internal divisions, with a case of quasi-incest, of dubious marriage practices, marred by the contrast between the strong and the weak in faith, disorderly in their assemblies, and even in need of being recalled to faith in the resurrection!

b. The above English translation is found in both passages, for instance, in NAB (1986). RSV (1971) and JB (1961) are closer to Penna's desired reading with "called to be saints," and indeed in JB 1 Cor 1:2, "called to take their place among all the saints" seems to be deliberately trying to avoid a moralistic understanding.

b) The members of the Church are on an equal footing, not only by their common holiness shared by them as a point of departure but also because all are called to carry out some ministry. The basic text in this regard is 1 Cor 12:4-11, which emphasizes the fact that "to each is given a specific manifestation of the Spirit for the common good" (12:7). Hence no one in the Church can be considered to be without some ministerial function, since the ministries are not concentrated in the hands of only a few. The same ecclesiological conception is found again in Eph 4:7 ("To each of us has been given grace according to the measure of Christ's gift") and 4:12, which says that the apostles-prophets-evangelists-pastors-teachers have the task of "preparing the saints for the work of service," i.e., to instruct the baptized for their ecclesial responsibility as Christian adults. Consequently, according to Paul, the Christian community is actually not dualistically divided as it were into producers and consumers of the sacred. Indeed, the whole Church is sacred, or better "holy," as a new "Temple of God" in a personal sense (see 1 Cor 3:16-17; 6:19; 2 Cor 6:16; Eph 2:20-22), which implicitly indicates that in such an unprecedented Temple, all the Christians are priests through participation in the priesthood of Christ.

c) But at certain points the Apostle witnesses the presence in various Churches of specific ministerial functions. We list the passages. In 1 Thess 5:12 we read of "those who labor among you who preside over you (προϊσταμένους) in the Lord and admonish you." In Rom 12:8 similarly among the other gifts is listed the one "who presides" (ὁ προϊστάμενος). In 1 Cor 12:28 we read of gifts of governance (κυβερνήσεις). In Phil 1:1, almost in passing, mention is made of ἐπίσκοποι and διάκονοι. In Eph 4:11 are listed "apostles, prophets, evangelists, pastors, and teachers." Then in the pastoral letters a clear distinction will be made between three functions affirmed in sequence, especially in 1 Tim: ἐπίσκοποι (3:1-7); deacons (3:8-13); presbyters (5:17-22; cf. Titus 1:5-9); here the task of presbyters is to preside (οἱ προεστῶτες), and it is not said whether this concerns times of worship, but their primary function is clearly concerned with the word, i.e., preaching and teaching.

None of these designations corresponds to any priestly activity of pagans or Jews (and furthermore, neither in Paul nor anywhere in the New Testament is the expression ἱερεῖς, "priests," used to designate a specific ministerial function within the Church); or better, never are the functions of those primarily responsible for the Christian communities described analogously to those of the priests of the Temple. This does not exclude the possibility of their having a special participation in Christ's priesthood, but Paul does not make it explicit.

II. Secularity and cultic categories

In Christian literature the first occurrence of the term λαϊκός (attributed to a person) is found in the Letter of Clement of Rome to the Corinthians from about A.D. 96, hence much later than Paul's letters. Here in an allusion to Judaism a distinction is made between high priest, priests, levites, and the *laikos* (chap. 40), to indicate that each must stand in the proper place and that the Christian community must be ordered within. And it is a type of discourse done in reference to sacred ceremonies (probably the first witness to a Christian liturgy), seeing that the Corinthians have "dismissed from the superintendency *(ἐπισκοπή)* those who have offered the oblations with holiness and perfection" (chap. 44). In all this we are faced with an evident evolution of the internal structures of the Church and their functions. True, the Letter to the Hebrews referred repeatedly to Jewish priestly practices as found in the Old Testament, but only to apply the categories to Jesus Christ (with the indication that he has surpassed them) and not to the ministers of the Church (designated in Heb 13:7, 17, 24 as "leaders," *ἡγούμενοι* in a general sense).

In Paul, as we have seen, the community leaders are never identified in priestly terms. Still, in his letter we must note a certain use of language derived from the priesthood but applied to various subjects in a completely new way. We must distinguish three areas of application.

1) In the first place we note *the employment of certain cultic language with reference to Christ.* The cases are extremely rare, an evident sign that Paul's mental structure was not inclined to reflect on the event of the cross in priestly/sacrificial terms deriving from the Jerusalem Temple. In fact, there are only two such texts, the first of which, moreover, according to many exegetes, would be pre-Pauline in derivation: Rom 3:25 and 2 Cor 5:21. Unable to go into details here, we will have to limit ourselves to a few essential highlights.

In Rom 3:25 (literally, "God prepared him as an expiation in his blood, through faith") the Greek term ἱλαστήριον, "expiation," can only recall what Lev 16 says concerning Yom Kippur, the Day of Atonement, when for the only time of the year the high priest entered the Holy of Holies of the Temple to pour the blood of a bullock for his own sins and that of a goat for those of the people, on the cover of the Ark of the Covenant (*kappôret* in Hebrew, ἱλαστήριον in Greek). Jesus comes, then, to fulfill the functions of the instrument of expiation par excellence, and so to cancel all the sins of human beings in general.

Moreover, 2 Cor 5:21 ("God made the one who knew no sin to be sin for our sakes") is an extremely strong statement. The sacrificial sense of the expression "made him to be sin," ἁμαρτίαν ἐποίησεν, is disputed; some would deny it (see the recent commentary of V. P. Furnish). But we must note that the same terminology appears in Lev 4:24, where the sacrifice for sin is simply called by the abbreviated term "sin" (in the Hebrew MT *ḥaṭṭa't hû'*; in the Greek LXX ἁμαρτία ἐστιν). Even the phrase "for us" (or "in favor of us") recalls the salvific goal of the event of the cross (see 2 Cor 5:14, 15). Isaiah 53:10 must also be compared: this says that the servant offered himself "in expiation" (MT: *assam*; LXX: περὶ ἁμαρτίας).

2) There is also cultic terminology *used by Paul concerning himself*. But it is interesting to note that this is never used in the proper sense, but rather in a transferred sense, i.e., not to describe properly cultic acts but to describe non-cultic acts of Paul's ministry in a cultic way. Essentially there are three cases.

In the first case, Phil 3:3 ("[we] who worship God in the Spirit") and Rom 1:9 ("the God whom I worship in my spirit, proclaiming the gospel of his Son"), the word λατρεύειν is used. Strictly speaking, in classical Greek this means only "to render a service" in general, but it is rare in cultic usage; however, in the biblical Greek of the LXX it indicates religious service in general, by all the people (e.g., Deut 10:12: "The Lord your God requires of you . . . you shall love him and *serve* [MT: *'abad*; LXX: λατρεύειν] the Lord your God with all your heart and all your soul"), while the cultic service of priests is indicated by the word λειτουργεῖν. Especially Rom 1:9 indicates in what such "service" consists: in proclaiming the gospel!

In the second case, Phil 2:17 is important ("Even if my blood must be poured out as a libation on the sacrifice and the offering of your faith, I am content and rejoice in it with you all"). Here the technical cultic terms are the two nouns θυσίᾳ καὶ λειτουργίᾳ (literally, "sacrifice and service") and the verb σπένδομαι ("poured out as a libation"). But their application concerns realities that are completely outside the strictly cultic realm. For the two nouns designate the faith of the Philippians, while the verb refers to the possible martyrdom of Paul, i.e., to the shedding of his blood (the letter is written from a dramatic situation in prison). Libations consisted in the pouring out of wine on the sacrificial offerings, and were practiced in both Israel (see Lev 23:13, 18) and the gentile world (the action is often depicted in paintings on pottery), where the libation at the beginning of the family meal was also important.

In the third case we have the more significant passage in Rom 15:16, where Paul says of himself that he has been designated as a "minister (λειτουργός) of Jesus Christ among the gentiles, exercising the sacred office (ἱερουργόν) of the gospel of God in order that the gentiles may become an acceptable oblation (προσφορά), sanctified by the Holy Spirit." The strongest term in this passages is surely λειτουργός. In the Greek of the Septuagint this is practically equivalent to ἱερεύς, "priest," as we can deduce from Neh 10:40; Sir 7:30; Isa 61:6 ("You shall be called priests of the Lord, ministers of our God shall you be called," where the synonymous parallelism between the two terms is evident). But perhaps the verb ἱερουργεῖν is just as significant with its technical meaning of "sacrifice, accomplish sacred rites." From this perspective, Paul's task of proclaiming the gospel to the gentiles is surprisingly identified as, or better, equated with, an act of sacrifice, suggesting that it has the same redemptive value (cf. the parallel in the rabbinic work *Abot de Rabbi Natan* 4: "The study of Torah is more pleasing to God than holocausts. . . . When the wise man sits to explain the Torah to the assembly, the Scripture counts for him as if he had offered fat and blood on the altar"; but this was written when the Temple was no more, while Paul's apostolic ministry takes place completely within the period of the so-called Second Temple).

From these passages we can deduce Paul's innovative conception of apostolic ministry, the principal function of which, the proclamation of the word, substitutes for and is equivalent to the specific cultic acts performed by priests in the Temple precincts. This indicates both that preaching has a preeminent dignity, and that it is capable, if accepted in faith, of bringing about human salvation (see Rom 1:16-17).

3) Finally, Paul also makes use of a certain cultic language *with regard to all Christians*, but only to describe their everyday life.

This is especially true of Rom 12:1: "So I exhort you, by God's mercy, to offer (παριστάνειν) your bodies as a living (ζῶσαν) sacrifice (θυσίαν), holy (ἁγίαν) and acceptable (εὐάρεστον) to God, your spiritual worship (λογικὴ λατρεία)." The verb παρίστημι in itself means "present, put at someone's disposal, place before," and as such can also have a technical cultic meaning (see, e.g., Xenophon, *Anabasis* 6:1:22). This is the sense in which Paul uses it here, since the object is a "sacrifice," or better, a "sacrificial victim" (θυσία). The important new thing is that the sacrificial matter consists of "your bodies." What does this mean? Of course, it is not a question of offering oneself on the altar (cf. 1 Cor 13:31)! Underlying this expression is a Semitic anthropology, according to which the human body is simply the human being, for it is incomprehensible to try to distinguish the person from that person's corporality. And then the sacrifice to which the Christian is called consists in a total offering of self to the Lord, in standing before God as a sacrificial victim in all the events and all the components of one's life, and thus in exercising one's priestly role upon oneself rather than on something external or foreign to self (see Eph 1:4: "to be holy and irreproachable in his sight, in love''). This is the sacrifice everyone can offer, one that is living, holy, and acceptable to God.

Paul identifies all this as "spiritual worship." In what sense? The expression in itself does not refer to the Holy Spirit. The adjective λογικός means "spiritual" only insofar as it is opposed to the physical, the material. Some light is shed on the subject by a text from Philo of Alexandria (*De spec. leg.* 1:203, 277) "The spirit of one who sacrifices must be sanctified by good and appropriate thoughts, and that person's life must consist in the finest actions. . . . What counts before God is not how many offerings are made but the extreme purity of the rational spirit *(πνεῦμα λογικόν)* of the offerer." Essentially this is an appeal for interiority of the cult—not so much to give an interior dimension to the outward cult, but to lead the outward cult back to that which is inward. Basically, the offering of self is all the cult that Paul knows as far as Christians are concerned. Even the next verse indicates this: "Do not conform to the mentality of this age . . ." (Rom 12:2); but we must also remember those texts where the act of faith itself is described as an "obedience," and hence a submission to God (see Rom 1:5; 6:16; 10:16; 16:19, 26). Hence there is a thematic affinity to 1 Pet 2:5, where the baptized are identified as "living rocks, built up as a spiritual edifice, as a holy priesthood, to offer spiritual sacrifices *(πνευμάτικας θυσίας)* pleasing to God, through Jesus Christ"; and it is also similar to Heb 13:16: "Do not forget to do good and to share what you have, for God is pleased by such sacrifices" (cf. also Heb 13:15; "Let us continually offer a sacrifice of praise to God").

There is also a second Pauline text that describes the Christian life in cultic terms, in 2 Cor 9:12: "The ministration of this sacred service not only provides for the needs of the saints. . . ." Paul here speaks of the collection that the Corinthian Church is asked to take up for the poor Christians of Jerusalem. He identifies such a social duty as διακονία τῆς λειτουργίας ταύτης (literally, "the ministration of this liturgy"). Considering the rather general sense of the Greek term λειτουργία (see above), the scholarly opinion has been expressed that it has a strictly profane semantic value (as also in Phil 2:30). But others (more probably right) think that Paul has invested the term with cultic sense considering the following observations: 2 Cor 9:12 goes on at once to say that it is not just a service rendered to the saints in Jerusalem, but also a service rendered to God himself (''but it has even greater value through the many thanks given to God''). Elsewhere the same collection is described with terms rich in theological flavor (note χάρις, "grace, in 8:4, 6, 7, 19; 9:8; and εὐλογία, "blessing," in 9:5). Finally, the above cited Heb 13:16 explicitly identifies acts of generosity as θυσίαι, ''[cultic] sacrifices.'' Paul, then, is very free in transferring the language of cult to the most concrete daily behavior of Christian existence, particularly to the enterprises most concerned with supplying the needs of other Christians. And here it is not just in relation to God that Paul sees the realization of an unprecedented "communion": that of reciprocal love (see 2 Cor 9:13: "the generosity of your communion with them and with all"), which more than cultic sacrifices is able to "cover a multitude of sins" (Jas 5:20).

III. Conclusion

At the end of this brief analysis let us draw a simple conclusion. What is new in Paul can be accurately assessed only if we situate it in the context of his activity in religious history. With his Pharisaic formation, he doubtless attributed enormous importance to the priestly function of the Jerusalem Temple before his conversion; and this Temple continued to function normally throughout his whole life. And yet, as we have seen, he completely prescinds from this perspective; even less does he want to extend to Christians the levitical rules that the Pharisees expropriated from the priests and applied to the whole people of Israel.

Paul certainly did not transfer to the Christian community the socio-religious dualism of priests and laity that was current in both Israel and the pagan world. In the second century the so-called *Letter of Barnabas* will simply lump together the Jerusalem Temple and the pagan temples (chap. 16) in saying that Christians have nothing to do with these cultic categories. And Tertullian at the beginning of the third century attests with regard to incense that "more of it is used—and at greater expense—for Christian funerals than to incense the gods." He goes on to report the complaint of pagans that the attendance at the temples has gone down because of conversions to Christianity, to which he responds: "It is true, but what do you want? We can't help both needy humans and your begging gods. And besides, we don't believe we need give to those who do not ask; if Jupiter holds out his hand, he'll get a few coins, since our generosity gives more in the streets than yours gives in the temples" (*Apologet.* 42). This paralleling of the streets with the temples says a good deal about the secularization of Christian faith and life. And it corresponds perfectly to Paul's conception of reality, according to which it is not in ceremonies that priesthood is exercised but in the common, existential dimension of every day, whether eating, drinking, or doing anything else (see 1 Cor 10:31), and even more so in the solicitous care of those in need.

We could actually say that for Paul there are no lay persons, or better, that all Christians are lay or secular if their identity is measured only in relation to a priestly caste, which for him simply does not exist in the Church. Now, it is true that in the Church there do exist specific ministerial functions which not all possess and which have considerable importance. It is here that distinctions do emerge (see above). But Paul (and the whole New Testament with him) does not use the category "lay," whether because the term in Greek is late and very rare, or because it tends to suggest more than a distinction, but a real separation, which is inappropriate for those who participate without distinction in the same benefits of redemption. Rather, all, while exercising different ministries, give glory to God by helping to build up the body of Christ in harmony and love.

Chapter 27

"Love Builds Up":
Ecclesiological Aspects of *Agape* in Saint Paul

Among the New Testament writers, it is surely Paul who most richly and most explicitly develops the treatment not only of the Church but also in particular of the close relationship between the Church on the one hand (we might better say, of the reality of single concrete Christian communities) and love on the other. In practically all his letters we find more than one shorter or longer treatment of the intimate relationship between these two basic aspects of Christian life. I must therefore confess myself surprised to discover that a relatively recent German work concerning the Church as communion in Saint Paul has absolutely no examination of the relationship between κοινωνία and ἀγάπη, thus ignoring Paul's deep theological sense that the former reality is impossible without the latter.[1]

I must confess that in dealing with this subject one is immediately tempted to systematize Paul's thought here. It lends itself to such treatment. But to do so would be to lose the freshness and concreteness. So I shall indicate the method of approach. Since biblical theology belongs to the genus of history,[2] I shall substantially follow the chronological order of the Pauline letters, seeking to grasp the development that Paul actually experienced, or at any rate manifested, in this area of his thought. As in the case of other theological issues, here also we get a good view

---

1. The work is the volume by J. Hainz, *Koinonia. "Kirche" als Gemeinschaft bei Paulus,* BU 16 (Regensburg, 1982); this author simply classifies and discusses the individual Pauline passages where the word "κοινωνία" occurs, without ever asking himself the larger and deeper question about the themes interrelated with this κοινωνία, and especially its foundations in love. So much so that in Phil 2:1b at least, the term is literally surrounded by two explicit mentions of agape: in 2:1a and 2:2. But see the excellent study by E. Franco, *Communione e partecipazione. La koinônia nell'epistolario paolino,* Aloisiano 20 (Brescia, 1986).

2. As J. Ph. Gabler already maintained in 1787: see W. G. Kümmel, *The New Testament: The History of the Investigation of Its Problems* (London, 1973 [Italian: 1976]) 98–101.

of an evolution that is vitally affected by the various events and developments that take place in his encounters and the correspondence with the communities he founded. We certainly do not intend to produce a dull, prosaic description of the matter, say by just giving a statistical account of each text. Anything but that. Rather, we intend to sketch just how it was that Paul little by little came to visualize for himself the relationship between Church and *agape*, as his thought grew ever richer on the basis of successive experiences in the history of his pastoral care.

One last word before proceeding. I shall not be translating the Greek term ἀγάπη, which, despite the quotation derived from the RSV in the title of this chapter, I shall leave in the original.* The various translations adopted, "love," "charity," do not take into account that this is a typical, creative expression of Christian speech, which in order to avoid confusion precisely has every right to its own existence in the vocabulary of modern languages.[3]

I. The labor of *agape* (1 Thess 1:3)

Paul already writes of *agape* in the first lines of his first work. Addressing the Christians of Thessalonica, he assures them that before God he remembers their "work of faith" and "labor of *agape*" and the "endurance of hope in our Lord Jesus Christ" (1 Thess 1:3). It will be worth our while to dwell briefly on the second phrase of this triad, which first appears here but will become a cliché, "labor of love," though in a different sense. In Greek the text reads τοῦ κόπου τῆς ἀγάπης. This κόπου means "strenuous work," "exertion," and hence "fatigue," as suggested by the traditionally used English term "labor."[4] Paul means not that the love put into practice by the Thessalonians is something practical, dynamic, as opposed to mere declaration in words, but rather that the display of love (which is taken for granted as put into action) is something that is not

---

* Here and elsewhere in this chapter Penna takes issue with a translation of the C.E.I., the translation of the Italian Bishops' Conference. In such cases I alter the text to fit a current English translation if appropriate, but here and in note 4 retain the philological information while omitting the polemic.—T.P.W., translator.

3. See C. Spicq, in the collection *Foi et salut selon S. Paul (Epître aux Romains 1,16)*, AB 42 (Rome, 1970) 226. For the characteristic meaning of New Testament *agape*, we recommend the basic works of C. Spicq, *Agape in the New Testament*, trans. M. A. McNamara and M. H. Richter, 3 vols. (St. Louis, 1963–) and A. Nygren, *Agape and Eros*, trans. P. Watson (London, 1982 = 1952 [Italian: 1971]).

4. See P. Rossano, *Lettere ai Tessalonicesi*, La Sacra Bibbia (Turin, 1965) 59: "Paul frequently uses the term (nineteen times) to indicate not only physical work by himself and Christians but especially apostolic work done in the Church on their behalf."

only demanding but costly; it is not easy.[5] In the other recurrences of the word κόπος in 1 Thess 2:9 and 3:5, Paul writes of "our labor," giving us a better idea of the meaning of the expression, which is used not of the Thessalonians alone but also in this context with reference to Paul's evangelizing activity in their city.

Actually, chapters 2–3 are an outpouring of feeling to which Paul abandons himself as he remembers how much he had to suffer at Thessalonica in order to found a Christian community there, which is especially dear to him just because of this labor. And after decisively denying any base motive of self-interest or profit or vainglory, he continues heart in hand, as it were: "We were tender *(ἤπιοι)* among you, as a mother nursing and caring for her own children. With such affection *(όμειρόμενοι)* for you, we would have wanted to give you not just the gospel but our very lives, for you had become dear *(ἀγαπητοί)*. You do remember, brethren, our labor *(κόπον)* and our torments, working night and day so as not to be a burden to anyone we announced the good news to you. . . . Like a father toward his children . . ." (2:7-9, 11).

This short section teems with expressions of two intimately related ideas: Paul's love for the Thessalonians, and the hardships through which he expressed it. Paul's love for the Thessalonians is costly, and he had already indicated it in 2:2, recalling: "After first having suffered and been mistreated at Philippi, as you well know, we had the boldness of our God to announce to you the Good News of God in the midst of many sufferings." This, then, is how a Church is born! From a costly love, where κόπος provides the matter of *agape*, and the latter provides the form of the κόπος. It is no accident that in these lines Paul joins a rich agapic vocabulary ("tender," "affection," "dear," "like a mother," "like a father") to strong allusions to endurance and hardship ("labor," "torments," "working night and day," wanting "to give our very lives").

It is natural to associate this reality with the exquisite pains of childbirth; and Paul must have had the idea tacitly on his mind if a little later in 1 Cor 4:15 he writes directly, "You may have ten thousand pedagogues in Christ, but not many fathers, for it is I who begot you in Christ Jesus, through the gospel." What shows through in these texts is the implicit comparison of a Christian community and a family. Parents know the sacrifice it takes to raise children, but it is also only they who know how much love goes into that sacrifice. That is also why at the end of the letter

5. The BJ renders quite well "le labeur de votre charité," which corresponds to the *labor caritatis* of the New Vulgate, implying clearly the idea of the burden of love. Curiously the Vulgate, perhaps sensing the Greek to be unusual, had separated the two terms, translating, . . . *et laboris et charitatis,* "the work of your faith and labor and charity"!

Paul fervently asks the recipients to treat "those who labor *(κοπιῶντας)* in your midst with much *agape*, on account of their labor" (5:12-13). And again we see here the labor of love, now attributed to the local church leaders. But in addition to the analogy with the human realities of child-birth and family, there is another term of comparison underlying Paul's text that more closely corresponds to the specifically Christian dimension of speech, and even more of the reality, namely, the dedication of Jesus shown in his death on the cross. But properly speaking, what we have here is not just an extrinsic comparison but a recalling and a reactualiza-tion of a pattern derived from the Archetype. For in Gal 2:20 Paul will say of Christ, "He loved me and gave himself up for me": and this it is that every Church (and every Christian) should be able to say of their first founders and their own pastors.

II. The First Letter to the Corinthians

When writing First Corinthians, Paul already had behind him not only the apostolic experiences of Philippi and Thessalonica but his long stay in Corinth. There he had founded an *"ἐκκλησία"* (1 Cor 1:2), i.e., a Chris-tian group that assembled together (see 11:18). It had cost him dearly even at the time of its establishment (see Acts 18; 1 Cor 2:1-5). But it gave him even more concern now that he was no longer there, because, besides some individual cases of immorality (see chaps. 5; 6; 7), the whole Church was undergoing the trial of a threefold fragmentation from within: (a) in the Church as a whole through opposing factions (see chaps. 1-4); (b) in the more specific question of contrasts between the "weak" and the "strong" in questions of conscience (chaps. 8-10); (c) and also in the mutual rela-tions among a proliferation of ecclesial ministries of various kinds (see chaps. 11-14). In the letter, then, the theme of the ecclesial dimensions of *agape* is extensively developed, in response to the many concrete cir-cumstances provided by the Church, which might be better described as "lively" than "living."

Paul's responses are based on two perspectives. First of all, and above all, Paul refers to the precise circumstance in Corinth. Of the three prob-lem areas noted above, Paul approaches the second one especially with the need of love. For regarding the first, the division brought about in the name of various personages, he tries to obviate it with a rich reflec-tion on the relationship between the wisdom of the world and the wis-dom of the cross, indicating that when the gospel is proclaimed we are all equal before it, and that our acceptance of the gospel gives equal dig-nity to all; meanwhile, the preachers are identified only in terms of instrumentality, being only "ministers through whom you came to believe" (3:5; cf. 3:21-23). It is only at the end of the section that Paul will threaten his audience in half serious terms: "Do you want me to come with a stick, or with love and a spirit of meekness?" (4:21).

But in facing the concrete problem of the idolaters, and seeing some Christians led astray through the free, uncaring, and unrestrained behavior of others, Paul tries to formulate the alternative choices. Which counts most: Is it the liberty of the one who "knows" that one's relationship to God does not depend on the thin line of just which kind of meat can be eaten, or is it rather the magnanimous and indeed agapic attitude of one who knows how to understand, excuse, and tolerate? It is precisely concerning this that he declares the principle that we here paraphrase slightly: "The pure conscience concerning things can puff a person up with pride; agape is constructive" (ἡ δὲ ἀγάπη οἰκοδομεῖ: 8:1b). The traditional rendering, "love builds up" (NAB; RSV), which we use as title for this chapter, could be understood in a rather sweet, even sentimental way.

But the decisive thing is to grasp the theological and specifically ecclesiological significance of the Pauline concept of οἰκοδομή. This term in the New Testament is characteristic of Paul (including Ephesians seventeen out of eighteen times), who invariably uses it in a transferred sense,[6] and moreover (except in one case, 2 Cor 5:1) always in relation to ecclesial life. The idea connected with it is no more and no less than that of modern pedagogy: the building up of the personality, or in a community sense, the building of the identity of a group through the exercise of respect, assistance, and mutual fellowship. So that, though on the one hand Paul certainly includes the basic reality of divine intervention (1 Cor 3:9: "You are God's construction"), on the other he often repeats, "try to excel in building up the ἐκκλησία" (1 Cor 14:12); "Everything goes, beloved, toward building you up" (2 Cor 12:19); "We seek for one another what goes toward building up" (Rom 14:19); "Let us each seek to please the next in good to build that person up" (Rom 15:2).

Now, 1 Cor 8:1 is the only text that immediately associates *agape* with such "building." And it is as if Paul were saying, it is love that builds up the Church! *Agape* is, after all, on the one hand, always a sign of personal maturity, of adulthood, especially when, as in our case, it is still exercised even when one is aware of one's right to do the contrary (note 8:1a: "We know that we all have knowledge"; 8:9: "see to it that your right does not become a stumbling block for the weak"). But on the other

6. Meanwhile the Pauline letters use the verbs, ἐπ-, συν-, οἰκοδομέω, only sixteen times (out of forty-two in the New Testament); but here, too, the use in a transferred sense is typical. See O. Michel, TDNT 5:136–148.

hand, love is, simply, constructive, i.e., it is fertile in the promotion of human persons and of the Church (note 8:12b-13: "By wounding their weak consciences you sin against Christ; and therefore if food causes my brother or sister to fall, I shall never eat meat again so as not to cause one of them to fall.") Actually, there is not a real choice between knowledge and love, and Paul says as much with a kind of play on words: "If one thinks one knows something, one does not yet know as one should know" (8:2). Here he is not so much echoing the Socratic saying, according to which one only knows if one knows one does not know,[7] as expressing a typically Christian expectation, that no knowledge is complete and perfect unless it is integrated with love; for knowledge actually is in danger of remaining on a dis-incarnated level, whereas love always includes a sympathetic adherence to concrete reality, especially to concrete persons and so (provided Christians are not content to be mere dreamers) can transform concrete situations.

In the second place, in 1 Corinthians Paul also makes *agape* an object of consideration in its own right. I refer, of course, to the famous chapter 13, the literary genre of which can best be identified as a praise of Christian love (see vol. 1 of this work, chap. 12). Actually, we have here a passage inserted in a very specific context that places such a hymn in close relation to the situation at Corinth. Specifically, in the context of a reflection on and exhortation to harmonious coexistence, indeed cooperation in the various charisms in the Church (chaps. 12-14), Paul inserts this passage to indicate the "best way of all" (12:31b), as if to say that while the charisms by their nature represent an element of differentiation (and sometimes of division) in the Church, *agape* on the other hand is a uniting, a bonding element.[8] Thus chapter 13 accomplishes a very specific function within the discourse on the Church's ministerial character; Paul's subject is not so much the existence of the ministries as their wide variety, all working together "for the common good" (12:5) within the one body of Christ (note 12:12-27).

But we must also note that some authors would have it that this text does not have its original site here[9] and that this is why it proceeds at such a solemn pace and is so well constructed, with the celebration of *agape* in its universal significance, largely prescinding from the immediate context. *Agape* is actually personified, made the subject of various actions

---

7. See Diogenes Laertius, *Vitae phil.* II:32.

8. Besides the commentaries, see S. Lyonnet, "Agapé et charismes selon 1 Cor 12,31," in L. De Lorenzi, ed., *Paul de Tarse, apôtre de notre temps* (Rome, 1979) 509-527.

9. See the authors cited by C. Spicq, *Agapé dans le Nouveau Testament. Analyses des textes,* II (Paris, 1966³) 55 [omitted in the English edition: see II, 140].

and attitudes, without receiving any grammatical specification: Is it God's *agape* for humanity? the Christian's *agape* for God? the mutual love of Christians among themselves? In any case, the present redactional location of the encomium not only in the nearest chapters that frame it but also in the larger view of First Corinthians, which is so much concerned with the ecclesial dimension of Christian life, absolutely constrains us to recognize in the text a definite reference to the life of the Church, if not actually to its intimate nature. If love is indispensable in the relations among the various ministries, it is even more irreplaceable than they precisely as the καθ' ὑπερβολὴν ὁδόν, setting the Church in a situation of movement and tension, but also already in the state of arrival, of achieving its goal, since it is the "greatest" reality (13:13).[10]

III. The Second Letter to the Corinthians

As we go on to Second Corinthians, we meet a new stage in Paul's apostolic experience. His relationship to the Corinthian Church was surely the most complex, and of all his missionary and pastoral activities the most fraught with difficulty and suffering. And of this, Second Corinthians is our evidence.

The letter reveals certain new facets of Paul's specific function, which he creatively and effectively describes as that of the paranymph (the young person who in Greek custom accompanied the bride to the house of the groom), but which could also be understood as that of the father of the betrothed: "for I promised you to one man, to present you to Christ as a pure virgin" (11:2). In the foreground of this text, even more than the spousal relationship between the community of the baptized and Christ, is the Apostle's acute sense of responsibility: he explicitly admits to experiencing for his Christians "a kind of divine jealousy" (ibid.), in the (well founded!) fear that they are following "another Jesus than the one we have preached" (11:4). All the polemic that he develops even in sharp terms in chapters 10–13 (see vol. 1 of this work, chap. 15),[11] is actually aimed at expressing this jealousy, in order to keep intensely alive the sense of the community's belonging exclusively to Jesus Christ, crucified and risen, the center of Paul's gospel. We might, of course, ask how we can

10. See Spicq, *Agape in the N.T.*, 2:144: "Charity is not a way of perfection in the sense of being a means, it is perfection itself. Whoever walks on this way is perfect. . . . Christ himself is the 'living way.' Anyone who has reached Christ has already arrived." We have here the Christian equivalent of the Stoic principle that *virtue* is its own end (see, for example, Seneca, *Epist.* 81:19; 89:8).

11. It is altogether plausible that in these chapters there has come to us at least part of the letter "written with tears" (2:5) that dates between 1 Corinthians and 2 Cor 1:9.

reconcile *agape* with the harsh tones of such a polemic. But apart from the fact that every literary genre has its laws,[12] what seems to cause a difficulty in theory should be put into proportion by the measure of the experience.

Now, in Second Corinthians we find two different levels of agapic behavior of Paul toward his addressees. In the first place, it is valuable to observe his attitude toward the anonymous figure of the "offender" (7:12) who, probably during an intermediate trip of Paul's from Ephesus to Corinth (not mentioned in Acts), brought him much in the way of "affliction . . . anguish . . . tears . . . pain" (2:4-5). The case is somewhat mysterious because the exact historical contours escape us,[13] but it concerns only personal relations between Paul and a single member of the Corinthian community. And yet we must note that Paul involves the whole community in the case. And this in two ways: because, he maintains, the offense was done to the whole community, but especially because he urgently invites the Church to show open kindness toward the offender: "I urge you choose *agape* toward him" (2:8). So, while in 1 Cor 5:1-5 he had required a severe but carefully limited disciplinary intervention for an incestuous member of the same Christian community of Corinth, here on the other hand Paul entrusts to the love of the whole community one who is guilty of lack of charity, thus perceiving a clearly redemptive and rehabilitating dimension in ecclesial *agape*. I should say that here we see the purest biblical kind of love, which covers a multitude of sins (Prov 10:12; Tob 12:9; 1 Pet 4:8; Jas 5:20),[14] as well as the sense of the preaching of Jesus, who requires only love in response to the work of the wicked (see Matt 5:45-48). The only new thing in Paul's case is that here the principle of *agape* is applied on a community level, and in a situation of concrete experience rather than on the level of theoretical exhortation.

In the second place, and as a result, the dimensions of *agape* widen out from one single Christian to the whole local Church of Corinth. In an extremely affectionate tone, almost overflowing with feeling, Paul assures the Corinthians: "Our heart is wide open to you" (6:11), asking for reciprocation: "Make room for us" (7:2; cf. 6:13). What he wants is to connect the circuit of *agape* to allow the life-giving energy of love to pass freely

---

12. Note already Saint Jerome, *Epist.* 47:13: When you are engaged in polemic, "carry your arguments where you want, say one thing, turn it into something else; show them a loaf of bread, as they say, while holding a rock in your hand."

13. See C. K. Barrett, " Ὁ ἀδικήσας (2 Cor 7,12)," in *Festschrift G. Stählin* (Wuppertal, 1970) 149–157.

14. F. Mussner, *Der Jakobusbrief* HThKNT (Freiburg–Basel–Vienna, 1981⁴) 233, rightly proposes seeing in the act of "covering" something that concerns not just the sins of the one who loves but also those of the one who is loved; in fact, see Prov 10:12; 25:22; Test. Ben. 5:4.

from one pole of the ecclesial reality to the other. And this is the context in which a phrase is formulated that will become a programmatic axiom in Christian tradition, especially of pastoral spirituality: "For I have said before that you are in our hearts *to die together and live together*" (7:3). This *ad commoriendum et ad convivendum* has been interpreted in various ways;[15] since the idea is attested in profane literature,[16] it is disputed whether the two verbs imply a reference to Christ, and hence to the dynamic of the paschal mystery. It seems to me that such a reference basically shines through with sufficient clarity, considering that our letter repeatedly alludes directly to the mystery (see 1:5; 4:10-12; 5:14-15; 12:9; 13:4). But what we really want to note here is the agapic sharing of life and death, which at any rate is certainly present in the text, which unites together Paul and the whole Corinthian Church. "For the Apostle, dying and living with his beloved children is nothing other than dying and living with Christ: it is, in fact, the concrete form of the total gift of self that he has made to Christ."[17]

We cannot help but hear in this text the words written earlier in the letter, when Paul proclaimed: "It is Christ's love that holds us in its power" (5:14: trans. H. D. Wendland *Die Briefe an die Korinther* [Göttingen, 1978]). Although the Greek verb συνέχει is traditionally translated "urges" or the like (BJ, CEI, TILC, NAB "impels," etc.), it actually means "hold together, encompass, contain, enclose," and also "keep united, support" (and from this last, "confine, compress, distress"); analogously Plato states, "Community [κοινωνία] holds gods and men together" (*Gorgias* 507d-508a). The significance is that not only the apostolic ministry but the whole of Christian and ecclesial existence is supported and held together[18] by the love of Christ, i.e., the love with which Christ faced death for those who belong to him (see 5:14b; Gal 2:20). The Church's very existence has its (historical and mystical) foundation precisely in this event.

IV. The Letters to the Galatians and the Romans

Galatians and Romans doubtless represent a final stage in Paul's apostolic experience. Close to one another chronologically and themati-

---

15. See the discussion by J. Dupont, "Ad commoriendum et ad convivendum (2 Cor 7,3)," in *Teologia Liturgia Storia. Miscellanea in onore di Carlo Manziana Vescovo di Crema*, ed. C. Ghidelli (Brescia, 1977) 19-28.

16. R. Bultmann, *The Second Letter to the Corinthians*, trans. R. A. Harrisville (Minneapolis, 1985) 178; besides 2 Kgs 15:21 LXXX, he cites Euripides, *Orest.* 307-308; *Ion* 852-853, 857-858; Horace, *Carm.* III:9:24; and Athenaeus VI:54.

17. Dupont, *Ad commoriendum*, 28.

18. Bultmann, *Der Zweite Brief an die Korinther*, 146, translates "beherrscht uns" ("controls us").

cally, they treat the idea that gradually forced itself on Paul's attention: justification by faith apart from the works of the Law. Any ecclesiological interest would seem to be extraneous to this idea. And, in fact, the history of both the exegetical and the dogmatic interpretation of the idea of the *justificatio impii*, the justification of the ungodly (Rom 4:5), shows just how traditional is the treatment of the issue from an individual, not to say grossly individualistic, perspective.[19] Various attempts have been made to evade such an approach: by placing Paul's reasoning against the background of his missionary task, typified as it is by the conception of the universality of salvation, to which are called gentiles as well as Jews;[20] or else even more, by inserting the Church, i.e., the community dimension of Christian existence, in the very event of justification, in which is embodied God's intervention on behalf of the true progeny of Abraham, and so of a whole people that through this means comes to be conformed to God's plan of salvation.[21] In our two letters the πνεῦμα, "Spirit," is the determinative factor of justification and of the new life of the justified (see Gal 3:1-5; Rom 5:5). "[The Spirit's] action makes of the community a communion, which—without ignoring its own weakness and the threatening reality of the world—lives only through the assurance of justification and of the unwavering love of God."[22] So actually *agape* itself is here indissolubly associated with the Spirit. And this is true in two ways.

In the first place, love characterizes God's justifying intervention for us: "God's *agape* has been poured out in our hearts through the Holy Spirit, which has been given to us" (Rom 5:5; cf. Gal 5:5). Various basic matters are present in this declaration. First of all, it is God who is the subject of love, of the only love which counts and which will a little later allow Paul to cry out that no possible difficulty or opposition can ever separate us from the love of the One who has loved us in Christ Jesus (see Rom 8:35-39; and even from the initial address of the letter the recipients are called ἀγαπητοί θεοῦ, "beloved of God": 1:7). It is then clearly said that this divine *agape* comes to the Christian by means of the πνεῦμα given to us, a discreet allusion to baptism (cf. 1 Cor 12:13) and faith (cf. Gal 3:2, 14). But then it is important to note for our purposes that this pouring out of the Spirit takes place "in our hearts." This frequent Pauline ex-

---

19. See U. Meyer, "Der Herkunft und Überwindung des protestantischen Individualismus," EvTh 24 (1964) 267–272.

20. See, e.g., K. Stendahl, "The Apostle Paul and the Introspective Conscience of the West," HThR 56 (1963) 199–215; now in Stendahl, *Paul Among Jews and Gentiles, and Other Essays* (Philadelphia, 1976).

21. See especially W. Klaiber, *Rechtfertigung und Gemeinde. Eine Untersuchung zum paulinischen Kirchenverständnis* FRLANT 127 (Göttingen, 1982).

22. Klaiber, *Rechtfertigung*, 192.

pression (see also 2 Cor 1:22; 3:2; 4:6; Gal 4:6) is not meant only to indicate the personal depths of the human individual but is normally connected with ideas of "adopted children . . ." *(υἱοθεσία)* and eschatological "inheritance" *(κληρονομία)*. Hence a direct line runs from God's love to our adoption as children. And from this fact we can gather not only the soteriological dimension of the new Christian anthropology, as is generally done, but also the ecclesiological, less evident perhaps but no less real. For we cannot afford to forget that Paul is writing to Churches, whether in Galatia or Rome, and so uses the plural pronouns "you" and "we"; it is no accident that the only time he uses the first person singular in an anthropological sense (Rom 7:9-25) it is to describe the unredeemed human person, far from Christ, and so in a hopeless situation. In contrast, it is to a communitarian "we" that the Spirit and God's *agape* give life, one that bears the signature of peace and joy because established on the unmerited, free event of our justification by God (see Rom 5:1).

And in the second place, Paul sets *agape* first among the gifts of the Spirit's fruitfulness: "The fruit of the Spirit is *agape*, joy, peace, patience, kindness, goodness, faithfulness, meekness, self-control; against these there is no law" (Gal 5:22-23). And a little earlier in the command "You shall love your neighbor as yourself," Paul has summarized the whole law (see 5:14 and Rom 13:8-10). What he says is not abstract but is aimed at the concrete community life of the addressees, and this is confirmed by the ironic and biting admonition that follows, "But if you bite and devour each other, watch out lest you be completely consumed by one another" (Gal 5:15). Evidently the Churches were imperiled by internal dissensions, probably provoked by different interpretations of Paul's gospel concerning the sufficiency of Christ for salvation; indeed, in the long list of vices and "works of the flesh" (5:19), a full half (seven of fourteen) identify situations of "enmity, discord, jealousy, dissensions, divisions, factions, envy" (5:20-21). This is why *agape* is presented as the first fruit of the Spirit, thus appearing again as the basic factor of ecclesial life.

But here too, following the themes of the letter, agape is in essential relation to faith, which gives it the seal proper to Christian identity. In the same chapter 5 Paul actually makes clear that what counts in Christ is nothing but "the faith that works through *agape*" (v. 6). This means that even within the Church the only anchorage of love is justifying faith *(πίστις)*.[23] The *agape* of the Church thus also has a "pistic" root, i.e., it presupposes our shared condition as sinners, the free redemptive inter-

23. In 1984 at the Pontifical Biblical Institute, P. M. Meagher, S.J., presented an unusual doctoral thesis on this very theme: *Faith Active Through Agape (Gal 5:6): A Study of the Formation of a Christian Community of Agape According to the Letter to the Galatians.*

vention of God in the cross of Christ that is equal toward all, our shared situation of salvation by grace, our complete liberty from any justifying claim on the part of other persons, norms, institutions, and hence the necessity of manifesting this situation with the resulting "works of love," of *agape*, without which faith would be "a fanatical abstraction, a pure vanity and a dream of the heart."[24] It is faith, then, that by its nature presses on, leading to the ecclesial dimension of love.

V. The Letter to the Ephesians

Ephesians in all probability is to be considered deutero-Pauline. The ecclesial situation it presupposes corresponds to the generation after the Pauline period.[25] It is now for the first time that the idea of the "Church" is treated by itself and no longer in response to an occasion, while the related letter to the Colossians had begun to refer the term no longer just to a local community but with a universal range (see Col 1:18, 24). But while Colossians still could use the word with restricted reference (see 4:15: domestic church of Nympha; 4:16: Church of Laodicea), in Ephesians it never refers to anything but the whole Church in general, almost abstractly (nine times out of nine: Eph 1:22; 3:10, 21; 5:23, 24, 25, 27, 29, 32). With this being the case, what the author has to say about *agape* also takes on a new, broad dimension. Here we find a repeated affirmation concerning the ultimate source of *agape*, in God and in Christ. This had already been said clearly enough in Galatians–Romans. But now the declaration is made with no reference at all to the perspective of anti-legalistic polemic and of justification by faith. What remains and is emphasized in the eyes of Paul's disciple is the pure greatness of God's *agape*. Thus is celebrated "the great love with which God has loved us" (2:4).

But the author especially emphasizes the Christological component of this *agape* to which our salvation can be traced (see 2:5-8). Already 3:19 proclaims fulsome praise of the "*agape* of Christ that surpasses all understanding," the all-comprehensive character and inexhaustibility of which is pressed home with an implicit reference to the four cardinal directions, with reference to its "length and breadth and height and depth,"[26]

24. Thus M. Luther, W.A. XL/1, p. 266: cited by V. Subilia, *La giustificazione per fede* (Brescia, 1976) 201.

25. Besides the New Testament introductions, see K. M. Fischer, *Tendenz und Absicht des Epheserbriefes*, FRLANT 111 (Göttingen, 1973); and the recent commentary by R. Schnackenburg, *Ephesians: A Commentary* (Edinburgh, 1991).

26. See the study of N. A. Dahl, "Cosmic Dimensions and Religious Knowledge (Eph 3:18)," in *Jesus und Paulus. Festschrift W. Kümmel* (Göttingen, 1975) 57-75: on the basis of biblical (wisdom/apocalyptic) and Greco-Roman documentation, the author demonstrates that the

as if to say that henceforth this *agape* is the place in which Christians must be present and conscious, in which they must move, that it is a space of wide horizons, in which each person can be sure to find room.

But it will be especially in chapter 5 that both the noun ἐκκλησία and the verb ἀγαπᾶν more often occur together. Significantly, this says repeatedly in different terms that "Christ loved you and gave himself up for us" (v. 2) and, in more openly ecclesiological terms, that "Christ loved the Church and gave himself for her" (v. 25). And if we note that these statements are made in the context of a marriage paraenesis, the exceptional reality, or to use the sacred writer's term, the "mystery" (v. 32), of such a relationship of love stands out all the more.[27] This is so true that a Gnostic reinterpretation of this passage in the second or third century rereads the text as presenting two partners of a syzygy pre-existing within the divine pleroma.[28] Surely no greater dignity could have been attributed to the Church than this, seeing it as this grand independent reality, recognizing it as the sole object of Christ's transport of love. This ὑπὲρ αὐτῆς of 5:25c represents the final stage of the formulation of Christian faith that began with the "for our sins" of the primitive kerygma (1 Cor 15:3), developed through similar variant formulas (note 2 Cor 5:14: "for all"; Gal 2:20: "for me"; 3:13: "for us"; Rom 5:6: "for the godless"; Col 1:24: "for his body"), so that the totality of the faithful are finally now personified in the feminine figure of the Church: it is precisely "for her" that Christ has given himself wholly, moved by a love that is not just a subjective attitude but is objectively effective; indeed, in removing the spots and wrinkles (5:27), it is creative of her beauty.

In the letter, then, these theological reflections also become moral exhortations. And in this regard it is interesting to note that the phrase ἐν ἀγάπῃ, which occurs only four times in the authentic letters of Paul (1 Cor 4:21; 16:14; 2 Cor 5:6; 1 Thess 5:13), is found five times in Ephesians alone (1:4: "to be holy and stainless before him in *agape*"; 3:17: "rooted and founded in *agape*"; 4:2: "putting up with one another in *agape*"; 4:15:

---

four dimensions have the rhetorical function of forming a simple preamble to other statements on which the principal accent falls (in our case, then, the love of Christ, which surpasses all understanding).

27. See R. Penna, *Il "mysterion" paolino. Traiettoria e costituzione,* Suppl. RivBibl. 10 (Brescia, 1978) 75–79.

28. See Irenaeus, *Adv. haer.* I:8:4; also I:11:1 (= the Valentinian dyad *Anthropos/Ekklesia,* "Human Being/Church"); Clement of Alexandria, *Excerpta ex Theodoto* 58:1; among the Nag Hammadi writings, see *Exegesis on the Soul* II:132:7-12; *Gospel of Philip* II:82; *Valentinian Exposition* XI:31:36-37; *Tripartite Tractate* I:136:1; 138:10-11. See Fischer, *Tendenz und Absicht,* 176–200; E. H. Pagels, "Adam and Eve, Christ and the Church: a Survey of Second Century Controversies Concerning Marriage," in *The New Testament and Gnosis: Essays in Honor of Robert McL. Wilson,* ed. A. H. B. Logan and A. J. M. Wedderburn (Edinburgh, 1983) 145–175.

"speaking the truth in *agape*";[29] 4:16: from Christ "the whole body . . . receives growth, that it may be built up in *agape*"; 5:2 "walk in *agape*"). The preposition ἐν in these phrases has not so much a local as a Semitic type of instrumental sense, hence a modal usage.[30] However, it is also possible that the phrase has a descriptive value, to be translated "agapically," "lovingly." Thus it indicates a dimension of life, a characteristic, a mode of being that identifies the members of the Church (cf. 4:16: "according to the way of working proper to each of the members"). The author's insistence on this obligation has its specific historical motivation in the need to recall the Christians converted from paganism to respect and even love for those who came from Judaism (note 2:11-22).

But the theme's importance comes to have a more universal, perennial value, concerning the nature and life of the Church in general. For the exhortation to *agape* has a function in presenting the Church itself as "temple of the Lord" (2:21), in which both Jews and gentiles are "built up to become God's dwelling in the Spirit" (2:22), as "the whole body, fitted together and knit together through each joint" (4:16), in order to achieve "full maturity in Christ" (4:13). The copious use of images of architectural and physiological origin fully emphasizes the fact that the frequent appeal to *agape* in the context makes this love the indispensable element, without which the building cannot stand nor the body live. Moreover, it is only love that in this context does not belong to the technique of literary imagery, since it derives from the realm of social attitudes and behavior, and hence from the real interpersonal daily life.[31] The Church itself, then, or surely at least its living pulse, can be defined by the love of its members for one another without distinction if the well-known Scholastic adage is true, that "love either finds all equal or makes them so."[32]

29. R. Schnackenburg, *Ephesians*, 187–188, rightly notes that this obligation concerns not just the preachers but the whole Church (cf. 4:13: "all of us").

30. See Blass-Debrunner-Rehkopf, par. 219.

31. Note M. Barth, *Ephesians*, II, Anchor Bible 34A (Garden City, N.Y., 1974) 451: "Just as in I Corinthians a paean of love was inserted between two chapters describing the life of the body and the edification of the Church, (see I Cor 12–14), so also in Eph 4:16 'love' is denoted as the ground, the sphere, the instrument of the church's existence. This love has at least three dimensions: it is the love of God and Christ for man, man's reciprocal love of God and Christ, and the mutual love of the saints. A church in which this manifold love is at work will not occupy herself with the erection of a tower of Babel and an empire vying for world dominion. Rather the structure erected will have the character of a building useful for rendering service to many people. It will resemble, e.g., a pilgrim's inn or a halfway house. It will have gates that are open day and night for all who wish to enter (cf. Rev 21:25; 22:14). The mystery of this building is both contained and revealed in God's promise to dwell in it (2:22). Without the rule of love, the Church is not built up but scattered (Calvin)."

32. Spicq, *Agapé*, II, 233, n. 1 [omitted in the English edition] cites a passage from the commentary of Cajetan on Eph 4:16: ". . . that we might understand that the true growth of

VII. Conclusion

Beginning with First Thessalonians, the theme of the relationship between *agape* and Church and of the importance of the one for the other develops to its culmination in Ephesians. It is significant to note that Paul does not begin by reflecting on the nature of such a relationship. Actually, he never does come to such a reflection. This had to wait for an anonymous disciple of his in different historical circumstances (= Ephesians). Instead, Paul lives the *agape* for the Church and requires it of his addressees as a primary reality, indispensable for the Church's life. Of course, this is not a love that has no motives. He begins with a basic discovery of faith. Christ loved me, and in his love God's own love is revealed. This love, becoming an event, by its very nature demands to be given, shared, experienced repeatedly. The φιλανθρωπία of God (Titus 3:4) must be transformed into φιλαδελφία (1 Thess 4:9; Rom 12:10). All the more must this be pursued, because in the Church, besides the natural tendency toward egocentric assertion of self, the existence and exercise of the ministries call for something extra in the demand for an "unfeigned love" (ἀνυπόκριτος: Rom 12:9; 2 Cor 6:6; N.B. the ὑποκριτής in Greek is the theater actor, the simulator). But just by living it himself and demanding it in all his letters, Paul shows that *agape* is really the *forma Ecclesiae*, provided that individual Christians not simply hide behind the social character of the Church, finding therein the excuse for their own dearth of *agape*.

It can be useful to note that in writing to his Churches, Paul is regularly generic in his exhortations to *agape*. There are two areas that are an exception to this, where his speech becomes more specific: one concerns the weak in faith and conscience (see 1 Cor 8; Rom 14:1–15:13); the other concerns ministers (1 Cor 12–14; Rom 12:3-10; cf. Eph 4:11-16). These are two preoccupations that should perhaps never be neglected, because the one aims to make the whole ecclesial community keep growing all together, without some racing ahead and forgetting those lagging behind, while the other reminds the ministers that their power to "build up" stands not in contradistinction of roles, much less in tyranny, but no more and no less than in διακονία, in service (see 1 Cor 13:13).[33]

We must make one last observation that is anything but secondary. Paul's treatment of the theme, repeated in different ways (sometimes as proclamation and other times as paraenesis), should invite Christians, and

---

the body of the Church consists not in the building of doctrine, preaching, prophecy, and the like, but in the building of itself in love, in the increase of love."

33. See R. Penna, *La diakonia nelle lettere ai Corinti*, in the volume of collected studies *Il diaconato permanente* (Naples, 1983) 211–218.

ministers all the more, not to turn *agape* into a platitude, since deception and self-deception are possible precisely where things are taken for granted and not looked straight in the face. If the duty of love is obvious for the baptized, it should not therefore be immune to continuous intelligent and self-critical examination. After all, *agape* is a κόπος, a strenuous labor (1 Thess 1:3), and is therefore not always immediately gratifying. And likewise, if one thing is perfectly clear in Paul's letters and in the New Testament as a whole, it is that love (whether within the Church or moving outward from it) must never be considered a means, reduced to a strategy to achieve something else, since a Church that is deeply characterized by *agape* (that which descends from God and that which the baptized extend to one another) already represents the *eschaton* within time (see 1 Cor 13:13).[34]

---

34. "Love for the neighbor is love for him in all his strange, irritating, distinct created-ness. . . . Love is eternal, leveling righteousness (Kierkegaard), because it justifies no man according to his desire. Love edifies the fellowship because it seeks fellowship only. Love expects nothing, because it has already reached the goal. Love does not intend, because it has already done. Love asks no questions, it already knows. Love does not fight, it is already the victor. Love is not EROS, that lusteth ever, it is AGAPE that never faileth" (K. Barth, *The Epistle to the Romans*, trans. E. C. Hoskyns [London–Oxford–New York, 1968 (1933)]: commenting on Rom 13:8-14: "The great positive possibility.")

Chapter 28

The Dialectic Between Seeking and Discovering God in the Pauline Epistles

I intend here to examine the thought of the Apostle Paul (and of New Testament Paulinism), prescinding from the "Pauline" speeches of the Acts of the Apostles. Even though the precise expression "to seek God," ζητεῖν τὸν θεόν, is found in Acts in Paul's words (Acts 17:27), it scarcely reflects Paul's typical thought. Actually, in the letters the vocabulary of seeking (ζητέω, ἐπιζητέω, ἐκζητέω, συζητέω, ζήτησις) never does take "God" as the object of the action of the seeking; indeed, when the two terms come together it is precisely to deny the possibility or at least the fruitfulness of such a quest. It is true, the idea actually is expressed with a different rich vocabulary of seeking (see below), but this normally no longer refers to the "natural" God, but the "revealed," "Christian" God; the quest, then, describes the postbaptismal and "pistic" (believing) state of the Christian. The same observation applies analogously for the correlative vocabulary of finding (εὑρίσκω, "find"; καταλαμβάνω, "grasp"; ἐπιτυγχάνω, "attain to," etc.).

Therefore, in what follows, after certain preliminary observations pertinent to the subject (1. the quest for God in the contemporaneous environment of Paul; 2. the meaning of the autobiographical silence about Paul's quest before conversion; 3. the significance of the formula εἰς αὐτόν, "unto him"), we shall divide the exposition into three parts, concentrating it especially on the examination of certain key texts of the Pauline correspondence.

I. The crisis of the natural quest for God (with specific reference to and explicit examination of Rom 1:19-23; 1 Cor 1:20; Rom 10:20).

II. The qualitative "leap" represented by the discovery of the Christian God revealed in the cross of Christ (vocabulary of revelation/apparition, and examination of Gal 2:17).

III. The specific positive topic of quest following discovery that is offered us in certain texts (1 Cor 2:10: the function of the Spirit; Col 3:1), but also in the normal vocabulary of quest/attraction, and finally in the characteristic formula πρὸς τὸν θεόν, which expresses the theocentric teleological orientation of Christian life.

Preliminaries

1) *The contemporaneous cultural environment*

It has been suggested that the Mediterranean world of the first century of this era had risen to its feet and, under the impulse of a renewed persistent religious spirit and of philosophy, was headed toward Christianity. This judgment, which does not originate with us,[1] must be reconsidered, for the Christian message does not actually correspond to the spirit and the direction of the quest that was typical of the time.

Let us then briefly examine some typical exponents of both the Roman and the Jewish milieux that will be the first to encounter and bear the brunt of this newborn Christianity, of which Paul was the proponent with the broadest horizons.

a) *The Greco-Roman milieu.* Here the movement with the greatest originality and religious intensity was surely Stoicism.[2] The idea of the *deus internus*, "the God within," is widespread: especially in Seneca (*Ep.* 41:2: *spiritus sacer intra nos sedet,* "The Sacred Spirit sits within us"; 66:12; 73:16; 92:30; Ovid, *Ars amat.* III:549: "There is a God in us, we are in touch with heaven" [trans. J. H. Mozley (Cambridge, Mass., 1935²)]); and in Epictetus (*Diatr.* I:14:13: ὁ θεὸς ἔνδον ἐστὶ, "God is within"; II:8:11: θεὸν περιφέρεις, "you carry God about").

Still, one would seek in vain the use of the verb ζητεῖν, *quaerere*, "seek," in a theological sense.[3] The only texts that can be quoted seem to be in

---

1. See A. Jagu, "Saint Paul et le Stoicisme," *RvSR* 32 (1958) 225–250, 228, quoting G. Boussier, *La religion Romaine* (Paris, 1900⁵) 2:402. See also A. J. Festugière, *L'enfant d'Agrigent* (Paris, 1941) 110–112.

2. See M. Pohlenz, *Die Stoa,* I–II (Göttingen, 1948 [Italian: 1987]). More generally, see also U. von Wilamowitz-Moellendorff, *Der Glaube der Hellene,* I–II (Berlin, 1931); A. J. Festugière, *L'idéal religieux des grecs et l'Evangile* (Paris, 1932²); M. P. Nilsson, *Geschichte der griechischen Religion,* I–II (Munich, 1941–51); E. Des Places, *La religion grecque* (Paris, 1969).

3. See, e.g., the index in J. von Arnim, *Stoicorum Veterum Fragmenta,* I–III (Leipzig, 1903–5). We know that Chrysippus wrote a Περὶ ζητήσεως in two books (see Diogenes Laertius VII:191), but we don't know the content, and could surmise that the perspective is purely philosophical. Even in Plato, "the frequent juxtaposition of ζητεῖν and εὑρίσκειν [only] represents one of the ways of acquiring knowledge" in general (E. Des Places, *La religion grecque,* 356); see *Gorgias* 503 d 4: ἐὰν ζητῇς καλῶς, εὑρήσεις, "If you seek well, you will find" (at most one could

Epictetus (*Diatr.* IV:1:51: "Seek and you will find [ζήτει καὶ εὑρέσεις]; for nature has well endowed you to perceive the truth") and in Seneca (*De benef.* VI:23:6: *vide animi quantum audeant, quemadmodum soli aut noverint deos aut quaerant et mente in altum elata divina comitentur*, "See how bold souls are, how they alone come to know the gods, or seek, and with minds raised on high attend on the divine realities"; cf. Cicero, *Acad.* 1:5:19: *neque ullā aliā in re nisi in naturā quaerendum esse illud summum bonum*, "this supreme good is not to be sought in any other thing but nature"). Indeed, in this philosophical environment, as throughout the rest of the classical tradition, the use of the verb γινώσκειν, "know," with its derivatives is prevalent, as Norden documents:[4] the typical highly intellectual character of the Greek approach to the deity is well known (see *Corpus Hermeticum* 5:2: "Only thought [νόησις] sees God, who, like it, is invisible"; and Iamblicus *Myst.* 2:11: "Who does not acknowledge that consciousness of true being comes the closest to the divine cause?").

Now, the precise verb "seek" in a religious sense is clearly of Jewish character, as can be verified by the Bible[5] and also Qumran and Philo of Alexandria (see below). This does not mean that the pagan authors have no religious vocabulary to describe the relations with the divine; indeed such speech is abundant and intense. Epictetus is surely the richest, with expressions like "venerate" (εὐσεβεῖν and derivatives), "serve" (ὑπηρετεῖν), "obey" (πείθεσθαι), "follow" (ἀκολουθεῖν), "thank" (εὐχαριστεῖν),[6] worship (προσκυνεῖν), praise (ἐπαινεῖν), please (ἀρέσκειν), and also in the nouns "servant" (διάκονος), "witness" (μάρτυς), "herald" (κῆρυξ), "friend" (φίλος). Nor are we thinking only of a purely passive, purely intellectual attitude; indeed, a text like *Diatribe* III:24:114 ("appointed to such a service," i.e., in the fullest and most free adherence to the divine will "*do I not strain toward God*, οὐχὶ δ' ὅλος πρὸς τὸν θεὸν τέταμαι, toward God's commands and ordainments?")[7] underlines the whole dynamic and hence af-

investigate κατὰ τὸν θεόν, i.e., in a manner befitting God: *Apol.* 23b); still, see *Leg.* VII:821a. And see Cicero, *Acad.* II:26: "It is reason that first sought, . . . since reason was fortified by seeking."

4. E. Norden, *Agnostos Theos* (Darmstadt, 1971⁵) 87–115.

5. See G. Turbessi, "Quaerere Deum. Il tema della 'ricerca di Dio' nella S. Scrittura," RivBibl 10 (1962) 282–296. By the same author see also: *Quaerere Deum. Il tema della 'ricerca di Dio' nell'ambiente ellenistico e giudaico, contemporaneo al N.T.*, SPCIC, II (Rome, 1963) 383–398; the study perhaps goes too deeply into the philosophical-religious system of Stoicism in general, while failing to take other cultural currents into account.

6. The sense of gratitude amply represented in Epictetus (see *Diatr.* II:23:5-6, 23; also I:29:46-50; II:16:42; III:24:112-113; 26:28) contrasts with Paul's negative judgment in Rom 1:21; this reveals his compactness and the tendential preaching style.

7. It is worth noting that here Epictetus uses the verb τείνω (in perfect middle), the same as used by Paul in Phil 3:13 (though there in a compounded form: ἐπεκτεινόμενος) in an analogous sense.

fective attraction of the philosopher toward union with God (see IV:1:99; 7:20; also II:23:42; III:24:95-118; IV:3:9-10).[8]

Besides Stoicism, in the first century we must point out Dio of Prusa (known as Dio Chrysostomus; ca. A.D. 40-120), the principal representative of the second sophistic movement. His *Oratio XII* is a quasi-tractate on natural moral theology. Even though the verb ζητεῖν does not appear there, we do read this powerful declaration: "All human beings have a strong desire to honor the divine from close at hand" *(ἰσχυρὸς ἔρως πᾶσιν ἀνθρώποις ἐγγύθεν τιμᾶν καὶ θεραπεύειν τὸ θεῖον)*. Such ἔρως is based on a conception of God which is common to all the human race[9] and which has more than one source *(πηγή)*. Dio lists five: the first is innate in the nature of everyone (12:39a); the second consists of the stories and myths of the poets, sometimes unwritten, and the customs (12:39b-40); the third, the lawgivers (12:40-43); the fourth is the art of sculpture (12:44-45; cf. the lovely fictitious speech of Phidias: 12:55-83); the last source consists of the philosophers (12:47; defining the philosopher as "true and perfect prophets and exegetes of immortal nature"). In fact, the point of departure of the attraction toward God consists in the observation of nature, of the cosmos and of its phenomena, beginning already with "the first and most ancient human beings" (12:27b); "How could they have been ignorant, have had no conjecture about who sowed and planted them, and now kept and nourished them, filled as they were from all sides by the divine nature through sight and hearing and every sense?" (12:29). In 12:32 we actually read a text that comes close to Paul in conception (Rom 1:20): "Thus, experiencing all these things and reflecting thereon, they could not help but marvel at and love the divine" *(ἃ δὴ πάσχοντες ἐπινοοῦντες οὐκ ἐδύναντο μὴ θαυμάζειν καὶ ἀγαπᾶν τὸ δαιμόνιον)*. Granted these principles, we understand Dio's polemic against Epicureanism, whether because it reduces the divine to Pleasure, or because it deposes the gods from their rule, proclaiming the universe to be without governance (see 12:36-37).

b) *The Jewish environment.* Passing over the Old Testament precedents (among which we find the explicit expressions "seek God/the Lord/his face," in moral or cultic and mantic senses, e.g., Pss 24:6; 27:8; 83:16; 105:3f.; 2 Chr 7:14; 11:16; 15:12; 18:4, 7, but also the search *by* God as shep-

---

8. On the religious nature of Epictetus, which is the most developed of all pagan antiquity, see T. Colardeau, *Étude sur Épictète* (Paris, 1903); M.-J. Lagrange, "La philosophie religieuse d'Épictète et le Christianisme," RB 9 (1912) 5-21, 192-212; R. Bultmann, "Das religiöse Moment in der ethischen Unterweisung des Epiktet und das Neue Testament," ZNW 13 (1912) 97-110, 177-191; A. Jagu, *La religion d'Épictète* (Angers, 1946).

9. See ibid., 12:27: such a conception (δόξα καὶ ἐπίνοια, "praise and reflection") "is inevitable and innate (ἀναγκαία κατὰ φύσιν) in every rational being, without the help of a human teacher and free of the fraud of any mystagogue" . . . "for the Greeks and barbarians alike."

herd: Ezek 34:12-16), we limit ourselves to the Qumran community and the Alexandrine philosopher Philo.

At Qumran[10] we repeatedly find the verbal roots *drš* (thirty-eight times) and *bqš* (eight times), both of which mean "seek, investigate, search." In about eighteen texts these expressions are used with a precise theological significance. In this case, but when the sense is rather vague, the object of the quest may be the Law (1QS 6:7), the divine commandments (1QS 5:11), the will of God (1QS 5:9), peace (CD 6:21), the Covenant (1QH 5:9), and especially the Torah (1QS 6:6; 4QFlor 1:11; CD 6:7; 7:18). In the other texts the object of *drš* is God himself (*'l*): 1QS 1:1 ("book of the Rule of the Community *to seek God [lidrôs 'el]* with all one's heart and all one's soul"); 1QSb 3:20; 5:23; CD 1:10; 6:6; 1QH 4:6; 4:14-15 ("These seek you with a divided heart and do not stand firm in your truth, and . . . seek you among the idols"); 4:16. The semantic of this vocabulary is dominated by a characteristic ascetic component of conformity to the will of God, as is well expressed in the beginning of the Rule: ". . . to do what is good and just before him, as he commanded through Moses and all his servants the prophets" (1QS 1:2b-3). The Qumran "seeking of God," then, is located on the practical, moral, I should say legalistic level of faithfulness to the precepts of the Law. In Pauline language we could say that at Qumran God is sought by means of "works," in the sense of Rom 9:31-32a: "Israel, while seeking *(διώκων)* a law of justification, did not reach it. Why? Because they were based on works rather than faith." This parallel is all the more legitimate since one of the infinitive phrases at the beginning of the Rule of Qumran that follow the initial *to seek God*, reads thus: "and to give self to all good works" *wᵉlidboq bᵉkol ma'aśê ṭob* (1QS 1:5).

With Philo of Alexandria we have something altogether different. A Jew by birth and by faith, but irenically devoted to Plato and Stoicism in philosophy, he introduces into Greek philosophical and religious language the precise phrase ζητεῖν θεόν and the like. Actually, the theological vocabulary of quest is highly developed in Philo.[11] As object of seeking we find "things invisible" (*Dec.* 1; *Migr. Abr.* 89); "truth" (*Dec.* 65; *Spec. leg.* 164); "the beginning of creation" (*Leg. alleg.* III:78); "virtue" (*Omn. pProb. libr.* 68); "transmigration" (i.e., from passions: *Somn.* 1:45; *Migr. Abr.* 189; *Det. pot.* 154); "the nature of beings" (*Plant.* 79); "the Creator" (*Fug.* 164); the true God (*Abr.* 68). Objects of the noun ζήτησις are specifically "the One" (*Virt.* 215); "Being" (*Somm.* I:182; *Spec. leg.* I:345); "the Beautiful" (*Post.*

10. The investigation is based on K. G. Kuhn, *Konkordanz zu den Qumrantexten* (Göttingen, 1960); "Nachträge zur Konkordanz zu den Qumrantexten," RQ 4 (1963) 163-234.

11. See I. Leisegang, *Indices ad Philonis Alexandrini opera*, I–II (Berlin, 1926–30).

C. 21; 84) and "God, the best Being of all, the incomparable Being, the universal Cause" (*Fug.* 141; cf. *Spec. leg.* I:32; 40; *Migr. Abr.* 76).

But there are especially certain very important passages, including in the first place the following: "Nothing is preferable to the quest of the true God, even when the discovery of God escapes human ability": ἄμεινον γὰρ οὐδὲν τοῦ ζητεῖν τὸν ἀληθῆ θεόν, κἄν ἡ εὕρησις αὐτοῦ διαφεύγῃ δύναμιν ἀνθρωπίνην (*Spec. leg.* I:36; cf. I:40). Of course, "it is certainly difficult to conceive and comprehend the Father and Lord of all things, but that is no reason to refuse to undertake the quest" (I:32). Still, "With the friends of God who rise up in quest of Being, even though they never find it, we rejoice, because the search for the Good is itself sufficient to give abundant joy, even when the goal is not reached" (*Post. C.* 21; cf. *Leg. alleg.* III:47b). The object of the search for God is twofold: his existence and his nature (see *Spec. leg.* I:32-33).[12] The method is philosophical thought ("than which no more perfect good has entered human life": *Opif.* 54), but this presupposes one's going out of oneself, i.e., from the burdens of the body and of the presumptuousness of the intellect (*Leg. alleg.* III:47a), and must also take account of the possibility of self-revelation of God himself (see ibid.: "To many he did not show himself": πολλοῖς γὰρ οὐκ ἐφανέρωσεν ἑαυτόν;[13] cf. *Sacr. A. et C.* 64). As a whole, though, the reality is conceived of as rational; indeed, "those who want neither the discovery nor the quest gravely distort reason [τὸν λογισμόν]" (*Fug.* 121).

Another thing to notice for our purposes: if for Philo it is true that some seek without discovering, it is also true that others "discover without having sought" (*Fug.* 120; see 166-176).[14] But these are those who have in themselves an inspired awareness from on high; this intellectual perspective of Philo is not marred even by the example of the Promised Land received as a gift from God (with citation of Deut 6:10-11). Essentially the discovery corresponds to the terms of the quest; at the very most, those who have become "disciples of the Only Wise One" receive from God "quickly that which they seek," provided they are "well disposed" (*Sacr. A. et C.* 64). We conclude this panoramic description with a lovely text that approaches (but only partially! see III below) the Pauline theme

---

12. As for created beings, however, there is "a single extraordinary discovery (τοῦτο εὑρίσκει ἄριστον εὕρημα), namely, that absolutely everything is God's grace (χάριν ὄντα τοῦ θεοῦ τὰ σύμπαντα) . . ." (*Leg. alleg.* III:78; cf. *Deus immut.* 93).

13. We note that the same idea (and the same verb!) recurs in Rom 1:19: "God showed them . . .," with "what can be known of God" as object: τὸ γὰρ γνωστὸν τοῦ θεοῦ . . . ὁ θεὸς γὰρ αὐτοῖς ἐφανέρωσεν.

14. It is precisely the tract *De fuga et inventione* that proposes four distinct kind of persons: those who are interested neither in the discovery nor in the search (121-125); those who seek and find (126-142); those who seek and do not find (143-165); those who find without having sought (166-176).

(though in Philo the theme remains undeveloped): "Not to seek further belongs to the one who has faith": τὸ δὴ μηκέτι ζητεῖν ἔργον εἶναι πεπιστευκότος (*Div. rer. her.* 101).[15]

2) Paul's autobiographical silence

It certainly is a surprise to discover that Paul in his letters (but the same is true of the picture of him in Acts) never mentions the experience of a personal quest by himself before his conversion—for instance, in the way of suffering or as a liberation from distress. The most clearly autobiographical texts concerning this period are three: 1 Cor 15:8-10; Gal 1:13-17; Phil 3:4-8. Now in all of them all that we see are two extreme points of his journey: the period of the zealous persecutor under the Law and then the new and unexpected situation of one who has been "apprehended by Christ" (Phil 3:12). The total dichotomy between the two points is emphasized by two explicit Greek expressions for "but," δέ (1 Cor 15:10; Gal 1:15) and ἀλλά (Phil 3:7). Furthermore, in Phil 3 it is even further stressed by the two antithetic concepts of "gain" and "loss," κέρδη/ζημία, the latter, negative expression being repeated three times (twice as the noun, once as the verb ζημιόω: vv. 7-8) with the addition of an even stronger expression (σκύβαλα = "garbage": v. 8b). Moreover, the same idea of "gain" is repeated in the verb κερδαίνω, "gain," of v. 8b, but now applied to Christ with a reversal of roles.

All we can derive from these passages is that the Pharisee Saul of Tarsus was related to God according to the presuppositions and expectations common to traditional Judaism (Gal 1:14b: "irreproachable as concerns the justification that belongs to the Law"). His quest for God, then, was to be found in the moral and cultic track we outlined above (probably closer to Qumran than to Philo).[16] Actually, his later polemic, dealing more with the question of the possibility of reaching God through the Law than through reflection on the cosmos, leads us to suppose that his own quest had been precisely legalistic and moral in character.

Now, it is here that we must face the hermeneutical question of the "I" of Rom 7:7-25. No other Pauline passage makes more use of first per-

15. As we shall see, in the Pauline correspondence the quest belongs only to the one who already has faith. Evidently the idea of "faith" is different in the two cases (static in Philo, dynamic in Paul). But in each, at any rate, faith brings an end to a certain type of seeking.

16. The concept of "quest" in rabbinic tradition, closer to that of the Pharisees, really ought to be investigated. For example, see *Abôt* 6:4-6, where the one who pursues the law is exhorted to: reduced use of material things, diligent work, humility, attention, memory, reflection, purity of life, service of neighbor—and all this as a ceaseless enterprise: "If someone tells you, 'I have labored but not found,' don't believe them; 'I have not labored, but have found,' don't believe them either; 'I have labored and have found,' believe them" (*b. Meg.* 6b).

son singular forms than this.[17] Of course, almost no exegete today considers this text autobiographical,[18] which is better explained as *enallage* of person, substitution of one grammatical person for another. And yet, even if such an "I" has a universal value, for that very reason it in some sense also includes the experience of the Pharisee Paul. He, too, like every descendant of Adam, must have experienced the rending contradiction between the original human creatureliness, tending toward life, and the historical human condition in the power of sin, tending toward death.[19] Hence the quest for a safe way out: "Miserable as I am, who will deliver me from this body of death?" (7:24).

Even so, we must attend to the following issues. First of all, considering how generic the discourse is, this passage refers to Paul no more than it can refer to Adam; hence nothing really specific is found there such as would describe the specific, unique experience of the ex-Pharisee of Tarsus. In the second place, the whole of vv. 7-23 describes the hopeless situation of the person previous to any movement of any kind of quest, since it is only v. 24 that raises such a question (and briefly at that). Finally, we could say that precisely this question seems actually to be rhetorical, followed as it is by v. 25b, which returns to the previous theme of the human contradiction; but perhaps it is better to see the question as suggested to Paul by the experience of the Christian life in the Spirit (as appears in the following chapter, chapter 8). Hence we shall say that this question expressing a quest is now formulated from the point of view of one who has already been found through the "Spirit of life in Christ Jesus" (Rom 8:2).

And so not even Rom 7 can give us the concrete living experience of the pre-Christian Paul in search of a God different from the God known to tradition, whom we do know to have been subsequently amply surpassed. But Paul's obstinate silence surely has a precise meaning that we shall try to gather in two steps.

17. The attested grammatical forms are the personal pronoun in the nominative (ἐγώ, αὐτός, "I," "[my]self"); accusative (με, "me"); dative (μοί, ἐμοί, ἐν ἐμοί, "me/to me, in me"); genitive (μου, "my"); and especially first person singular verbs: indicatives (in present, aorist, and perfect) and participle (perfect passive)—fifty times in all!

18. The decisive study indicating this was by W. G. Kümmel, *Römer 7 und die Bekehrung des Paulus* (Leipzig, 1929; republished in *Römer 7 und das Bild des Menschen im Neuen Testament* [Munich, 1974]); the author appeals both to the thematic of the immediate context and to other passages of the correspondence where the "I" has a more general sense (e.g., Rom 3:7; 1 Cor 6:12, 15; Gal 2:18ff.), and also to Hellenistic parallels (pp. 126ff.) Further, see S. Lyonnet, "L'histoire de salut selon le chapitre VII de l'épître aux Romains," Bib 43 (1962) 117–151; see also the two most recent major commentaries: E. Käsemann, *Commentary on Romans* (Grand Rapids, Mich., 1980); H. Schlier, *Der Römerbrief* HThKNT (Freiburg–Basel–Wien, 1977 [Italian: 1982]).

19. See H. Schlier, 221–222.

a) The Christian God is not liable to investigation in his specificity. As such, he simply reveals himself (see II 1 below). A quest that would reach the God of Jesus Christ step by logical step as the God of the saving cross is quite impossible. In a certain sense, the human person has no predisposition to understand this God. The *a priori* of the search for God essentially can be either the Greek type (through application of the intellect to the experience of the cosmos), or the Jewish type (through moral application in the execution of God's commandments), or the two types combined together (as in Philo of Alexandria and the wisdom tradition in general). But the Christian God arrives unexpected,[20] while the person is still struggling in the sterility of the one attitude or the other (note Rom 3:21ff. compared with 1:18ff., and Rom 8:1ff. compared with 7:7ff.).

Paul himself is a case in point. He was not seeking God but rather came to encounter him only on the basis of an unexpected εὐδοκία, "favor," on God's part (see Gal 1:15-16; 1 Cor 1:21). Hence the autobiographical silence, necessitated by the fact that at first he knew "according to the flesh, but now no longer . . ., since in Christ the old things have passed, behold, they have become new" (2 Cor 5:16-17). Between the "first" and the "then" of the encounter (which is "pistic" in character! see below II) there is the same opposition as exists between flesh and spirit (see Rom 7 and 8): the former does not produce the latter; rather, it is the latter that not only surpasses but annuls the former (see Gal 5:17-18; Rom 8:2, 12-13).

b) The ignoring of the past is explicable by Paul's total and exclusive attention to the new object found, which takes all his attention: τὰ μὲν ὀπίσω ἐπιλανθανόμενος, τοῖς δὲ ἔμπροσθεν ἐπεκτεινόμενος, "setting aside what is behind, stretching out to the future" (Phil 3:13). This is why all Paul's vocabulary about "seeking" reflects only the post-baptismal stage of the Christian; but this stage is anything but passive and static (see below, III). Even so, other, anticipatory forms of quest are not condemned *en bloc*; indeed, something of God actually can be perceived through reflection on the cosmos (Rom 1:19-21a) or through observance of the Law, which is still "holy" (Rom 7:12). Indeed, to such enterprises one can even apply the concept of a preparatory function, as can be found in the image of the "pedagogue" in Gal 3:24. But whatever features are to be attributed to the function of the pedagogue in antiquity, they include not only its provisional character but also the qualitative discontinuity when it is finished.[21] In this regard it would be instructive to examine the recurrent Pau-

---

20. As in Blaise Pascal's "night of fire."
21. Commentators apply two different meanings to the image of the pedagogue, either negative (one who kept the minor child in a harsh condition of virtual servitude; thus H.

line pattern of ποτέ/νῦν, "once"/"now," which practically corresponds to the "behind/ahead" of Phil 3:13, and clearly sets up a contrast between two periods not only of universal history but also and especially of individual history (see, e.g., Gal 4:8-9).[22]

3) *The formula εἰς αὐτόν, "unto him"*

This formula recurs seven times in the Pauline letters, six instances of which are certainly of interest to us (Rom 11:36; 1 Cor 8:6; Col 1:16, 20; Eph 1:5; 4:15).[23] Grammatically it constitutes an adverbial phrase of motion toward-, and so indicates a direction, an orientation, a goal, actually implying some movement of seeking. The goal of such movement is personal: three times God and three times Christ. We shall examine it in three stages.

a) *The construction.* The subject of the movement "unto him" is three times the neuter plural τὰ πάντα, "everything" (Rom 11:36; Col 1:16, 20) and three times the pronoun "we" (1 Cor 8:6; Eph 1:5; 4:15). In four cases the phrase depends on various explicit verbs: ἐκτίσθη, "were created" (Col 1:16); ἀποκαταλλάξαι, "to reconcile" (Col 1:20); προορίσας, "planned" (Eph 1:5); αὐξήσωμεν, "grow up" (Eph 4:15); in the other two cases there is simply no verb, with a simple copulative being understood (Rom 11:36; 1 Cor 8:6).

b) *The context.* Our formula regularly returns in fixed and traditional literary forms: once in a doxology (Rom 11:36), once in a confession of faith (1 Cor 8:6), once in a eulogia (Eph 1:5), twice in a hymn (Col 1:16, 20); only once (Eph 4:15) does it occur in an ordinary discursive passage.[24] We can legitimately deduce that the phrase has been borrowed from extra-Pauline environments.

c) *The origin.* Since the expression has no precedent in the LXX biblical Greek, the common opinion is to attribute it to the Hellenistic or Hellenistic-

---

Schlier, *Der Brief an die Galater,* ad loc.) or more positive (one who guided the child to and from the teacher; thus more commonly, e.g., J. Bligh, ad loc.) But in either case, the function ends completely either on reaching adulthood or in the presence of the teacher.

22. On this subject we recommend P. Tachau, *"Einst" und "Jetzt" im Neuen Testament,* FRLANT 105 (Göttingen, 1972).

23. We ignore Phil 1:29, where the expression is πιστεύειν εἰς αὐτόν, "to believe in him (= Christ)": here the sense is determined more by the verb than the prepositional phrase (representing as it does a well-known New Testament formula), and so lies outside the subject we are investigating.

24. Still, M. Barth (Ephesians, I–II [Garden City, N.Y., 1974] 445) correctly points out the original character of the expression "to grow unto him who is the Head"; this has no parallel, whether in contemporaneous science (the opposite if anything) or in the Old Testament, or in Orphic or Gnostic literature.

Jewish environment. Actually, at least Rom 11:36 offers a surprising affinity to the formulation of the Stoic Marcus Aurelius,* *Thoughts*, 4:23: "O Nature, from you is all, in you is all, unto you is all": ἐκ σοῦ πάντα, ἐν σοὶ πάντα, εἰς σὲ πάντα" (see also Philo of Alexandria, *Spec. leg.* I:208).[25] Surely 1 Cor 8:6 is similar, both because the phrase there too is lapidary, understanding a simple copulative, and because the goal of the movement is strictly theological in character and not yet Christological.[26]

d) *The use.* Paul's use of the formula is not all of a kind. The text closest to the timbre of the original Stoic use is surely Rom 11:36. Also 1 Cor 8:6 is for the most part similar, but here the neuter "all things," τὰ πάντα, is replaced with the personal pronoun "we," ἡμεῖς, which shifts the attention from the cosmic perspective to something more personal in conception. Even so, this does not detract from the characteristic reference to attraction toward God, which is rendered all the more significant by the fact that the formula occurs only in the first part of a confession of faith in binitarian structure (while in v. 6b, with its Christological content, we find only an adverbial phrase of means, δι' αὐτοῦ, "through him"); the "we" further seems to have a semantic horizon of universal weight, as a simply human and not specifically Christian "we," for a relationship of synecdoche with the immediately preceding "all things," τὰ πάντα, is easily recognized (v. 6a: ἐξ οὗ τὰ πάντα καὶ ἡμεῖς εἰς αὐτόν, "from whom are all things, and we are unto him," with the personal pronoun appearing as a simple personalistic restriction of the cosmic "all," πάντα). Meanwhile in Eph 1:5 the εἰς αὐτόν still has a *theo*-logical value, but the subject of the attraction ("we," ἡμᾶς) is clearly restricted to the ecclesial "us," the theme of the whole blessing in 1:3-14. Then in the three other texts (Eph 4:15; Col 1:16, 20) the Christologizing of the formula has been completely accomplished, since the phrase εἰς αὐτόν, "unto him," stands only for Christ, even though in Col 1:16, 20 the subject of the movement is again "all things." The formula, then, never occurs again, strictly speaking, in connection with the specific theme of "seeking God."

e) *The meaning* of the formula, at least in the most archaic Pauline texts (Rom 11:36 and 1 Cor 8:6), is basically that of the Hellenistic matrix: God, who is the point of departure of all, is also their necessary point of arrival, the only and definitive goal of the existence of "all things" and of "us" in particular. Thus is affirmed an original and universal orientation

---

25. For further documentation, see E. Norden, *Agnostos Theos*, 240-250 ("Eine stoische Doxologie bei Paulus: Geschichte einer Allmachtsformel").

26. See A. Feuillet, *Le Christ Sagesse de Dieu d'après les Épîtres Pauliniennes* (Paris, 1966) 59-85 ("La profession de foi monothéiste de 1 Co, VIII, 4-6"). See also R. Kerst, "1 Kor. 8⁶—ein vorpaulinisches Taufbekenntnis?" ZNW 66 (1975) 130-139.

"unto him," in Augustine's sense, "You have made us for yourself alone" (*Conf.* 1:1). It is in this perspective that we can locate and justify every attempt of quest that brings about a thrust and signifies an attraction toward our final end, and that of all things. This end, then, is simply identified as "God," θεός (Rom 11:36), or at most as "God the Father," θεὸς ὁ πατήρ (1 Cor 8:6). But we should note that this last description as "Father" does not yet have the Christological sense of "Father of our Lord Jesus Christ" (as in Eph 1:3, which thus identifies the "unto him" of 1:5), but only a cosmic and hence universal value, since it is also used in the same sense even by Philo of Alexandria (*Opif.* 7; *Spec. leg.* 1:32; etc.)[27] Finally, we must say that our formula guarantees a creaturely substratum (natural but established by God himself) and hence the possibility of receiving some revelation by God himself—and such revelation according to Paul (as we shall see) far surpasses the independent human power of discovery. The εἰς αὐτόν, "unto him," however, indicates that God's self-revelation presupposes and is rooted in this inborn capacity, even if by itself it would remain fruitless.

I. The crisis of the natural quest

Concerning the natural human propensity for the search for God, Paul makes two declarations, one positive and the other negative. The former, however (apart from the expression εἰς αὐτόν, "unto him," remaining too vague anyhow) is not developed as a theme and actually receives very little treatment, as we shall see in Rom 1:19-23, which we are now about to examine.

1) *The significance of Rom 1:19-23*

This passage is found in a context that paints a dark picture of human ἀσέβεια καὶ ἀδικία, "ungodliness and unrighteousness" (v. 18), understood as idolatry and the source of manifold moral perversions (vv. 24-32).

Obviously this is no place to embark on a detailed exegesis of the pericope.[28] Here we will describe only the most striking aspects of the message, considering them in two stages corresponding to the two parts of

27. This value of "Father" is not biblical (the Old Testament uses the title only in reference to the people of Israel and their king), but comes from a Greek tradition, where Homer already identified Zeus as "Father of humans and of the gods," art. πατήρ in TDNT 5:951–958.

28. Besides the commentaries, see, e.g., A. Feuillet, "La connaissance naturelle de Dieu par les hommes d'après Rom 1,18-23," *Lumière et Vie* 14 (1954); S. Schulz, "Die Anklage in Röm 1,18-32," TZ 14 (1958) 161–173.

the passage (in which the particle οὐχ of v. 21 forms a logical watershed, separating a positive section from a negative section).

a) In vv. 19-21a: to arrive at some aspect of the divine nature is not only possible but actually a fact of human experience. We note here a certain affinity of vocabulary with both Dio of Prusa and Philo of Alexandria. In common with the first, Paul employs the idea of νοῦς, "mind," applied actively to the experience of visible things (νοούμενα, "understood," in Rom 1:20; ἐπινοοῦντες, "conceiving," in Or. 12:32)[29] and the term δύναμις, "power," as quality of God discovered by human beings (Rom 1:20b = Or. 12:35). This latter parallelism is all the more remarkable in that for Paul it is the only case (out of forty-eight uses) in which the word has a theo-cosmological significance.

With Philo, Paul shares the concept of δύναμις, "power" (though Philo uses the plural: Opif. 7)[30] whether that of a divine "revelation" expressed with the same verb in the aorist ἐφανέρωσεν, "showed" (Rom 1:19b = Leg. alleg. III:47): when Philo denies the universality of this revelation ("To many he did not show himself"), he thereby does confirm the reality (cf. the Philonian concept of "God's grace" applied to the whole cosmos: Deus immut. 93). Now this is the only time (out of twenty-two occurrences) when Paul uses the verb with a cosmological value.[31] The means of such manifestation (note also the adjective φανερόν, "manifest," in v. 19a) is explained immediately after in v. 20a: "from the creation of the world,[32] his invisible qualities are perceived through reflection on things that are made."[33] Verse 20b, then, tells what is the object of this possible and even

29. In terms of the ideas, it is useful to compare the καθορᾶται, "is perceived," of Rom 1:20 with the verbs θαυμάζειν καὶ ἀγαπᾶν, "marvel and love," of Or. 12:32. A similar comparison could be made between Paul's concept of τὸ γνωστὸν τοῦ θεοῦ φανερόν ἐστιν ἐν αὐτοῖς, "What is known of God is manifest to them" (Rom 1:19), and that of Dio, Or. 12:27: ἐπίνοια . . . ἀναγκαία ἐν παντὶ τῷ λογικῷ, "conception, . . . necessary in all reasoning beings."

30. See also his question of the nature of visible things (compare Rom 1:20a with Opif. 54: τίς ἡ τῶν ὁρατῶν δὴ τούτων οὐσία, "what is the nature of these visible things?") as a source of philosophical knowledge (ibid.) Still, for Philo God cannot be grasped by the νοῦς, "mind," which however does tend "toward the incomprehensible nature of God, τὴν ἀκατάληπτον θεοῦ φύσιν, of whom nothing can be comprehended save only that he exists, μὴ πρὸς τὸ εἶναι μόνον" (Det. pot. ins. 89).

31. At any rate, this observation has its significance: natural "revelation" is set parallel precisely to that of "God's righteousness" (Rom 3:21), "the mystery hidden" (Rom 16:26; Col 1:26), "the life of Jesus" (2 Cor 4:10-11), etc.

32. See Dio of Prusa, Or. 12:27.

33. We can compare Paul's expression "perceived in the things that are made" (τοῖς ποιήμασιν νοούμενα) to the lovely text of Philo, which plays on the double meaning of ποίημα as "work/poem": "Anyone who is able to hear the poetry of God (τῆς θεοῦ ποιητικῆς) is of necessity happy and joins the joy of those who were hearers thereof in the past. In God's poetry neither meter nor rhythm is found, nor the vocal cadence that seduces the ear with music; rather the most perfect works of nature can be seen, whose harmony is found in chance;

actual perception: "his eternal power and divinity" *(ἥ τε ἀΐδιος αὐτοῦ δύναμις καὶ θειότης)*. By this hendiadys Paul indicates that one can come to know of a dynamic deity, as if to say that reason can go no further. For Paul this achievement is doubtless scanty but should represent a minimum adequate for appropriate religious comportment. But in actual fact this is not what happens.

b) Verses 21b-23: the sterility of the natural quest for God. Negative phrases abound here: "They neither glorified nor thanked," "grew futile," "were darkened," "senseless hearts," "became foolish" (emphasized by juxtaposition with "declaring themselves wise"); see also the contrast between "the glory of the immortal God" and "the image of the mortal human, birds, beasts, reptiles" (v. 23).[34] This evidence emphasizes the great gap, actual as well as possible, between the knowledge of God and the appreciation of God. And the lack of thankfulness is only one aspect of this. It also appears in the stupid divinization of the cosmic realities,[35] with inevitable consequences on the level of individual and interpersonal experience, consequences that are both sign and cause of "God's wrath" (vv. 18, 24-32).

This theme of the sterility of the quest for God and its deleterious results is picked up again at the end of this first section (1:18-3:20) of the Letter to the Romans, indicating a kind of logical inclusion. For actually, in 3:10-11 Paul cites Ps 14:1-3 LXX freely: "There is not one who is just, there is none who understands, *none who seeks God (οὐκ ἔστιν ὁ ἐκζητῶν τὸν θεόν).*" The clear observation of the psalmist, which Paul makes his own, understands the "seeking" on a concrete, existential level, much more than intellectual (as indicated by the whole citation, note vv. 12-18); and this is also the meaning of the peremptory saying of v. 9, "Jews and Greeks alike, all are subject to sin" (cf. v. 19b: "so that . . . the whole cosmos should be found guilty before God"). Surely if we think of Paul's near contemporaries, Seneca, Dio, and even more Epictetus, not to mention Philo of Alexandria, these judgments of Paul seem rather drastic, summary, hasty, preconceived. Actually, he is speaking from the point of view of one who has found, not by his own search, but by God's free revelation. From the viewpoint of faith he is able to measure the whole distance between God's wisdom (not his own!) and the foolishness of the world. Only thus can we explain and accept all the paradox but also all the truth of what he claims (see also vol. 1 of the present work, chap. 6).

---

just as the mind that sets itself to listen to the poems/works of God is overjoyed, (καθάπερ δὲ ὁ νοῦς ἀκροατικῶς ἔχων τῶν θεοῦ ποιημάτων χαίρει), so . . ." (*Det. pot. ins.* 124–125).

34. On this whole theme see also 4 Esdr 8:60.

35. See Philo, *Opif.* 7: "They exalted the world beyond measure."

2) Explicit polemic

There are at least two texts where Paul clearly states that one gets oneself in a blind alley by seeking God only on the basis of one's own natural capacity, obstinately choosing to limit oneself to this: 1 Cor 1:20 and Rom 10:20.

a) "*Where is the seeker of this world?*" (ποῦ συζητητὴς τοῦ αἰῶνος τούτου;— 1 Cor 1:20). We understand this question as a descriptive title of the whole section 1 Cor 1:17–3:23. Moreover, we identify the grammatical character of the genitive as subjective, with "this age" as a theological attribute of the "seeker," but also of the "sage" and the "scribe." The threefold question accentuates the subject (who is described in various ways), to affirm the total discomfiture not only of the person but of the person's theological proposals.[36] The rhetorical question, which implies a negative response, is occasioned and also confirmed by the preceding biblical citation of Isa 29:14 LXX (which semantically reinforces the concept by causing it to be repeated, and which within itself is composed of a synonymous parallelism: "I shall destroy the wisdom of the wise and shall put down/humble the cleverness of the clever").

The simple statistics of the vocabulary confirm that the general theme of this whole section of the letter is wisdom.[37] We have a contrast between the "wisdom of the cosmos," σοφία τοῦ κόσμου (1:20b; 3:19; see 2:6: σοφία τοῦ αἰῶνος τούτου, "wisdom of this world/age") and the "wisdom of God," σοφία τοῦ θεοῦ (1:21, 24; 2:7): the former, which is implicitly recognized as having a specific identity, by its very nature is incapable of giving rise to the latter; this latter actually has its very own ways of emerging, in the last analysis rooted in the εὐδοκία, "gracious choice," of God's own self (1:21b).

The explicit theme of "quest" is present not only in the substantival adjective συζητητῆς, "seeker" (1:20) but also in the verb "seek," ζητοῦσιν (1:22b: "The Greeks seek wisdom"); note also the neighboring αἰτοῦσιν, "ask for" (1:22a: "The Jews ask for signs"). The negative outcome of this effort of seeking is described by the category "did not know," οὐκ ἔγνω,

---

36. From the formal point of view, we can find a similar triple question in ποῦ, "where?," in Isa 33:18 LXX: ποῦ εἰσιν οἱ γραμματικοί; ποῦ εἰσιν οἱ συμβουλεύοντες; ποῦ ἐστιν ὁ ἀριθμῶν . . ., "Where are the scribes? Where are the advisors? Where is the one who counts?" Its sense and use in the diatribe are confirmed by Epictetus, *Diatr.* III:10:17. Also note its affinity to Isa 19:11-12; Bar 3:14-16. Probably the first of the three nouns, "sage" (σοφός) has a general meaning, referring to both the Jewish and the Greek quest; this is specified by the second, the "scribe" (γραμματεύς), in a Jewish sense, and by the third, "seeker" (συζητητῆς), with a Greek meaning (thus U. Wilckens, *Weisheit und Torheit. Eine exegetisch-religionsgeschichtliche Untersuchung zu 1. Kor 1 und 2* [Tübingen, 1959] 28).

37. The term σοφία, "wisdom," occurs in Paul 29 times, 18 of them in 1 Cor 1-3. Similarly, the adjective σοφός, "wise": of 16 occurrences in Paul, 10 are in 1 Cor 1-3.

of v. 21a ("In God's wisdom the world *did not know* God through wisdom.")[38] It is not improbable that behind the Corinthian understanding is the Hellenistic Jewish tradition represented by the Alexandrians Wisdom and Philo, mediated by the Alexandrian preacher Apollo, and tending to reduce the Christian message to speculative philosophy.[39] The consequence of such a quest, at least at Corinth, essentially consists in a form of marked overconfidence[40] (see 1 Cor 1:29, 31; 4:8), which leads to a stance of disdainful intellectual self-sufficiency, with painfully divisive effects within the Christian community. That such a quest misses the target is confirmed by the unexpected content of the apostolic kerygma, which unpredictably views the dynamic presence of God in the cross of Christ (1 Cor 1:17-18; 2:2), and by extension in that which is "foolish . . . weak . . . ignoble and despised" (1:27-28).

There is a reason, then, why the conception of "power" *(δύναμις)* no longer identifies a property of God related to the cosmos, but the unexpected salvific intervention of God in Christ crucified, and by way of parallel in the preaching of the cross.[41] "It is precisely *the proclamation* about

38. We prefer to understand this "in God's wisdom" as "a scheme, or plan, prepared and enacted by God" (with C. K. Barrett, *A Commentary on the First Epistle to the Corinthians* [London, 1971²] ad loc.) rather than cosmologically as *divine* "wisdom poured out upon all [God's] works" (against A. Feuillet, *Le Christ Sagesse de Dieu*, 75–76, who inappropriately cites Job 38:1-39, 40; Sir 1:7; thus also H. Conzelmann, ad loc.). In the whole context, in fact, in the precise phrase "God's wisdom," σοφία τοῦ θεοῦ, the genitive has a clear subjective and not just descriptive sense (note the interconfessional Italian New Testament translation [Turin, 1976] ad loc. reads, in effect, "With all their wisdom, people were unable to know God and his wisdom").

The apparent contradiction between "did not know God," οὐκ ἔγνω . . . τὸν θεόν, and the statement of Rom 1:21, "knowing God," γνόντες τὸν θεόν, is resolved by giving different meanings to the same verb and also to the object "God." Romans 1:19-21 is in a cosmological context and affirms the accessibility of God, but with very precise limits ("his eternal power and divinity"; see above); whereas 1 Cor 1:18ff. is in a soteriological context and affirms the inaccessibility of the specifically Christian God, who reveals himself in the cross of Christ. A third passage in the semantic of Pauline vocabulary is found in Gal 4:8-9: "Once, *not knowing God* [οὐκ εἰδότες θεόν], you were subject to gods who are not gods; but *now that you have known God* [νῦν δὲ γνόντες θεόν], or better, that you are known by God [μᾶλλον δὲ γνωσθέντες ὑπὸ θεοῦ]. . . ." As we see, the expression "knowing God" repeats that of Rom 1:21, but with a completely different meaning, since in this context (Gal 4:1-7) it refers to the God manifested by Christ and his Spirit, and no longer to the God of creation; meanwhile the οὐκ εἰδότες θεόν, "not knowing God," corresponds to the οὐκ ἔγνω, "did not know," of 1 Cor 1:21, the past value of which is emphasized in Gal 4:8 by a perfectly clear τότε ("then," "once," i.e., before the encounter with the *Christian* God, whose personal initiative is attested by the aorist passive participle γνωσθέντες ὑπὸ θεοῦ, "having come to be known by God").

39. Thus R. A. Horsley, "Wisdom of Word and Words of Wisdom in Corinth," CBQ 39 (1977) 224–239.

40. See J. Sanchez Bosch, *"Gloriarse" según San Pablo. Sentido y teología de καυχάομαι,* AB 40 (Rome, 1970) esp. 124–133.

41. See vol. 1 of this work, chap. 10; S. Virgulin, "La croce come potenza di Dio in 1 Cor 1:18-25," in *La sapienza della croce oggi. Atti del Congresso Internazionale: Roma, 13–18 ottobre 1975* (Turin, 1976) 144–150.

the cross, foolish as it seems, that reveals the bankruptcy of human wisdom. . . . No wise man could ever have discovered that God would do
this. God's action is the kind of surprise that makes startlingly clear the
ultimate inanity of the deepest human intelligence"[42] (cf. Rom 11:33: "How
inscrutable are his judgments, and unsearchable his ways!"). And it is
this that is passionately confirmed by many a convert just as in the case
of Paul.[43]

b) *"I was found by those who did not seek me (εὑρέθην τοῖς ἐμὲ μὴ ζητοῦσιν),*
I was revealed to those who did not ask" (Rom 10:20 = Isa 65:1). Paul
knows that he is producing a paradoxical text and actually introduces this
quotation with "Isaiah dares *(ἀποτολμᾷ)* to say." Between the prophet and
the Apostle the sense of the saying differs only in details;[44] the main difference is that in Isaiah it is still the traditional God of Israel who commends
himself to those who *no longer* sought him, while in Paul we have a sudden displacement of reference, to the God of the faith in Jesus Christ, who
surpasses the order of Israel to offer himself to those who had not sought
him at all (including Israel itself). The more universal reference acquired
by the Isaian passage in Paul is revealed by the context in which it is now
inserted, a context of missionary character with considerable reflection on
the relationship between Israel and the gentiles in salvation history.

The language of the text related to our theme emerges especially in
three passages of the context: Rom 9:30-32 ("What then are we to say?
That the gentiles, who were not seeking [μὴ διώκοντα] righteousness,
received [κατέλαβεν] righteousness, but the righteousness derived from
faith; whereas Israel, which did seek [διώκων] a Law of righteousness,
did not accomplish [οὐκ ἔφθασεν] the Law. And why not? Because they
based themselves on works rather than faith"); 10:3 ("Not knowing God's

42. W. F. Orr and J. A. Walther, *I Corinthians,* Anchor Bible 32 (Garden City, N.Y., 1976) 159.
43. Note, for instance, what was written on the basis of his own conversion by the French
convert Maurice Clavel, one of the so-called *nouveaux philosophes:* "It is only through God
that we can know God. Indeed, if God has personally taken the trouble to reveal himself
to humanity, he inflicted on himself that sacrifice, those emotions, those sufferings of which
we read in the Bible; I mean that humans could not come to know God in any other way,
especially not with the power and resources of their own spirit. . . . How is it possible after
that, that the Christian religion could somehow have become respectability, practically the
prey of the wise and learned? . . . A doctrine, a doctrinal whole, which was termed 'an
absurdity,' 'stupidity,' 'foolishness,' 'impossible,' of what value could this ever be in the
marketplace of human thought—all of which is not worth one nail from the cross?" *Ce que
je crois* [Paris, 1975] 18, 19, 26).
44. Apart from the fact that Paul simply inverts the LXX order of the two verbs *(εὑρέθην*
and *ἐμφανὴς ἐγενόμην),* we should note that in Isaiah the phrase probably indicates those who
stayed in Jerusalem during the Exile, participating in paganizing cults, and found in this state
by the returning Jewish community (cf. Isa 65:10: "My people will seek me again," and 64:4:
"You go the opposite way from those who practice righteousness"). But in Paul the text is
applied precisely to the gentiles.

righteousness and seeking to establish their own, they did not submit to God's righteousness"); 11:7 ("What should we say, then? Israel has not reached what it sought [ὅ ἐπιζητεῖ], but rather the elect have reached it; the others were hardened").[45]

The quotation reported by Paul does assume a clear distinction between Israel and the gentiles: only the latter "did not seek" God, while the former actually did. We have no intention here of discussing what kind of "seeking" was done by Israel, especially according to the witness of the Old Testament. What is important is that such a quest did not encounter the Christian God (see Isa 55:8-9) and that therefore this God is confirmed as the God for those who are far off, for sinners and even atheists (see H. Schlier, ad loc.)[46] But we must emphasize the missionary context of Rom 10:20. The ideas of proclamation, mission, hearing, obedience to the gospel, word of Christ, geographical extension constantly succeed one another (especially in vv. 14-18). But basically there is an element of surprise and a resulting anguish that the gospel was accepted precisely by those for whom it was not originally meant. Not even the "quest" of the gentiles was at all directed toward the God of the gospel, and yet they found him and accepted him (see 9:30: κατέλαβεν, "accepted"; 11:7: ἐπέτυχεν, "reached").

In this salvation-history type of contrast it is not hard to read an implied preference of Paul for the gentile quest: the philosophical and even the idolatrous seeking of God would seem to constitute a better possibility of acceptance (a *praeparatio evangelica*), precisely because it was farther from the point and so imposed less in the way of conditions than the Jewish quest, based as this was on an overconfident understanding of self, that has its own starting point, its own hypothesis, and fails to meet the One who has other thoughts and other ways (see 9:31: οὐκ ἔφθασεν, "they did not arrive"; 11:7 οὐκ ἐπέτυχεν, "they did not reach").

The discovery of the Christian God

The quest of God, which is after all a connatural aspect of the human condition, fails its goal because unexpectedly the specifically Christian God

---

45. See J. Gnilka, *Die Verstockung Israels* (Munich, 1961). See also C. K. Barrett, "Romans 9:30-10:21: Fall and Responsibility of Israel," in the collection *Die Israelfrage nach Rom. 9-11*, ed. Lorenzo De Lorenzi, Monographische Reihe von "Benedictina." Biblisch-ökumenische Abteilung, 3 (Rome, 1977) 99-121.

46. See again M. Clavel, *Ce que*, 24: "As for the atheist, to whom I feel closer, nothing separates us except the abyss" (cf. a later reflection: "I do not think faith to be the prolongation or satisfaction of a psychic appetite. I do not think it expands our being by complementing it; rather faith renews it by turning it on its head." [I have been unable to trace this quotation in the original. In view of the relative length of the Italian edition (which Penna cites, and where it is on p. 226) and the French, it should be about p. 286.—T.P.W., translator.]).

is simply not where this quest looks (see Rom 9:16). God is to be found only by self-revelation, not by human search. God's accessibility is itself a free gift.

We do not intend really to develop this theme, because to do so could well lead us far afield. But we must simply sketch it rapidly so as to be able to recognize the sudden displacement of reference in the human enterprise of seeking God.

1) One thing stands out: in the whole Pauline correspondence, while "God" is never explicitly called the object of seeking (except, perhaps, in Rom 1:20, but at least never with the vocabulary of ζητέω, "seek"), this God is frequently identified as subject of *an initiative of revelation or appearance.* To describe this, the correspondence makes use of essentially four verbs: γνωρίζω, "make known"; φανερόω, "manifest"; ἀποκαλύπτω, "reveal"; ἐπιφαίνω, "appear."[47] Not that these always refer to an already accomplished manifestation of God; sometimes the reference is eschatological or simply profane, or has Paul himself as subject. If we include the nouns ἀποκάλυψις and ἔνδειξις, "revelation" and "demonstration," with the first three expressions, we can find twenty-four references to the manifestation of God in history.

Still, it is important to note that the object of this revelation is never God in himself. The object of God's revelatory action is thus identified: twelve times the μυστήριον ("mystery" of God, of God's will, of Christ, or the like: Rom 16:25 [twice], 36; Col 1:26-27; Eph 1:9; 3:3 [twice]; 3:10; 1 Tim 3:16), to which should be added two further texts reflecting the idea (1 Cor 2:10a; 2 Tim 1:10);[48] four times the δικαιοσύνη θεοῦ (Rom 1:17; 3:21, 25, 26); twice Jesus Christ (Gal 1:12, 16); one time faith (Gal 3:23; cf. 3:25); the power of God (Rom 9:22); the riches of his glory (Rom 9:23); his word (Titus 1:3). As for the etymological unit φαιν-, subjects of the verb are "the saving grace of God" (Titus 2:11) or "the goodness and kindliness of God our Savior" (Titus 3:4), while the noun ἐπιφάνεια (which occurs in the already cited 2 Tim 1:10) takes "our savior Jesus Christ" as its object.

A methodological observation is called for: most of this vocabulary is late Pauline (if not deutero-Pauline). The authentic Paul, or at least the earlier Paul, essentially uses the verbs φανερόω-ἀποκαλύπτω and the noun ἔνδειξις, and sees the object of this manifestation by God as "his righteousness" (Rom 1:17; 3:21, 25, 26), Jesus Christ (Gal 1:12, 16) and faith itself (Gal 3:23). We must at once observe how *faith* has a determinative role

47. A fifth verb (δείκνυμι–ἐνδείκνυμαι, "show") is not used relevantly in connection with our topic, unlike the derived noun ἔνδειξις (in Rom 3:25, 26). In our statistics we naturally ignore the passages where the subject of the revelation/apparition is Christ (by whatever title).

48. On mysteriological texts and themes, see R. Penna, *Il 'mysterion' paolino: Traiettoria e costituzione* (Brescia, 1978).

in the structure of revelation itself, and this very fact helps to undermine any supposition of independent discovery in the quest of God.[49] This faith identifies a new economy, a new system in the relationship between human beings and God. Paul almost personifies it, affirming that it has "arrived" (Gal 3:25: ἐλθούσης δὲ τῆς πίστεως, "faith having arrived") with an arrival in time, in the history of salvation, thus indicating as it were the watershed between two eras of history and two religious worlds.[50]

The faith-principle comes down to a single element of content, which, however, appears in two stages. The one is objective: the revelation of God's merciful justice in the death of Christ on the cross (note Rom 3:21ff.); the other is subjective and personal: the revelation of God to Paul himself (see Gal 1:12-16; Phil 3:7ff.; Eph 3:3). In this regard it is helpful to note that the subject of the initiative is actually God, while Jesus Christ is the content of it: "for I have not received it [i.e., the gospel] from a human being, nor have I been taught it, but *through the revelation of Jesus Christ,* δι᾽ ἀποκαλύψεως Ἰησοῦ Χριστοῦ" (Gal 1:12);[51] that this genitive is objective is confirmed by the following vv. 15-16. This means that the act of revelation is traced back to the supreme agent, which is God himself (v. 15: ὅτε δὲ εὐδόκησεν ὁ θεός), but Paul leaves us wishing to know more about the concrete ways in which understanding came.[52]

2) Paul only uses the verb ζητέω, "seek," once with reference to the time and content of what Christians discover, namely, in Gal 2:17: "*But if while seeking to be justified in Christ (εἰ δὲ ζητοῦντες δικαιωθῆναι ἐν Χριστῷ),* we too were found to be sinners. . . ." We note from the beginning that δικαιωθῆναι, "to be justified," is a discreet allusion to an act of God himself;[53] hence the seeking of which he here speaks is concerned with God (so that the ἐν Χριστῷ, "in Christ," simply indicates the instrument of

---

49. Cf. Philo, *Migr. Abr.* 220: πολλοῖς καὶ μεγάλοις πόνοις, "with many great labors. . . ."

50. Note the great distance between this "coming" in a Pauline sense and the "coming" in simple natural religion, of which Seneca writes: "God comes to persons, indeed, what is more accurate, God comes into persons: no mind is good without God. Divine seeds are sown in human bodies" (*Ep.* 73:16).

51. Paul's claim, which excludes any human intervention from without, recalls the natural understanding of God according to Dio of Prusa: "the *glory* (δόξα) and *understanding* (ἐπίνοια) of the Sovereign of all things . . . is produced according to nature, *without the help of any human teacher or mystagogue*" (*Or.* 12:27). But between the two authors there is all the distance between the natural God and the God of Jesus Christ.

52. See K. Kertelge, "Apokalypsis Jesou Christou (Gal 1:12)," in *Neues Testament und Kirche. Für Rudolf Schnackenburg,* ed. J. Gnilka (Freiburg–Basel–Vienna, 1974) 266–281; see also A.-M. Denis, "L'investiture de la fonction apostolique par 'apocalypse.' Études thématiques de Gal 1:16," RB 64 (1957) 335–362.

53. Grammatically the verb δικαιόω in the Pauline letters always (27 times) appears either in the passive (13 times) or middle (7 times) or in the active with "God" as the explicit and only subject (7 times; e.g., Rom 4:5: it is God "who justifies the godless").

justification or the living space of the justified). So our text makes this justification in Christ proclaimed by God (cf. Rom 8:33: θεὸς ὁ δικαιῶν, "God who justifies") an object that is sought.

We must point out that grammatically ζητέω, "seek," followed by an infinitive is practically equivalent to an auxiliary verb ("want to") and that normally, as in our case, the subject of the infinitive is the same as that of the governing verb[54] (see also Gal 1:10). The action described, therefore, is completed in the subject of the action. In effect, the verb here is equivalent to "strive to, do all one can to . . .": specifically in order to be truly the object of divine justification. The immediate context indicates two things in which this personal effort consists.

a) In v. 16a ("*knowing* that one is not justified by works of the Law . . . we have believed in Christ Jesus") the participle εἰδότες, "knowing," discreetly alludes to a labor of reflection or meditation on the Christ-event compared with certain Old Testament passages (as witnessed by Rom 3–4 and 9–11; see also Gal 3:1-14), whence springs the awareness that a quest of one's "own righteousness" is misguided and impossible (Rom 10:3).[55]

b) In the second place, v. 18 ("If I rebuild what I have torn down, I reveal myself as a transgressor") refers to the not implausible risk (the text, after all, follows the account of the confrontation between Paul and Peter at Antioch: vv. 11-14) of restoring in practice regard for the discredited principle of the Law as way of salvation. It is precisely on this concrete level that the strenuous "quest" must be pursued to maintain intact the "scandal of the cross" (5:11; cf. 2:21: "I therefore do not nullify God's grace, for if righteousness is through the Law, Christ died for nothing") so as not to "fall from grace" (5:4). The context, then, directs the quest not so much toward acquiring righteousness as toward maintaining it.[56]

III. Seeking after having found

Philo's principle that "No longer to seek belongs to the one who has faith" (*Div. rer. her.* 101; see above) is only partially applicable to Paul.

54. Blass-Debrunner 392:1a.
55. This very passage, Rom 10:3 (ἀγνοοῦντες γὰρ τὴν τοῦ θεοῦ δικαιοσύνην καὶ τὴν ἰδίαν ζητοῦντες στῆσαι, "not knowing God's righteousness but seeking to set up their own . . .") can be understood as an antithetic parallel to our Gal 2:16-17 (εἰδότες ὅτι οὐ δικαιοῦται ἄνθρωπος ἐξ ἔργων νόμου . . . ζητοῦντες δικαιωθῆναι ἐν Χριστῷ, "knowing that one is not justified by works of the Law . . . we seek to be justified in Christ"): note the contrasts of "not knowing/ knowing," "one's own [righteousness]/in Christ," and the use of participial constructions and of ζητέω, "seek," with the infinitive.
56. H. Schlier is basically right: "the ζητεῖν δικαιωθῆναι [seeking to be justified] does not differ materially from πιστεύειν [believing] (Seiffert)" (*Der Brief an die Galater*, in the note on v. 17); only we should clarify that "believing" here is seen in its more properly existential aspect.

This is true as far as it concerns the natural quest of God, which is rendered superfluous, or at least quite limited by God's intervention in Christ (see I.1-2 above). But the principle does not fit insofar as for Saint Paul faith entails its own specific type of quest, which already appears in Gal 2:17 but is developed especially in other texts and in other significant expressions. Thus a certain characteristic dynamism intrinsic to faith itself imposes itself; this is not just something of an intellectual character, *fides quaerens intellectum*, Anselm's "faith seeking understanding," but is configured on a specifically mysterious and existential level as *fides quaerens Deum*, "faith seeking God."[57] This faith through the movements of the Spirit of baptism comes to characterize the normal life of the Christian in this world (Col 3:1 and all the other vocabulary of "seeking/attraction"), directing it constantly and with an implied liturgical nuance πρὸς τὸν θεόν, "toward God."

1) *The sense of 1 Cor 2:10:*
   "For the Spirit searches everything, even the depths of God"
   (τὸ γὰρ πνεῦμα πάντα ἐραυνᾷ καὶ τὰ βάθη τοῦ θεοῦ).

The text enters the framework of our theme both because of the precise Hellenistic verb ἐραυνάω (classical ἐρευνάω), which is typical of the vocabulary of quest, and because of the object identified here. In itself the verb means "track, ransack, explore, dig up, search, examine, investigate" and is used in the Greek world in a religious and philosophical sense.[58] Meanwhile the expression τὰ βάθη τοῦ θεοῦ, "the depths of God" (= v. 11: τὰ τοῦ θεοῦ, "the things of God") can be equivalent simply to God's self (thus H. Conzelmann) or more specifically to the unsearchable eschatological deliberations of God (thus U. Wilckens, p. 83; cf. also Rom 11:33), and is attested in Judeo-apocalyptic sources (1 Henoch 63:2; 1QS 11:19; 4 Esdr 4:21; 10:35, 38; *Syr. Bar.* 14:8-9; 54:12-13).[59] The most original thing

57. In other New Testament authors, especially in the Fourth Gospel, this idea is already expressed in the simple formula πιστεύειν εἰς [θεόν], "to believe in [God]," but this is missing from Paul and is only rarely used with a Christological reference (Gal 2:16; Phil 1:29). Here there is found only once the expression πίστις πρὸς τὸν θεόν, "faith toward God" (1 Thess 1:8), which is, however, less "dynamic" than the other.

58. See G. Delling, art. ἐρευνάω, TDNT 2:655–657. The texts of Pindar are useful (frag. 61, where the verb takes as object the θεῶν βουλεύματα, "plans of the gods") and of Sophocles (frag. 80: "Do not investigate everything; it is good for many things to remain hidden," μὴ παντ' ἐρεύνα πολλὰ καὶ λαθεῖν καλόν); Philo Alex., in particular, uses it often in the sense of "Know yourself" (see *Migr. Abr.* 138; *Agr.* 72; *Somn* I:54) or taking the object "the reason for being of every creature" (*Deus imm.* 167).

59. The Gnostic use of the expression is secondary, at least in terms of attestation; it is found in the mouth of the Naasenes, "who called themselves Gnostics, since they say that they alone know the depths" (thus Hippolytus, *Ref.* V:6:4, beginning of third century).

in Paul's text is the subject of the action, the "Spirit," πνεῦμα, for elsewhere examples are not to be found of "seeking" as something done by the Spirit.

A first text that can illuminate Paul's statement, albeit only partially, comes from Philo: "*The mind, ὁ νοῦς* . . ., rising still higher, *searches out the divine and its nature, ἐρευνᾷ τὸ θεῖον καὶ τὴν τούτου φύσιν*, with unspeakable love of knowledge" (*Leg alleg*. III:84). Here, of course, the subject of "searches out" is the νοῦς, "mind," which is also present in the Pauline passage (v. 16: ἡμεῖς δὲ νοῦν Χριστοῦ ἔχομεν, "But we have the mind of Christ"), where certain recent authors understand it as equivalent to the Spirit. However, we have elsewhere stated the impossibility of such an equation.[60] For Philo, then, unlike Paul, the quest of the divine is an autonomous act belonging properly to human reason, even if we must note the "unspeakable passion," δι᾽ ἔρωτα ἄλεκτον (cf. the "strong passion," ἰσχυρὸς ἔρως, in Dio of Prusa, *Or*. 12:60). It is true that in another passage the Jewish philosopher states about Moses that "the prophet . . . prays to learn from God who God is in himself *(εὔχεται παρ᾽ αὐτοῦ μαθεῖν τοῦ θεοῦ, τίς ἐστιν ὁ θεός)*; indeed he did not hope to be able to know him from anyone else. . . . Even so, he could not search out anything of the essence of the Existent *(μηδὲν περὶ τῆς τοῦ ὄντος ἐρευνᾶν οὐσίας)*" (*Fug*. 164–165, with citation of Exod 33:23).

We note that the philosopher differs from the Apostle in at least three things: (a) the subject of the quest, which we have already mentioned (the intellect rather than the pneuma); (b) its object, granted that τὰ βάθη τοῦ θεοῦ, "the depths of God," has essentially the dynamic salvation-history significance of "intention, deliberation" (cf. the "mysterious wisdom of God" in v. 7 and the "mind of the Lord" in v. 16), or simply "gifts" (v. 12b), while we look in vain for properly philosophical terms φύσις and οὐσία, "nature" and "essence" (the latter term being totally absent from the correspondence). (c) The third difference is the total inability of the human person to search out the divine essence. For Philo, God is completely ἀκατάληπτος, "incomprehensible,"[61] which contrasts with the af-

---

60. See R. Penna, *Lo Spirito di Cristo; Cristologia e pneumatologia secondo una originale formulazione paolina* (Brescia, 1976) 276–277, note 8.

61. See especially *Deus imm*. 62; *Poster*. 15; *Det. pot*. 89; *Somn*. I:67. "That God is ἀκατάληπτος [incomprehensible] is a verity repeated by Philo to satiety. It is discussed whether he was the first to propose this concept explicitly: see Wolfson, II, 110–126, favoring originality; and on the contrary, A. J. Festugière, *Révélation*, IV, p. 307, note. At any rate, if Philo did not invent it, he certainly made it current: we can truly say that he 'stabilized a vocabulary' that will be that of negative theology" (I. Feuer, *Quod deterius potiori insidiari soleat. Introduction, traduction et notes*, Les Oeuvres de Philon d'Alexandrie 5 [Paris, 1965] 76, n. 1). In any case, what we have is not agnosticism but simple apophatism, which always implies dynamic elan and adoration.

firmation of our Pauline text, already anticipated in vv. 9-10a ("what eye has not seen and ear has not heard, nor has it entered the human heart, what God has prepared for those who love him").[62] But in any case there is a certain correspondence: God does not come to be known by anyone but God himself (see above: *Fug.* 164), just as in Paul: "For the things of God no one can know but the Spirit of God" (1 Cor 2:11).

In this matter, the text closest to Paul's is found at Qumran in 1QH 12:11-13: "But I, who am wise, know you, my God, by virtue of the Spirit[12] you have put in me *(wa'anî maškîl y⁵da'tîkâ 'elî bāruâḥ 'ašèr nātatta bî)*, and I have attentively listened to your marvelous secret *(sôd)*. In virtue of your holy spirit *(b⁵rûaḥ qôd⁵sèkâ)* you have opened in me the consciousness of the mystery of your wisdom *(pātaḥtâ l⁵tôkî da'at b⁵raz śikl⁵kâ)*, the fountain of your power" (after the translation of L. Moraldi, vocalization of E. Lohse). This is the only documented passage in which, as in 1 Cor 2:10, a cognitive function exercised upon God himself is attributed to the Spirit.

But it is important to note that precisely on the basis of this Qumran parallel,[63] the Pauline text does not mean the Spirit abstractly or absolutely as personalized, so as to refer his action to an intratrinitarian relationship. Rather, it is important to note that the reference is to the *rûaḥ* "that you have placed in me" (1QH 12:12; cf. 12:13: "in me"; see also 1QH 13:19; 16:11; 17:17; Hymn frag. 3:14). This is further confirmed simply by the context of the Pauline passage, where we observe an interchangeability between the Pneuma and the Pneumatic. Verse 10b actually is echoed in v. 15a: "The Pneumatic (masc. sing.) judges all things," ὁ δὲ πνευματικὸς ἀνακρίνει τὰ πάντα.[64] This passing from neuter to masculine is especially anticipated in v. 12a: "we have received [ἐλάβομεν] not the spirit of the world but the spirit that is from God." Therefore, the spirit that searches the depths of God is the one that is present in the Christian on the basis of faith and baptism (actually it is to these two realities that the aorist

---

62. As for the original formulation of this unknown quotation (v. 9a: "as it is written"), it is probably a citation from memory fusing various biblical texts (see Isa 64:4; 52:15; 65:17; Jer 3:16; Sir 1:10), the result of which admirably fits the present context. See the commentaries; K. Berger, "Zur Diskussion über die Herkunft von 1 Kor II.9," NTS 24 (1978) 270–283 (= apocalyptic derivation).

63. We must not be deceived by the Qumran expression *rûaḥ qôd⁵sèkâ*. "It would seriously falsify the sense of this expression if it were translated 'the Holy Spirit,' introducing the Christian theology of the Trinity. In fact, at Qumran, as in the Old Testament, this indicates only the sanctifying influx of God, and is completely parallel to 'the spirit of tenderness' (16:9)" (J. Carmignac and P. Guilbert, *Les textes de Qumran traduits et annotés,* I [Paris, 1961] 155).

64. The verb ἀνακρίνω, "judge," can be considered synonymous with ἐραυνάω, since its significance is also "to investigate, examine" (even though normally in a judicial function). See F. Büchsel, art. ἀνακρίνω, TDNT 3:943–944.

ἐλάβομεν/ἐλάβετε refers when it is regularly used of the Spirit in Gal 3:2, 14; Rom 8:15; 2 Cor 11:4).[65]

There is, then, a typical Christian quest that characterizes the pistic condition of all baptized persons on the basis of their pneumatic endowment; this makes it possible for them to fit the ancient principle that any object is known only on the basis of a similarity of nature (v.11):[66] since the God of Christian faith is different from that perceptible by the human intellect [νοῦς] alone, the very Spirit of God allows to the human person an affinity between subject and object, renewing the capacity of the one adequately to the newness of the other. It is in this sense that the terminology πνευματικός/ψυχικός should be understood, whatever be its historical derivation.[67] The consciousness of the pneumatic person is no different from that faith (see 2:5) that actually makes one "perfect" (2:6); indeed, for Paul perfection is not only the goal but the *status* of every believer. The distinction between believers of superior or inferior standing derives from the fact that Paul's addressees do not really correspond to the *status* they have been given.[68]

We should also note the constant use of the first person plural in the whole of 1 Cor 2:6-16. This "suggests that the *locus operandi* of the Spirit is the fellowship of the Christian community. The examination which produces spiritual comprehension is not properly conducted by one person in isolation but in the common life of the church."[69] The repeated τὰ

65. The "Spirit [that] searches the depths of God" is parallel to "our Spirit" in Rom 8:16, which has not only an anthropological meaning but indicates essentially the "elevating" intervention of the specifically divine Pneuma; see R. Penna, *Lo Spirito di Cristo*, 216–219.

66. The principle that like is known only by like was already described by Democritus (see H. Diels, 68B, 164) and runs throughout all ancient literature up to the *Corpus Hermeticum* XI:20 (see H. Conzelmann, ad. loc.) On this type of pneumatic investigation through affinity and affection a beautiful text of Saint Bonaventure is interesting: "And therefore the Apostle says that this mystical wisdom is revealed through the Holy Spirit. If you want to know how this happens, ask grace not doctrine, desire not intellect, the groaning of prayer not the study of reading, the bridegroom not the teacher, God not man, darkness not brightness, not light but the fire that burns completely, and that through overwhelming unctions and burning affections transports [one] into God [in Deum transferentem]" (*Itinerarium mentis in Deum*, 7:4).

67. "For Paul the πνευματικος man is the one who walks according to the Spirit of God in the light of what he has received from God (v. 12; cf. Rom. 8) apart from any created potentiality in himself. . . . The 'psychic' man, for Paul, is one who has only natural possibilities apart from the eschatological gift of the Spirit, and cannot attain to 'the things of the Spirit of God" by virtue of anything within himself' " (B. A. Pearson, *The Pneumatikos-Psychikos Terminology in I Cor. A Study in the Theology of the Corinthian Opponents of Paul and Its Relation to Gnosticism* [Cambridge, 1973] 40–41); according to this author, Paul "has skillfully used the language of his opponents, and has turned it back against them by interpreting their language in an apocalyptic fashion" (41). See also M. Winter, *Pneumatiker und Psychiker in Korinth. Zum religionsgeschichtlichen Hintergrund von 1. Kor 2,6–3,4* (Marburg, 1975).

68. H. Conzelmann, *1 Corinthians*, Hermeneia (Philadelphia, 1975) 59.

69. W. F. Orr and J. A. Walther, *I Corinthians*, 166. This communitarian component is not diminished by the distinction between "pneumatic" and "psychic" persons. At any rate,

πάντα in vv. 10b, 15a discreetly suggests that there simply is no possibility of any limitation or censorship being imposed on the dynamism of exploring the abyss of God's depths (see 2 Cor 13:8), even though in the context these depths are all gathered together in the ἐσταυρωμένος, the Crucified One (1:23; 2:2; cf. 1:17, 18; 2:8). Such seeking is exercised with regard not to God's essence nor to the identity of Christ and his personal stature, but rather with regard to the specific wisdom of the Christian God, to the rich fruitfulness of his unexpected and inexhaustible plan of salvation, which of necessity includes the cross of Christ.[70] The participle συγκρίνοντες (v. 13), considering the sense proper to the verb ("unite, compound, compare, measure, evaluate, interpret"),[71] here indicates the method of seeking, which is done not with passive waiting for some improbable infused knowledge, but consists in the loving and attentive comparison of various elements, which all converge symphonically to manifest the true identity of God.

2) The meaning of Col 3:1: "seek the things on high"
(τὰ ἄνω ζητεῖτε)

Colossians 3:1 is the only passage in the Pauline correspondence where the specific verb ζητέω, "seek," assumes a positive meaning with evident reference to the post-baptismal condition. For it is inserted in a theological-literary contextual framework that uses many verbs in the past tense to describe the turning point that has taken place in the life of the recipients,[72]

---

this does not apply to the Church of Corinth, where all are still "psychic," if not "carnal," because of the internal divisions (see 1 Cor 3:1-3). Even so, the "we [pneumatics]" refers not so much to the elite circle of apostles or certain few Christians (actually 2:6-16 is surrounded and almost constricted by the singular "I": 2:1-5; 3:1-2), as it does to the Corinthian community as united to Paul and idealized, or better, considered in its real pneumatic potentiality (baptismal and pistic), the explicit development of which, however, is hindered by the division.

70. I think the splendid work of M. Pesce, Paolo e gli Arconti a Corinto. Storia della ricerca (1888-1975) ed esegesi di 1 Cor 2,6.8 (Brescia, 1977) 255 and 385, makes a somewhat too clear distinction between the figure of Christ and the "wisdom of God." We should remember that Christ is not outside the plan of God, which at least turns on an axis that is clearly soteriological (if not Christological), so that the "Crucified One" is fully an integral reality of the "depths of God" and not just the external agent who reveals them.

71. See F. Büchsel, art. συγκρίνω, TDNT 3:953-954 (the author attributes a masculine sense to the dative plural πνευματικοῖς, "for spiritual men"; others opt for the neuter).

72. Such a transformation is repeatedly stated in the letter with different verbs and expressions: ἐρρύσατο/μετέστησεν, "rescued, transferred" (1:13); ἀποκατήλλαξεν, "reconciled" (1:22); τῇ πίστει τεθεμελιωμένοι, "founded in faith" (1:23); Χριστὸς ἐν ὑμῖν, "Christ in you" (1:27); συμβιβασθέντες ἐν ἀγάπῃ, "knit together in love" (2:2); περιετμήθητε, "were circumcised" (2:11); συνταφέντες, συνηγέρθητε, "buried together, raised together with him" (2:12); συνεζωοποίησεν, "brought you back to life" (2:13); ἐξαλείψας, "canceled" (2:14); ἀπεκδυσάμενοι, "disarmed" (2:15); ἀπεθάνετε, "you died" (2:20); περιπατήσατε, "you walked" (3:7); ἀπεκδυσάμενοι/ἐνδυσάμενοι, "stripped"/"clothed" (3:9, 10).

while the many present tenses (indicative, subjunctive, imperative, participial) describe the new character acquired and call for its manifestation in daily life. The imperative here in v. 1 is placed right between two aorist indicatives, συνηγέρθητε, "have risen" (v. 1a), and ἀπεθάνετε, "you died" (v. 3), which show its precise semantic framework; that is, they define the viewpoint, showing that for the Christian it is not a question of an absolute quest that starts with zero and tends toward something completely new to discover. On the contrary, the Christian quest is already based on the event and the experience of a qualitative leap or discontinuity brought about by God.

The generic neuter plural τὰ ἄνω, "the things above," is specified by the following adverbial phrase of place: "where Christ is seated at the right hand of God." This fragmentary confession of Christological faith, which alludes to the frequently cited Ps 110:1, here has a secondary sense dependent on its use in this context, emphasizing specifically the divine sphere into which not only Christ has entered, but radically so has every Christian (see 2:12, 20!)[73] This means that τὰ ἄνω on the one hand does not have a Platonic-Aristotelian impersonal value in the philosophical sense of "transcendence," since it is defined by Christ, but on the other hand it does not have simply a "Christological" sense but is more precisely *theo*-logical, since the "on high" in Jewish tradition is the seat of God (see Gen 11:15; Exod 24:9-10; Ezek 1:26; Dan 7:13; 1 Henoch 17:2; 71:1; Qoh 5:1; Jub 2:2, 11, 30; Matt 6:9).

But there is a thematic relationship between the indicative and the imperative; indeed the ζητεῖτε, "seek," of Col 3:1 presupposes and joins itself to the affirmation that "our citizenship is [already] in the heavens" (Phil 3:20): "But if you have died with Christ to the elements of the world, why do you submit, as if you still lived in the world, to rules like 'do not handle, do not taste, do not touch'?" (Col 2:20-21). We thus understand that while the "Colossian philosophy" was Empedoclean, Platonic, and Neo-Pythagorean in character,[74] and so favored ascesis as a means of access to the higher world, for the author of Colossians the Christian must not undertake any flight from the world. The quest of the "the things above" has not a local significance,[75] nor does it entail a rupture or abstention from bonds to the cosmic realities (in this sense precepts are hence-

---

73. Against E. Lohse, *Colossians and Philemon*, Hermeneia, trans. W. R. Poehlmann and R. J. Karris (Philadelphia, 1971) 133; better, see E. Schweizer, *The Letter to the Colossians* (Minneapolis, 1982) 172–174.

74. See the excursus by E. Schweizer, *Kolosser*, 103–104 ("Die kolossische Philosophie").

75. Contrast, for instance, with Philo of Alexandria: "The soul of one who loves God *is hurled up from the earth toward heaven* (ἀπὸ γῆς ἄνω πρὸς οὐρανὸν πηδᾷ), takes wings and flies through the clouds" (*Spec. leg* I 207).

forth nailed to the cross of Christ: 2:14). It is just that the world is no longer norm, goal, or meaning of the Christian's existence.[76]

The parallel τὰ ἄνω φρονεῖτε in 3:2 implicitly becomes an invitation henceforth to place the quest on the level of the value judgment, of "faith in God's power" (2:12: διὰ τῆς πίστεως τῆς ἐνεργείας τοῦ θεοῦ), which gives assurance that henceforth "our life is hidden with Christ in God" (3:3).[77] The object of the quest, then, can be recognized in this ἐν τῷ θεῷ, i.e., "in God" in whom we live and move and have our being: but not in the naturalistic sense of Acts 17:27, but in the more specifically Christian meaning whereby the God of the cross and of baptism becomes the new environment for the life of the believer. In this perspective a detailed ethic (see 3:5-4:1) becomes possible and even necessary for the baptized, not as a means of salvation but as its lived manifestation. Thus it will be simply an expression of a seeking of God, not to lift one up self-sufficiently above the natural human experiences, but immersing oneself deeply in God's ἐνέργεια, "working within," making room for these experiences (according to 3:5-4:1) in the specific events of individual, familial, and social life.

3) *The remaining Pauline vocabulary of religious attraction and quest*

Here we give simply the list of verbs, and other expressions or procedures whereby the Pauline correspondence richly describes the dynamic attraction of the Christian toward God, even though the object of the quest is never specifically called God.[78] The abundance of the material indicates well enough the many facets of Christian relationships to God.

ἐπεκτείνομαι = "strain after" (Phil 3:13), takes as object "the things that are ahead" (τοῖς ἔμπροσθεν);

διώκω = "pursue, strive" (Phil 3:12, 14; 1 Tim 6:11; 2 Tim 2:22), takes as object τὸ βραβεῖον, "prize" (Phil 3:12-14), τῆς ἄνω κλήσεως, "of the upward call" (Phil 3:14), or δικαιοσύνη "righteousness" (1 Tim 6:11; 2 Tim 2:22) and εὐσέβειαν, "reverence" (1 Tim 6:11);

καταντάω = "arrive at" (Phil 3:11), which has the "resurrection of the dead" as object; this fits into our theme in that "knowledge of God"

---

76. See E. Schweizer, *Kolosser,* 166 and 172.

77. To some extent the τὰ ἄνω, "things above," of Col 3:1, 3 coincides with the expression of Ephesians, ἐν τοῖς ἐπουρανίοις, "in the heavenly [places]" (at least of Eph 1:3; 2:6), understanding τόποις, "places," metaphorically. Where the spiritual blessing of God is at work, there the Christian finds a heaven, even in the "worldly" context of life.

78. We omit the etymological derivatives in σεβ- ("reverence . . ."), which in the letters are late and have no significant religious import. But for the concept of "fear of God" (φόβος, φοβέομαι) see C. Romaniuk, *Il timore di Dio nella teologia di san Paolo* (Brescia, 1967).

actually entails its dynamic aspect in God's intervention to raise the dead (see 1 Cor 15:34!; Rom 4:17);

τρέχω = "run": in Rom 9:16 it is intransitive, while in 1 Cor 9:24, 26 it has as object "to take the prize" *(λαμβάνειν/καταλαμβάνειν τὸ βραβεῖον);*

καταλαμβάνω = "seize, grasp": in Rom 9:30; 1 Cor 9:24; Phil 3:12-13 it occurs in a context of dynamism and describes an act that follows upon quest or attraction (cf. also Eph 3:18);

ἐπιλαμβάνομαι = "take hold of," with "eternal, true life" as object (1 Tim 6:12, 19);

"become *imitators of God,* μιμηταὶ τοῦ θεοῦ" (Eph 5:1; cf. Plato, *Phaedrus* 252–253);[79]

εὐχαριστέω = "to thank" (and also the noun "thanksgiving"); see the introductory thanksgivings;[80]

εὔχομαι = "pray" (2 Cor 13:7); the prefixed verb προσεύχομαι never takes an object, but "God" is always understood (see, e.g., Rom 8:26; 1 Thess 5:17).

δουλεύειν = "serve" (1 Thess 1:9; Titus 1:1; see Gal 4:8-9);

ἀγαπάω = "love" God (Rom 8:28; 1 Cor 2:9; 8:3);[81]

ἐπικαλέω = "call upon" (Rom 10:12-14; 2 Cor 1:23);

ἐξομολογέω = "confess, acknowledge, praise" (Rom 14:11; 15:9);

δοξάζω = "glorify" (Rom 15:6, 9; 1 Cor 6:20; 2 Cor 9:13; Gal 1:24); we should add the expressions "to God's glory" (1 Cor 10:31), "to him the glory" (Gal 1:5);

προσκυνέω = "adore" (1 Cor 14:25);

ἐπαινέω = "praise" (Rom 15:11); note also the expression "to the praise of God" (Phil 1:11; Eph 1:6, 12, 14);

ᾄδω = "sing" (Col 3:16; Eph 5:19);

τὰ γόνατα κάμπτω, "bend the knees" (Phil 2:10; Eph 3:14; cf. Rom 14:11);

Sometimes γινώσκω, "know," and its derivatives have God himself as object (note the texts already examined above: Rom 1:21; 1 Cor 1:21; 2:10-11; Gal 4:9; see also Rom 11:33; 2 Cor 10:5; Rom 1:32; Col 1:6; Rom 1:28; Eph 1:17; Col 1:10; 2:2);[82]

---

79. On the theme of ὁμοίωσις or "assimilation" to God, see P. Rossano, "L'ideale dell'assimilazione a Dio nello Stoicismo e nel Nuovo Testamento," in the collection *Scrinium Theologicum. Contributi di scienze religiose,* II (Alba, 1954) 7-71.

80. See M. Del Verme, *Le formule di ringraziamento postprotocollari nell'epistolario paolino* (Rome, 1971).

81. These few texts should be kept in mind to correct the aim of the theses of A. Nygren, *Agape and Eros. A Study of the Christian Idea of Love* (London-New York, 1953).

82. On this issue see R. Bultmann, art. γινώσκω, TDNT 1:689-719; J. Dupont, *Gnosis. La connaissance religieuse dans les épîtres de S. Paul* (Louvain-Paris, 1949). For Paul, however, the utter reversal of the direction of the act of knowing is something more specific: also impor-

To all these verbs we must add the various examples of prayer actually being done by Paul, as for instance the doxologies (Rom 11:33-36; 16:25-27; Eph 3:20-21), the grateful blessing (2 Cor 1:3ff.; Eph 1:3-14) and the many thanksgivings with God as object.[83]

4) *The Orientation of Christian Life* πρὸς τὸν θεόν

It is useful to examine Paul's use of the preposition πρός, "to, toward" with the accusative, used to describe interpersonal relations. Apart from the very frequent use with personal pronouns alluding to humans ("you [sing. and pl.], me"), thirteen cases should be noted in which God is the object (nine times θεός, "God"; twice κύριος, "Lord"; twice πατήρ, "Father").

> *The situation.* In five passages (the largest number) the formula occurs with explicit and direct reference to prayer: Rom 10:1; 15:30; 2 Cor 13:7; Eph 3:14 (πατήρ, "Father"); Phil 4:6.
> Twice the formula is present in a context dealing with the salvific value of the death of Christ on the cross, in that this opens up access to God: Rom 5:1; Eph 2:18 (πατήρ, "Father").
> Two more times it describes the act and content of conversion (with the vivid verb ἐπιστρέφω): 1 Thess 1:9; 2 Cor 3:16 (κύριος).[84]
> Two more texts refer to the apostolic ministry: Rom 15:17 to the Apostle's boast, and 2 Cor 3:4 to his confidence.
> Once the formula is used to describe the strength of a personal adherence to faith: 1 Thess 1:8 (πρὸς τὸν θεόν, "in God"); to this we should add another text in which, atypically, the object is not God but "the Lord Jesus": Phlm 5 (πρὸς τὸν κύριον Ἰησοῦν).
> Finally, once it refers to the appearance before the Kyrios after death: 2 Cor 5:8.

In the light of all this, it seems we can draw the following conclusions. First of all, we should observe that the use of the preposition πρός expresses not just a general dynamism of the Christian "toward God" but

---

tant is "being known by God" (Gal 4:9; cf. K. Barth, *cogitor ergo sum*, "I am thought, therefore I am").

83. On prayer in Saint Paul in general, see G. P. Wiles, *Paul's Intercessory Prayers: The Significance of the Intercessory Passages in the Letters of St. Paul* (Cambridge, 1974); C. Marcheselli-Casale, *La preghiera in S. Paolo* (Naples, 1975).

84. On the first of these two texts, see T. Holtz, " 'Euer Glaube an Gott.' Zu Form und Inhalt von 1 Thess. 1,9f," in the collection *Die Kirche des Anfangs. Für Heinz Schürmann* (Freiburg-Basel-Vienna, 1978) 459–488: the text has been compared to *Jos. As.* 54:10 (Batiffol). On the second, see R. Penna, *Lo Spirito di Cristo*, 193–194.

access and appearance face to face *before* God.[85] Perhaps it is just for this semantic nuance, which maintains the distinction in the relationships, that Paul much more often uses the formula πρὸς τὸν θεόν, "to/toward God," than that studied above, εἰς αὐτόν, "unto him," which, let us not forget, is probably of Hellenistic-Stoic (pantheistic) origin. The formula πρὸς τὸν θεόν is of clearly biblical derivation; it is extremely common in the Greek of the LXX, especially in Exodus (see 2:23; 8:29, 30; 19:8, 21, 23, 24; 24:2; 32:30) and in Psalms (18:6; 30:8; 43:4; 57:2). In the same sense we should compare the equivalent πρὸς τὸν κύριον, "to/toward the Lord" (see Exod 8:8, 12, 28; 9:28, 29, 33; Ps 3:4; 5:3; 30:2, 8; 69:13; 88:9, 13). But the most important thing to note in these Old Testament passages is that this formula normally occurs in contexts simply of prayer (e.g., Ps 18:6 LXX: "In anguish I cried *to my God*") or more specifically cultic (e.g., Exod 24:2 LXX: "Moses shall advance alone *toward the Lord God*").

This means that even in Saint Paul the formula has a liturgical connotation that serves to identify the Christian (or apostolic) life as taking place in the solemn presence of God.[86] This is confirmed by the use of προσαγωγή ("approach" or "bring near"), which appears only a few times in Paul (and nowhere else in the New Testament), but always along with the formula "to God" *(πρὸς τὸν θεόν):* Rom 5:2; Eph 2:18; 3:12. In profane Greek as well as that of the Bible, the noun, and even more so the verb προσάγω (since the noun is unknown in the LXX), is a normal part of sacrificial language (offering a victim or various gifts). To this there is added secondarily juridical language (in the LXX) and ceremonial court language (in Greek literature).[87] In every case this vocabulary carries the idea of "be presented, approach, appear before," either as a cultic offering or to attain legal justice or as one admitted in audience. The first use is surely the most prominent, not only for the reasons already indicated but also and even more because of Paul's use of "worship," λατρεύω (Rom 1:9; Phil 3:3; 2 Tim 1:3) and λατρεία (Rom 12:1), which expresses a service of religious character. Thus Christian life appears as worship rendered to God and exercised through the stuff of common human and ecclesial existence,

---

85. Let us note the difference from εἰς, "into, to, in": while εἰς indicates movement that "is continued right on into the object," which thus constitutes the "end" of the movement, πρός rather expresses a movement that "breaks off at the border of the object sought (see B. Reicke, art. πρός, TDNT 6:720–725, 721).

86. This sense is suggested by the various Pauline texts that use adverbial prepositions like ἐνώπιον, κατενώπιον, κατέναντι, "in the presence of," that take the genitive θεοῦ/κυρίου, "of God/the Lord" (see Rom 14:22; 2 Cor 2:17; 7:12; Gal 1:20; Eph 1:4).

87. For the documentation, see K. L. Schmidt, art. προσάγω-προσαγωγή, TDNT 6:131–134. See also the Paulinizing text of 1 Pet 3:18 ("to bring you near to God").

involving one's own corporal existence (Rom 12:1), i.e., with one's whole self in the normal context of world and community.[88]

The last thing to demonstrate is that in the use of all this vocabulary *(πρὸς τὸν θεόν, προσαγωγή, [κατ]ενώπιον, λατρεύω)* the constantly recurring object is precisely "God," *θεός*, and not "Jesus Christ":[89] it is to *God* that one approaches, and before God that in the last analysis the Christian life unrolls. Christ's role is that of mediator[90] and "presenter" (see the Paulinizing 1 Pet 3:18), since the Christian truly does not so much "approach" or "present oneself" to God, but *"is* presented" or *"is granted* access" to God. In any case, the ultimate term of the tendency remains without question "God." And so Saint Paul's Christian is not a Christ-worshiper; the truth rather is that it is "God whom I worship in my spirit, announcing the gospel of his Son" (Rom 1:9).

Conclusion

Against the background of a world which, in the reflection of the learned as well as in the common practice of religion, is markedly inclined toward the quest for and union with God, Saint Paul sets the theme of "seeking God" in a new perspective, one that is irreducible to the Greco-Roman and Jewish cultural and religious worlds alike. While he does acknowledge the possibility of a rational access to the Deity (see Rom 1:19-21a) and does describe the Jewish life of the Law as "holy" (Rom 7:12), he reveals an essentially negative judgment on both fronts of the human attempt to approach God. When all is said and done, the former arrives at a paltry theological achievement, characterized by idolatry of the cosmic realities (traditional and popular religion) or by an aristocratic exaltation of wisdom (Stoicism) or agnosticism (Epicureanism) or an esotericism given to zealotry and naive mythology (mystery cults), and ultimately leads people astray from their vocation to individual and interpersonal dignity (see Rom 1:18-32). The latter, even while preserving an altogether noble and original theological worldview, emphasizes a vision of the human per-

88. See H. Schlier, *Der Römerbrief,* 355–358. Paul's positive evaluation of the "body" in one's relations with God stands out all the more by comparison with the negative judgment of Philo of Alexandria: "For it is impossible while dwelling in the body in the midst of mortals *(οὐ γὰρ ἔστι κατοικοῦντον ἐν σώματι καὶ τῷ θνητῷ γένει δυνατόν)* to find union with God *(θεῷ συγγενέσθαι),* but one can do so only if liberated by God from one's prison" (*Leg. alleg.* III:41).

89. The only exception for the formula *πρὸς τὸν . . .,* "for," is Phlm 5 *(κύριον Ἰησοῦν);* but we should remember that here it is a reference to "faith," and that it is in any case counterbalanced by the corrective of 1 Thess 1:8 *(πίστις πρὸς τὸν θεόν,* "faith in God"). As for the adverb *ἐνώπιον* ("in the presence of)," *Χριστοῦ* ("Christ") is only *associated* with *θεοῦ* ("God)," and in the late texts of 1 Tim 5:2 and 2 Tim 4:1 at that.

90. See W. Thüsing, *Per Christum in Deum. Studien zum Verhältnis von Christozentrik und Theozentrik in den paulinischen Hauptbriefen* (Münster, 1969²).

son that in practice risks basing the possibility of approaching and pleasing God on an inflated conception of one's own moral achievements (see Rom 9:11; 1QS 1:1ff.).

The quest of the Jew and the Greek alike undergoes a radical transformation as a result of encountering the unexpected εὐδοκία of God, who in Christ and in his cross and resurrection on his own initiative proposes a startling new way of conceiving God and of relating to him (see 1 Cor 1:18-25)—not that there is a pessimistic condemnation under every aspect of whatever rational or ethical elements exist in the human attraction, but the Christian God takes it up and places it where it can be seen from a completely different direction. This produces a completely different situation in the relationship between the human person and God; however, this is not a resigned quietism but a renewed dynamism, which is offered only a new end, the God of faith. As a result, we recognize the existence of a new dialectic of search and discovery in the thought of the Apostle, which looks something like this:

The first stage is the apparently autonomous human effort to undertake the quest of God, of God's nature or God's will. But this movement unfolds in a manner completely inadequate to the "mysterious hidden wisdom of God, which God decreed before the ages" (1 Cor 2:7), and so even what is discovered turns out to be inadequate to God's plans and to true human liberation as well.

The second stage (logical but also chronological) consists in an autonomous revelation of self by God, who by an unexpected disclosure not only of self but also of his own plan of salvation (centered on the justification of the ungodly through faith in the fecundity of Christ's blood) overcomes, indeed uproots the presuppositions, the *a priori* of the human quest, showing himself to be far more vast than had been presupposed, with far greater intellectual and ascetical potential. God thus becomes unexpectedly the object of a freely granted discovery (see Rom 10:20).

But there follows upon such a gift, as a third stage, not a satisfied stasis where one can indulge oneself tranquilly in the passive contemplation of a possession henceforth under complete control. For the quest is not interrupted but simply continues in new terms, for the Christian is always faced with the "deep things of God," which the baptismal Pneuma helps to investigate (1 Cor 2:9-10), with the aspiration, not to flee, but to immerse oneself in the "things of below," in the common framework of daily life (Col 3:1 and context).[91] Thus, every stage of Christian existence can represent a possibility of access to the God who through Christ and in the

---

91. We must always emphasize that the Christian (Pauline) quest of God is never a flight from the world. Whereas this idea runs through the whole of extrabiblical ancient literature:

Spirit has turned our natural modes of tending toward him upside down, only by coming to us in his true identity as Savior in history and gratis, something we could never know on our own. We could say that in a certain sense the natural εἰς αὐτόν, "unto him," has simply been transformed into the more exact and biblical πρὸς τὸν θεόν, "to/toward God."

But there is always something new to discover, since God (not only the natural God but even more the Christian God) is "unsearchable" and "inscrutable" (Rom 11:33). Every journey of faith, even every groping of one's way is justified, for faith, far from arrogantly disposing of God, means simply placing oneself humbly in the ocean of his mystery. It is not without reason that the Pauline author of Ephesians prays "that the God of our Lord Jesus Christ, the father of glory, may give you the spirit of wisdom and revelation to understand . . . what is the overwhelming greatness of his power toward us believers" (Eph 1:17, 19; cf. 3:18).

---

from Plato (*Theaet.* 176a: "We ought to try to escape from the earth to the dwelling of the gods as quickly as we can; and to escape is to become like God, so far as this is possible": trans. H. N. Fowler [Cambridge, Mass., 1967 = 1921]) to Plotinus (note the conclusion to the *Ennead* VI:9:11: "This is the life of the gods and of divine and blessed human beings: separation from the remaining things here below, life that no longer takes pleasure in earthly things, flight of the person alone to the Alone"), and continuing especially through Gnosticism with its well-known devaluation of the world. But this can be claimed extraneous to the New Testament, and to Paul in particular, where the kerygmatic *a priori* is not the attraction of the person outside of self to the divine, but the loving quest undertaken by God himself with regard to human beings, who are seen and are left in their "worldly" reality, only purified of sin (see Rom 5:8-9; 1 Cor 7:20-24; Col 2:20-22) and exposed to the eschatological reversal (see Rom 8:19-25; 1 Cor 7:29-31).

Chapter 29

Problems and Nature of Pauline Mysticism

The Apostle Paul is, of course, the very first extant Christian writer, and in him we immediately perceive the originality of a message that is partly new in relation to both Judaism and Hellenism, a message that in part repeats previous tradition and in part is enriched by contributions of his own thought that are by no means marginal.

We ask, Does the Christian tradition as presented by the Pauline mediation include mystical components? We could answer immediately, at the cost of appearing hasty, that there are indeed such components, but that they reflect the personal theology of Paul more than the patrimony of pre-Pauline preaching. For before him there is no mystical tradition properly speaking, neither in the group of the Twelve nor in Stephen's circle and its possible derivatives (perhaps at Antioch?). But to what extent can Paul be described as a mystic? And what is mysticism? There is a problem in speaking of mysticism in Saint Paul. (I) So we will begin with this, by clearing the conceptual field and attempting some methodological reflections; (II) then we will go on to examine the foundations of Pauline mysticism and (III) its dimensions.

I. Preliminaries

1) *History of the problem*

The idea of mysticism in Paul was first discussed in the nineteenth century. The decisive stimulus came from the famous study of Adolf Deissmann on the formula "in Christ," which he understood as referring to "finding oneself in the pneumatic Christ in a *local* sense."[1] But it was

---

1. A. Deissmann, *Die neutestamentliche Formel "in Christo Jesu"* (Marburg, 1892) 97.

especially R. Reitzenstein, with his volume on the Hellenistic mystery religions,[2] who first inserted the Apostle into the great current of Hellenistic-Oriental mysticism, as this is expressed in the mystery cults and in the gnosis of the Hermetic literature, especially the *Poimandres*. Paul would actually have undergone these influences before his conversion, and his mysticism would then have merged into his Christian theology. It is to Hellenism, then, that he would have been indebted for all that is best in his letters, not only individual expressions and images but even the fundamental conceptions.[3] As we see, the problem arises with the attribution to Paul of a concept of mysticism derived from the pagan environment, where this was in fact quite identifiable, and so of paradigmatic value.

Certain other scholars have reacted quite strongly, either completely denying the existence of a mysticism in Paul,[4] or else reducing it to the pure mysticism of faith, i.e., to a mere subjective relationship with Christ and with God on the level of awareness.[5] If the obvious response to the former is that some correspondences of Paul with the Hellenistic environ-

2. *Hellenistic Mystery-Religions: Their Basic Ideas and Significance* (Pittsburgh, 1978 [Leipzig, (1910) 1927³]) 533–543 (and 426–500); see also idem, *Poimandres. Studien zur griechischägyptischen und frühchristlichen Literatur* (Leipzig, 1904); *Das iranische Erlösungsmysterium* (Bonn, 1921); R. Reitzenstein and H. H. Schaeder, *Studien zum antiken Synkretismus* (Leipzig, 1926); W. Bousset, *Christos Kyrios.* (Nashville, 1970 [Göttingen, (1913) 1921²]) 164–172. For a somewhat excessive evaluation of the so-called mystical genitives in Saint Paul, see O. Schmitz, *Die Christusgemeinschaft des Paulus im Lichte seines Genitivsgebrauchs* (Gütersloh, 1924).

3. For documentation we here report on certain Hellenistic texts: in at least three magical papyri we find the formula "For you are I and I am you" (σύ γὰρ εἶ ἐγώ καὶ ἐγώ σύ: R. Reitzenstein, *Poimandres*, cit. 17, 20f., 21); in another we read, "We rejoice because even though we are in our bodies, you have divinized us with knowledge of yourself" (ἀπεθεώσας τῇ σεαυτοῦ γνώσει: K. Preisendanz, *Papyri Graecae Magicae. Die griechischen Zauberpapyri*, I [Leipzig–Berlin, 1928] 58). In the *Corpus Hermeticum* I:26, the assurance is given, "This is the blessed end for those who have knowledge: to be divinized [theôthênai]"; "The one who is born will be different, will be God's child, the all in the all, composed of all powers" (ibid. XIII:2). See also the rite of initiation of Lucius into the mysteries of Isis in Apuleius of Madaura, *Metamorphoses* XI.

On the basis of these and other texts, the following elements are generally considered characteristic of mysticism, whether Hellenistic or not: pantheism, divinization, accentuated consciousness, ecstasy, rebirth, anti-somatic attitudes, magic ritual, individualism. Some of these factors influence Pseudo-Denis the Areopagite, a disciple of the neoplatonic philosopher Proclus, who did mystical theology in a Christian environment; see especially his *De mystica theologia*.

4. See especially E. von Dobschütz, *Der Apostel Paulus I. Seine welt-geschichtliche Bedeutung* (Halle, 1926) 42: "Proper to mysticism is especially the tendency to become only one thing with the Deity, to become free of the 'I,' to become lost in the infinite. Mysticism is always only a religion of feeling, deliriousness in the love of God, a retreat of ethical and active aspects. And this simply cannot be said of Saint Paul." See also P. Feine, *Der Apostel Paulus. Das Ringen um das geschichtliche Verständnis des Paulus* (Gütersloh, 1927).

5. In this sense see especially K. Deissner, *Paulus und die Mystik seiner Zeit* (Leipzig, [1918] 1921²); H. E. Weber, "Die Formel 'in Christo' und die paulinische Christusmystik," *Neue Kirchliche Zeitschrift* 31 (1920) 213–260; "'Eschatologie' und 'Mystik' im Neuen Testament. Ein Versuch zum Verständnis des Glaubens* (Gütersloh, 1930).

ment are inevitable (see below), the latter had to be reminded that if the human spirit is not merely feeling but also substance, and if the supernatural activity of God stands on the level of reality, then reflection on mysticism must take account of this objectively.[6] Moreover, the reminder was voiced that there is not one single mysticism as such, κατ᾽ ἐξοχὴν, but that each religion historically develops its own, with its own particular characteristics.[7] Meanwhile, a distinction was proposed that has become widely accepted, between mystical and prophetic religions,[8] with the latter safeguarding the distance between God and humanity, or the element of hope, which directs the human person not only upward but especially forward.

It was against this background that Albert Schweitzer's book *Die Mystik des Apostels Paulus* appeared,[9] which succeeded in again raising the question in a new and comprehensive manner. First of all, he denies that Paul can be explained on the basis of Hellenism, since only Judaism, and particularly its eschatology, is the key to an adequate interpretation. But especially, Schweitzer decisively recalled attention to what is at the center of Paul's thought, namely, that the resurrection of Christ constitutes the irruption of the *eschaton* in history, so that the fundamental problem becomes the theological evaluation of the period between the resurrection of Jesus and his parousia. Now, "What is decisive for the character of the period . . . was not outward appearance but the nature of the powers which were at work in it. Through the Resurrection of Jesus it had become manifest that resurrection powers, that is to say, powers of the supernatural world, were already at work within the created world. Those who had insight, therefore, . . . conceived of the intervening time between His Resurrection and the beginning of the Messianic Kingdom as a time when the natural and supernatural world are intermingled. With the Resurrection of Jesus, the supernatural world had already begun, though it had not as yet become manifest" (pp. 98–99).[10]

6. These points were made by E. Peterson, "Zur Theorie der Mystik," *Zeitschrift für Systematische Theologie* 2 (1924) 146ff.

7. See L. Baeck, *Ursprung und Anfänge der jüdischen Mystik* (Giessen, 1927) 94: "We encounter not mysticism in general but the mysticism of Buddhism, Taoism, Neoplatonism, Judaism, Christianity, Islam."

8. See F. Heiler, *Die Bedeutung der Mystik für die Weltreligionen* (Munich, 1919), dependent on N. Söderblom.

9. (Tübingen, 1930 [= 1954]): English edition *The Mysticism of Paul the Apostle*, trans. W. Montgomery (New York, 1968 = ca. 1931); for a critical evaluation see M. Bouttier, " 'La Mystique de l'Apôtre Paul.' Rétrospective et prospective," RHPhR 56 (1976) 54–67; and especially E. Grässer, *Albert Schweitzer als Theologe*, Beiträge zur historischen Theologie 60 (Tübingen, 1979) 176–205.

10. Note the adverbs *"bereits . . . noch nicht"* ("already and not yet"), which became a stereotypical formula to describe the basic ambivalence of Christianity.

And so Schweitzer speaks of "eschatological mysticism," through which the Christian already today, in the temporality of the present, lives the eternity of the future, dying and rising with Christ. This mysticism is not only subjective, for it is doubly based in objective reality: in the death/resurrection of Jesus and in the sacrament of baptism. To be in Christ, then, means that "in Him I know myself as a being who is raised above this sensuous, sinful, and transient world and already belongs to the transcendent; in Him I am assured of resurrection, in Him I am a Child of God" (p. 3).[11] In all this we are dealing not with a God-mysticism, a *Gottesmystik*, but only a Christ-mysticism, a *Christusmystik*, which safeguards the real distance between the infinity of God and human finitude (see pp. 3 and 378).

After Schweitzer the discussion of the issue includes two interventions by Martin Dibelius,[12] who accepts his basic understanding of the placement of the Christian "between the times—*zwischen die Zeiten*" (p. 97);[13] however, he rejects the excessive distance Schweitzer places between Paul and Hellenism, and specifies that mysticism is only "*one* element" (p. 98, emphasis his) of Pauline spirituality, and that it is inserted in a prophetic framework. Consequently "the theme 'Paul and mysticism' within theology today finds a place for itself only with notable limitations" (p. 136).[14]

Among Catholics, apart from the good descriptive exposition of J. Huby,[15] the only notable study was and remains that of Alfred Wikenhauser, *Die Christusmystik des Apostels Paulus*, best known in its second edition.[16] The author is moved by two basic preoccupations: to demonstrate the objectivity of Pauline mysticism as not reducible only to the level

---

11. Below (II.2, n. 56 and its context) we shall touch on Schweitzer's hasty judgment concerning justification by faith as central to Pauline mysticism. The least enduring aspects of his work are the idea of an intermediate messianic reign and the resultant idea of a twofold resurrection (see *The Mysticism*, 90–98; E. Grässer, *Albert Schweitzer als Theologe*, 186–187).

12. In 1931, "Glaube und Mystik bei Paulus"; in 1941, "Paulus und die Mystik." Both are printed in *Botschaft und Geschichte*, Gesammelte Aufsätze, II (Tübingen, 1956) 94–116; 134–159.

13. "The decisive perception that being a Christian was not a judgment about *all that [was alles]* has taken place through Christ, but the experience *that all [dass alles]* has already taken place through him. . . . And so [in Paul] the early Christian tradition about the life and suffering of Jesus plays a relatively minor part" (p. 108); "The mystic's consciousness of having and seeing includes only half of this [Christian] existence; the other half consists in not having—and believing" (pp. 115–116).

14. "To be Christian means to live according to the final time *[endzeitlich]*, but not yet perfectly *[endvollendet]* so . . ., and thus being a Christian is not presented by Paul essentially as mystical" (pp. 104–105); the supposed "aristocratic character of all gnosis, of being closer to God than the others, is shattered in favor of the command to love these others. The egoism of the mystic must recede before the altruism of the gospel" (p. 153).

15. *Mystiques paulinienne et johannique* (Bruges–Paris, 1946 [Italian: 1950]) 11–141.

16. Freiburg i. Br., 1956² (first edition: Münster i. W., 1928). *Pauline Mysticism*, trans. J. Cunningham (New York, 1960 [Italian: 1958]).

of faith, and to distinguish it in its milieu from the parallel Hellenistic conceptions. He therefore goes so far as to define it, in scholastic terms, as "a physical-accidental union between Christ and his faithful" (p. 58); even though based on the same baptism that is equal for all Christians, we can identify as mystics only those persons who "conform this union on the level of being with the glorified Lord, based objectively on baptism, to a truly *actual* communion of life on the religious and ethical level, offering themselves with their whole soul to Christ and allowing the heavenly forces to act upon them and in them" (pp. 66–67). Actually, the posing of the question by Wikenhauser is too anthropological: he begins at once by treating the formula "in Christ," while the saving intervention of God is considered only in relation to baptism (pp. 70–86) and the call of Paul himself (86–97), and then in the final pages he sets up a comparison with Hellenistic mysticism.[17] But on the whole he does not give the death and resurrection of Christ their due prominence as Schweitzer[18] and Dibelius alike had done.

An original critical position is represented by Lucien Cerfaux, who treated the issue twice.[19] He rejects the expression "Christ-mysticism" (and "God-mysticism") and also the "ontological mysticism" of Wikenhauser. Determining that "Paul is fond of precise theological ideas and not a vague mysticism" (*Le chrétien*, 326) and that "the term 'mysticism' . . . is not suggested by Pauline vocabulary, and even partly contradicts it" (p. 328), he subjects even the very theological foundation of the theory of *Christus-mystik* to criticism (reducing various Pauline images such as "putting on Christ" to metaphor; reducing the significance of the preposition *en* and the many so-called mystical genitives; understanding metonymically various terms that express only being "Christians"; and giving even to the verb "live" in Gal 2:20 an unspecific and general meaning of a global experience of consciousness). But Cerfaux himself proposes to speak of *experiential mysticism—mystique expérimentale*, consisting simply in the fact that Paul has *lived* his theology in an intimacy with God, which he requires

17. According to Wikenhauser, the basic differences distinguishing Pauline mysticism from that of the Hellenistic Orient are essentially five (pp. 166–167, 199–208, 228ff.): Jewish monotheism; the eschatological orientation; the relationship to Christ as a historical person; its provisory character (but he exaggerates on p. 200 when he writes that eschatological union with Christ is *eine Ganz andere Art der Gemeinschaft,* "an utterly different kind of fellowship," from the present "being in Christ"); and its connection with ethic.

18. Also, inexplicably and I should also say inexcusably, Wikenhauser in the second edition of his study does not engage at all with Schweitzer, whom he cites only once (apart from the initial bibliography).

19. First in *Christ in the Theology of St. Paul,* trans. J. Webb and A. Walker (New York, 1959 [Italian: 1969]) 324–339, and especially in *Le chrétien dans la théologie paulinienne* (Paris, 1962 [Italian: 1969]) 353–371; English edition: *The Christian in the Theology of St. Paul* New York, 1959.

of all Christians; "Paul's interest is in the 'situation' of Christians and with the perceptual conclusions that derive from it: liberation from the old Law, replacement of the justice of the Law by an inner justice, the obligation for Christians to conform their conduct to the spiritual 'nature' of this life within them" (p. 364). Even if not everything is clear in Cerfaux's proposal, which even runs the risk of becoming a purely extrinsic or psychologizing relationship of the Christian with Christ,[20] still, his warning against a facile use of mystical vocabulary to explain Paul is well taken.

Apart from the re-edition of Wikenhauser's pre-war work, after the Second World War the *topos* "Paul and mysticism" has in fact faded away almost completely. An interesting study of Eduard Schweizer published in 1966 can be cited:[21] on the basis of the apocalyptic and eschatological value of the formula "with Christ," the author perceives the anticipation of future communion with Christ in the present life of the Christian, based on baptism, and in the last analysis on the saving intervention of God in the death and resurrection of Jesus. The question of which is more important in Paul, the mystic line of the new creation or the juridic line of forensic justification by faith, is resolved precisely by reference to "the absolute precedence of the action accomplished in the cross and resurrection of Christ" (202), which calls to faith and obedience, and through the Spirit places humanity under a new lordship. Of this reality Paul speaks in both juridic and mystical language, since both are found side by side (e.g., 2 Cor 5:14-17; 1 Thess 5:10). In any case we must exclude any merely anthropological solution to the question, whether by making it consist only in mere conversion/repentance or by limiting it to the new behavior of the convert.

Following Rudolph Bultmann, who does not recognize any individual mystical dimension to the formula "in Christ" but only an ecclesiological and eschatological import,[22] his disciples Günther Bornkamm and Hans Conzelmann deny any properly mystical dimension to Paul: "For an essential element in mysticism is the blurring of the boundary between God and man—the two become one. With Paul, however, the qualitative differences of both are preserved. Christ remains Lord . . . and the liberating union with Christ comes about in his service."[23]

---

20. Even so, on explaining the Pauline formula "body of Christ," Cerfaux speaks of "mystical identification with the body which belongs to Christ personally" and of "participation through some mystic identification with the life of the risen Christ" (*Christ*, 339; see *The Church in the Theology of Saint Paul* [New York, 1959] 270).

21. "Die 'Mystik' des Sterbens und Auferstehens mit Christus bei Paulus," *Evangelische Theologie* 26 (1966) 239ff. (= *Beiträge zur Theologie des Neuen Testaments* [Zurich, 1970] 183–203).

22. See *Theology of the New Testament*, trans. K. Grobel, 2 vols. (New York, 1951, 1955) 312, 327–328.

23. G. Bornkamm, *Paul*, trans. D. M. G. Stalker (London, 1975 [Italian: 1977]) (= *Paulus*, Stuttgart, 1969). See also H. Conzelmann, *Outline of the Theology of the New Testament* (New

A more recent and refreshing contribution, which has revitalized the discussion, has come in the large and stimulating (and sometimes provocative) study by E. P. Sanders, *Paul and Palestinian Judaism: A Comparison of Patterns of Religion*.[24] Though the greater part of the volume (31–428) describes and defines the "pattern" of Jewish religion,[25] the author is actually identifying what it is in comparison to "the heart of Paul's thought." In this regard he returns to A. Schweitzer, with whom—despite his criticism at points—he shares two basic complementary data: the secondary character of justification by faith (and hence of the juridical categories for describing the already effected salvation of the Christian), and correspondingly the primary nature of the realism of incorporation into Christ (and hence of participative or "participationist" categories). But the term "mysticism," Sanders maintains, "has generated so much misunderstanding . . . that perhaps it is better to drop it than to hedge it by repeated definitions."[26] He does not seem to want to propose a substitute term (he states that there is no category to express the real participation in Christ and the real possession of the Spirit that would mediate between the mere revised self-understanding of Bultmann and a naive magical conception: p. 522), and yet, he clearly prefers to speak of *transfer* of lordship, expressed by Paul in the concepts of participation in the death of Christ, freedom, transformation or new creation, reconciliation, and finally also justification and righteousness (see 463–472). "The heart of Paul's thought is not that one ratifies and agrees to a covenant offered by God, becoming a member of a group with a covenant relation with God and remaining in it on the condition of proper behavior, but that one dies with Christ, obtaining new life and the initial transformation which leads to the resurrection and ultimate transformation, that one is a member of the body of Christ and one Spirit with him, and that one remains so unless one breaks the participatory union by forming another."[27]

York, 1969) 208f. and 184. Also, but more moderately, M. Bouttier, *Christianity According to St Paul* (London, 1966) has considerably reshaped mystical language, preferring to speak of communion, relation, presence, condition of life (see 32ff.; the analogy of p. 41 is suggestive: "Life in Christ is out of our reach, beyond our experience. . . . It is like the gold bars that lie in the vaults of a bank and cover the value of the paper money that passes from hand to hand and deteriorates a little every time it is used. . . . What we can see of it is never the criterion; the only thing that counts is the promise. . . .").

24. Philadelphia–London, 1977; Italian edition 1986.

25. Which the author identifies as "covenantal nomism" (see 75, 236, 426–428).

26. 435–436, including n. 19.

27. P. 514. Cf. also 549: "The pattern of Paul's religious thought is this: God has sent Christ to be the savior of all . . .; one participates in salvation by becoming one person with Christ, dying with him to sin and sharing the promise of his resurrection; the transformation, however, will not be completed until the Lord returns; meanwhile, if one who is in Christ has been freed from the power of sin and the uncleanness of transgression, his behavior should be determined by his new situation; since Christ died to save all, all men must

It is only at the end of the book (549) that Sanders is able to name the *pattern* of Paulinism a "participationist eschatology." This is hardly the place for a complete critique of E. Sanders.[28] For us, it is enough to note that for the author, what separates Paulinism and so°defines it in relation to Judaism is precisely the "participationist" thematic of Paul (what others would have called "mystical").

2) *Methodological questions*

First of all we must observe that if we want to preserve the specific original sense of the words, we will have to avoid terms like "mysticism" and "mystical" simply because even the adjective μυστικός is never used by Paul.[29] Moreover, even the concept of the "mystical" in the strict sense, which implies an autonomous tendency independent of history toward the overcoming of self and of the abyss that separates the finite from the infinite, with a concomitant depersonalized submersion of self in the abyss of the divine,[30] does not apply to the Bible in general nor to Paul in particular.

Still, we are not without "points of contact."[31] But these should not be sought on the lexical level. Actually, the verb μυέομαι (to be initiated, i.e., consecrated, with esoteric awareness), which is found only once in

---

have been under the domination of sin, 'in the flesh' as opposed to being in the Spirit." This final clause is explained from the author's viewpoint, since according to him, in opposition to Bultmann, the point of departure of Pauline theology is not anthropological (the sorry human condition under sin), but soteriology (what has taken place in Christ illuminates the preceding human condition): that is, for Paul the solution precedes the problem (see 442–447).

28. He would seem sometimes not to avoid the risk of the truism, or of begging the question, the *petitio principii* (see 505: for Paul "it is the right kind of righteousness that cannot come by works of the Law, and the reason for this is that it comes only by faith in Christ''; 552: "In short, *this is what Paul finds wrong in Judaism: it is not Christianity*" [emphasis his]!) See the reviews by N. A. Dahl and S. Sandmel, RSR 4 (1978) 159–160; J. Neusner, *History of Religions* 18 (1978) 177–191; W. Horbury, *The Expository Times* 90 (1979) 116–118; J. Murphy-O'Connor, RB 85 (1978) 122–126.

29. [The sentence in the text above is somewhat adapted from the Italian because in English we have had to use the term "mysticism" to refer to the Italian *la mistica*, an abstraction that covers mystical experience and all ways of talking about it.—T.P.W., translator]. Originally, the adjective referred to the Greek mysteries (see Liddell-Scott-Jones, *sub voce*,) and in Thucydides V:28:2 the plural neuter noun *ta mystika* is clearly equivalent to *ta mystéria* of 28:1.

30. See Th. Ohm in *Lexikon für Theologie und Kirche*, VII[2] (Freiburg i. Br., 1962) 732; L. Richter in *Religion in Geschichte und Gegenwart*, IV[3] (Tübingen, 1960) 1237ff.

31. R. Schnackenburg in *Lexikon für Theologie und Kirche*, VII[2], cit. 733; K. H. Schelke, "Im Leib oder ausser des Leibes. Paulus als Mystiker," *Theologische Quartalschrift* 158 (1978) 285–293. Especially illuminating on the subject of Pauline mysticism is the article of F. F. Bruce, "Was Paul a Mystic?" *The Reformed Theological Review* 34 (1975) 66–75, which clearly distinguishes between mystical experiences and theology, and correctly notes that for Paul the latter does not derive from the former.

Phil 4:12 (the only time in the whole New Testament), is used in a mundane context of the apostolic ministry in such a way that it loses its mystical meaning.[32] The more frequent term, which would seem to be closer to Hellenistic mysticism, is μυστήριον; but actually in Paul's letters this takes on a new semantic reference, closer to that of apocalyptic Judaism.[33]

Thus we would also go astray if we tried to emphasize more than does Paul his experience of rapture "into the third heaven" (2 Cor 12:2; cf. v. 4: "into paradise"), where he "heard unspeakable things that one cannot express" (v. 4). This evidently alludes to an ecstatic condition, in which the bodily aspect becomes secondary (vv. 2b, 3b), and the unusual aspect of the specific time of the event is emphasized (v. 2a: "fourteen years ago"). But besides speaking of it in the third person, that is, distancing himself, he attaches no importance to it with reference to either his Christian existence or his apostolic life. Indeed, the chronology given brings the event to about A.D. 40, so that it does not correspond to his vocation on the road to Damascus, and so is not determinative for his missionary role, nor does he ever mention it elsewhere in his autobiographical passages. Moreover, this is a single experience dated to a single time, never repeated, and so an indication that this was not habitual with Paul. Finally, he definitely speaks of it unwillingly (12:1: "It is not fitting"), and his decision to do so is only because in the Corinthian Church such phenomena were granted a particular esteem, which Paul, however, seeks to minimize: "It would obscure the fact that it is to his gospel, and not to himself, that men should attend, and that he is a more effective witness to Christ crucified if he endures suffering and disgrace."[34] Actually, this is precisely the way Paul's passage develops, climaxing with the answer received from Christ: "My grace is enough for you, for [my] power reaches its completion in weakness" (12:9a), and with the paradoxical conclusion of the Apostle: "All the more, I shall glory in my weakness in order that the power of Christ may rest on me" (12:9b). Therefore ecstatic or mystical experiences are for Paul at least indifferent or useless, if not actually misleading. Against these he places the experience of the

---

32. See R. Penna, *Il "mysterion" paolino: traiettoria e costituzione* (Brescia, 1978).
33. Ibid.
34. C. K. Barrett, *The Second Epistle to the Corinthians* (London, 1976²) 313; see also E. Käsemann, "Die Legitimität des Apostels," ZNW 41 (1942) 33–71, esp. 69; R. Bultmann, *The Second Letter to the Corinthians*, trans. R. Harrisville (Minneapolis, 1985) 224: "What is at issue, then, is a mystical experience whose meaning is its *fruitio* [enjoyment or advantage]. . . . Paul is speaking of the third heaven, not of Christ. . . . For Paul, Christ certainly does not denote the object of a *fruitio* but the δύναμις [power] of activity." See also A. T. Lincoln, " 'Paul the Visionary': The Setting and Significance of the Rapture to Paradise in II Corinthians XII.1-10," NTS 25 (1979) 204–220.

suffering of the apostolic mission, with its daily total dedication, not in the third heaven but concretely "in the city, in the wilderness, on the sea" (11:26), "always carrying the death of Jesus in the body" (4:10). "For when I am weak, then I am strong" (12:10).

A proof of this typical Pauline attitude is to be had in Paul's critical intervention in the situation that had developed in the Corinthian Church as this is attested in 1 Corinthians. At Corinth there had developed a grossly exaggerated esteem for what is sometimes called "realized eschatology,"[35] characterized by a strong emphasis on a γνῶσις, or esoteric wisdom, by boasting of one's pneumatic experiences and by depreciation of the future resurrection. Hence the tendency to undervalue the message of the cross and that which the cross entails on the practical level of esteem for the "weak" moral life and intra-ecclesial relationships. In a word, this situation could be labeled "enthusiasm" in its technical meaning of self-sufficient religious exaltation, of which the Corinthian glossolalia was only the most apparent and most superficial manifestation.[36]

Paul's intervention, as seen in the various sections of First Corinthians, tends precisely to recall the Corinthians to the realistic wisdom of the cross of Christ (chaps. 1–4); not to consider themselves emancipated from specific concrete moral norms, which can then be reduced to the fundamental norm of ἀγάπη (chaps. 5–10 and 13); to assume their role of service within the Church with a sense of balance and common responsibility (chaps. 11–14); and finally to recognize that their relationship with God is not exhausted in the "today" of the Spirit already given but necessarily demands the future of bodily resurrection, and hence an anthropological transformation yet to come (chap. 15.) Paul explicates this whole rich patrimony precisely in opposition to a mysticizing of Christianity by which some considered themselves to have reached the goal, the τέλος, of their perfection through a pneumatic condition that left nothing to be desired (note Paul's irony in 1 Cor 4:8 and in the way he treats the ecstatic phenomena in chapter 14).

Paul opposes any spiritual experience which not only tends to be overly confident but which goes to create an elitist and isolationist situation (with its resultant rending of the fabric of the community, as seen in the Corin-

35. See A. C. Thiselton, "Realized Eschatology at Corinth," NTS 24 (1978) 510–526. For a good description of the Corinthian situation, see also G. Barbaglio, *Le Lettere di Paoli*, I (Rome, 1980 [1990²]) 199–206.

36. See, for example, O. Kuss, "Enthusiasmus und Realismus bei Paulus," in *Auslegung und Verkündigung* (Regensburg, 1963) 260–270. "The theological and practical conquest of enthusiasm was the first test to which the young Church was exposed; and nothing less than its whole existence and future depended on its mastery of the problem"—E. Käsemann, *Perspectives on Paul*, trans. M. Kohl (Philadelphia, 1971 [Italian: 1972]) 123.

thian factions.) Nor does his own distinction between "pneumatics" and "psychics," the spiritual and the natural (2:13-15), subvert his preoccupation. This does not describe different degrees within the Corinthian community; actually this community was, on the one hand, still all "psychic" at the time of evangelization (3:1-2a), and even now can be described as "carnal" because of their internal divisions (3:2b-3), while on the other hand it is all on the way to becoming "pneumatic." Actually, only faith (2:5) makes the Christian "perfect" (2:6), in union with the gift of the Spirit (2:10; 12:13), whereas the adjective "psychic" in 2:14 describes not so much the imperfect Christian as the non-Christian (or the Christian who deviates from the very Christian identity by rejecting the Crucified One).[37] Hence, the "perfect" (2:6) are simply those who accept the mysterious wisdom of God revealed in the crucifixion of Christ and oriented "for our glory" (see 2:7-8). But the whole community is concerned and involved, for either it is all at this level or it does not exist: to be Christian means to be "perfect" in this way.[38] Hence, a "mysticism" of a few privileged persons is inconceivable and unacceptable.

Having identified these negative elements, we must now consider what positive elements specifically characterize the so-called Pauline mysticism.[39] First of all, we must recognize that Paul employs formulas, terms, ideas that are interrelated and also recall a mystical language: die and rise with Christ; live in Christ; Christ in me; be clothed with Christ; new birth; be transformed; know and be known (by God); see; communion; God all in all. And there is in this terminology an undeniable semantic of participation: the human person sets up a relationship not only with the "divine" in an impersonal sense but with "God" and especially with

37. Actually, the concept of *môria*, "foolishness," that is associated with it (2:14) is used by Paul to describe the negative reaction of the pagan (see 1:18, 23); see B. A. Pearson, *The Pneumatikos-Psychikos Terminology in 1 Cor. A Study in the Theology of the Corinthian Opponents of Paul and Its Relation to Gnosticism* (Cambridge, 1973) 40-41; R. A. Horsley, "Pneumatikos vs. Psychikos: Distinctions of Spiritual States Among the Corinthians," HThR 69 (1976) 269-288. According to Chr. Senft, *La première épître de st. Paul aux Corinthiens* (Neuchâtel, 1979) 49, the "psychic" are neither pagans nor believers of lower rank, but "those members of the community who judge the word of the cross unworthy of them" (note the position of K. Barth there).

38. "For Paul, perfection is not only the goal, but also the status of every believer . . . the division between believers of a lower and higher order arises from the fact that the addressees do not correspond to the true status conferred on them" (H. Conzelmann, *1 Corinthians* [Philadelphia, 1975] 59). See particularly U. Wilckens, "Das Kreuz Christi als die Tiefe der Weisheit Gottes. Zu 1. Kor 2,1,16," in *Paolo a una Chiesa divisa (1 Cor 1-4)*, ed. L. De Lorenzi (Rome, 1980) 43-81, esp. 54-59, 69-72 and 77-78.

39. We use the expression "mysticism" provisionally and methodologically, both because other terms proposed (e.g., by E. P. Sanders) are not exhaustive of all the reality concerned and in order to avoid various circumlocutions and paraphrases. The term is used simply as a linguistic instrument; these pages are intended precisely to define what should be understood by Pauline "mysticism."

"Christ," and moreover, this relationship is not exhausted on a purely extrinsic level limited to a merely intellectual relationship that would make of God and Christ only a passive object of perception or term of comparison.[40] Paul's statement, "You are all children of God through faith in [ἐν] Christ Jesus" (Gal 3:26), is very close to this other, "You are all one in [ἐν] Christ Jesus" (Gal 3:28). And this closeness is not just their location within two verses of one another, but touches the meaning of each in itself and in comparison with the other. That is, "faith in Christ" cannot be separated from "being in Christ" but inevitably demands it, and vice versa, this personal condition of communion "in him" cannot be realized except by beginning with, presupposing, and involving a relationship of faith.

But to say "faith" means to recognize the existence of a relationship of otherness, of non-confusion of persons, even of distinction, so that we read in Eph 3:17: "May Christ *dwell* in your hearts *through faith*." "Faith" indicates a face-to-face, made up of humility, confidence, obedience, confession, hope, and fear.[41]

Still, Paul in fact thinks of a κοινωνία that, while it also extends to a community dimension, is primarily realized in vertical relations with the Lord. It begins with the basic sacraments of baptism (Rom 6:3-5) and the meal (1 Cor 10:16), passes through the whole Christian life ("I in Christ" and "Christ in me"), with special emphasis on the apostolic sufferings (Phil 3:10; 2 Cor 1:5, 7; 4:10), and finally is displayed on the eschatological plane (2 Cor 1:9; 5:8; Phil 1:23). Actually, the Christian community is not only a people on the way nor solely a structured ἐκκλησία, but it is especially the "body of Christ," an expression that simultaneously indicates belonging and identification (see below).

The simple conclusion from these preliminary observations is that the Christian is not called to live some sort of autonomous piety, neither perceiving the Divine as an isolated completely foreign reality, in no way accessible to the human person,[42] nor making the Divine an object of an "erotic" attraction consisting in intellectual understanding or in magic art.[43] The fact is that according to Greek, especially Platonic, tradition, mystical union, ἕνωσις, "union" (or ὁμοίωσις, "similarity"), is possible because

---

40. Perhaps as in Jas 2:19: "Even the demons believe [that there is only one God] and tremble."

41. See the excellent description of Pauline *pistis*, "faith," in Bultmann, *Theology*, I, 314–324.

42. See Aristotle, *Nic. Ethics* VIII:7, 1159a, 12: "if one of the parties is separated by a great distance, as happens in the case of God, friendship is no longer possible"; see also Epicurean theology (Lucretius, *De rer. nat.* II:1090ff.).

43. See the concept of ἔρως in theme of the quest of God, both in the Jewish Philo of Alexandria, *Leg. Alleg.* III:84, and in the slightly later pagan Dio of Prusa, *Oratio* XII:60.

it presupposes a basic connaturality or *synergeia* between the human and the divine,[44] something unknown to Paul, and from which Christianity has always kept its distance.[45] Correlative to the Platonic concept of assimilation to God is that of flight from the world.[46] These two linked concepts found a new synthesis in the Gnosticism of the second century, certain elements of which could conceivably have been already developing at the time of Paul.[47] In any case, Paul is distinct from the religious environment of the time (even from the Hellenistic Jewish world represented by Philo of Alexandria).[48] There are essentially two differences.

First of all, for Paul the overcoming of the distance between God and the human person, which is both ontological and moral in character, is accomplished by God himself, in an intervention that in turn has two characteristics: God intervenes by an act of *grace*, which is therefore totally free; and this act is accomplished concretely in Jesus Christ in *history*, so that to want to interpret its proclamation allegorically would be to betray it. And so any talk about Pauline "mysticism" must begin with this, with the basic foundation of every divine-human relation, in which the ascending movement is always anticipated by a descending movement:

44. On this, see especially E. Des Places, *Synergeia. La parenté de l'homme avec Dieu d'Homère à la patristique* (Paris, 1964); also J. Pépin, *Idees grecques sur l'homme et sur Dieu* (Paris, 1971) 1-20.

45. The statement of Acts 17:28b-29a ("we are God's offspring"), though found on Paul's lips, is actually to be attributed to the Lukan redaction of the work (prescinding from the considerable bibliography, we refer only to R. Fabris, "La ricerca di Dio nell'opera di Luca," in *Quaerere Deum:* Atti della XXV Settimana Biblica dell'Associazione Biblica Italiana [Brescia, 1980] 235-260, esp. 238-240). Cf. Clement of Alexandria ("we have no relationship of nature with God . . . we are not consubstantial with him": *Strom.* II, 16:74:1) and Saint Jerome (on Matt 5:45), both cited by E. Des Places, *Synergeia*, cit., 184.

46. See Plato, *Theaetetus*, 176ab; Philo, *Gig.* 14; *Rer. div. her.* 82; Plotinus, *Enn.* VI:9:11.

47. See K.-W. Tröger, ed., *Gnosis und Neues Testament. Studien aus Religion-wissenschaft und Theologie* (Berlin, 1973) 281-339; E. Pagels, *Paul the Gnostic: Gnostic Exegesis of the Pauline Letters* (Philadelphia, 1975: the author refers only to the Valentinian system of the second century, and maintains in any case that it is not appropriate to judge Paul with later categories); W. Schmithals, "The 'Corpus Paulinium' and Gnôsis," in *The New Testament and Gnôsis: Essays in Honour of R. McL. Wilson* (Edinburgh, 1983) 107-124.

48. Note the typical Philonian expression "sober inebriation," *sobria ebrietas = nêphalaia methê* (*Opif.* 71; *Leg. alleg.* I:84; III:82; *Ebr.* 32; *Fug.* 152; *Mos.* I:187; *Omn. prob. lib.* 13), which characterizes mystical delirium; and see H. Lewy, *Sobria ebrietas. Untersuchungen zur Geschichte der antiken Mystik*, Beihefte zur Zeitschrift für die neutestamentliche Wissenschaft 9 (Giessen, 1929); F. N. Klein, *Die Lichtterminologie bei Philon von Alexandrien und in den hermetischen Schriften*, Untersuchungen zur Struktur der religiösen Sprache der hellenistischen Mystik (Leiden, 1962); D. S. Winston, "Was Philo a Mystic?" in *Society of Biblical Literature, 1978 Seminar Papers*, I (Missoula, Mont., 1978) 161-180. On the beginning of mystical tendencies in Palestinian Judaism, see (besides n. 7) J. Abelson, *Jewish Mysticism* (London, 1913); G. Scholem *Major Trends in Jewish Mysticism* (New York, 1946) esp. 13-93 *Jewish Gnosticism, Merkabah Mysticism, and Talmudic Tradition* (New York, 1965) 1-19; J. Neusner, *Early Rabbinic Judaism* (Leiden, 1975) 181ff. See also D. J. Halperin, *The Merkabah in Rabbinic Literature* (New Haven, 1980). For the experience of an already present salvation at Qumran, see H.-W. Kuhn, *Enderwartung und gegenwärtiges Heil. Untersuchungen zu den Gemeindeliedern von Qumran* (Göttingen, 1966).

the quest by a revelation, conquest by a gift, ἔρως by ἀγάπη. The reverse tendency would simply risk missing the mark, i.e., arriving at a God who does not correspond to the God of the Christian biblical message.[49] This basic point of departure includes the events of appropriation of the saving event: faith and justification; baptism and the Spirit; the condition of life "in Christ." This whole conceptual world belongs to the *foundations* of Pauline "mysticism," and to these we will dedicate the first part (section II) of the following treatment.

In the second place, in Paul certain effects of God's saving intervention and of its anthropological impact are so delineated that it appears that the "mystical" is a state that affects all Christians. All the baptized are called to, and are already even participants in, communion with the Lord; hence the only differences are found in the comparison of the present with the common eschatological goal, τέλος, to be reached (see Phil 3:12-13; 1 Cor 9:24), and not by comparisons among one another as categories of Christians located in different degrees of perfection. Not that we should distort the picture of the Christian community with a naive, unrealistic judgment. At Corinth there is a whole series of cases requiring the strong corrective intervention of the Apostle. And still, all the members of this Church, to whom the letters are addressed, are called "sanctified in Christ Jesus" (1 Cor 1:2) and simply "saints" (2 Cor 1:1). There is, thus, a common denominator in virtue of which growth and maturation are both possible and imperative (see Col 1:10; 2:19; Eph 2:21; 4:15).[50]

But this common denominator is not just a minimum to get along with, but is already the maximum, which only must be made to bear fruit. To put it in Pauline terms, the Spirit poured out in the hearts of the baptized (see Gal 4:6) is not something imperfect, as if perfection consisted in having another reality different from the Spirit: rather, it is called a "down payment" (2 Cor 1:22; 5:5), and concerning it, it is said that it must manifest itself in "fruit" (Gal 5:22). But especially, it is true that "through the Holy Spirit given to us, the ἀγάπη of God has been poured into our hearts" (Rom 5:5), and that "through the Spirit God has revealed to us what eye has not seen nor ear heard, nor has it entered the human heart" (1 Cor 2:10, 9). On these bases we identify specific characteristics of Christian being and life that form the typical dimensions thereof: individual, communitarian, intellective, ethical, eschatological. The second part of our exposition will investigate this conceptual world.

---

49. See above, chap. 28.
50. See B. M. Ahern, "Pauline Mysticism," *The Way* 18 (1978) 3–12.

II. The fundamentals

1) *The revelation of God's love in Jesus Christ*

This is the starting point of all discourse about the "mystical" participation of the Christian: a deliberation by God and its execution. Paul describes it not so much with the neutral and extrinsic terminology of a merely subjective decision (θέλημα, βουλή, βούλημα, εὐδοκία: rarely used), as rather with positive terms that immediately demonstrate its salvific content: "grace" *(χάρις)*, "love" *(ἀγάπη)*, "righteousness" *(δικαιοσύνη)*, "gift" *(δώρημα)*, with the adverb "gratis" *(δωρεάν)*.[51] "The grace of God and the grace granted thanks to one single human being, Jesus Christ, have been poured out abundantly on all" (Rom 5:15). "God, who is rich in mercy, through the great love with which he loved us, dead though we were through sins, brought us to life again with Christ: for by grace you have been saved" (Eph 2:4-5). "Now God's righteousness has been revealed independently of the Law . . .; God's righteousness by means of the faith in Jesus Christ" (Rom 3:21-22).

These various ideas converge upon two basic affirmations. (a) The first addresses an unmerited divine initiative, freely undertaken "while we were still sinners" (Rom 5:6, 8). Hence, from Paul's point of view no communion with God is possible except on the basis of God's condescension (see 2 Cor 8:9), which means on the basis of his preceding communion with humanity. Human mysticism, as attraction, knowledge, and experience of God, is always preceded, if we can say so, by a "divine mysticism" as attraction, knowledge, and experience of the human by God himself. "He emptied himself, taking the condition of a servant and becoming in the likeness of humans" (Phil 2:7). "Now you have known God, better, you have come to be known by God" (Gal 4:9). All this, obviously, implies a specific and original image of God, which affects precisely the new concept of "mysticism."[52] The God of Paul and of the Christian is

---

51. See these expressions in the *Theological Dictionary of the New Testament*, trans. G. W. Bromiley (Grand Rapids, Mich., 1964-74). Also K. Romaniuk. *L'amour du Père et du Fils dans la sotériologie de Saint Paul* (Rome, 1961).

52. See A. Nygren, *Agape and Eros*, I (London, 1982 [Italian: 1971]) 105-145. Very imaginative is the position of Denis the Areopagite, who works out an original fusion of the Platonic concept of ἔρως (as conquering or ascending love) and the New Testament/Pauline idea of ἀγάπη (as giving or descending love), describing the former with characteristics of the latter: "This divine yearning brings ecstasy *(ἔρως ἐκστατικός)* so that the lover belongs not to self but to the beloved. . . . The very cause of the universe in the beautiful, good superabundance of his benign yearning for all is also carried outside of himself in the loving care he has for everything. He is, as it were, beguiled by goodness, by love, and by yearning and is enticed away from his transcendent dwelling place and comes to abide within all things, and he does so by virtue of his supernatural and ecstatic capacity to remain, nevertheless, within himself"

no longer the distant and inaccessible deity of classical Greek philosophy, nor the impersonal and pantheistic universal principle of the Stoics, nor a mythical and naturalistic god like those of the mystery cults, nor yet again a good personality dualistically opposed to an evil divine entity and gathering all into his own πλήρωμα, as in Gnosticism. Nor is even the rigorous transcendence of the Jewish God maintained, who at most tends to make human observance of the Law the means of communion with himself. Rather, henceforth for Paul God is the "Father of our Lord Jesus Christ" (2 Cor 1:3; 11:31; Rom 15:6; Col 1:3; Eph 1:3), so that if the baptized also can address him with the familiar invocation "Abba!" this is only because they have received in their hearts "the Spirit of his Son" (Gal 4:6; see Rom 8:15). But this all means that now God has come to encounter humanity by passing through the cross and resurrection of Jesus Christ, which henceforth become his indelible identification. And so, "to cancel out the grace of God" (Gal 2:21) is simply equivalent to "having nothing more to do with Christ" (5:4), and that is to remove "the scandal of the cross" (5:11).

b) The second basic affirmation is this: God's love for the human person, while rooted *in the past* in an eternal calling (see Eph 1:4) and oriented *for the future* to an eschatological glorification (see Rom 8:23; Phil 3:21), is manifested in history—indeed said to be "now" (Rom 3:21), in the "fullness of time" (Gal 4:4), which thus becomes "the end of the ages" (1 Cor 10:11). For the Christian, God is now the one "who raised Jesus our Lord from the dead, who was put to death for our sins, and was raised for our justification" (Rom 4:24-25).

What is generally called the "paschal mystery" becomes the place par excellence where the Christian God is revealed. Here God is presented and declared as the one who gives true life through death, in the first place through the death of Jesus (see Col 2:13-15). For the terms "suffering, death, cross, blood" are not abstractions but as vividly as possible report the total gift of self that God has made in Christ. And the Pauline concepts of expiation, redemption, reconciliation, ransom, liberation are simply thematic variations on the basic reality of the cross of Christ.[53] But God's glory is shown not only in the (fertile) impotence of the cross but also in the resurrection of Jesus (see Rom 6:4). In fact, properly speaking,

---

(*De div. nom.* IV:13; trans. Colm Luibheid with Paul Rorem, *Pseudo-Dionysius,* The Classics of Western Spirituality [New York, 1987] 82); but the perspective is one of ontology rather than salvation history.

53. See H. Schlier, *Grundzüge einer paulinischen Theologie,* (Freiburg–Basel–Vienna, 1978) 132–140, 158–173; see also chapter 19 above.

this is the eschatological act of God.[54] There God shows his *dynamis,* "power," over death, while with the exaltation of Christ he offers a Lord for the living and the dead (see Rom 14:9), who "sits at his right hand" and becomes dispenser of the Spirit and life-giver to his community of believers. "If Christ is not risen . . . you are still in your sins" (1 Cor 15:17). But "now he is always beyond death and sin in his permanent love; now the love that bore sin works in him forever and for all human persons; now his earlier existence in favor of those in need also proves to be for us and for all; now his dying is revealed as actually having-died-for-us."[55]

2) *The role of faith and of justification*

One's first contact with the God of grace comes through faith in him and in the saving intervention accomplished in Christ Jesus, "through whom we have obtained access, through faith, to this grace in which we stand" (Rom 5:2). This is a contact characterized by awareness of one's own insufficiency, since "all have sinned, and are deprived of the glory of God" (3:23); by an immense openness to accept "the abundance of grace and of the free gift of righteousness" (5:17) in obedience to the way of the cross which he has chosen (see 1:5; 16:26); and by an attitude of rejoicing and gratitude for all that has been done for us by God (see 8:31; 1 Cor 15:57).

This contact, undertaken in humility and in the joy of faith, brings about that process of anthropological renewal the first act of which Paul calls "justification" (see Gal 2:16; Rom 3:28). The term expresses a concept derived from the law court, and so it has been assigned a secondary role in Pauline theology even by some recent Protestant authors who are anxious to overcome a merely juridical and hence extrinsic conception of salvation in favor of one that is more attentive to the participatory dimension.[56] But one really ought not to stress the two poles of Pauline thought

54. See B. Rigaux, *Dieu l'a ressuscité* (Gembloux, 1973 [Italian: 1976]) 432–467. Concerning the preference of Pauline language that makes "God" the agent of the resurrection of Jesus, see R. Schnackenburg, "Zur Aussageweise 'Jesus ist (von den Toten) auferstanden,' " *BZ* 13 (1969) 1–17.

55. H. Schlier, *Grundzüge einer paulinischen Theologie*, 149.

56. Already W. Wrede, *Paul* (Boston, 1908 [Tübingen, 1904, 1907²]) 122–124, identifies the doctrine of justification as a polemical teaching, a *Kampflehre*, understandable only on the basis of Paul's confrontation with Judaism and Jewish Christianity. However, this did not mean, as is often thought, that Wrede devalued the doctrine (this point is correctly made by U. Wilckens, "Was heisst bei Paulus: 'Aus den Werken des Gesetzes wird kein Mensch gerecht,' " in the collection *Rechtfertigung im neuzeitlichen Lebenszusammenhang* [Gütersloh, 1964] 84–85, n. 17). It was rather P. Wernle, *The Beginnings of Christianity* (London–New York, 1903–

excessively. In fact, it is not a question of an opposition or an alternative. E. P. Sanders correctly notes that the verb "justify" is used differently in 1 Cor 6:11 (with reference to the forgiveness of a series of *sins,* listed in vv. 9-10) and in Rom 6:7 (where it refers rather to the overcoming of *sin* as the area of a dominion from which one escapes, so that *participation* in sin is replaced by participation with Christ).[57] But he ignores the fact that the Pauline expression "die with Christ" is used in a baptismal context (see Rom 6:8; Col 2:20; and similarly 2 Cor 5:14) and that hence this participatory event is preceded by the fact that "Christ died for us," an event that is basically verifiable by faith only.

In any case, it remains true that even faith and the justification associated with it cannot be reduced to a purely juridical declaration of absolution and a passive acceptance thereof, as if the person were not affected inwardly; rather they already signify a *transfer,* i.e., a passage from one dominion to another, and hence a change that also involves a whole way of being of the human person. "Justified by his blood . . . we have become reconciled with God" (Rom 5:9, 10): this text, as we see, brings about a clear merging of two different ways of speaking and clearly shows that even if justification is different on a logical level from the other stages of the process of salvation, it is not actually separated from, much less opposed to, a participatory dimension, which rather deeply inheres in it. Also in 2 Cor 5:21 we find the two formulas "for us" and "in him" closely associated with one another. And hence it is right to maintain that "Paul did not see any contradiction between Christ's death for transgressions and his death as providing the means by which believers could participate in a death to the power of sin, and he saw no contradiction between the reconciliation provided by God's overlooking the past transgressions and the new creation provided by being in Christ."[58]

1904) 309, who first identified it as "one of his most disastrous creations." And A. Schweitzer, *The Mysticism,* 220–225, saw it only as a subsidiary crater, a *Nebenkrater,* of Pauline theology, which failed to establish a logical link between justification and ethic. Similar judgments are passed by both W. D. Davies, *Paul and Rabbinic Judaism* (London, 1955²) 221–222, and E. P. Sanders, *Paul and Palestinian Judaism,* 502–508, who sees "the real bite" of Pauline theology only "in the participatory categories" and denies that justification there appears as entrance into the new life.

57. See E. P. Sanders, *Paul and Palestinian Judaism,* 503; see also 471–472; 545.

58. Thus E. P. Sanders himself, *Paul and Palestinian Judaism,* 502: "Righteousness by faith and participation in Christ ultimately amount to the same thing" (506). Here, with the same author (508) we can perceive only a terminological difference in that the "juristic" terms and the "participationist" terms correspond to two different conceptions of the same human situation without Christ: that which emphasizes transgressions as individual punishable acts, and that which prefers to stress a type of bond and communion with sin in general that is incompatible with union with Christ; rather, they are simply alternative conceptions (as, for instance, in 1 Cor 6:12-20; 10:6-14.)

Precisely the Pauline emphasis on faith and justification (in relation to the event of the crucifixion/resurrection of Christ) shows us why the Apostle in his theology on the one hand gives no space to the ideas of guilt and repentance (the language of "conversion," μετανοεῖν, and ἐπιστρέφειν, "repent and turn back," is all but irrelevant), and on the other hand takes no account of the efficacy of the whole expiatory system of Judaism (sacrificial cult, the "atonement," *kippûr*, fasting, etc.) This is because his point of departure is not so much anthropological as kerygmatic: the proclamation of the death and resurrection of Jesus, and the faith that in him God has come to humanity with a gracious deed, which actually "passes over previous sins" (Rom 3:25) and renders every other system of salvation useless (see 2 Cor 3:14; Eph 2:15; Heb 8:13).[59] Nor is this a question of a merely "imputed" justice but of a real transformation of the individual, as now is generally acknowledged by our Protestant brothers and sisters. Paul is, after all, sufficiently clear when he says, "Anyone who is in Christ is a new creation" (2 Cor 5:17; see below, III.1)[60]

3) *Baptism and Spirit*

That which according to Paul constitutes the properly mysterial[a] foundation of the new anthropological reality is the gift of the Spirit: "The love of God has been poured out in our hearts through the Holy Spirit that has been given us" (Rom 5:5). "You have been washed, you have been sanctified, you have been justified in the name of the Lord Jesus Christ and in the Spirit of our God" (1 Cor 6:11): these three verbs evi-

59. Note the important pages 442–447 of E .P. Sanders, indicating that for Paul "the solution precedes the problem"; on p. 500 he finally admits that "the characteristic act of Christians was to *believe* in the gospel message" (although he refers this only to Jesus' resurrection, inexplicably ignoring the crucifixion). See also the pertinent words of A. Oepke in TDNT 1:541: "In Paul there is no suggestion of cleavage between a forensic and a mystical mode of thought. Forensic justification leads to pneumatic fellowship with Christ. The *justitia Christi extra nos posita* aims ceaselessly to become the *justitia Christi intra nos posita*, [the justice of Christ granted from without—the righteousness granted within us]. There is here no leap, and a transition only insofar as justification is not conditioned by the new life, but the new life by justification, so that a distinction of thought is demanded." See also S. Kim, *The Origin of Paul's Gospel* (Tübingen, 1981) 307.

60. See B. Bultmann already in *Theology of the NT*, 277 (not "as if," . . . but "truly righteous"); while E. P. Sanders, *Paul and Palestinian Judaism*, 492, n. 57, could not be more explicit: "The term 'forensic' is somewhat ambiguous, since it can refer to God's declaring one to be righteous (though he is not), a meaning conveyed by the term 'imputation' and the catch-phrase *'simul justus et peccator* [simultaneously just and sinner]. This meaning derives from Luther's theology . . ., and it is a meaning I do not find in Paul"!; and 495: "The righteousness terminology . . . may be used as the equivalent of salvation and life. . . ."

a. I use this rare English adjective derived from the noun "mystery" to represent Penna's "misterico," an adjective that neutrally reflects all that concerns the "mystery"—T.P.W., translator.

dence the clear disjunction from the preceding situation, while the expression "in the name of . . ." clearly enough indicates baptism, which is here explicitly associated with the mention of the Spirit.[61] Of course, Paul connects this gift with faith as well: "Is it through the works of the Law that you have received the Spirit, or by having believed the preaching?" (Gal 3:2), and from the context the answer is clearly the latter (cf. 3:5, 14). But habitually, its linkage is with the sacramental event (see 1 Cor 12:13; 2 Cor 1:21-22; Eph 1:13; 4:30; and the relationship in Romans of chapter 6, which treats of baptism, with chapter 8, which spells out the theme of life according to the Spirit).[62] Also in Galatians Paul connects the divine filiation of Christians with baptism (in 3:26-27) and with the Spirit as well (4:6). This last text reads: "And that you are sons, the proof is the fact that God has sent into our hearts the Spirit of his Son, which cries, 'Abba, Father.'" Various things worth noting appear here.[63]

First: The theme is the $\nu\iota o\theta\varepsilon\sigma\iota\alpha$, i.e., the adoption as children as expressed by the new relationship of humankind before God, as overcoming a condition of slavery or minority (note 4:1-3); this gives the right of inheritance, whether this is understood as present participation in the Christian fulfillment of ancient promises or as future reception of eschatological benefits.

Second: The new filiation consists in a previously unknown relationship of extreme familiarity and intimacy with God, as shown by the Aramaic cry "Abba." This demonstrates that the new filial condition of the baptized is unachievable by nature because it consists in a conformity to Jesus himself, for whom such intimacy with God was habitual and profoundly connatural; for the new character of the Christian is brought about by the Spirit of "the Son," which therefore puts the baptized in a situation analogous to that of Christ himself.

Third: All this is a gift of grace, for at its origin is God in person, who "sends" the Son and also "his" Spirit, in a sovereignly free decision. Paul, then, to show the new Christian reality, appeals not only to its pneumatic foundation but also to the fact that its unearned reality is a pure, free

---

61. Besides the commentaries, see R. Schnackenburg, *Baptism in the Thought of St. Paul*, trans. G. R. Beasley-Murray (Oxford, 1964) 18–21 and 86. See also P. E. Deterding, "Baptism According to Saint Paul," *Concordia Journal* 6 (1980) 93–100.

62. On the relationship between baptism and justification, see K. Kertelge, *"Rechtfertigung" bei Paulus* (Münster i. W., 1967) 228–249 [Italian: Brescia, 1991]); and especially E. Dinkler, "Römer 6:1-14 und das Verhältnis von Taufe und Rechtfertigung bei Paulus," in *Battesimo e Giustizia in Tm 6 e 8*, ed. L. De Lorenzi (Rome, 1974) 83–103.

63. See R. Penna, *Lo Spirito di Cristo. Cristologia e pneumatologia secondo un'originale formulazione Paolino* (Brescia, 1976) 207–235 (also regarding the relationship with the parallel passage of Rom 8:15-17ab); see also Penna, "Lo Spirito di Gesù Cristo," *Parola Spirito e Vita* 4 (July-Dec. 1981) 160–172.

divine intervention (cf. Wis 9:17: "Who has known your thought if you have not granted them wisdom and have not sent them your holy spirit from on high?")

Fourth: By saying "in our hearts," Paul alludes to the personal depths of the human individual, who is thus touched and so transformed down to the most hidden roots. It is not without reason, according to Saint Paul, that Christians are "the temple of the Spirit" (1 Cor 6:19; 3:16), while elsewhere he claims that, beholding the glory of the Lord as in a mirror, "we become transformed into that same image, from glory to glory, according to the action of the Spirit of the Lord" (2 Cor 3:18).[64] It is only the Spirit that accomplishes the true metamorphosis of the Christian.

Fifth: The most unimaginable thing is that the baptized is inserted into and, as it were, immersed in the very mystery of the Trinity. And it is precisely the Spirit that produces this thing unheard of, for, having been sent by God, it reaches us in a typically Christological manner, then returns to the supreme Sender in the form of a filial cry. The Father-Spirit-Son take us up into their communion, in the vortex, as it were, of their mutual relations; and in this circular movement, in which the Christian is entirely bound up and as it were absorbed, consists precisely the whole dynamic and mysterial structure of human redemption—its sublimity and at the same time its dailiness.

Sixth: These things hold for all the baptized without distinction (according to Gal 5:4, only those who seek justification in the Law have "fallen from grace"); hence there are no privileged classes in the Church, not even a group of "mystics" who can certify their superiority over "simple" Christians, since all the "simple" Christians are fundamentally "mystic"; and Paul insists on this basic reality (see the insistence on "all" in Gal 3:26-28; Rom 3:22-24; 5:15, 18-19) against any dangerous tendency to put one's confidence in oneself and to set up boundaries of inequality within the Church.[65] This contention, then, is not prejudiced by the fact that certain persons have, for various reasons, a deeper experience of God.[66]

The whole of Christian existence is, then, a life according to the Spirit: "For all who are led by the Spirit are children of God" (Rom 8:14; see Gal 5:16, 18).[67] And it is in this light that we understand the frequent Pau-

---

64. After the Italian Episcopal Conference version; for another translation cf. R. Penna, *Lo Spirito di Cristo*, 190-191. On the prayer of the Spirit in Rom 8:26-27, see E. Vallauri, "I gemiti dello Spirito Santo (Rom 8,26s.)," RivBibl 27 (1979) 95–113.

65. See, for example, the use of expressions of "boasting" (καυχάομαι, καύχημα, καύχησις) and the opposites related to humility (ταπεινοφροσύνη).

66. And it remains true that the Pauline language about "growth" (αὔχησις, οἰκοδομή) is never segmentary but always concerns the whole community of the baptized.

67. See W. Pfister, *Das Leben im Geist nach Paulus* (Fribourg en Suisse, 1963); I. De La Potterie and S. Lyonnet, *The Christian Lives by the Spirit* (Staten Island, 1971 [Italian: 1971²]);

line expression "in the spirit" (see Rom 2:29; 14:17; 1 Cor 6:11; 2 Cor 6:6, etc.).

In such discourse, however, we must always be mindful of the Christological component, which also affects the pneumatological reality. For baptism is for Paul a "dying and rising with Christ," i.e., it symbolizes and produces a solidarity of destiny between creature and Lord (as we find especially in Rom 6:1-11; cf. Col 2:12-13). Communion with him is not only personal and static but is existential, since it takes place first in the sacrament and then in life and even in suffering (2 Cor 4:7-14),[68] and also in the eschatological future. Still, this relatively infrequent expression prepares for the more frequent and significant term "in Christ," ἐν Χριστῷ.

4) "In Christ"

The formula occurs very often (about 170 times, including "in him," "in whom," "in the Lord") and is characteristic of Paul. Actually it was from the study of this expression that the discussion of Pauline mysticism began some one hundred years ago (see above I.1). And a correlative, much rarer phrase is "Christ in you" (eight times). Our expression is the constant cross and delight of Pauline scholars.[69] Sometimes it is reducible simply to a Semitic-sounding instrumental phrase, "by means of Christ" or the like.[70] Other times it can be translated simply with the adjective "Christian";[71] see, for example, 2 Cor 12:2: "a person in Christ." But we cannot ignore the usual semantic density of the phrase, which makes it a cipher for Christian identity, not so much on the level of a sociological

---

I. De La Potterie, "Le chrétien conduit par l'Esprit dans son cheminement eschatologique," in *The Law of the Spirit in Rom 7 and 8,* ed. L. De Lorenzi (Rome, 1976) 209-241.

68. See R. Schnackenburg, "Baptism in the Thought of St. Paul," 139-177; and especially R. C. Tannehill, *Dying and Rising with Christ* (Berlin, 1967), who demonstrates that the expression emphasizes the eschatological and inclusive dimension of the event of the cross (so that it is not just a *repetition* of what Christ did) and that dying and rising with Christ inserts the individual in the broad context of a new world that begins precisely with the death/resurrection of Christ, and in the transfer of one's submission from the dominion of sin to the dominion of Christ himself (and thus the reality cannot dissolve into a purely subjective-mystical experience).

69. See esp. F. Neugebauer, *In Christus. Eine Untersuchung zum paulinischen Glaubensverständnis* (Göttingen, 1961); M. Bouttier, *En Christ. Etude d'exégèse et de théologie paulinienne* (Paris, 1962); F. Neirynck, "Paul's Teaching on 'Christ in Us' and 'We in Christ,'" *The Presence of God,* Concilium 50 (1969) 141-154.

70. This is especially true in the Letter to the Ephesians, where the formula is found all of 34 times; see J. Allen, "The 'In Christ' Formula in Ephesians," NTS 5 (1958-59) 54-62.

71. See F. Büchsel, "'In Christo,'" ZNW 42 (1949) 141-158. According to F. Neugebauer, *In Christus,* 171ff., the formula would be interchangeable with "by (or through) faith," since it also is related, like faith, to the salvific events centered upon Christ; but this solution does not account for all the profundity, and in some sense the realism, of the Pauline expression.

designation as in the newness of the person's being, referring to the baptized in their personal totality. For example, the phrase of Gal 3:28, "You are all one *in Christ* Jesus," absolutely cannot be reduced to the mere significance "You are all Christians," since the accent is placed on the unity (almost numerical! note the Greek masculine "one," εἷς, rather than neuter ἕν) formed by all the baptized and based precisely on being "in Christ Jesus," so that even the phrase of the following verse, "if you are *of Christ*," alludes to a belonging that touches the deepest levels of the person. In this sense it would be better to recognize a *sociative* value for the preposition "in," as expressing the close solidarity of Christians with the Redeemer.[72]

A text of utmost significance is Rom 6:11: "Consider yourselves as dead to sin, but alive to God in Christ Jesus." The sentence, actually, can be considered a contrasting parallel to the preceding v. 2: "We who are now dead to sin, how can we still live in sin?" As we can see from the parallel, "living in Christ Jesus" is the exact opposite of "living in sin." This does not just mean that Christ Jesus and sin are mutually exclusive, but that each constitutes an environment for life, a sphere of influence and action, in which each of these exercises its own dominion. With baptism the enslaving dominion of sin is eliminated and is replaced by the liberating dominion of Jesus Christ. In this sense, while not accepting A. Deissmann's (see note 1) local realism, we should preserve a generally local but metaphorical sense for the preposition "in," to say that henceforth Christ determines and represents the field in which his disciple now lives. Christ is not just a term of comparison, but especially the root and that which itself constitutes holiness, i.e., Christian identity.[73] "In Christ Jesus" is a formula with which Paul describes the vital sphere of Christians, which is opened up to them through the intervention of God in the cross and resurrection of Jesus and given to them through faith and baptism. And it is the living space of the new creation (see 2 Cor 5:17), "in which they

---

72. See M. Zerwick, *Biblical Greek* (Rome, 1963) nn. 116–118 [86–88]. R. C. Tannehill, *Dying and Rising with Christ*, 24, speaks of "corporate" and "inclusive patterns of thought."
73. See H. Schlier, *Der Brief an die Epheser* (Düsseldorf, 1957 [Italian: 1957²]) on 1:1 and 1:3: Christians "are not only in Laodicaea or Hierapolis or in some other place: their residence, their living space . . . is also Christ Jesus. . . . He is our 'transcendental' place. . . . We are thus, thanks to God, blessed to the very roots of our existence, both in the depth of our own being, and, in the midst of the abysses of the powers of the world, safeguarded in Christ insofar as we are blessed in him" (34, 48). See Schlier also in *Der Römerbrief*, on 6:11: As a Christian one "no longer lives on the basis of one's earlier, ancient origin [Adam], through which one rather dies (see 1 Cor 15:22); one no longer lives ἐν σαρκί, 'in the flesh' (Rom 7:5; 8:8-9 [Eph 2:3; Col 2:11]), on one's own, no longer 'in the world,' ἐν κοσμῳ (Col 2:20), in confined dimensions of the world and of one's own powers, but rather ἐν Χριστῷ Ἰησοῦ, 'in Christ Jesus,' in whom, and through whom, one is open to God in one's being and one's existence, and so in life."

are delivered from eschatological condemnation [cf. Rom 8:1], sanctified [1 Cor 1:2; 6:11], and freed from the Law [Rom 8:2; Gal 2:19]; for God's love is the force that rules this space [see Rom 8:39; 1 Cor 16:24], and in it all Christians, though each is distinct as a human being, are only one reality (see Gal 3:28) as one body (see Rom 12:5) and by the action of the one Holy Spirit all the charisms constitute their riches [see 1 Cor 1:5]."[74] Not that the formula sets up a place in which everything is static; indeed, if one is so to speak captured (see Phil 3:12) by Christ, it is only to find a new way of living, in relation to God and to other human beings, in the present world and in the world to come, a way that is determined by the Lord Jesus.[75]

What is original about the Pauline expression, and at the same time what is utterly remarkable about its meaning, can be appreciated only by comparing it to other expressions that are grammatically similar or semantically related, whether negatively ("in sin," "in the world," and especially "in the flesh") or positively ("in the Pneuma"). Now, these realities are all either impersonal or at least grammatically neutral in gender (like the Greek πνεῦμα); and for that reason they are less surprising and more comprehensible. But "Jesus Christ" is an individual, specific person, who remains such even after resurrection from the dead, and as such is called "Lord" (see 1 Cor 12:3; Phil 2:11). But if Paul writes that he wants nothing but "to be found in him" (Phil 3:9), the logical question raised by this expression is overcome and resolved only in the mysterial stature of this Jesus, who "was designated as God's Son in power" (Rom 1:4) and "sovereign of the dead and the living" (14:9), so much so that he does not just stand before the Christian as someone other,[76] but above all is the "life" of the Christian (Col 3:4; cf. Phil 1:21; and also Ignatius, *Ad Eph.* 3:2; *Ad Smyrn.* 4:1; *Ad Magn.* 1:2). Whoever belongs to him (or is "of him": 1 Cor 15:23; 2 Cor 10:7; Gal 3:29) has overcome sin, death, the flesh, and is precisely in grace, in life, in the Spirit.[77]

---

74. See U. Wilckens, *Der Brief an die Römer,* Evangelisch-katholischer Kommentar VI/2 (Einsiedeln–Neukirchen Vluyn, 1980) 19.

75. See M. Bouttier, *En Christ,* 86; see 133: "*In Christ* can be understood only in relation to history (what Jesus has done for us), to eschatology (what the Lord will do with us), and finally to mysticism, if by that we mean what God accomplishes in us, the communion that unites the Lord and those who belong to the Lord, which finds its expression in the communion of these among themselves."

76. It is just this that definitively explains Paul's silence about the historical Jesus: he is not interested in him as a personage of the past, nor as teacher of doctrine, nor as marvelous miracle worker. What Paul strongly emphasizes is rather the present, actual, fresh relationship with him; see 2 Cor 5:16-17.

77. We shall not here dwell on the antithetic pair "flesh/Spirit," which is nevertheless typical of Paul and would have a role in the discussion of Pauline mysticism; for this we refer to R. Penna, *Lo Spirito di Cristo,* 243–248. On the parallel formulas "in the Spirit" and "the

Galatians 2:20 illuminates what we are saying from another point of view: "I live, now no longer I, but Christ lives in me, but my present mortal life I live in the faith of the Son of God, who loved me and gave himself up for me." As we see, the perspective here is not so much that of "myself in Christ" as it is "Christ in me." But the mystical union described is not such as to cancel the individual personality of the Christian, as if an identification between the person were declared. The explicit allusion to faith maintains a distinction between the two, between which there is a matter not just of a superimposition but of a relationship.

Moreover, there is talk of "mortal life" (literally, "life in the flesh"), i.e., an existence that is anything but absorbed in glory, but rather corruptible and ephemeral, *within* which is experienced union with Christ. And moreover, the title "Christ" alludes to the salvific (paschal) realities, which are at the origin of the new Christian reality and guarantee it. "Through Christ the new eschatological age is already introduced, thus dissolving the old era determined by the Law. The expression 'Christ lives in me,' then, without losing its ontological character, comes to be understood in an eschatological sense. It is precisely because Christ, the initiator and the foundation of the new age, lives in the baptized that these already live in the saving future of the lordship of Christ, which has already begun."[78] For it is essential not to dissolve the figure of Christ in an impersonal abstraction (or a pneumatic abstraction, as does A. Deissmann); he remains the one who historically "loved me and gave himself for me." In this way Paul's certainty is vindicated: "Who will now separate us from the love of Christ?" (Rom 8:35), which sounds like a challenge. "In Christ" means precisely to exist within the radius of the life-giving effect of this love, which "holds us in its power," (2 Cor 5:14),[79] and in which, with faith and baptism, Christians are already "rooted and founded" (Eph 3:17).

Spirit in us," see *Lo Spirito di Cristo,* 248–257. For a *status quaestionis,* see L. Lopez de las Heras, "Cristo y el espíritu en nosotros: veinte años de investigación paulina," *Studium* 20 (1980) 349–390.

78. F. Mussner, *Der Galaterbrief,* HThKNT, IX (Freiburg-Basel-Vienna, 1974) 182–183. The "I" of Gal 2:20 is not so much autobiographical as collective; the experience of union with Christ here described is not exclusively concerned with Paul, since in the context the "I," which begins already with v. 18, appears only as a specification and individuation of the "us" (Jewish Christians) of the previous vv. 15-17. Paul means to say that the individual person now bears Christ's signature as such a person had originally borne that of the Law, an experience that is specifically his own but is simply presented as Christian, and therefore characteristic of all the baptized.

79. Following H. D. Wendland in *Briefe an die Korinther,* NTD (Göttingen, 1978), who thus well translates the Pauline *synechei hêmas* (in place of the Vulgate *urget nos,* "presses us"); cf. R. Bultmann, ad loc., *beherrscht uns;* C. K. Barrett, "controls our action"; J. Héring, *nous posède.*

III. The dimensions

1) *The "new creation" (individual dimension)*

Granted the fundamentals of which we have spoken, the result on the anthropological level cannot help but be something absolutely original. Paul is aware of this and affirms it with a very pointed axiom: "If one is in Christ, one is a new creation; the old things have passed away, behold they have become new" (2 Cor 5:17); and also: "It is not circumcision that counts nor uncircumcision, but the new creation" (Gal 6:15). Parallel to these are expressions about the "new human being" (Col 3:10; Eph 2:15; 4:24) and the "new dough" (1 Cor 5:7), which are in turn contrasted with the "old human being" (Rom 6:6; Col 3:9; Eph 4:22) and the "old leaven" (1 Cor 5:7).[80]

The crucial text 2 Cor 5:17 treats not just a new "world" coming into existence, or a "creation" in the cosmic sense of the term, or, considering the whole general context, the framework of the life of the baptized person, who at least is involved in it, nor do we have only a creative intervention of God considered as an act.[81] Rather, the attention is concentrated on the concrete, individual single human person: εἴ "τις" ἐν Χριστῷ. The pronoun τις, even if indefinite and impersonal, is grammatically masculine or feminine, not neuter, in gender; and it is singular, not plural. So it cannot help but refer to what happens in each single baptized person, time after time. The "new creation" refers to and defines each Christian personally. And this constitutes the first dimension of Pauline mysticism as Christian identity.

Thus, the Christian—each Christian—is made the equivalent of the "new creation," and the term "creation" refers to a new beginning, a re-creation, a re-making that transforms one's deepest roots. For Paul, "the justification of the human person signifies an ontic transformation, concretely: the reintegration of the original condition as image of God corresponds to the original creation."[82] It is not, then, a question of mere

---

80. See B. Rey, *Créés dans le Christ Jésus. La création nouvelle selon St. Paul* (Paris, 1966); P. Fiedler, "Wozu erlöst Erlösung? Der 'Neue Mensch' nach Paulus," *Bibliothek der Kirchenväter* 33 (1978) 2–6.

81. Compare, for instance, the commentary of J. Héring (or M. Bouttier, *Christianity According to St Paul* [London, 1966: *La condition chrétienne selon Saint Paul* (Geneva, 1964)] 95: "A new genesis is coming into being," *Une nouvelle genèse s'accomplit*). The translation proposed by C. K. Barrett ("There is a new act of creation") distracts attention from the single human individual *of whom* Paul says that this is a καινὴ κτίσις; much better is the rendering of R. Bultmann, *Wenn jemand in Christus, ist, so ist 'er' ein neues Geschöpf*, "If anyone is in Christ, that person is a new creation."

82. P. Stuhlmacher, "Erwägungen zum ontologischen Charakter der *kainê ktisis* bei Paulus," *EvTh* 27 (1967) 1–35, 2; the Lutheran author is presently New Testament professor at the University of Tübingen.

imputation but of a real transformation, which the Letter to Titus identifies as "palingenesis (rebirth or regeneration) and renewal" (Titus 3:5); and on this point Lutherans now agree with Catholics.[83] "There is now no condemnation for those who are in Christ Jesus. For the law of the Spirit who gives life in Christ Jesus has freed you from the law of sin and death" (Rom 8:1-2). Note how very much personalized this language has become with the singular pronoun "you," and how it returns to constitutive ideas of the new creation, namely, freedom in the Spirit (see 2 Cor 3:17; Gal 5:1) and the fruits implicit therein (cf. Gal 5:22).

We can perceive and even measure the original weight of the fresh new Pauline affirmation if we remember that in Jewish apocalyptic the "new creation (or creature)" is associated only with eschatological palingenesis: "From the day of the new creation, when the heavens, the earth, and all their creatures shall be renewed" (Jub 1:29); "God has appointed them (the spirits of truth and injustice) until the time chosen for the new creation" (1QS 4:25).[84] What in these texts is barely perceived on the horizon of hope, Paul proclaims without reticence to be already fully realized (though leaving room for further completion). The only terms of comparison for the "new creation" resulting from faith and baptism (which therefore is where the act of creation takes place) are two: the protological moment of the creation of humanity and the eschatological moment of its future transformation. But in a certain sense we can say that in the Christian everything begins again from the beginning, and at the same time everything is anticipated proleptically. The "new human being" is a synthesis of different levels, of opposite moments, but is the product of the same free, gratuitous intervention of God, who acts in the baptized as he acted "in the beginning" and as he will act in the end. "We are his work, created in Christ Jesus. . . . Thus you are no longer strangers and guests but are fellow citizens with the saints, and members of God's family" (Eph 2:10, 19; cf. Col 1:12-14). In this sense the Christian is truly a "work of art" of God, "God's masterpiece."[85]

---

83. See above, note 60.

84. Other texts: Jub 4:26; 1 Hen 72:1; Ap Bar 32:6; 44:12 (cf. 4 Esdr 13:26); 1QH 13:11f.; cf. 1QH 3:19-22; 11:13-14. Meanwhile, Hellenistic Judaism is closer to Paul, as testified in the pseudepigraphal *Joseph and Asaneth;* here Joseph prays to the Lord for his gentile betrothed, Asaneth: "Bless her, give her life, and *renew her* with your Holy Spirit" (8:9); and the angel announces to Asaneth: "Take courage . . . from this day you will be *renewed and re-formed* and re-vivified" (15:4, 5). For rabbinism see P. Stuhlmacher, "Erwägungen zum ontologischen Charakter," 14; W. D. Davies, *Paul and Rabbinic Judaism,* 119–120 (*Gen. R.* 39:4: "If one leads to God and converts a gentile, it is as if one had created that person"; cf. the rule: "The proselyte is like a newborn baby," in Strack-Billerbeck, II:423).

85. See M. Barth, *Ephesians, I,* Anchor Bible 34 (Garden City, N.Y., 1974) 226.

2) *All of you are one in Christ Jesus (community dimension)*

The Pauline theme of "new creation" is not limited to certain members of the Christian community but has general, collective validity. The indefinite pronoun τις of 2 Cor 5:17 opens onto a vast, unlimited horizon.[86] Actually the whole community (actually the whole of the communities: see below) is under the sign of "newness," i.e., of a transforming communion with Christ. See, for example, the language of Eph 5:8 in the plural: "Though you were once darkness, now you are light in the Lord."

The words of the title of this section are taken from Gal 3:26-28, which in brief logical succession presents certain basic realities of the new economy of salvation from an anthropological perspective. This economy is based on faith and baptism (vv. 26-27) and centered on the figure of Christ (whose name occurs four times in vv. 26-28 alone). The passage is enclosed between two very similar expressions that form a strict *inclusio*: "For you all are children of God in Christ Jesus by faith" (v. 26) and "for you all are one in Christ Jesus" (v. 28b). But the obvious parallelism is not so much synonymous as climactic. For "one [Greek: εἷς in the masculine, therefore presumably personal!] in Christ" is not explicable only through *unity of faith*, of which v. 26 speaks, but through *union with Christ*, since we here perceive the resonance of 3:16 (which comments rabbinically on Gen 12:7): "[Scripture] says not, 'and to your offsprings,' as if they were many, but: 'and to your offspring,' that is to one only [Greek: ἐφ᾽ ἑνός], who is Christ."

The clear dialectic tension attested here between the one and the many is resolved by Paul through the assumption of the insertion of the many in the one. The ultimate meaning is not "You, the baptized, are united among yourselves, that is, you form only one thing, if you are in Christ," but rather, "You, the baptized, all together, form only one reality with Christ; you are like one only son in him who is the only Son," i.e., "the oneness of his sonship extends to you, who share therein; he includes you in his sonship, and so with him you become the one true offspring of Abraham" (see the context). Christians, then, are "one" in the one who is "one." The perspective is one of profound participation and communion; it is, properly speaking, "mysterial" (mystical, if you will).[87] Now,

---

86. Perhaps we should note that this pronoun does not substitute for "Christian" (as if it were possible for a Christian not to be "in Christ"!: for Paul this would be a contradiction in terms); rather, it stands simply for "human being" or "natural human creature," who becomes "new" precisely through insertion "in Christ."

87. [See note *a*, after n. 60 above.—T.P.W.] "Baptism marks the point of 'entry into' the person of Christ, an entry which Paul appears to conceive of in genuinely spacial, directional terms," as the preposition εἰς of v. 27 suggests (B. Byrne, *"Sons of God"—"Seed of Abraham." A Study of the Idea of the Sonship of God of All Christians in Paul Against the Jewish Background,*

this reality applies to "all of you," which in this text refers not to a single community but to a totality of Christian groups, since the letter is addressed "to the Churches of Galatia" (1:2). The dimension of this mysterial communion with Christ, then, is clearly communitarian.

Here we must consider the exclusively Pauline theme of the "body of Christ," which so much characterizes Paul's ecclesiology and which is best understood if we consider it in the light of the formula "in Christ" (see above, II.4). In fact, Rom 12:5 reads: "Many though we are, we are one body *in Christ.*" But if in this text the "body" can still be understood as referring to the Christians associated with one another, elsewhere the expression *"of Christ"* is used instead, so that an equation is being made definitively between the Christian community and Christ himself: "For as the body is one but has many members, and all the members, though many, are one body, so it is with Christ" (1 Cor 12:12; cf. 12:13, 27). Here the term of comparison with the human body is not the community but is simply Christ in person, not in his physical body but in his ecclesial body. The comparison is not between Church-body and Christ, but between the (human) body and Christ-Church. So in the last analysis, the expression "body of Christ" means at the same time the community of the baptized and the person of Christ. The two concepts are superimposed.

From this we conclude that the meaning of the expression is not metaphorical but proper and real, so that in 1 Cor 1:13, in a context dealing with the factions in Corinth, Paul asks his addressees whether Christ (not the Church!) is divided. "Baptism . . . consecrates us to one and the same body, the body of Christ with which it identifies us in a mystical way."[88] But it is especially to the "supper of the Lord" (1 Cor 11:20) that

---

Analecta Biblica 83 [Rome, 1979] 169). The image of "putting on Christ" (v. 27) also "has essentially the same meaning as the formula 'being in Christ'; that is, the baptized are surrounded and identified by the being of Christ, they participate in what he is; they are inserted into his state, his mode of being as Son of the Father. . . . Through this identical clothing, all the baptized in Christ constitute the one person, the offspring of Abraham in the spirit, through whom the promise comes true (see v. 16)" (W. Beyer and P. Althaus, in *Die kleinere Briefe des Apostels Paulus*, NTD (Göttingen, 1962 [Italian: 1962]).

88. L. Cerfaux, *La théologie de l'Église suivant Saint Paul* (Paris, 1965³ [Italian: Rome, 1968]) 229, and the more popular English edition, *The Church in the Theology of Saint Paul* (New York, 1959) 270 (note also the more specific treatment of p. 228, n. 2, or 268–269, n. 13). Meanwhile P. Benoit, "Corps, Tête et Plérôme dans les épîtres de la captivité," *Exégèse et théologie* (Paris, 1961 [Italian: 1964]) 112 (= RB 63 [1956] 9), speaks precisely of "a very real, physical union of the Christian to the body of Christ." See also H. Lietzmann, *An die Korinther*, I, II (Tübingen, 1949⁴) 62 (on 12:12): "For Paul this is not just a comparison but a mystic verity"; E. Käsemann, *Leib und Leib Christi* (Tübingen, 1933; p. 159: the theme of the body-organism is only subsidiary with regard to the theme of the Church as Christ's body); Käsemann, "The Theological Problem Presented by the Motif of the Body of Christ," *Perspectives on Paul*, trans. M. Kohl (Philadelphia, 1971 [Italian: 1972]) 149–172 (see p. 151: "To deny that these are assertions of identity affects the whole of Pauline theology"; p. 117: "Pauline ecclesiology is

we can trace the origin and the sense of this Pauline expression, as we read in 1 Cor 10:16b-17: "The bread we break, is it not participation in the body of Christ? Since there is only one bread, we, though many, are one body." It is not a question of two bodies but of one body in two forms.[89] In my opinion, the denial of this sort of identification (which is not confusion) voids the profundity of Paul's discourse on the subject, reducing the relationship between Christ and Church to something purely extrinsic.[90] All this indicates that the foundation of the Church's mysterial nature is not in itself but drawn completely from Christ, and not so much from a Christ considered only as founder-ancestor, as from Christ as present "partner," who actually identifies himself with her and hence is, so to speak, her other face.

This overall view is particularly true of the so-called major Pauline letters. In the letters from prison, on the other hand, the Christological ideas of "head" (Col 1:18; 2:19; Eph 4:15; 5:23) and of "spouse" (see Eph 5:25-32) seem to emphasize a certain separation between Christ and Church, showing the subordination of the latter with regard to the Lord. But while acknowledging that this aspect of the problem has permanent theological value, we must remember Eph 1:23, where the Church is proclaimed the body of Christ with this literal explanation: "the fullness of him who fills every part of it completely," or in other terms, "the fullness of him who in it becomes fully completed." Now actually, this sentence in the original Greek is not so easy to understand and translate.[91]

---

basically Christology," i.e., one belongs to the Church to the extent one belongs to Christ, rather than that one belongs to Christ to the extent one belongs to the Church); H. Conzelmann, *1 Corinthians*, 212: "The body of Christ is preexistent in relation to the 'parts' "; E. Schweizer, art. σῶμα in TDNT 7:1068-1071, distinguishes judiciously between figurative expressions (1 Cor 12:27; Rom 12:5) and proper expressions (1 Cor 10:16; 12:12-13; Gal 3:26-29; note 1070-1071: "The one body of the community is no other than the body of Jesus Christ himself").

89. See L. Cerfaux, *The Theology of the Church*, 263ff.; G. Bornkamm, "Herrenmahl und Kirche bei Paulus," in *Studien zu Antike und Christentum. Gesammelte Aufsätze*, II (Munich, 1963²) 138-177. For other possible origins of the expression "body of Christ," see K. M. Fischer, *Tendenz und Absicht des Epheserbriefes* (Göttingen, 1973) 52-78.

90. But see in this direction R. Schnackenburg, *The Church in the New Testament* (New York, 1965 [Italian: 1973]) 169: " 'Mystical identification' remains disputed. . . . The union . . . is created by the Spirit"; C. K. Barrett, *A Commentary on the First Epistle to the Corinthians* (London, 1971² [Italian: Bologna, 1979]) 287f.; R. H. Gundry, "*Sōma*" in Biblical Theology with Emphasis on Pauline Anthropology (Cambridge, 1976); P. Dacquino, "La Chiesa 'corpo di Cristo,' " RivBibl 29 (1981) 315-330, who refers to the theme of the "corporate personality." Meanwhile, Chr. Senft, *La première épître de Saint Paul aux Corinthiens* (Neuchâtel, 1979) 161, speaks of " 'metaphysical' and 'metaphorical' aspects" combined (but see p. 162: "The Church is not in the first place a sociological phenomenon. . . . The idea of the 'corporative' Christ that would cancel the idea of the essential, 'metaphysical' antecedence of Christ is harmful if it becomes more than a hypothesis—unlikely at that—about the possible origin of the Pauline notion of *sōma Christou*").

91. Besides the commentaries, see I. De La Potterie, "Le Christ, Plérôme de l'Église (Eph 1,22-23)," Bib 58 (1977) 500-524, and the critical observations of R. Penna, "La proiezione

Still, it seems to me that such words allude to a true and proper Christological immanence in the Church, which derives not only its vitality but even its identity from the risen Christ. In Eph 5:28b-29a the love of the husband for the bride, which outside the metaphor is the love of Christ for the Church, is called love for "himself, his own flesh." Evidently between the two poles there is not just distinction, but intertwining and mutual compenetration.[92]

3) "For a deeper understanding of him" (intellectual dimension)

A rich vocabulary concerning knowledge is displayed in the Pauline correspondence (γινώσκειν/γνῶσις, "knowledge . . ."; ἐπιγινώσκειν/ἐπίγνωσις, "understanding . . ."; εἰδέναι, "know, understand . . ."; καταλαμβάνειν, "grasp . . ."; συνίημι/σύνεσις, "understand . . ."; σοφία/σοφός, "wisdom") and to a large extent is used in religious-theological contexts.[93] Of special interest are the passages that deal specifically with the "mystery," i.e., God's plan of salvation; see, for example, Eph 1:8-9: "In all wisdom and intelligence, [God] makes known to us the mystery of his will."[94] The Christian, then, is characterized by a unique patrimony of wisdom. Actually, what is at stake is a progress along the way of perception and a deepening interior grasp of God's will: "May the God of our Lord Jesus Christ, the Father of Glory, give you a spirit of wisdom and revelation for a deeper understanding of him. May he enlighten the eyes of your heart that you may know what is the hope to which he has called you, what the treasure of glory of his inheritance among the saints, and what the extraordinary greatness of his power for us believers" (Eph 1:17-19; see Col 1:9: "We do not cease to pray for you, asking that you may be filled with the knowledge of his will, with all spiritual wisdom and understanding").

These texts raise a question: What is the knowledge here spoken of? And what are its effects? In the *Corpus Hermeticum* we read that "this is

---

dell'esperienza communitaria sul piano storico (Ef 2,11-12) e cosmico (Ef 1:20-23)," RivBibl 26 (1978) 163–186, 177f., n. 28.

92. See R. Penna, *Il "mysterion" paolino*, 70–71. This does not mean that Christ is completely and exclusively in the Church, since he remains greater than it; the term "head" also has—perhaps even primarily has—a universal cosmological import (see Col 2:10; Eph 1:10, 22); and hence Christians, even as a community, cannot claim to reproduce the whole unapproachable stature of Christ. But the inverse of this actually is true: that the Church is completely and exclusively in Christ; if anything were outside Christ, it would be only a dry, dead branch (cf. John 15:6). Hence, though Christ's identity subsists even without the Church, the Church finds its living identity only in Christ.

93. See J. Dupont, *Gnôsis. La connaissance religieuse dans les epîtres de Saint Paul* (Louvain, 1949); H. Conzelmann, "Paulus und die Weisheit," NTS 12 (1965–66) 231–244.

94. See R. Penna, *Il "mysterion" paolino*, 39–45; on what constitutes this "mystery," see ibid., 51–85.

the excellent goal of those who have obtained knowledge [γνῶσιν]: to be divinized [θεωθῆναι]" (I:26). And the Gnostic *Gospel of Philip*, found among the Nag-Hammadi manuscripts (= NHC II), declares: "You have seen the Spirit and have become Spirit. You have seen Christ and have become Christ. You have seen the Father, and will become the Father" (61:29-31); and again: "Such a one is no longer a Christian but a Christ" (67:26-27). It is evident that in these texts the knowledge/vision tends to a literal identification with the divine, especially with Christ.[95] Should Paul be read in this strictly mystical sense?

Despite its abundance, the "gnostic" (or better, the "gnoseological") vocabulary of Paul is not put at the service of any divinization and certainly not effected through the exercise of the human intellect. For two reasons. In the first place, knowledge is requested in prayer and is thus understood as grace;[96] that is, the decisive element is not knowledge of self but divine revelation. Cf. 1 Cor 2:11b: "No one has understood the secrets of God except the Spirit of God." It is like saying that like is known only by like, after an ancient and generally accepted gnoseological principle, attested variously: at Qumran (see 1QH 12:11-12: "I know you, my God, in virtue of the Spirit you have placed in me"); in Philo of Alexandria (see *Praem. poen.* 46: "they are on the way of truth who perceive God through God, and light through light"); in the *Corpus Hermeticum* (XI:20: "Unless you become equal to God you cannot understand God: for like is comprehensible only to like [τὸ γὰρ ὅμοιον τῷ ὁμοίῳ νοητόν]").

In the second place, in Colossians and Ephesians the object of knowledge is not the divine in general (much less the divine in itself) but "his will" (Col 1:9) and "him" (Eph 1:17; specified not by his nature but by his salvific interventions, specifically the resurrection of Christ). The cultural background, then, appears in the Old Testament (Hos 6:6; Isa 1:3; 11:9; Hab 2:14) and at Qumran (see 1QH 12:12-13; 13:18-19; 14:25), where knowledge fundamentally consists in perceiving the saving plan of God

---

95. On these Nag-Hammadi Gnostic texts, see E. Pagels, "Gnosis: Self-Knowledge as Knowledge of God," in *The Gnostic Gospels* (New York, 1979 [Italian: 1981]) 119-141. Particularly, there we can distinguish three central issues (for texts see *Nag Hammadi Library* [Leiden, 1988]): emphasis on ignorance as the basic evil: see *Gospel of Truth* 17:10-16; 29:8-30:12; 24:32-25:3; *Dialogue of the Savior* 134:1-22; the necessity of knowing oneself as indispensable means of liberation: see *Teachings of Sylvanus* 106:30-117:20; *Gospel of Truth* 21:11-22; 15; 32:31-33:14; *Gospel of Thomas* 32:19-33:15; the perception of the supreme knowledge as silence, light, and beatitude: see *Discourse on the Eighth and the Ninth* 57:31-58:22; *Allogenos* 52:15-21; 59:9-37.

96. G. MacRae, "Prayer and Knowledge of Self in Gnosticism," *Tantur Yearbook* (Jerusalem, 1978-79) 97-114, very opportunely distinguishes in Gnostic texts between a prayer of petition for light and a prayer of simple praise proper to a mystical experience; the former, according to MacRae is characteristic of Christian Gnostic texts, the latter of non-Christian texts.

through faith and accomplishing God's will concretely.[97] This is also essentially true of 1 Cor 2, which speaks of the "wisdom in the mystery" (v. 7) and of the Spirit who "searches . . . the depths of God" (v. 10): a fair exegesis of this section leads one to identify the former with the divine plan of salvation centered on Christ crucified (note vv. 2, 8), the latter with the "gifts" (v. 12) of salvation, which one receives from those depths.[98] It is precisely in this direction that the Christian is called to direct the "eyes of the heart" (Eph 1:18; cf. 1QS 2:3: "May he bless you . . . and enlighten your heart").

4) *"To walk in a new life" (ethical dimension)*

In Gal 5:25 Paul proposes a perfectly explicit axiom: "If we live by the Spirit, let us also walk in the Spirit." Now, in the Pauline letters the verb περιπατέω always has only a figurative value, i.e., it indicates ethical behavior, a style of life (see 8:4; 2 Cor 4:2; Phil 3:18; 1 Thess 4:1). We do well to note that it takes the second place, after the affirmation of life in the Spirit (Gal 5:25: "If we live . . . let us walk . . .") or after the evocation of death with Christ in baptism (Rom 6:4; cf. Rom 7:4: "Having *died* to what kept us prisoners, in order to serve in newness of Spirit").

Christian moral life presupposes and derives everything from the basic reality of being "in Christ" and "in the Spirit." Indeed, it is a manifestation of these realities, and more than that, a necessity. We might say in a simple slogan that for Paul mysticism is the basis of the ethic, or, more precisely, that mysticism should be the basis of the ethic, which means that the latter has a secondary value with respect to the former; but still that its role is not accessory but rather essential—though derived. This is also expressed and confirmed by the typical, well-known Pauline procedure of the relationship between indicative and imperative (e.g., 1 Cor 5:7: "*Clean out* the old leaven, since you *are unleavened*"), an antinomy that is resolved only by recognizing that the kerygmatic indicative is pri-

---

97. See S. Lyonnet, "Saint Paul et le gnosticisme. L'épître aux Colossiens," in *Le origine dello gnosticismo*, ed. U. Bianchi (Leiden, 1967) 538–551, esp. 539–541; especially see B. Antonini, "La conoscenza della volontà di Dio in Col. 1,9b," in *La cristologia in San Paolo*. Atti della XXIII Settimana Biblica dell'Associazione Biblica Italiana (Brescia, 1976) 301–340. See also F. Garcia Bazan, "San Pablo y el problema de la gnosis," *Revista Bíblica* 41 (1979) 109–128.

98. It is significant that U. Wilckens, after having first maintained the Gnostic background of the section *(Weisheit und Torheit. Eine exegetisch-religionsgeschichtliche Untersuchung zu 1. Kor 1 und 2* [Tübingen, 1959]), later completely modified his position: "Das Kreuz Christi als die Tiefe der Weisheit Gottes. Zu 1. Kor 2,1-16," in *Paolo a una Chiesa divisa (1 Cor 1-4)*, ed. L. De Lorenzi (Rome, 1980) 43–81, esp. 68ff. For a critical comparison with Philo of Alexandria see above, chap. 28 (Preliminaries, 1).

mary, and that from it derives the paraenetic imperative.[99] Essentially Paul means, "Become what you already are in Christ!"

Hence it is evident that here Paul's "mystical" discourse does not really detract from ethical obligation, nor does it propose some sort of flight or quietism, much less a condemnation of the world, of humanity, of the body, for the sake of a Platonizing or Gnosticizing dualism.[100] Pauline mystical doctrine rather leads to daily life and calls for love, in which is summed up every other commandment (see Rom 13:8-10).

But it has been rightly said that for Paul "ethics are just as natural a resultant phenomenon of the dying and rising again with Christ as is liberation from the flesh, sin, the law, or the bestowal of the Spirit."[101] Even so, it is not true that he associates ethic "only with the mystical being-in-Christ" and "never . . . [with] the righteousness by faith."[102] For Gal 5:6 is clear enough: "In Christ, what counts is . . . faith working through love"; and I know no better explanation than that which sees the root and precondition for love and for the fruits of the Spirit precisely in faith,[103] just as faith is the basis for the grace of being in Christ (Rom 5:2). And finally, in 2 Cor 5:7 we read, "We walk by faith, and not yet by vision," and precisely in this condition "we strive to be pleasing to him" (5:9).

A very specific topic of Pauline ethic concerns the experience of pain, especially the apostolic sufferings. Paul writes of it in an absolutely "mystical" perspective, i.e., one of intimate participation in Christ, even speak-

99. See J. Murphy-O'Connor, "The Contemporary Value of Pauline Moral Imperatives," *Doctrine and Life* 21 (1971) 3–16 (see also his *L'existence chrétienne selon Saint Paul*, Lectio Divina 80 [Paris, 1974] 103–114); M. Adinolfi, "La dialettica indicativo-imperativo nelle lettere paoline," *Antonianum* 52 (1977) 626–646; W. D. Dennison, "Indicative and Imperative: The Basic Structure of Pauline Ethics," *Calvin Theological Journal* 14 (1979) 55–78; L. Alvarez Verdes, *El imperativo cristiano en San Pablo. La tensión indicativo-imperativo en Rom 6. Análisis estructural* (Rome, 1980).

100. It is important to remain aware that the exhortation of Col 3:1, "Seek the things that are above," is an invitation not to flight (as in Philo, *Spec. leg.* I:207) but to the vivification of the present historical life with an ethic, the very specific negative (vv. 5ff.) and positive (10ff.) prescriptions of which follow immediately. Meanwhile, it is through this same letter that we learn of the existence of the so-called "Colossian heresy" with its ascetical coloring of Platonic and neo-Pythagorean character (see E. Schweizer, 103–104; English: *The Letter to the Colossians*, (Minneapolis, 1982) 131–133.

101. A. Schweitzer, *The Mysticism*, 225.

102. Ibid., 294.

103. Meanwhile E. P. Sanders, *Paul and Palestinian Judaism*, 439–441 and n. 48, while not accepting precisely the position of A. Schweitzer (objecting that Schweitzer fails to perceive the internal connection between the terminology of justification through faith and that of life in Christ and in the Spirit, which according to Sanders coincide, though with the participationist categories taking the first place), refuses to ascribe to justification by faith the role of entryway into the new life (506–507; see above II.2). The recent interesting work of J.-F. Collange, *De Jésus à Paul. L'éthique du Nouveau Testament* (Geneva, 1980) places faith among the "ethical forces" (after freedom and love) but is vague about both the problematic aspect of its real relation to ethic and the question of the "mystical" foundation of ethic itself.

ing of "Christ's sufferings in us" (2 Cor 1:5), of "suffering together with" him (Rom 8:17), and of "always and everywhere carrying the death of Christ in our bodies" (2 Cor 4:10). Paul's language on this existential level is just as explicit as on the sacramental level, a clear sign that there is no real break of continuity here.[104]

5) "We will always be with the Lord" (eschatological dimension)

If, as we have seen (II.4 above), the formula "in Christ" is more or less the synthesis of Paul's Christian mysticism in referring to the present historical life of the baptized, the formula "with Christ" (also typical of and even exclusive to the Apostle) embraces the two different aspects, historical and eschatological, of Christian life. For communion with the death of Christ (see Rom 6:4, 5, 6, 8; Gal 2:19; Col 2:20) will be followed by participation in his resurrection and his glory (see Rom 6:5, 8; 2 Cor 4:14; 13:4; Col 3:4; 1 Thess 4:14; 5:10). The same eschatological life is described as "to be always with the Lord" (1 Thess 4:17) or "to be with Christ" (Phil 1:23). It is God who calls us to "communion with his Son Jesus Christ, our Lord (1 Cor 1:9; see Rom 14:9)."[105]

Let us not here ask whether such communion follows only upon the parousia or already on individual death.[106] What is important is to note and emphasize that the "new creation," strictly speaking, is not mortal, since it is the divine spirit that vivifies it: "It is God who has destined us for this, who gave us the down payment of the Spirit" (2 Cor 5:5). So that "even if our outer person is disintegrating, our inner one is renewed day after day" (4:16). With life "in Christ" and "in the Spirit" there begins something that is never to cease—a dynamic process of transformation (see 2 Cor 3:18; 1 Cor 15:51; Phil 3:20), which can be disrupted only by rejecting the saving lordship of Christ, but not by death. To maintain the op-

104. The question, then, as in baptism, is of *daily* dying and rising with Christ, as N. Baumert appropriately entitles his study, *Täglich sterben und auferstehen. Der Literalsinn von 2. Kor 4:12–5:10* (Munich, 1973). On the subject see also E. Güttgemanns, *Der leidende Apostel und sein Herr* (Göttingen, 1966); R. Penna, "Sofferenza e salvezza come participazione al mistero pasquale nella Seconda Lettera ai Corinzi," in the collection *Sofferenza e salvezza* (Rome, 1981) 75–89; M. D. Hooker, "Interchange and Suffering," in *Suffering and Martyrdom. Studies Presented to G. M. Styler*, ed. W. Horbury and B. McNeil (Cambridge, 1981) 70–83.

105. See J. Dupont, *"Syn Christôi." L'union avec le Christ suivant St. Paul* (Bruges, 1952); P. Siber, *Mit Christus leben. Eine Studie zur paulinischen Auferstehungs-hoffnung* (Zurich, 1971); E. Schweizer, loc. cit. (see above, n. 21).

106. The question is complex. Probably even Paul's thought knew an evolution on the issue (see P. Benoît, "L'évolution du langage dans le Corpus paulinien," in the collection *Apocalypses et théologie de l'espérance* [Paris, 1977] 299–335). The Pauline texts most favorable to an individual intermediate eschatology are two: Phil 1:23 and 2 Cor 5:1-10; for the former we refer to the commentaries.

posite would mean making death a power greater than God's power. But Paul is explicit: death "cannot separate us from the love of God in Christ Jesus our Lord" (Rom 8:38-39). This is the "good hope" (2 Thess 2:16) given to the Christian.

Thus the life of the baptized is characterized not only by the vertical dimension of an actual communion with Christ, which, if this were all, could promote the Corinthian "enthusiasm" of an already realized eschatology; it has the horizontal dimension of a forward impulse toward a future completion. "We are saved in hope . . . . But if we hope for what we do not see, we await it with perseverance" (Rom 8:24, 25; see Gal 5:5; Eph 1:18).[107] And it is precisely this that is the principal watershed separating all biblical mysticism from the general pagan mysticism.

The final goal, realized with the final coming of Christ, is that "God be all in all" (1 Cor 15:28). This is "a phrase which in itself has a mystical sound"[108] and plausibly could be based on pantheistic Greek terminology, describing or celebrating the cosmic Deity under the viewpoint of macro-human being.[109] Now, similar language is found in the Bible (see Sir 43:27; Wis 12:1; Zech 14:9; Acts 17:28) and even in the Pauline correspondence (1 Cor 12:6; Col 3:11; Eph 1:23). But the context suggests no identification between God and the cosmos; rather it envisages a divine lordship exercised totally and directly; "It is the state of things God had in mind in raising Christ up again."[110] It is just this diffuse, undisputed, and intimate presence of God in things and in human persons that brings to consummation that communion already begun in history, which belongs to him by right and which confers on us "the stature of the com-

107. It would be useful also to develop the theme of a participation of the Cosmos itself in the "freedom of the Children of God" (Rom 8:21), to note that Christian life also preserves a dimension oriented toward nature, and is always integrated in creation. Hope also involves the world. And that means that there cannot exist a mysticism so myopic as to be reduced merely to interpersonal relations, leaving out of its perspective the great cosmic context in which it is inserted (cf. St. Francis of Assisi's "Canticle of the Creatures"). On Rom 8:18ff., we refer to the commentaries, esp. O. Kuss, E. Käsemann, H. Schlier, U. Wilckens; see also S. Lyonnet, "Redemptio cosmica secundum Rom 8,19-23," *Verbum Domini* 44 (1966) 225–242; J. G. Gibbs, "The Cosmic Scope of Redemption According to Paul," Bib 56 (1975) 13–29.

108. H. Conzelmann, *1 Corinthians*, 275. We do not accept the version of the Italian Episcopal Conference [and RSV 1971] "that God may be everything in [to] everyone," for the neuter rather than the masculine seems to be understood by the phrase en pâsin (thus most of the commentators).

109. See, e.g., *Orphic hymns*, frag. 167, 168, 169 (= Zeus is the only divine form in which all things are encompassed); Musaeus: "All things are generated by the one, and in the one all things dissolve again" (in *Diogenes Laertius* I:3); Magic Papyrus V: "The sun and the moon are his eyes, his cape is the sky, his body the ether, his feet the earth. . . . You are the Lord who generates all, nourishes them and causes them to grow" (see also Macrobius, *Saturn.* I:20:11, 17.)

110. Chr. Senft, *La première épître*, 200.

pleted person, in the measure corresponding to the full maturity of Christ" (Eph 4:13).

IV. Conclusion

At the end of this chapter we must again emphasize a basic distinction concerning the idea of mysticism in Paul that always excludes its pagan Hellenistic sense.[111] If by "mysticism" we mean merely extraordinary ecstatic phenomena, we can hardly deny that Paul was the beneficiary of such (see 2 Cor 12:1-4 and 1 Cor 14:18). But he absolutely does not base his own theological thought on such experiences, which he even slights and clearly tends to minimize (see above, I.2). But if by "mysticism" we mean a knowledge of and communion with God that is out of the ordinary, then his letters are full of it. But in this case the "not ordinary" means "not natural," in the sense of 1 Cor 2:14: "The unspiritual person does not recognize what belongs to God's Spirit." But what belongs to the Spirit of God becomes "ordinary" and "natural" for the Christian. For those whom Paul calls "perfect" or "pneumatic" (1 Cor 2:6, 15), though these are not in fact all the baptized, certainly represent the normal stage that these should reach, or better, that they should make explicit in their life, since "we [Paul and his addressees] have received not the spirit of the world but the Spirit of God to know all that God has given us" (1 Cor 2:12). And the whole understanding of the world's transformation "is nothing other than the eschatological conception of redemption looked at from within,"[112] i.e., a salvation already realized and experienced as prolepsis of the future, so that the whole of Christian life is signed with grace: with reference to the past, *a parte post,* with the salvific event of the death and resurrection of Jesus; with reference to the future, *a parte ante,* with the promise of an ultimately assured inheritance. The existence of the baptized, located between these two poles, is mystical precisely in the measure in which it participates in, i.e., is based and is nurtured on, "what God has given us" (1 Cor 2:12), and allows all the innate virtuali-

---

111. See notes 3 and 4 above. It would also be interesting to set up a comparison in the Pauline letters between two formulas of movement aimed at God: εἰς αὐτόν ("into him"; six times) and πρὸς τὸν θεόν ("to him" or "toward him" or "before him"; thirteen times). In the New Testament both can be considered characteristic of Paul. But while the former is of Hellenistic-Stoic derivation (since there are no precedents in the LXX Bible) and carries the idea of dissolution in the Deity, the later, more frequent phrase rather provides a kind of corrective. Drawn from euchological and cultic contexts of the Old Testament, it maintains the distinction between the two personal terms (human person and God) with the sense of "turn, approach, present oneself, appear before"; and to this is related the exclusively Pauline noun *prosagôgê,* "access." Generally, see chapter 28 above.

112. A. Schweitzer, *The Mysticism,* 112.

ties to come to fruit: "That I may know him, the power of his resurrection, participation in his sufferings, becoming conformed to him in his death, in hope of arriving at resurrection from the dead" (Phil 3:10-11).

There is no doubt that this condition constantly typified Paul in person. But it is above all evident in his writings that he thus taught, and that he wished his Christians so to be: "to share in the inheritance of the saints in light" (Col 1:12).

In all this, the figure of Christ is absolutely determinative. The mystical relationship does not just run directly from the human person to God and from God to the person. It inevitably passes through Jesus Christ and his Spirit. This is a qualifying mediation, which makes explicitly Christian an experience that would otherwise be only Jewish or pagan. "To be conformed to the image of his Son" (Rom 8:29) is at once the reality and the goal of Christian life. And to say that the life of the baptized is of mystical character is almost redundant, since it is such by its nature. But its relation to Christ is essential, not only to avoid falling into some other, alienating participatory relationship (to the Law, sin, the flesh) but also to perceive the concrete, human, essential, yes the agapic character of this relationship. For Christ is—if for Paul not so much the incarnate Son of God—the Crucified Son of God, the basis of the exhortation "Accept one another as Christ has accepted you" (Rom 15:7). Pauline and Christian mysticism does not indicate a spiritual aristocracy in the Church, a kind of half idealistic, half prideful apartheid. Ultimately it has nothing to do with the (Platonic, Stoic, Gnostic, Neoplatonic) abstraction from the human world because of devaluation or simply indifference.[113] Nor can it prescind from ἀγάπη, which is its origin and essence, and which reveals it: "Even if I knew all mysteries . . . but have not love, I am nothing" (1 Cor 13:2). And ἀγάπη means to be-with-and-for-others.

In all this, the case of Jesus provides the paradigm, according to the hymnic passage of Phil 2:6-11: the condition of the servant obedient to the death of the cross is not just a presumably accessory point of passage between the two highpoints of preexistence with God and exaltation as the Risen One. The basic outline of the hymn is not Neoplatonic (from the One to the many, then returning to the One) but Christian-apocalyptic (the Son of Man comes on the clouds of heaven, experiences death and then resurrection). The final state is not that of a return but of a new acquisition for humanity, since the Deity had already acquired the human condition through emptying of self, through κένωσις. And the intermedi-

---

113. Thus the desire to "be released and be with Christ" (Phil 1:23) is overcome by the awareness of having to remain in his obligatory relations: "however, it is more necessary for you that I remain in the flesh" (Phil 1:24).

ate stage is absolutely essential, so that it is presented as the condition, and therefore the cause (v. 9: διὸ = "therefore") of what succeeds it. But the dialectic remains: the Son, while not losing what he is, becomes what he was not (cf. 2 Cor 8:9). In short, union with God can never be an obstacle to communion with human beings, indeed it requires it, as if to say that Christian *being* precedes and also demands *doing*. And finally, the context of the hymn in the epistle is paraenetic, and its introduction reads thus: "Have this mind in you, which is also in Christ Jesus" (Phil 2:5).[114]

What is important for the Christian, then, is that one undertake the search for oneself, to discover in one's depths one's own received identity, to marvel thereat and joyfully to give thanks to God, who makes it possible for one to live in "the breadth and the length and the height and the depth" (Eph 3:18) of a space that is truly unlimited, for God has created it with "the surpassing lavishness of his grace through his goodness toward us in Jesus Christ" (Eph 2:7).

114. Besides the commentaries (esp. J. Gnilka, *Der Epheserbrief* [Freiburg, 1971] ad loc.), see especially J. Heriban, *Retto φρονεῖν* e *κένωσις. Studio esegetico su Fil 2,1-5.6-11*, Biblioteca di Scienze Religiose 51 (Rome, 1983); and for a theological perspective: L. Iammarrone, "La teoria chenotica e il testo di Phil 2,6-7," *Divus Thomas* 82 (1979) 341–373.

Chapter 30

The "'Visio Pauli'' and the Apocalyptic Ascents of the *Divine Comedy*

In Canto II of the "Inferno," Dante Alighieri, to express his unworthiness and his fear to undertake the journey through the lands of the afterlife, compares himself with those who had gone before him. Correctly he completely ignores the evocation of the dead by Ulysses in Book XI of the *Odyssey*, since that is something completely different.[1] But neither does he refer to the journey of Muhammad to both paradise and hell, which is narrated in the Arabic work called *al Mi'rag* (*The Ascension*, or *The Book of the Ladder*, which in Dante's days already existed in Castilian, French, and Latin versions).[2]

In fact, the poet mentions only two precedents: that of Aeneas, who though "still corruptible, passed to the immortal world with his senses" (vv. 13-15), and then that of Paul in vv. 28-30:

Later the Chosen Vessel travelled there.
to bring us back assurance of that faith
with which the way of our salvation starts.[a]

1. The *nekuia* is no journey: Ulysses does not go to the dead, but the dead come to him. Furthermore, he is alone, without a guide (having only received instructions from Circe: *Od.* X 468–539). Finally, the Beyond consists of only one subterranean, lugubrious place, Hades (note XI 94); see below.

2. See the edition of the French and Latin text with various added studies, E. Cerulli, ed., *Il "Libro della Scala" e la questione delle fonti arabo-spagnole della Divina Commedia*, Studi e Testi 150 (Città del Vaticano, 1949; photoreprint 1974); idem, *Nuove ricerche sul Libro della Scala*, Studi e Testi 271 (Città del Vaticano, 1972). See also C. Kappler et al., *Apocalypses et voyages dans l'au-delà* (Paris: Cerf, 1987) 267–320.

a. The texts from Dante are quoted from *The Divine Comedy of Dante Alighieri*, trans. Allen Mandelbaum (New York: Bantam Books, 1982–86: originally published by the University of California Press, 1980–84)—T.P.W., translator.

I will not here deal with the reference to Aeneas, which refers to Virgil's *Aeneid* VI 236–899. Rather, I consider the mention of Saint Paul (identified by a title derived from Acts 9:15), asking: To what literary text is Dante alluding as the ultimate source of his discourse? We think at once of Second Corinthians, where Paul writes of himself in the third person: "I know a person in Christ, who fourteen years ago . . . was taken up to the third heaven; and I know that this person, whether in the body or out of the body, I know not, God knows, was taken up into Paradise and heard unutterable words, which no one may speak" (12:2-4). Now this passage may reverberate in Canto I of the *Paradiso*, where Dante writes:

> I was within the heaven that receives
> more of his light; and I saw things that he
> who from that height descends, forgets or can
>   not speak. (4-6)

However, the Pauline text speaks only of a "third heaven" and of "paradise," i.e., the place of the blessed, but does not so much as mention a purgatory, much less a hell, whereas Dante uses the reference to Paul as a preface to the whole *Comedy*, as though he had also visited the other places of ultra-terrestrial retribution.

So Dante must presuppose another source.

I. Actually, as has long been recognized,[3] Dante must have been using not a canonical book but an apocryphal work known as the *Apocalypse of Paul* (or the *Vision of Paul*), already known in the third century to the great Alexandrian Origen (and thus *not* the document of Gnostic character found recently among the manuscripts of Nag-Hammadi). It is hard to say whether Dante used it directly (and if so, in which version, since the text has reached us in codices written in some fifteen languages)[4] or through the mediation of other medieval authors.

In any case, a dependence is sufficiently verifiable, as certain examples will show. In the first ring of the seventh circle of Hell, Dante places those

---

3. It would seem that the first to propose a dependence of Dante on the *Apocalypse of Paul* was A.-F. Ozanam, *Dante et la philosophie catholique au treizième siècle* (Paris, 1845) 345; [this seems to be missing from the English edition, *Dante and Catholic Philosophy in the Thirteenth Century* (New York, 1913), which omitted a final section on sources].

4. For a presentation (introduction, Italian translation, and notes), see M. Erbetta, *Gli Apocrifi del Nuovo Testamento*, III (Turin: Marietti, 1969) 353–386, on which the following translation is based. The major study of this work remains that of Th. Silverstein, *Visio Sancti Pauli: The History of the Apocalypse in Latin together with Nine Texts*, Studies and Documents IV (London, 1935); see also G. Riccioti, *L'Apocalisse di Paolo siriaca*, I–II (Brescia: Morcelliana, 1932; on the relations to Dante, I 27–31), and C. Kappler et al., *Apocalypses et voyages*, 237–266.

who are violent against others, set in boiling oil to various levels, depending on the gravity of their sins (*Inf.* XII).

> Now, with our faithful escort, we advanced
> along the bloodred, boiling ditch's banks,
> beside the piercing cries of those who boiled.
> I saw some who were sunk up to their brows. (100-103)

> A little farther on, the Centaur stopped
> above a group that seemed to rise above
> this boiling blood as far up as their throats. (vv. 115-117)

> Then I caught sight of some who kept their heads
> and even their full chests above the tide. (121-122)

> And so the blood grew always shallower
> until it only scorched the feet. (124-125)

Now in paragraph 31 of the *Apocalypse of Paul*, the Apostle, who describes himself as being led beyond the ocean, where "there was no light . . . only darkness, mourning, and sorrow," states: "There I saw a river of fire burning strongly. There were a great many men and women, sunk to the knees, others to the navel, still others to the lips and to the hair"; but when he again enumerates each category of the damned, he refers to the last as "those in it up to the eyebrows."[5]

Here the Dantean imitation is even literal: "I saw some who were sunk up to their brows" (*Inf.* XII 103), not to mention the same outline treating four levels of immersion—and in an analogous boiling liquid (fire for the *Apocalypse*, blood for Dante.)

But besides these material details, we should also find in this same passage of the apocryphal *Apocalypse* a theme which is formulated there in a perfectly clear manner and which is essentially realized in Dante's *Commedia*. This is the law of equivalent retribution, by which every sin receives a punishment in the afterlife exactly corresponding to its gravity. This is illustrated precisely here in the commensurate immersion of the body in the boiling swamp or in chapter 31 of this *Apocalypse* (which, in chapter 35 offers the example of a bishop who is immersed to the knees and "who now receives the recompense according to his wickedness and his actions") as well as in Canto XII of the *Inferno*, which is a kind of paradigm for all three of Dante's books.

---

5. The Latin text, edited by M. R. James, *Apocrypha Anecdota. A Collection of Thirteen Apocryphal Books and Fragments* (Cambridge, 1983) 1–42, renders: "usque ad superlicia [= supercilia] vero dimersi sunt qui innuunt sibi, malignitatem insidiantur proximo suo."

For the just also, our apocryphon, which interestingly places the vision of the just before that of the wicked (in chapters 19–30; and the same order is found in the *Book of the Ladder*), measures the recompense according to a tripartite heavenly geography: the paradise of the "Third Heaven" (in reference to 2 Cor 12:2); the "Promised Land" (a preliminary sketch of Purgatory, since the souls of the just are sent there temporarily); and the "City of Christ" (in which there are distinguished seven further areas).[6] And a further parallel can be drawn between our *Apocalypse*, where the first stage of the City of Christ contains "all who have afflicted their souls, and for love of God have not done their own will, separating themselves from the world" (chap. 25), and Canto III of Dante's *Paradiso*, where the monastic woman Piccarda Donati cries:

> Brother, the power of love appeases our
> will so—we only long for what we have;
> we do not thirst for greater blessedness. . . .

> And in his will there is our peace. (vv. 70-72, 85)

Finally, we note that even the famous tercet on the vision of earth from the heights of heaven,

> . . . The little threshing floor
>   that so incites our savagery was all—
> from hills to river mouths—revealed to me
> while I wheeled with eternal gemini. (XXII 151-153)

has a parallel in the *Apocalypse of Paul*: "I looked down on the earth from heaven and observed the whole earth; it seemed to me like nothing to the sight. . . . I marveled, and said to the angel, 'Is this what human greatness is?' The angel replied, 'That it is. And these are they who do evil from morning to night' " (chap. 13).[7]

II. But the comparison of the *Visio Pauli* raises the more general issue of the various apocalyptic forerunners of the *Divina Commedia*. Even the *Apocalypse of Paul* is largely indebted to an *Apocalypse of Peter* of about one century earlier, and already placed by the Muratorian canon (of the sec-

---

6. I.e., a river of honey (for the prophets, who have given up their own will); a river of milk (for infants and for the chaste); a river of wine (for those who give hospitality to strangers); a river of oil (for those without pride); a place of twelve great walls (where "one surpasses the other in glory"); the golden thrones (for the monks: "Without knowing scripture or many psalms, they are mindful only of the chapter of the commandments of God"); and finally a towering altar (beside which David "with psaltery and harp chanted praise, singing 'halleluia!' ").

7. See the similar subject treated by Lucian of Samosata *Icaromenippus*, esp. par. 18.

ond half of the second century) on exactly the same level of dignity as the more famous *Apocalypse of John*. But the *Apocalypse of Peter* is distinguished from that of Paul by its delay of recompense completely till the end of time, and by a detailed descriptive list of nineteen types of sinners, with their relative torments (in chaps. 7–12 of the Ethiopic text), with nothing similar done for the blessed (presumably finding it more fun to relate the torments of the dead than their joys). And what Dante wrote in Canto XXXI of the *Paradiso* about the "rose" of the blessed,

> Their faces were all living flame; their wings
> were gold, and for the rest, their white was so
> intense, no snow can match the white they showed (vv. 13-15),

is actually anticipated in the *Apocalypse of Peter*, where the blessed are described: "When we saw them we were astonished: their bodies were whiter than snow ever was, and redder than any rose" (Akhmîm fragment 8). But if we note that these words reflect an earlier Jewish apocalypse known under the name of *Ethiopian Henoch* (106:10-11: the work is named after the language of the only known text, which was translated from a Semitic original), then we realize that the *Divina Commedia* stands at the end of a long process of development, both literary and thematic.

In putting Dante's *Commedia* in the category of apocalyptic I am well aware of the limitations of such an enterprise. The very concept of "apocalyptic" is disputed among scholars because of the difficulty in identifying a criteriology that would let us make some kind of homogeneous grouping of a literature that is so vast in numbers, so disparate in contents and expository techniques as well.[8] For example, a fundamental quality in classical apocalyptic is pessimism about concrete history, and hence the "absolute 'no' . . . to this world-age,"[9] tempered only by the expectation of a total eschatological reversal. This seems foreign to the *Commedia*, where Dante is simply transferring personages, events, judgments, and monumental historical pictures of all sorts into the afterlife, and this not only in the *Inferno* but in the *Purgatorio* and most important the *Paradiso* (we need only think of Canto VI in each book).

Further, while classical apocalyptic presents an eschatology that involves universal history and the whole cosmos in a catastrophe (whence

---

8. See, for example, K. Koch, *The Rediscovery of Apocalyptic*, trans. M. Kohl (London, 1972 [Italian: 1977]); P. Sacchi, "Jewish Apocalyptic," SIDIC 18 (1985, 3) 4–9; idem, *L'apocalittica giudaica e la sua storia*, BCR 55 (Brescia, 1990).

9. W. Schmithals, *The Apocalyptic Movement: Introduction and Interpretation* (Nashville, 1975 [Italian: 1976]) 45; on the concept of the "two aeons" see Schmithals 20ff., and D. S. Russell, *The Method and Message of Jewish Apocalyptic* (Philadelphia, 1964) 266ff.

arises the rather restricted popular concept of "apocalypse"), Dante tends essentially to limit himself to the personal destiny of individual persons.

But conceding this, we still should recognize how much Dante's master-work, rather than depending on precisely identifiable written sources, is debtor to a whole tradition that even antedates Christianity, since it had its origins and principal development in the Judaism preceding the present era. Here we intend only to cite limited evidence regarding certain elements, with no intention to treat exhaustively an issue that calls for further research.

First, we recall the propensity of apocalyptic to include various bizarre representatives of the animal kingdom, often with a symbolic dimension. Consider, for instance, the Lamb, the dragon, and the four horses of the Johannine *Apocalypse*. Dante is less flamboyant in this. But Canto I of the *Inferno* describes three animals ("a leopard," v. 32; "a lion," v. 45; "a she-wolf," v. 49) blocking the poet's way as we read in the apocalyptic *Slavic Henoch or Book of the Secrets of Henoch* (first century B.C.): "I saw the guardians of the key of hell, standing before the gates, like great serpents, with faces like smoldering lamps, with eyes like faintly glowing fire, and with teeth bared to the breast" (42:1 B). Though these animals are of a different genus, their function as an obstacle is analogous.

Second, we mention the role of guide exercised by an angelic companion in the journey beyond the grave. Studies of apocalyptic speak of the interpreting angel, the *angelus interpres*, who from time to time explains the meaning of the visions or encounters to the beneficiary of the journey (thus we have the Archangel Gabriel in the *Book of the Ladder*). It is true that a similar function is assigned in the *Aeneid*, Book 4, by the Cuman Sybil and by Anchises, father of Aeneas. And Dante's picture of Virgil and then of Beatrice follows the same direction of humanizing the guide to the afterlife. Nevertheless, their presence is so emphatic and so systematic that they recall the constant appearance of a heavenly emissary throughout apocalyptic literature who could well be described in Dante's words to Virgil, "O guide, master, teacher" (*Inf.* II 140); and furthermore, the picture of Beatrice is thoroughly angelic, as an authentic messenger of the divine world, already when she first appears to Dante in Canto II of the *Inferno:*

> For I am Beatrice, who send you on;
> I come from where I most long to return;
> love prompted me, that love which makes me speak (70-72);

as well as when she is revealed to Dante in *Purgatorio* Canto XXX, "within a cloud of flowers" (v. 28) and "her dress . . . flame red" (v. 33). Moreover, just as in the Johannine Apocalypse a heavenly voice indicates to the seer, "What you see, write in a book and send it to the seven Churches" (1:11), so Beatrice invites Dante:

". . . and thus, to profit that world which
lives badly, watch the Chariot steadfastly
and, when you have returned beyond, transcribe
    what you have seen" (*Purg.* XXXII 103-105).

But there is a final, profoundly fundamental aspect to which I should like to attract attention. It concerns the "blessed people" (*Inf.* I 120), and the subject is the subterranean place of the just. Virgil's Aeneas as well as Homer's Ulysses encounter both the blessed and sinners in a completely subterranean afterlife. What Virgil wrote in the *Aeneid* VII 267, "things sunk in the deep earth and darkness," is equally true of Tartarus and the Elysian Fields. It is obvious that the Latin poet did not yet know that Copernican revolution concerning the geography beyond the tomb that transferred the dwelling of the just to Heaven, separating it from the primitive common location in the lower regions. In fact, such a differentiation is already attested in the ancient Indian books of the *Upanishad* (eighth century before Christ) and at least in one pre-Zoroastrian Persian literary work.[10]

But for Greece and Israel alike, in a first stage of their religious evolution there was only one fate for the dead, destined as they all were to share the same subterranean dwelling place (Hades or Sheol). Heaven was reserved exclusively as the seat of the gods or of God. True it is that the *Odyssey* IV 563 speaks of an ἠλύσιον πεδίον, or "Elysian Field," reserved for Menelaus, though some critics would see this as a later redaction,[11] and at any rate it is a question of an earthly place, located "at the ends of the earth," as is also the case of the "island of the blessed" in Pindar (*Ol.* II 71-72).[12] Only later are human beings able to attain to the destiny of dwelling in heaven, in company with the gods or with God. As far as I can determine, in Greece this is first documented in the fifth century

10. See the *Kaushitaki Upanashad* (which distinguishes between a lunar and a solar way) and the Persian work *Namak* (where Ardāi Virāz completes a journey to heaven and hell alike); see G. Widengren, *Die Religionen Irans* (Stuttgart, 1965) 5:37-38, and especially C. Kappler et al., *Apocalypses et voyages*, 367–368.

11. See already E. Rohde, *Psyche. Seelencult und Unsterblichkeitsglaube der Griechen* (Tübingen, 1925 [Italian: 1983]) 69–70; English edition: *Psyche: The Cult of Souls and Belief in Immortality Among the Greeks* (New York, 1966).

12. In Greece the cult of the heroes is quite another thing. Already Homer, *Odyssey* XI 601–602, distinguishes between the "imaging," εἴδωλον, of Heracles in Hades and "himself," *autós*, who "is among the immortals." In the Old Testament cf. the figure of Henoch (Gen 5:4) and especially Elijah (2 Kgs 2:1-18).

B.C. by the Pythagorean poet Ion of Chios in Aristophanes, *The Peace*, 832–833: "When we die we become like stars in heaven"; but the idea was accepted only slowly.[13]

In Israel, biblical literature reveals this idea only rather late (see 2 Kgs 2:1, 11; and the deuterocanonical Wis. Sol. 5:15; 6:19: "Immortality causes one to be near God"), whereas in the New Testament it is standard. But apocryphal literature gives abundant witness to the new doctrine, especially in apocalyptic, as we read for example in *Ethiopian Henoch* 104:1-2 *(Epistle of Henoch)*: "I swear, O just, that in heaven the angels will remember you . . . and the gates of heaven will open to you"[14] (cf. also 53:6; 108:12; *Ass. Mos.* 10:3-9, etc.).

This is confirmed on the terminological level by the use of the expression "paradise." Persian in origin (see the Avestan *pari-daiza*, "garden enclosed"), this first appears in Greek literature in the fourth century B.C. with Xenophon, *Anabasis* I 2:7 *(παράδεισος)*, in its original material, territorial (one might say ecological) sense, and this usage remains current, even in Hellenistic Judaism (see LXX, Philo Alex., Flavius Josephus, Sibylline Oracles). But the semantic leap takes place in apocalyptic literature,[15] already to some extent in *Ethiopian Henoch*, which clearly mentions "paradise, in which are the elect and the just" (60:80), and then also in *Slavic Henoch*, where we read, "Henoch ascended to paradise: and there I saw a blessed place, and all blessed creatures, and they all lived in joy and in the infinite felicity of eternal life" (42:2-3 B). But while here this is already a reality, in the apocalypse of 4 Esdras it is reserved for the eschatological times (see 4:7; 6:2; 7:36, 123; 8:52).[16]

So we perceive two conceptions: in the one, paradise is put off to a future time, at the end of history (thus 4 Esdras;[17] in the New Testament

---

13. See the word *Himmel* by S. Morenz in *Die Religion in Geschichte und Gegenwart*, III (Tübingen, 1959³), col. 331; but see also I. P. Couliano, *Esperienze dell'estasi dall'Ellenismo al medioevo*, BCM 926 (Bari: Laterza, 1986) 40; and also the texts cited by G. Lohfink, *Die Himmelfahrt Jesu*, SANT 26 (Munich, 1971) 37, nn. 34, 35. In Plato also the related speculations are complex: thus, *Gorgias* 524a speaks of the "Isles of the Blessed," while *Phaedrus* 249a mentions a "heavenly place" (but in the perspective of metempsychosis); see also the various fates of the dead in *Phaedo* 113d–114c (divided into four categories), and the myth of Er in the *Republic*, 614b–621b (esp. 614c–615a).

14. After the translation of L. Fusella, in *Apocrifi dell'Antico Testamento*, I, ed. P. Sacchi, Classice delle Religioni 38 (Turin, 1981) 658.

15. See A. T. Lincoln, *Paradise Now and Not Yet: Studies in the Role of the Heavenly Dimension in Paul's Thought*, (Cambridge, 1981 [Italian: 1985]) 79–80.

16. See also *Ethiopian Henoch* 32:3 *(Book of the Watchers:* "And I arrived in the garden of Righteousness," the earthly paradise, now uninhabited); 60:23 and 61:12 *(Book of Parables)*; *Test. Levi* 18:10: "And he [the Messiah] will open the gates of Paradise and will deflect the sword pointed at Adam"; *Sibylline Oracles* fr. 3:46-48 (= Lactantius, *Div. inst.* II 12:19).

17. This apocryphal work already shows a tendency to compromise between the ancient and the later conception of the destiny of the just in the afterlife, for after death they can

perhaps Rev 2:7; and then the apocryphal *Apocalypse of Peter*); in the other, paradise is already a place that can be enjoyed at the end of the individual life (thus *Slavic Henoch;* in the New Testament Luke 23:43, and perhaps 2 Cor 12:2-4; and also the apocryphal *Apocalypse of Peter*).

Dante is decisively in the camp of this latter conception. But in contrast to the apocalypses (of Paul and John alike), which have more extensive description of the heavenly city than of its inhabitants, our poet optimistically emphasizes this personal aspect, as he writes in Canto XXX of the *Paradise:*

> Into the yellow of the eternal Rose
> that slopes and stretches and diffuses fragrance
> of praise into the Sun of endless spring,
>   now Beatrice drew me as one who, though
> he would speak out, is silent. And she said:
> "See how great is this council of white robes!
>   See how much space our city's circuit spans!
> See how our seated ranks are now so full
> that little room is left for any more! . . ." (vv. 124-132).

contemplate the fate of the damned (7:81-87) and the blessed (7:92-98) alike for a period of seven days, after which they must return to their common dwelling (see 7:101); see Strack-Billerbeck IV/2 1026–1029.

Index of Subjects

Agape, 143–144
  ecclesial dimension of, 192, 197
  in Letter to the Ephesians,
    196–198
  in relation to faith, 195–196
  labor of, 186–188
Apocalyptic, 279–282. *See also*
  Dante

Baptism, 253–256. *See also* Spirit
Blood of Christ
  cipher for Death of Christ, 34
  cosmic reconciliation in, 35–37
  eight texts in Paul on, 25
  in relation to New Covenant, 30

Christian secularity, 175–177
Church, foundation of the, 45–51.
  See also Cross of Christ; *Ekklesia;*
  Faith; Word of the Cross
Cross of Christ. *See also* Redemption; Word of the Cross
  foolishness of, 54–55
  origin of salvation, 20–22
Cultic language
  with reference to Christ, 179
  with reference to Christians,
    180–183
  with reference to Paul himself,
    180–181

Dante and the ''Visio Pauli,''
  274–282
Death of Christ, 43. *See also*
  Blood of Christ; Redemption

Death of martyrs, 21, 32
Dio of Prusa, 204, 213
Discovery of God, 218–221.
  See also Quest for God

Εἰς αὐτόν. See Unto him
Ekklesia, 177
Ethic, 267–269. *See also* Mysticism;
  Paul's moral teaching

Faith, 246. *See also Agape;*
  Church, foundation of the
Faith and works. *See also Agape;*
  James and Paul; Justification;
  Philo of Alexandria
  in James, 96, 98
  in Judaism, 93–94
Filiation, 254
Freedom, 131–134

Γραφή and *Γράμμα. See* Scripture
  and letter
Guilt, 16

''In Christ,'' 256–259

James. *See also* Faith and works
  Christology of, 100–101
  sapiential nomism of, 102–104
James and Paul. *See also* Faith
    and works
  convergences between, 108–112
  divergences between, 98–107
  representing two currents within
    Judaism, 102–107

Index of Scriptural Texts